The Rule of Law in Retreat

The Rule of Law in Retreat

Challenges to Justice in the United Nations World

Edited by
Sławomir Redo

LEXINGTON BOOKS
Lanham • Boulder • New York • London

Published by Lexington Books
An imprint of The Rowman & Littlefield Publishing Group, Inc.
4501 Forbes Boulevard, Suite 200, Lanham, Maryland 20706
www.rowman.com

86-90 Paul Street, London EC2A 4NE, United Kingdom

British Library Cataloguing in Publication Information Available

Library of Congress Cataloging-in-Publication Data Available

ISBN 9781666911565 (cloth) | ISBN 9781666911572 (ebook)

Contents

Foreword

Diego García-Sayán

I am very honored by the generous invitation to write this foreword. As a special rapporteur, I have always given special importance to academic or scholarly contributions that are a result of a thorough analysis of a diversity of experiences of building rule-of-law processes.

In 2012, after the adoption by the United Nations General Assembly of the "Declaration on the Rule of Law at the National and International Levels," its president emphasized that the declaration recognized the importance of national ownership in rule-of-law activities, and stood at the heart of the social contract between a state and its citizens. He urged world leaders to draw inspiration from Montesquieu: "There is no nation so powerful as the one that obeys its laws, not from principles of fear or reason, but from passion."[1] In some 700-word text, there is no intergovernmental definition of the rule of law.

Six years later, in 2018, the General Assembly endorsed the definition of the rule of law and due process. It "recognizes that respect for the rule of law, due process and access to justice are fundamental to all aspects of migration governance. This means that the State, public and private institutions and entities, as well as persons themselves, are accountable to laws that are publicly promulgated, equally enforced and independently adjudicated, and are consistent with international law."[2]

Concerning independent adjudication, this definition combines subjective/mental element reminding of Montesquieu's *principe interieur*—innate principle "residing in the hearts of all men"[3] with external criteria which should be consistent with international law.

In regard to the latter, the United Nations Human Rights Committee opined that the notion of "impartiality" in article 14(1) of the International Covenant on Civil and Political Rights "implies that judges must not harbor preconceptions about the matter put before them, and that they must not act in ways that promote the interests of one of the parties."[4]

More comprehensive was the European Court of Human Rights. It stated that the notion of "impartiality" indeed contains two elements: subjective and objective. Not only must the tribunal be impartial, in that "no member of the tribunal should hold any personal prejudice or bias," but it must also "be impartial from an objective viewpoint," in that "it must offer guarantees to exclude any legitimate doubt in this respect."[5]

Recently, regarding the guarantees of impartiality and independence, the Court of Justice of the European Union went further. It pointed that these guarantees should protect "from the direct or indirect influence of the . . . legislature and executive."[6] This includes autonomous legal or administrative court reform to which is entitled any EU member state, provided that its impact does not infringe judges' independence or impartiality. It must not affect their disciplinary regime of responsibility, if prompted by their making "a reference for a preliminary ruling to the Court of Justice," or putting "questions to the Court, as well as the system of judicial cooperation between the national courts and the Court of Justice established by the Treaties in order to secure uniformity in the interpretation of EU law and to ensure the full effect of that law."[7]

If the above renderings could protect us—as Montesquieu could have hoped—from "the designs of men stronger than ourselves, men who could hurt us in a thousand different ways, and could do so most of the time with impunity,"[8] then this would be a milestone in international jurisprudence and humankind's resolve to pursue the rule of law to promote social progress and better standards of life in larger freedom, as stated in the Universal Declaration of Human Rights. Be that as it may, coincidentally the last verdict involves the infringements of the independence of judiciary in Poland—a country which I visited in 2017 shortly after the legal and administrative court reform started there. In my report on that issue, I emphasized that "Poland is entitled to reform the judicial system. However . . . the main effect—if not the main goal—of the measures adopted by the ruling majority has been to hamper the constitutionally protected principle of judicial independence and to enable the legislative and executive branches to interfere with the administration of justice." I recommended to "review the measures adopted in the light of international norms and standards relating to the independence of the judiciary and the separation of powers."[9]

Regarding Hungary, I expressed my concern over reportedly politically motivated and rather inordinate new eligibility criteria for the appointment to the office of the president of the Supreme Court, its chambers and offices of judges at the ordinary courts.[10] Further, regarding Hungary (but also Poland, Brazil, and Turkey), judges from these countries informed about disguised measures affecting their conditions of service. They involved the transfer to a different court or tribunal as a punishment and to deter others from following her or his example. This measure has reportedly been used sometimes under the threat of dismissal or the imposition of disciplinary sanctions, in order to prevent a judge from adjudicating on a particular case or to punish and marginalize a judge regarded as too independent or unsympathetic to the government's interests. In some of these countries, there have been malicious and often simultaneous use of disciplinary proceedings, civil suits, and/or prosecution as a retaliatory or coercive tactic to force a judge to dismiss the consideration of a particular case, move to another court or tribunal, or resign.[11]

These are just a few annotations relevant to the case studies on Power Politics versus the rule of law provided in this book in which Montesquieu's vision of separation of powers is confronted with the "designs of the men stronger than ourselves"—Machiavellian one may say, if to interpret these designs so. In this sense, using Machiavelli's literary *topos*, this book entered a path, perhaps, "hitherto untrodden by any."[12] But in contrast with his quest for "new modes and systems"[13] (*modi ed ordini nuovi*) involving more usurpatory laws for the executive branch (by the way—politics is as old as this world), this book's contributors look into democratic measures for larger freedom with the rule of law for the United Nations world.

In 2004, Kofi Annan, then the United Nations secretary general, said that "advancing the rule of law at both the national and international levels is at the very heart of the United Nations."[14] Ban Ki-moon, his successor, reemphasized: "At the national level, the rule of law is at the heart of the social contract between the State and individuals."[15]

In any country which indeed pursues such a social contract, the state must guarantee the independence of judges and impartiality of prosecutors. Yet, even if justice is residing in the hearts of all men, contemporary authoritarianism jeopardizes social justice progress. This is a global reality on the rise. The United Nations is at the forefront of this challenge. Kofi Annan also said: "We need to champion democracy . . . Democracy's enemies are spending billions to undermine it, both in practice and through misinformation. In a world of "alternative facts," who do we believe? We must not let them win by abdication. Democracies have to reclaim the lost ground by defending and promoting liberal ideas, just as they did against democracy's past ideological enemies. We should remember that democracy is always a work in progress. We must cherish, reform, and defend democracy, or else it may be lost for future generations. As Thomas Jefferson put it, "the price of liberty is eternal vigilance.""[16]

In line with this priority, one of the major challenges in the world for the judicial systems is how society and individuals may have effective access to a judicial system. A well-known figure is that at least 1.5 billion persons in the world had already no access to justice before the pandemic. The figure has increased and the situation worsened during and after the pandemic. The other major challenge is an independent judiciary and respect for the function of lawyers as fundamental rights of the society as a whole, and not only of judges or lawyers.

As this book is being published, at this stage it is inevitable to state a very clear and well-known fact: The pandemic has severely affected the functioning of judicial systems, increasing the risk of not having a functioning, accessible, and independent justice system. Its impact has been uneven and differentiated in each country but has tended to disproportionately affect vulnerable groups.

While some of the pandemic's impacts on access to and functioning of justice, as well as judicial independence, are temporary, others will generate definitive changes. How these challenges may affect human rights and judicial independence is a matter of particular concern.

The protection of fundamental rights by an independent judiciary and access to the judicial system become, in this context, particularly relevant. During the pandemic, I have publicly warned, as a special rapporteur, of the variety of dangers to human rights and rule of law. Judicial systems generally operated in an atypical manner, interrupting, suspending, and/or affecting the normal development of their services.

During the pandemic as well, there have been attacks, threats, and harassment, as well as stigmatization or discrediting campaigns, against justice operators who investigate or are in charge of cases of great public interest and social impact. Crimes against health and economic and financial crimes have increased due to the corruption of extraordinary public funds for the emergency.

Quarantine or confinement measures have, in turn, led to a significant increase in cases of domestic, gender, and sexual violence facilitated by confinement. Gender-based violence is a serious issue of particular concern. Measures put in place to mitigate the spread of COVID-19 have caused a 40 percent increase in reporting in some countries. In the United States, the number of complaints increased by 8.1 percent since the quarantines were put in place.

Several issues are arising as challenges to be dealt with.

One has a connection with the impact of corruption during the response to the pandemic. Important not to ignore the so-called "COVID millionaires." Other is the *impact on the prison population* considering that in most countries the prison population lives in overcrowded conditions generating a special vulnerability. Any form of confinement, isolation, or quarantine should only be imposed as a last resort and based on independent medical assessments.

There are several *challenges to judicial independence and accessibility for the protection of human rights.* Judicial institutions in several countries have expressed some concerns regarding the impact that the use of technical means of communication for the transmission of images and sound could have, both in criminal and civil proceedings, on the rule of law and fundamental rights. As well concerns were expressed, how the digital divide affects access considering that the use of digital means presupposes access to electronic media and technological knowledge which is not the case for the great majority of the population and even lawyers.

To emerge stronger from this crisis, it is of particular importance to address the risks and threats of corruption, both in the short-term response and in the recovery phase, with a special emphasis on the functioning and operation of justice systems.

The state is responsible for guaranteeing access to justice, the functioning of an independent justice system, and its proximity to the people. The judicial system should be considered an essential public service, and its personnel and the role of lawyers among them as essential in pandemic contexts, including vaccination processes still ongoing in most parts of the world.

In this critical context, countries should adopt urgent and sustained measures to close the digital divide that affects access to justice and generates exclusion. States must promote appropriate policies to achieve universal access to the Internet and information technologies and ensure real and effective access to justice by guaranteeing connectivity and the availability of appropriate software and equipment, as well as adequate training for judges, judicial officials, and lawyers.

The critical situation caused by COVID-19 is not only a serious problem but also an opportunity to adopt public policies that ensure the independence and effective functioning of justice systems and that facilitate the population's access to justice under a gender perspective and with respect for human rights. States should be guided for these purposes by international human rights treaties, the "Basic Principles on the Independence of the Judiciary" (1985), the "Guidelines on the Role of Prosecutors" (1990), and the "Basic Principles on the Role of Lawyers" (1990).

How in the variety of contributions in this book the issue of human rights and justice is addressed is connected not only to previous and permanent challenges but to the new ones being raised in the contemporary evolution of societies. Placing human rights, rule of law, and independence of justice vis-à-vis these challenges as three basic key ideas or concepts, as is the idea of this book, is a very valuable contribution to which I am very grateful to have been invited to join.

Diego García-Sayán
Geneva, August 2021

NOTES

1. UN doc. GA/11290, World Leaders Adopt Declaration Reaffirming Rule of Law as Foundation for Building Equitable State Relations, Just Societies, 24 September 2012.

2. UN doc. A/RES/73/195, Global Compact for Safe, Orderly and Regular Migration, § 15 (d).

3. Charles L. de Secondat Montesquieu, *Persian Letters: With Related Texts*, ed. Raymond N. Mackenzie (Indianapolis/Cambridge: Hackett Publishing Company, Inc., 2014), Letter 83, 125.

4. Communication No. 387/1989, Arvo O. Karttunen v. Finland (Views adopted on 23 October 1992), in UN doc. GAOR, A/48/40. Report of the Human Rights Committee (vol. II), 120, § 7.2.

5. Eur. Court HR, Case of Daktaras v. Lithuania, judgment of 10 October 2000, § 30. For the text see the Courts's web site: http://echr.coe.int.

6. Judgment in case C-791/19 Commission v. Poland, https://bit.ly/3ipigB5.

7. Judgment in case C-791/19 Commission v. Poland.

8. Montesquieu, *Persian Letters*, Letter 83, 125.

9. UN doc. A/HRC/38/Add.1 Report of the Special Rapporteur on the independence of judges and lawyers on his mission to Poland. 5 April 2018.

10. UN doc. AL Hungary 2/2021, https://bit.ly/3kB9sZQ.

11. UN doc. A/75/172, Disciplinary Measures against Judges/Use of "Disguised" Sanctions, 17 June 2020.

12. Niccolò Machiavelli, *Discourses on Livy,* trans. Ninian Hill Thompson (Mineola, NY: Dover Publications, 2007), Preface, 1.

13. Machiavelli, *Discourses*, Preface, 1.

14. UN doc. S/2004/616, The Rule of Law and Transitional Justice in Conflict and Post-Conflict Societies. Report of the Secretary-General. 23 August 2004, § 6.

15. UN doc. A/66/749, Delivering Justice: Programme of Action to Strengthen, 16 March 2012, § 4.

16. Kofi Annan, *The Crisis of Democracy*, Published on September 14, 2017, https://bit.ly/3eo7lX2.

BIBLIOGRAPHY

Annan, Kofi. The Crisis of Democracy, Published September 2014, 2017. https://bit.ly/3eo7lX2.

Communication No. 387/1989, Arvo O. Karttunen v. Finland (Views adopted on 23 October 1992), in UN doc. GAOR, A/48/40. Report of the Human Rights Committee. Vol. II.

Judgment in case C-791/19 Commission v. Poland. https://bit.ly/3ipigB5.

Machiavelli, Niccolò. *Discourses on Livy,* trans. Ninian Hill Thompson. Mineola, NY: Dover Publications, 2007.

Montesquieu, Charles L. de Secondat. *Persian Letters. With Related Texts*, ed. Raymond N. Mackenzie. Indianapolis/Cambridge: Hackett Publishing Company, Inc., 2014.

UN doc. A/HRC/38/Add.1. Report of the Special Rapporteur on the Independence of Judges and Lawyers on his Mission to Poland, 5 April 2018.

UN doc. AL Hungary 2/2021. https://bit.ly/3kB9sZQ.

UN doc. A/66/749. Delivering Justice: Programme of Action to Strengthen. 16 March 2012.

UN doc. A/75/172. Disciplinary Measures Against Judges/Use Of "Disguised" Sanctions. 17 June 2020.

UN doc. GA/11290. World Leaders Adopt Declaration Reaffirming Rule of Law as Foundation for Building Equitable State Relations, Just Societies, 24 September 2012.

UN doc. S/2004/616. The Rule of Law and Transitional Justice in Conflict and Post-Conflict Societies. Report of the Secretary-General. 23 August 2004.

Introduction

Sławomir Redo

In the past decade, the rule-of-law developments in the world have become tardy and contentious. Its idea, concept, and global implementation have met growing resistance. The 2012 United Nations (UN) "Declaration on the rule of law at the national and international levels," the 2015 declaration "Transforming our world: The 2030 agenda for sustainable development," and the 2018 "Global compact for orderly, safe and regular Migration" are the best examples of the repositioning of rule of law throughout the world.

At the 76th session of the United Nations General Assembly, António Guterres, the current UN secretary general, in his opening statement said:

> I am here to sound the alarm: The world must wake up. We are on the edge of an abyss—and moving in the wrong direction. Our world has never been more threatened. Or more divided. We face the greatest cascade of crises in our lifetimes. The COVID-19 pandemic has supersized glaring inequalities. The climate crisis is pummeling the planet. . . . A surge of mistrust and misinformation is polarizing people and paralyzing societies, and human rights are under fire. Science is under assault.[1]

This book offers insights into the globally relevant rule-of-law ramifications for human rights, constitutional law, and philosophy of law in the time of such considerable challenges to it. In their context and from this legal perspective, twenty contributors analyze the questions of independence of judiciary, liberal education, freedom of mass media, populism, and corruption. They discuss global civic education and other civic participation that help to meet these challenges and overcome poverty—material and of thought—while augmenting larger freedom in the 2030 (UN) world of evolving North-South values.

The book consists of fifteen substantive chapters, including Foreword, and Afterword. The book's table of contents may remind of a sinusoid waveform. (In mathematics, it consists of two sinusoidal excitations with a lower natural line in between.) Accordingly, the three initial chapters address—as if they were a part of a sinusoid waveform—the rule-of-law developments in general UN terms. Subsequent six chapters document natural frequency: regressive country-specific case studies on power politics versus the rule of law. These chapters involve Brazil, USA, India, Poland, Turkey, Hungary, and the European Union—all written from the idiosyncratic legal perspective. These six chapters are followed by another sinusoidal excitation of six chapters from the UN rule-of-law perspective. They give legal, criminological, philosophical, and artistic rule-of-law insights—all concluded by the Afterword. The only difference between the mathematical and the intended in this book sinusoidal design is the latter's orientation. According to the UN Charter, such a sinusoid should have a linear dynamic—socially just, relentlessly straightforward, progressive trend.

Amid its chatty political twists and turns (hence the book's cover) that make factual development nonlinear—cyclical or recurrent, but still progressive—this book opens with the Foreword by H.E. Diego García-Sayán, the UN special rapporteur on the independence of judges and lawyers. He sets the book's direction by recalling what the president of the 67th session of the United Nations General Assembly/UNGA (2012) said about the rule of law. In implementing it, the UNGA president urged world leaders to draw inspiration from Montesquieu: "There is no nation so powerful as the one that obeys its laws, not from principles of fear or reason, but from passion." But he also added that "If our aim is to strengthen trust between nations, then respect for accepted norms and standards cannot be ambiguous or selective."[2]

Regrettably, after a decade since that statement, the passion for pursuing the rule of law is waning, while ambiguity and selectiveness in applying international norms and standards is strengthening. The special rapporteur gives a short review of such regressive developments regarding the independence of judiciary. He pays special attention to them in the context of COVID-19 pandemic.

The next contribution comes from Mallika Mahajan, Pawan Kumar Sinha, in cooperation with Thomas Stelzer. They write about "Corruption of the Rule of Law and the United Nations." Since the 1948 adoption of the Universal Declaration of Human Rights, there has been a growing de facto recognition of the rule of law worldwide. However, only in 2004, Kofi Annan, the seventh UN secretary general, formulated its definition as the Secretariat's benchmark. While the experiences from the UN peacekeeping operations before and after those dates brought into the organization's approach to the rule of law new ideas and developments which differentiate what comes first in peacekeeping operations and for the implementation of the 2030 Agenda for Sustainable Development, in a broader spectrum of global peacekeeping, there are very serious challenges to the rule of law. This chapter reflects on such conceptual and practical UN developments on the rule of law in the light of political statements of the heads and leaders of governments and organizations which in 2020 celebrated the 75th anniversary of the UN.

Further, Megan Capp writes about "The Rule of Law in the Voluntary Reviews of the Implementation of the United Nations 2030 Sustainable Development Agenda." That is the only viable way in which one may monitor the implementation of that soft law. This chapter explores the tension between the declaratory value of the rule of law, and its practical application, within the context of the 2030 Agenda for Sustainable Development. It highlights the complex dichotomy that where rule-of-law monitoring and reform are most needed, data is most challenging to collect. The author notes that attempts by the international community to evaluate progress toward the 2030 Agenda for Sustainable Development have produced a broad debate on how to measure progress in the implementation of its crosscutting sustainable development goal (SDG) 16 "Peace, Justice and Strong Institutions" where the rule of law is listed (target 3: "Promote the rule of law at the national and international levels and ensure equal access to justice for all"). In 2017, a global indicator framework was adopted by the UN General Assembly which provides universal indicators for voluntary country-led review on each of the seventeen SDGs. In the interest of identifying how SDG 16.3 finds itself within this broader framework, this chapter analyzes these voluntary reviews and provides clues on the declaratory value of the rule of law in the context of the UN Sustainable Development Agenda.

Next, Eduardo Pinheiro Granzotto da Silva and Newton Tavares Filho turn our attention to "Power Politics versus the Rule of Law in Brazil: A Case Study." At the start they recall the most prominent initiative to fight corruption and money laundering in the history of Brazil, known as "Operation Car Wash." This criminal investigation changed the country's political landscape, putting the three powers of the republic on a collision course and pushing the boundaries of Montesquieu's separation of powers. The operation also had an impact on Brazil's leadership, having propelled Jair Bolsonaro, a right-wing conservative candidate to the presidency in 2018. Since then, the rule of law in the country has been tested to its limits. The coalition in power today promotes conservative principles, inspired by autocratic tendencies, and departs, in many ways, from the libertarian ideals that inspired the Constitution of 1988. In addition, attacks on the judiciary, the Brazilian Bar Association and the press, and pushes to discredit public universities have become frequent. In this context, and from the perspective of constitutional law, the authors explore on a case study basis the struggle between power politics and the rule of law in Brazil between 2018 and 2020, with a focus on three main topics: constitutionalism; the independence of the judiciary, the impartiality of the legal profession and university legal education; and the independence of mass media.

Murugesan Srinivasan and Varsha Vijayan in "Power Politics versus the Rule of Law in India: A Case Study" argue that power politics is an international construct which broadly denotes that power is the determining factor for the formation of international hierarchies of nations—divided into world powers, middle powers, and small states. Several scholars have expressed that an alternative to power politics should exist in the international sphere if the world community is to survive. The "Rule of Law" is the real alternative to power politics as it is one of the most important political ideals and one of the arrays of ideals constitutive of modern political morality. In India, the power derived from politics and political institutions is more colossal than the power derived from other sources that include bureaucracy, police, and judiciary. Operationally, in the Indian context, power politics may be understood as to how politics is used as a powerful tool to attain power. But politics and political institutions are influenced by several factors including caste and religion. With this opinion in mind, the authors of this chapter confront Indian realities such as caste, religion, caste, and communal politics that affect the implementation of the rule of law. The authors also attempt to demonstrate how these factors, the legal institutions and legal provisions, and last but not least, perpetual inequality, make the rule of law a paper ideal. Hence, the authors are of the view that the practice of the rule of law in the Indian context is influenced by the prevailing sociopolitical conditions.

Further, in "Power Politics versus the Rule of Law in the United States: A Case Study," Cora True-Frost discusses the limits of the constitution and system of law in the United States. Even before the notorious Capitol riots of January 6, 2021, American legal scholars warned of the imperiled impartiality of law and proposed various reforms of core domestic institutions such as the Supreme Court and Congress. This chapter's argument is straightforward: the United States has been alerted to the potential lasting damage that existing legal gaps may have on the balance between justice and impunity in the future. Legal reforms to the executive-media relationship and the pardon power are necessary to foreclose the possibility of these abuses in the future; reforms are also necessary to forestall some aspects of the erosion of the separation of powers.

Following that chapter is Şerife Ceren Uysal's chapter "Power Politics versus the Rule of Law in Turkey: A Case Study." She contributes to a discussion about Turkey's current rule-of-law status. In order to enable the assessment of the state of emergency period within the rule-of-law framework, her chapter addresses the regime of statutory decrees, constitutional amendment, and the Inquiry Commission on the State of Emergency Measures—the ad hoc mechanism—established in this period to review the appeals of the public officials that were discharged from service by a statutory decree. In conclusion, the legislation in Turkey will be evaluated in the context of the generally accepted criteria of the rule of law, including the judicial independence, the right to a fair trial, the current state of lawyers, and freedom of speech. Freedom of the press and academia will be assessed as a sign of the institutionalization of the state of emergency.

In the next chapter, "Power Politics versus the Rule of Law in Hungary: A Case Study," Bernadette Somody emphasizes that constitutionalism means limited public power in order to secure citizens' freedom. The judiciary and the constitutional court, the pluralistic media system, and the universities, even if in different roles, serve as the guarantee of freedom. Thus, their independent or autonomous status is crucial for constitutionalism. Her chapter presents indicators of the status of the above-mentioned institutions in Hungary from the period after 2010, from a constitutional law perspective. The indicators focus on the appointment of ordinary court judges and constitutional court justices, the independence of institutions in the media system, and the autonomy of universities. This overview points out that the constitutional and legal changes carried out by the governing majority allowed it to control the independent and autonomous institutions.

Rita Haverkamp, in her chapter "The Rule of Law and the European Union in the Time of Challenge," argues that the Rule of Law is a manifold fundamental principle. This chapter first traces the foundations of the rule of law and presents its conceptions ranging from thin to thick, formal to substantial. This analysis is essential to comprehend the substantial conceptions of the Rule of Law in the Council of Europe and the European Union, which are presented in light of the principles spelled out by the Venice Commission and the European Court of Human Rights as well as by the Union Rule of Law Framework and the European Court of Justice. Then the chapter sheds light on the alarming undermining of the rule of law, in particular in Hungary and Poland, that can be labeled as sad trendsetters for deteriorating the fundamental value in the Union. Due to its broad range of conceptions from thin to thick, the principle is somehow acknowledged all over the world. In Europe, its origins are rooted in England but also the French *Ėtat de droit* and the German *Rechtsstaat* are pivotal for the development of the rule of law. These concepts used to have a formal (thin) understanding in common, but as a result of the Nazi regime it changed to a substantive (thick) understanding which became established first in the Council of Europe and later in the European Union (EU). In the face of major setbacks in the rule of law in the twenty-first century, concern for its upholding in several EU member states has grown stronger in the European Commission and the European

Parliament. Due to continued violations, especially by Hungary and Poland, the Union as well as the Council of Europe worked out safeguards for the rule of law in member states. Consequently, the measures taken to counter the COVID-19 pandemic even fuel the decay of the rule of law. The Union encourages this process through financial subsidies that are vital to Hungary and Poland but are used to dismantle the rule of law further. Both member states, therefore, try to do everything in their power to avoid the danger of the withdrawal of funds through the newly introduced sanctioning mechanism.

In the next chapter, Yvon Dandurand and Jessica Jahn question "The Future of International Criminal Justice Cooperation: A Retreat from the Rule of Law?" This chapter reflects on the past and future of international criminal justice cooperation and the effectiveness of the legacy mechanisms on which such cooperation still relies. By drawing on issues identified by states parties in reviews of their implementation of the UN Convention against Corruption and those related to the UN Convention against Transnational Organized Crime, the text observes some of the fault lines and trends in the current international cooperation regime and questions the regime's sustainability. In the latter half of the chapter, given the many uncertainties that continue to prevail in that complicated yet crucial criminal justice policy area, a scenario-based discussion is offered that points at five possible futures in international criminal justice cooperation.

The subsequent four chapters break away with the above terse legal approach to the rule of law. In contrast with its regressive features exposed by the book's contributors, these subsequent chapters emphasize progressive features of the rule of law. Through a drama, pictures, and other liberal accounts, their authors document that the rule of law with its respect to fellow human beings is meant to emphasize our humanity, and serves mutual regard, that is, the Golden Rule.

It goes without saying that dialogue is an important and necessary tool for building relations between people. It prompts reflection, may entail empathy, and leads to some kind of transformation. The next section is opened by William Schabas's *Exordinum*, where he offers comments on the book's dialogue between Montesquieu and Machiavelli. This eminent author of global and regional human rights law commentaries points to the importance of more viable countering the autocratic attempts to dismantle the rule of law. Mindful of World War II genocide that prompted the establishment of the UN and the adoption of the Universal Declaration of Human Rights, Schabas agitates the readers by invoking the call of Marian Turski, the head of the International Auschwitz Committee. Reacting to the erosion of humanistic values, Turski said: "Thou shalt not be indifferent. Do not be indifferent when any minority is discriminated against. Democracy hinges on the rights of minorities being protected."

In this vein, Friedrich Forsthuber, Michael Platzer, Sławomir Redo, and Gerhard Reissner wrote together "Dialogue in Hell between Montesquieu and Machiavelli on Climate Change, Migration and the Rule of Law." The dialogue was inspired by Maurice Joly's book *The Dialogue in Hell between Machiavelli and Montesquieu: Humanitarian Despotism and the Conditions of Modern Tyranny* (translated, edited, and with commentary by John S. Waggoner, Lexington Books 2003)—first published in 1864. In that book, its French author, barrister, and progenitor of French civil society movement concerned with rising authoritarianism of Napoleon III (1848–1870), insightfully scripted corruption of democratic principles in France, eventually falling to absolutism. Montesquieu and Machiavelli, the two intellectual giants with opposing worldviews on how the world should be ruled, are the on-stage personages discussing their philosophical opinions on governance in the current North-South rule of law context, that is, in the age of climate change, migration, and interregionally changing values.

In the following chapter, Sławomir Redo comments "On the Dialogues in Hell between Machiavelli and Montesquieu," that is the above dialogue and the original dialogue by Joly. Both texts enable to throw more light on the inversion of humanistic values, exemplified in the book's chapter by the oxymoron "ideological blackmail by the Rule of Law." Next, the author casts other rule-of-law arguments into a broader UN context of the Universal Declaration of Human Rights and the 2030 Sustainable Development Agenda. The UN rule of law is challenged by popular sovereignty's "mobocratic spirit" as Abraham Lincoln would say, and exploited by unscrupulous power holders. The author calls to respond in kind through global civic education to counter intellectual and material poverty of thought—to address climate change, migration, and larger freedom in the 2030 UN world of evolving North-South values. He emphasizes that leaving people behind undermines their life chances and impedes development. Finally, in his opinion, the emancipative rule-of-law education in the Global North and South is the most promising and progressive way to pursue orderly, safe, and responsible migration in decades of sustainable livelihood hopefully to experience.

It also goes without saying that other forms of cultural expressions may likewise be helpful to solutions to justice issues. This message is conveyed in the penultimate chapter entitled "Faith in the United Nations and Arts Approaches to Conflict Prevention and Resolution." It was written by Marian Liebmann, f. activist of the Friends Committee for Consultations (Quakers), originally Quakers, established in England in the seventeenth century—the progenitor of the global civil society movement, now one of the stalwart members of the Alliance of the Non-governmental Organizations of the United Nations Crime Prevention and Criminal Justice Programme.

Marian Liebmann is a practitioner who built strong working relationships with diverse vulnerable groups. In her text, she first informs about religious ideas communicated by the Friends Committee for Consultations. She then brings to the reader's attention the like-minded artistic expressions for conflict resolution and prevention by mentioning the *Golden Rule* painting of Norman Rockwell, and the two other remarkable paintings by Sagenji Yoshida and Jan Henryk de Rosen—all in honor of the UN, where they are shown in its locations across the world. All these positive expositions introduce the reader to daily life experiences with faith and art approaches to conflict resolution at the restorative and social justice level, including art therapy with offenders.

Last but not least, Pedro R. David in his "Afterword" reflects on the constitutional and philosophical aspects of the rule of law, especially on the importance of the independence of judiciary. He does so against the background of research findings. They reposition the rule of law in the era of climate change, evidenced by the recent report of the Intergovernmental Panel on Climate Change—"a code red for humanity," as António Guterres alerted.[3]

Here, in a way of general conclusion, may be added that at the 75th-anniversary session of the UN General Assembly member states declared that "[o]ur world is not yet the world that our founders envisaged 75 years ago. It is plagued by growing inequality, poverty, hunger, armed conflicts, terrorism, insecurity, climate change and pandemics. People in different corners of the world are forced to make dangerous journeys in search of refuge and safety." Member states also declared to "continue to promote respect for democracy and human rights and to enhance democratic governance and the Rule of Law by strengthening transparent and accountable governance and independent judicial institutions."[4]

This book's contributors seek to do just that amid the everyday rule-of-law vagaries which contrast with their modest visions of progress.

My sincere thanks to all the authors for accepting my invitation to contribute to this book. I also thank Lexington Books staff: Mses. Becca Beurer, Carter Moran, Jade Bair and associate Ms. Monica Sukumar, for their enthusiasm and professionalism. Last but not least, I thank my family: my wife Jolanta, our son Piotr, my sister Elżbieta for their generous and constructive support. I am very fortunate to enjoy it.

Vienna, October 24, 2021
On United Nations Day

NOTES

1. Secretary-General's Address to the General Assembly, September 21, 2021, https://bit.ly/3hWRpwW.

2. UN doc. GA/11290, World Leaders Adopt Declaration Reaffirming Rule of Law as Foundation for Building Equitable State Relations, Just Societies, 24 September 2012.

3. *Secretary-General's Address.*

4. UN doc. A/RES/75/1, Declaration on the Commemoration of the Seventy-Fifth Anniversary of the United Nations, § 10.

BIBLIOGRAPHY

Secretary-General's Address to the General Assembly. September 21, 2021.

UN doc. GA/11290. World Leaders Adopt Declaration Reaffirming Rule of Law as Foundation for Building Equitable State Relations, Just Societies, 24 September 2012.

UN doc. A/RES/75/1 Declaration on the Commemoration of the Seventy-Fifth Anniversary of the United Nations, 21 September 2020.

Chapter 1

Corruption of the Rule of Law and the United Nations

Mallika Mahajan, Pawan Kumar Sinha, and Thomas Stelzer

INTRODUCTION

The 75th anniversary of the United Nations (UN) in 2020 provides us with a vantage point to trace the evolution of the concept of the rule of law within the UN system and the countries where it operated, covering its peacekeeping operations and extrapolating the trajectory toward achieving the sustainable development goals (SDGs) by 2030. This chapter draws evidence from various UN resolutions and existing literature and demonstrates how the UN recognized various roadblocks in the path of establishing and maintaining the rule of law and the extent it overcame them. This also includes the growing understanding of the vulnerability of the rule of law ascribed to corruption and heightened attention to it to ensure global security, development, and welfare of people. The chapter underscores that building capacities through research, education, training, and technical assistance at the international level is an imperative which requires immediate attention and resources.

After World War II, the UN establishment rested on three pillars—international security and peace, human rights, and development. All these three pillars are mutually reinforcing. The formation of the UN was "as a common endeavor for humanity (and) was established to save succeeding generations from the scourge of war."[1] The UN Charter did not explicitly specify the tenets of "the rule of law" or its definition. However, creating a governance structure in different countries to establish security and peace and protect human rights was the *sine qua non*. Further, the concept of *the international rule of law* was fledging at the time of the formation of the UN. However, it evolved over seventy-five years and is still evolving. **As also mentioned in the 2005 World Summit Outcome,[2] the aim is to uphold the resolution of disputes by peaceful means and conformity with the principles of justice and international law. The same resolution also acknowledged that the world requires collective security against transnational threats through effective cooperation of all countries following international law. However, from the various resolutions, it appears that focus on the corrosive factors that corrupted the rule of law itself were missing, especially corruption. There is a growing concern that corruption corrupts and weakens the rule of law, and in turn, a weak rule of law exacerbate corruption. This mutual reinforcement galvanizes the vicious cycle, which explains intractable "high corruption-weak rule of law" equilibrium in several countries. This has also adversely impacted the endeavors to achieve sustainable development in these countries. The UN is resolutely attempting to address with a mix of successes and failures. It would be prudent to trace various actions of the United Nations that display the UN system's continuous efforts at course correction to strengthen the rule of law for ensuring and maintaining peace, security, protecting human rights, fight corruption in all forms, and spur sustainable development. This chapter examines the relationship between corruption and the rule of law in the background above.

HISTORY OF THE CONCEPT OF THE RULE OF LAW AND GOVERNANCE

The history of the rule of law begins with the Code of Hammurabi, promulgated by the king of Babylon around 1760 BC. It was the first set of written laws, inscribed in stone and made publicly available. For Plato, the rule of law was an option second to that of philosopher king, whose absence warranted the rule of law. In contrast, Aristotle preferred the rule of law to that of any individual. Throughout this early period, the law was a method to rule and not a constraint on the ruler. The 1215 Magna Carta established limits on the exercise of power by the king with respect to the liberties of freemen. This remained a theory until the adoption in 1689 of the Petition of Rights. It became illegal for the sovereign to suspend or dispense with laws, establish his own courts, or impose taxes without parliamentary approval. It also provided free election of members of parliament, and that parliamentary scrutiny would guide parliamentary proceedings.[3] Since then, the concept of the rule of law has been variously interpreted or described by philosophers and thinkers such as medieval theorist Sir John Fortescue (1471), early modern period thinkers like Niccolò Machiavelli (1532), James Harrington (1656), John Locke (1689), Montesquieu (1748), A. V. Dicey (1885), and modern theorists F. A. Hayek (1944, 1960, and 1973), Michael Oakeshott (1983), Joseph Raz (1977), and John Finnis (1980), Lon Fuller (1964), Ronald Dworkin (1985), and John Rawls (1971), etc.[4]

THE RULE OF LAW DEFINED

The 1993 Vienna World Conference on Human Rights recommended that the UN should offer technical and financial assistance "in reforming penal and correctional establishments, education and training of lawyers, judges and security forces in human rights, and any other sphere of activity relevant to the good functioning of the rule of law."[5] A series of General Assembly resolutions endorsed this, each citing the rule of law as "an essential factor in the protection of human rights."[6] The Charter of the UN, together with the four pillars of the modern international legal system, namely, international human rights law, international humanitarian law, international criminal law, and international refugee law, constitute the normative foundation of the UN rule of law. Consequently, the UN tribunals can never allow capital punishment. There are no amnesties for genocide, war crimes, and crimes against humanity or gross violations of human rights in an UN-endorsed peace agreement.[7] The UN addition of human rights to the rule of law has made the concept foggier as different nations view human rights differently.[8]

The dissensus on its understanding is probably the reason for a high degree of consensus on the virtues of the rule of law. At the UN World Summit in 2005, member states unanimously recognized the need for "universal adherence to and implementation of the Rule of Law at both the national and international levels."[9] Over the years, member states of the UN have agreed with the explanation of the rule of law set out by the secretary general (SG) in his 2004 report, which is as under:

> The rule of law is a principle of governance in which all persons, institutions and entities, public and private, including the State itself, are accountable to laws that are publicly promulgated, equally enforced and independently adjudicated, and which are consistent with international human rights norms and standards. It requires measures to ensure adherence to the principles of supremacy of the law, equality before the law, accountability to the law, fairness in the application of the law, separation of powers, participation in decision-making, legal certainty, avoidance of arbitrariness, and procedural and legal transparency.[10]

The 67th session of the General Assembly on the rule of law at the national and international levels held on September 24, 2012, also affirmed this definition.[11]

On a broad categorization, the rule of law definitions fall into two categories. The first set emphasizes the end goals of this concept in society, such as (1) a government bound by law, (2) equality before the law, (3) law and order, (4) predictable and efficient rulings, and (5) human rights. The second set highlights the institutional attributes of the rule of law. John Locke enumerated the three primary institutions of the rule of law: (1) publicly known laws, (2) an independent and knowledgeable judiciary, and (3) a force to enforce laws, execute judgments, and maintain public peace and safety. An expanding array of institutions such as law schools, bar associations, prisons, intelligence services, bail systems, and the like support these institutions.[12] The UN articulation of the rule of law requires both human rights and democracy as necessary elements.[13] The UN transitional presence in conflict and post-conflict societies veers it toward the rule of law institutional building. However, the means and the ends must go tandemly. We demonstrate that anti-corruption, including within the UN system and international organizations, is the lever to push the rule of law institutions toward the desired outcomes.

To conclude this section, we quote a legal maxim modified by Koechler, "the rule of law is not *fiat justitia, pereat mundus* (Let justice be done, though the world may perish) rather it is *fiat justitia ne pereat mundus* (let justice prevail so that the world does not perish)".[14]

THREE BASKETS OF THE UN-LED RULE OF LAW

UN has three main "baskets" of the rule of law activity: the rule of law at the international level; in the context of conflict and post-conflict situations; and in the context of long-term development,[15] including the SDGs.

The UN and the International Rule of Law

The "international rule of law" means applying the rule of law principles to relations between states.[16] The UN Charter provides the core principles of the international rule of law to include sovereign equality of states, noninterference in internal affairs, prohibition of the threat, or use of force and the settlement of disputes by peaceful means.[17] The mediation of dispute settlement under international law is through the International Court of Justice, and other tribunals specialized in particular branches of international law, such as the International Tribunal on the Law of the Sea, the UN Commission on International Trade Law and the International Law Commission.[18]

Aside from the foundational concept of *pacta sunt servanda*,[19] the UN promotes the international rule of law through international protections for human rights and the codification of the content of international law.[20]

The International Convention for the Protection of All Persons from Enforced Disappearance has enhanced international legal protection. Also significant is the Optional Protocol to the Convention against Torture and Other Cruel, Inhuman or Degrading Treatment or Punishment that entered into force on June 22, 2006, which provides for in-country inspections of places of detention.[21]

Criminal trials in the transitional context have contributed to creating an international rule of law[22] by way of the development of rich jurisprudence for international criminal law.

The UN has expanded the content of "crimes against humanity" as a norm of international law. The Nuremberg Charter's article 6 (c) had narrowed the interpretation of "crimes against humanity," to acts connected to war. It was impossible to apply this interpretation to the conflict and post-conflict societies like that of Rwanda[23] because there was no "war" in the classic sense of an interstate or international armed conflict. The UN expanded the definition in 1992, as "Gross violations of fundamental rules of humanitarian and human rights law committed by persons demonstrably linked to a party to the conflict, as part of an official policy based on discrimination against an identifiable group of persons, irrespective of war and the nationality of the victim."[24]

The above definition was amplified by including acts such as the following: Murder and extermination; enslavement; deportation and population transfer; persecution; mutilation; cruel treatment; humiliating and degrading treatment; torture; unlawful human experimentation; apartheid.[25]

In 1951, Convention on the Prevention and Punishment of the Crime of Genocide on December 9, 1948, went into force. Article I of this Convention states that "genocide, whether committed in time of peace or in time of war, is a crime under international law," which ratifying states undertake to prevent and punish. Article II provides that:

> genocide means any of the following acts committed with intent to destroy, in whole or in part, a national, ethnical [*sic*], racial, or religious group, as such, killing members of the group, causing serious bodily or mental harm to members of the group, deliberately inflicting on the group conditions of life calculated to bring about its physical destruction in whole or in part, imposing measures intended to prevent births within the group, forcibly transferring children of the group to another group.[26]

Through the principle of *jus cogens*, the genocide convention bound even states that had not fully ratified it. *Jus cogens* have a peremptory status, and the prohibition of genocide applies to all members of the international community rather than merely to parties to the convention.[27]

The attribution of responsibility to the individual in *propria personam* has also become a part of customary international law.[28] Alongside states with predominant international responsibility, an individual, regardless of office or rank, is also responsible for war crimes, crimes against peace, and crimes against humanity.[29]

The concomitant principle is a *command responsibility*. Per this principle, a person who orders a subordinate to commit a violation for which there is individual responsibility is as responsible as the individual that actually carries it out. The Nuremberg Principles, adopted by the UN General Assembly on December 11, 1946, affirmed that even a head of state is not free from responsibility for the commission of a crime under international law.[30]

Under the UN, the national courts of third-party states have tried cases under the *universality principle*, an element of international law that holds that some crimes are so grave that all countries have an interest in prosecuting them. The use of *universal jurisdiction* is for the prosecution of only the most serious crimes and only in cases where the country's justice system that was home to the violations is unable or unwilling to do so.[31]

Lockerbie represents the best example of the UN upholding the international rule of law. In December 1988, a Pan Am flight 103 exploded midair over Lockerbie, Scotland. By resolution 731 of 1992, the UN Security Council decided that the Libyan government must comply with the requests of the governments of the UK, USA, and France to cooperate fully in establishing responsibility for the terrorist acts against Pan Am flight 103 and Union de transports Aeriens flight.[32] This case demonstrated an unprecedented step of establishing a national court of one country (Scotland) to conduct a trial in another country (the Netherlands). The Libyan government complied after member states imposed various sanctions against it.[33]

The UN Peacekeeping and the Rule of Law

In its peacekeeping operations, the UN experimented with various ideas for implementing the rule of law that can be useful in its anti-corruption efforts and eventually in the successful implementation of the 2030 Agenda for Sustainable Development. We, therefore, briefly trace this evolution.

The UN first used "the rule of law" in resolution 1040 (1996), when it decided to promote "national reconciliation, democracy, security and the rule of law in Burundi."[34] The earliest UN role in conflict societies was limited to "peacekeeping" that gradually expanded to "peacebuilding" that included the rule of law as an integral component. The 2000 Brahimi Report and the SG's 2001 report defined peacebuilding as "an attempt, after a peace has been negotiated or imposed, to address the sources of present hostility and build local capacities for conflict resolution."[35] After the 2005 World Summit, the rule of law became an integral part of all new peace operations. Previously, reform of the judicial and prison systems was rare outside of executive missions.[36] Transitional administrations in Kosovo and Timor-Leste even had direct responsibility for the administration of judiciaries, police, and prison services.[37]

Criticism of Building of the UN Rule of Law

There are scanty academic studies on the UN transitional administrations as a specific class of intervention or the rule of law initiatives by various missions. Some studies of the UN transitional administration, such as those by Chesterman (2004), Chesterman (2008), Wilde and Schrijver, Wilde and Caplan[38] have provided deeper insights yet the rule of law issues was not their primary focus. Other studies tend to fall into two groups: those that examine state-building under international intervention more generally; and those that examine the several rules of law issues in a single UN mission, or a single rule of law issue in one or two missions. Bull examines a broad set of the rule of law initiatives pursued by three of the four UN transitional administrations deployed to date: in Cambodia, Kosovo, and East Timor.[39] The key findings are (a) UN transitional administrations failed to build local commitment to the rule of law and (b) a state-based enforcement approach to establishing the rule of law proved ineffective as it largely ignored entrenched informal justice institutions.[40] Upham has pointed out that the World Bank adopted a "formalist model of law" instead of legal systems based on interconnections between the social and political linkages of the UN and other aid agencies.[41] Hammergren finds that the connection between judicial reform and human rights protection or good governance is unproven. Studies find that the stances of the political elite and various interest groups, including the judiciary, influence legal and institutional change.[42] In a study of Russian legal reform, Aron noted that even more debilitating is the fact that millions of Russians do not trust their legal system. Making good laws (supply) does not guarantee their proper use (demand), especially when a country suffered generations of state terror, lawlessness, and fraud where the courts, judges, and laws perpetrated a totalitarian state.[43]

THE UN SOLUTIONS TO THE RULE OF LAW IN CONFLICT AND POST-CONFLICT SOCIETIES

We find that the UN was not oblivious to these weaknesses and attempted to overcome them. By its own admission, it had underestimated the extent of the political will necessary to support an effective rule of law reform in post-conflict states.[44] Corruption, however, played a spoiler in its rule of law effort.[45]

The UN provided support for the building of courts and police stations and training of police units and judicial officers.[46] Concomitantly, it also attended to legal education, prison reform, victim protection, and property dispute resolution. Training in evidentiary rules and procedures elicited visible and significant results in Guinea, Liberia, Sierra Leone, Timor-Leste, and Somaliland.[47]

The UN rule of law initiatives moved beyond institutional formalism toward a more bottom-up approach. From 2011, the UN started promoting gender equality to establish the rule of law in transitional administrations. The UN set up specialized police units and investigative magistrates to investigate crimes of sexual violence. The UN also recognized reparations as an essential vehicle to address gender inequality.[48] In 2015, the UN committed to allocate 15 percent of UN-managed peacebuilding funds to projects that address women's specific needs. Most active peacekeeping missions have a senior gender adviser.[49] Such measures make women invested in the peace and the rule of law process. To ensure future peace in conflict and post-conflict societies, from 2011, the UN also kept the perspective of children in transitional justice processes. The Special Courts established in post-conflict societies started sanctioning individuals for child-specific violations.[50]

The UN used initiatives of reparations, truth-seeking, vetting, and dismissals to develop support for the rule of law among other groups in conflict and post-conflict societies. The UN's reparations programs for the violence-victims promoted reconciliation and restored victims' confidence in the state. Reparations also included nonmonetary elements, such as rehabilitation programs for victims and symbolic measures, such as official apologies, monuments and commemorative ceremonies.[51] Reparations strengthened victims' participation in reconstruction efforts.[52]

Vetting of the public service was another of the UN's trust-building measure. Vetting was a formal process for identifying and removing individuals responsible for abuses from police, prison services, the army, and the judiciary. The removal followed due process of natural justice that distinguished the UN vetting processes from the wholesale purges practiced in some countries.[53] Vetting played an essential role in enhancing the legitimacy of official structures, restoring the confidence and trust of the public in the institutions and building the rule of law.[54]

The Rome Statute of 2002 established the International Criminal Court to prosecute those responsible for war crimes, crimes against humanity, and genocide. The UN established a number of ad hoc criminal tribunals.[55] These included ad hoc international criminal tribunals for the former Yugoslavia and Rwanda, which used international judges and prosecutors.[56] The UN adopted an international criminal tribunal mode to remove all perception of bias.[57] The 2004 report of the SG, however, prioritized domestic justice systems as the first resort in the pursuit of accountability. This led to the establishment of "hybrid" mechanisms, such as in Cambodia (2006), Guatemala (2007). Hybrid mechanisms were composed of both international and national judges and prosecutors and were located *in situ* within the affected communities to build national justice systems' capacity.[58]

The UN made formal justice mechanisms accessible to the public in conflict and post-conflict societies through legal aid clinics and mobile courts.[59] Legal aid desks, for example, in Darfur prisons in Sudan benefited over 500 prisoners.[60] The UN recognized that ignoring indigenous and informal traditions for administering justice could exclude large sectors of society from accessible justice.[61] The UN ensured that their functioning was compatible with human rights. They did not perpetuate discriminatory social norms, and that their relationship with the formal justice system did not create further conflict. One mechanism to achieve this were training workshops for the capacity building of customary court judges and paralegals to protect women and children from sexual and gender-based violence.[62] Truth commissions developed by the UN are one such example. Truth commissions are official, temporary, nonjudicial fact-finding bodies investigating a pattern of abuses of human rights or humanitarian law committed over several years. These bodies take a victim-centered approach and conclude their work with a final report of fact-findings and recommendations. Such truth commissions fostered accountability, preserved evidence, identified perpetrators and recommended reparations and institutional reforms.[63]

CORRUPTION AND THE RULE OF LAW

A strong synergy between anti-corruption and the rule of law will lead to the desired rule of law outcomes. The UN is aware that inappropriate behaviors undermine its legitimacy. It issued special measures against sexual exploitation and sexual abuse, setting out minimum standards of behavior and conduct expected of all UN personnel.[64] The UN has acknowledged that building the rule of law fosters cultural beliefs that people can turn to legal institutions to resolve their disputes instead of resorting to self-help. However, before 2011, there was little guidance on anti-corruption to the international officials of UN peacekeeping missions.

In 2002, a corruption scandal was discovered. A senior UN official had transferred $4.3 million of Kosovo Energy Company's money to a bank account under his control in Gibraltar. The same official had also unlawfully obtained €220,000 of UN funds by submitting false invoices. In addition, he had also lied about his academic, professional, and personal achievements in his recruitment.[65]

The next year there were findings of systemic corruption in Kosovo's Pristina Airport. The special representative took no action because "staff in peacekeeping missions . . . are transient," and the events reported were "historical."[66] Audit firms from 2001 to 2003 had found that there were payments of commissions and kickbacks in procurements and incidences of the passage of salient information to favored bidders. The airport management required all airport charges paid in cash directly to airport officials. Some commercial airlines experienced extortion in the payment of fees for landing slots, a critical element of any commercial air carrier's flight scheduling. The special representative response to the investigation report by the UN Office of Internal Oversight Services (OIOS) was that as much time had passed since 2001 when the events had occurred, it would not be a good use of limited resources to pursue the matter further. The OIOS presciently forecast then that the reluctance by senior mission management to address fraud and corruption would have a devastating impact on public perception inside and outside of Kosovo, as the UN will appear to be escaping from the problems rather than solving them.[67] Another report of the OIOS in 2008 mentioned that the Kosovo Consolidated Budget's financial statements for 1999 through 2006 carried disclaimer opinions by its auditors. This was indicative of a weak internal control system and financial mismanagement. Audit reports of all public sector enterprises of Kosovo had similar disclaimers attached to them.[68]

Besides the continuous measures to deal with corruption within itself, the UN also took the lead in the global fight against corruption. The UN is the architect and administrator of implementing the United Nations Convention against Corruption (UNCAC).[69] This will be discussed separately.

In 2008, the UN stated that combating corruption was a crucial activity internationally and in conflict and post-conflict societies for long-term development.[70] In 2011, situations in Côte d'Ivoire, Egypt, Libya, South Sudan, the Syria Arab Republic, and Tunisia brought the UN's focus starkly on the importance of addressing corruption. In its 2011 report, the UN stated that profound capacity deficits in state justice and security institutions, exacerbated by widespread corruption and political interference, undermined the legitimacy and competence of state institutions.[71]

In a population survey in Afghanistan, it became apparent to the UN (November 2012), that 50 percent of Afghan citizens paid a bribe when requesting a public service and that officials from the key rule of law institutions received the highest amounts of bribes. The UN recognized that the result of this was that many Afghans could not gain access to the justice system. In Liberia, indicators highlighted corruption and insufficient accountability in the police system.[72]

A high-level meeting of the General Assembly on the rule of law at the national and international level in 2012 declared the following:[73]

> We are convinced of the negative impact of corruption, which obstructs economic growth and development, erodes public confidence, legitimacy and transparency and hinders the making of fair and effective laws, as well as their

> administration, enforcement and adjudication, and therefore stress the importance of the rule of law as an essential element in addressing and preventing corruption.

This statement demonstrated that the UN believed that strengthening the rule of law leads to enhanced integrity. In our opinion, there is a close, mutually reinforcing relationship between the two. Strong rule of law institutions will certainly inhibit corruption, but corruption itself can have a debilitating effect on the rule of law.

At the international level, the UN must walk the talk. Decisions by the committee administering sanctions are by consensus, in the absence of which the Security Council decides the matter where the veto power of the permanent five members applies. For the international rule of law, equality of all nations is still a contentious matter.[74] Additionally, many member states have not accepted the compulsory jurisdiction of the International Court of Justice.[75] These examples point to areas that need attention for stronger international rule of law, primarily led by the UN.

In transitional and developing countries, the feeling of a lack of equality before the law is so strong that ordinary people do not even attempt to test the principle with a time-consuming and expensive court case. Real equality depends largely on the absence of corruption within the judiciary because the rich can use bribes to escape equal justice. In many countries, the poor or marginalized will not risk bringing misdeeds of their "betters" before a court if they believe the courts will simply uphold the power structure of society.[76]

Likewise, corruption infinitely pollutes the end goal of the rule of law, that is, peace and security. If police capture criminals but a corrupt judge releases these criminals, the rule of law is corrupted. The police reform in Panama was successful, and the people turned to the police routinely for help. However, there was no law and order improvement as the corrupt judiciary released prisoners, particularly drug traffickers and organized criminals.[77] In transition societies, large-scale returns of displaced civilian populations bring to the fore disputes related to housing, land, property, and natural resource extraction. Corruption in such a sensitive scenario can spoil peace and security and the rule of law scenario.[78]

Corruption distorts another desirable goal of the rule of law, that is, predictable and efficient justice. Corrupt judges can delay judgments to favor one party that acts as a penalty to the other party before announcing an actual verdict.[79] Clerks can "lose" files, and law enforcement agencies can delay investigations for bribes just as easily. In Moscow, Belton found that during the roaring 1990s, for example, the going rate for stalling a criminal investigation was claimed to be $50,000.[80]

Anti-corruption training and measures are particularly necessary, as many of the UN rule of law initiatives can appear paradoxical. The rule of law requires that people settle disputes through the law rather than through violence. The use of armed force by the interveners themselves precede the post-conflict rule of law initiatives. This paradox, along with corruption, can totally negate attempts to foster a belief in the rule of law as an alternative to self-help.[81]

UN administrators in transitional countries admit that a critical component of transforming a territory along the rule of law is leading by example. However, there is also a feeling that since an international organization like the UN is involved, there is reduced pressure for effective accountability.[82]

This underscores the inescapable fact that corruption hinders the acceptance of external and transplanted legal institutions. The rule of law institutions is likely to be accepted and utilized if they are not corrupted.[83] Adherence to any rules system is reliant on the extent to which people commit voluntarily to it and central to this voluntary compliance is the question of legitimacy.[84] There is a normalization of violence in transitional societies due to protracted conflict, and crimes such as drug trafficking, human trafficking, smuggling, and corruption dominate public life.[85] Anti-corruption and integrity building measures can help build the process of legitimacy. Truth commissions can greatly benefit post-conflict societies in establishing the facts about past human rights violations, fostering accountability, preserving evidence, identifying perpetrators, and recommending reparations. A prime factor that can limit these potential benefits can be a corrupt justice system.[86] In one instance in western Sahara, the UN has received information that human rights defenders' trials were falling short of international fair trial standards,[87] which was a red flag for corruption.

While pursuing its goals to establish and promote the strong rule of law, the UN also push its global anti-corruption agenda through UNCAC. The Convention Preamble begins with the concern "about the seriousness of problems and threats posed by corruption to the stability and security of societies, undermining the institutions and values of democracy, ethical values and justice and jeopardizing sustainable development and the rule of law."[88] Through its Implementation Review Mechanism, the UN is making efforts to implement the standards to establishing an anti-corruption legal system in member countries. Yet, their process is time-consuming, and the gap between the promulgation of laws and the establishment of instruments on the one hand and effective use thereof to prevent corruption, convict wrongdoers, and recover end return assets is still exceptionally large and stark. While conceiving SDGs, the UN realized the importance of simultaneous focus on both the rule of law and corruption, which translated into Goal 16 of the SDGs. It is empirically proved that corruption negatively affects economic growth.[89] It would be pertinent to discuss how the rule of law is the median variable between corruption and sustainable development.

THE RULE OF LAW, ANTI-CORRUPTION, AND SUSTAINABLE DEVELOPMENT

Spearheaded by the United Nations, the SDGs are 17 aspirational "global goals" and 169 targets adopted in 2015 by the 193 UN member states. These "global goals" build on the millennium development goals (MDGs) and intend to steer policymaking and developmental funding for the next fifteen years.[90] Originally, "sustainable development" was defined in 1987 as "development that meets the needs of the present without compromising the ability of future generations to meet their own needs." Over time, the definition of sustainable development has evolved to capture a more holistic approach, linking the three dimensions of sustainable development: economic development, social inclusion, and environmental sustainability.[91] As the MDGs did not incorporate the rule of law, conflict-affected and fragile states were among the poorest achievers of the MDGs.[92] Wars, and the ensuing violence and corruption that accompany them, impede overall economic development—direct (e.g., infrastructure damage) and indirect costs (e.g., reduced tourism) draw substantially from state budgets and the gross domestic product.[93] Target 3 of Goal 16 of the SDGs, "promote the rule of law at the national and international levels and ensure equal access to justice for all," signifies the importance of the rule of law for achieving all other SDGs, besides underscoring its legal dimension, rather than merely its economic one.

Whether the focus is on health, equality for women and girls, or the discriminatory effects of climate change, SDGs recognize that the rule of law is an essential contributor. For example, in the Philippines, the rule of law has stabilized smallholders' land and put in place the proper incentives and services to ensure the protection of smallholder landowners.[94] Additionally, target 16.1 states "to significantly reduce all forms of violence and related death rates everywhere. It represents global recognition that development cannot succeed without peace and justice as components of the rule of law."[95]

Target 16.5 aims to reduce corruption and bribery in all their forms. However, there is a broad consensus in the anti-corruption community that the fight against corruption needs to encompass the entire SDG framework. Corruption affects all SDG-related sectors, undermining development outcomes and severely compromising efforts to achieve health, education, gender equality, climate action, water and sanitation, and other goals. Corruption occurs at every stage of the service delivery chain, from policy design, tax collection, and budgetary allocations to procurement and service provision. SDGs 3, 4, 5, 6 and 13 relate to sectors characterized by: (a) significant investments from national governments, foreign and multilateral donors, and private sources; (b) specialized goods; and (c) multiple points of service delivery, all of which make them especially vulnerable to corruption. Climate change action alone involves many sectors with extremely high risks of corruption, such as construction, forestry (logging), and the energy sectors. These, the automobile sector, and the fossil fuel lobby will exert influence to limit national ambitions to transition to renewable energy.[96]

There has been mention of the interrelationship between the rule of law and anti-corruption in earlier paragraphs. People cannot have confidence in institutions that do not operate fairly and transparently. A study based on household survey data from the Gallup World Poll has demonstrated a negative correlation between corruption and confidence in public institutions.[97] There are two concepts of trust: generalized trust and particularized trust. Generalized trust means generalized trust in people, legal framework, state institutions, civil society, and trust between or among anonymous economic actors. Trust in family, friends, and kin is particularized trust. Low generalized trust and high in-group trust form fertile ground for corruption. Low generalized trust and corruption have negative consequences for economic growth and thus threaten the SDGs. Nations can create and promote generalized trust through strengthening the rule of law backed by anti-corruption measures.[98]

Corruption directly impinges on development and growth-enhancing activities by misapplication of resources, distorted investments, subdued innovations, lower productivity, and causing various inefficiencies. Often the best-connected firm rather than the most efficient firm gets government contracts. Inefficiency and reduced competition caused by bribery prevent many firms from entering the market, thereby creating a "rent-seeking" environment. The companies either quit the market or fall into the informal sector if they are unwilling or unable to pay bribes. Unnecessary public investment and infrastructure projects are implemented for awarding contracts to cronies in return for corrupt gains. The survival of a small business is threatened in corrupt environments. Small firms are the engines of growth in most economies and generate employment, and hence corruption hurts an economy's growth rate. Low incomes due to corruption lead to limited access to essential resources as health care and education. Corruption undermines the rule of law by creating a corrupt environment that corrupts judicial systems' ability to enforce contracts. In short, corruption erodes the climate for development in all possible ways.[99]

THE WAY FORWARD

Under Article 47 of the 2030 Agenda, governments have the primary responsibility for the follow-up and review of the SDGs at the subnational and national levels. The UN high-level political forum does the global-level review and follow-up of the SDGs. At the regional level, the UN Regional Commissions convene annually Regional Forums for Sustainable

Development. The way forward is to integrate anti-corruption and the rule of law strategies across the SDGs and apply this amalgam to an expanded circle of stakeholders.

In 2013, the UN launched "Business for the Rule of Law" to mobilize the business community's support for the rule of law.[100] The business sector can also be mobilized as a prime agent for anti-corruption. Combining the rule of law and anti-corruption can be an effective model of sustainable development and economic growth. Another target group for sustainable development is civil society. This includes voluntary organizations that hold both government and business to account. It has philanthropies that support science, research, education, and help the poor. In addition, it includes "social enterprises," often with distinct legal status, that work on a business model yet do not pursue profit as their sole or main motive.[101] The UN Democracy Fund devoted half its total funding in 2013 to civil society projects in the field of the rule of law.[102]

The authors recommend similar funding and support by the UN to the organizations and educational institutions already engaged in anti-corruption capacity building. Nongovernmental organizations such as the US-based Open Society Institute, the associated Revenue Watch Institute, UK-based Global Witness, and the Publish What You Pay (PWYP) coalition can also be influential partners for sustainable development. PWYP advocacy campaign was the principal catalyst for the Extractive Industries Transparency Initiative. Fiscal transparency and political accountability can be the bedrocks of sustainable development.[103] Last but not least, there should be active engagement of local authorities and communities in sustainable development.[104]

The lessons learned by the UN during the evolutionary process of the international and national rule of law may also be applied to the fight against corruption through capacity-building measures namely: (a) education and training of investigators and prosecutors in evidentiary rules and procedures, (b) training workshops for customary court judges and paralegals, (c) achieving institutional formalism toward a more bottom-up approach, (d) making women invested in the fight against corruption, and (e) establishing reparations especially in the context of asset recovery and return.

Capacity building in anti-corruption and compliance will be an effective tool for the active engagement of all stakeholders in the sustainable development process. The authors argue to concretize the tools for capacity building for effective participation in furtherance of anti-corruption initiatives, which in turn will assist in building the rule of law and moving toward SDGs, such as:

(a) a free, timely, and online access to a global repository of legal information such as laws, statutes, regulations, caselaw, treaties, and academic works, and so on. Legal education will engage a larger audience of stakeholders and make many more people aware, at all levels, of both the laws that protect them and the laws that regulate behavior.

(b) building corruption control mechanism using information and communication technologies diffusion, as empirically established by Mohamed Sami Be Ali.[105] In 2014, the then UN SG Ban Ki-moon advocated harnessing the data revolution in support of sustainable development. New technologies can also be a powerful anti-corruption tool.[106]

(c) more countries now (127 countries) have freedom-of-information laws that serve to enhance empowerment and equality among all social groups.[107] Capacity training should include training on using these laws for anti-corruption purposes, including the appeal procedures.

(d) one of the main tools for delivering the SDGs is data collection and monitoring.[108] Here training people to disaggregate SDG data to extract the effects of corruption across the different SDGs would come in handy. Disaggregated data will highlight impediments in the realization of the SDGs, for example, whether corruption unfairly prevents women from accessing equal opportunities or leads to environmental degradation. Such vital information may enable timely course correction and the realization of sustainable development.

The SDG indicators mostly rely on data generated by government agencies. The reliability and credibility of official data may be open to question for two reasons. First, the task of producing data for 169 targets may simply overwhelm certain national statistics offices. Second, politically sensitive targets, such as those related to corruption and governance, require that governments assess their efficacy or corruption. This calls for independent analysis through third-party collection and validation of data. Training of multiple stakeholders in collecting proxy and actual data at various levels can capture both the SDGs' impact and progress.[109]

Finally, there is an urgent need to use technology to diffuse knowledge, conduct research, and impart anti-corruption education and training at affordable costs to a wider population. Sophisticated laws and emerging technologies cannot be harnessed to their potential unless people in every country can implement these. Every employee of the UN and connected organizations must also be trained in anti-corruption and compliance system. The report of the panel of the High Level Panel on International Financial Accountability (FACTI) observes:

> A host of international institutions do provide capacity building, but it has not been sufficient. Intergovernmental bodies and initiatives that assist countries in building capacity–including the International Anti-Corruption Academy, the Platform

for Collaboration on Tax, the Addis Tax Initiative, Tax Inspectors Without Borders, regional tax organizations, the Stolen Assets Recovery Initiative, and the African Legal Support Facility—should be further strengthened.[110]

The authors are in complete agreement with this observation.

CONCLUSION

The importance of establishing and maintaining the rule of law is a *sine qua non* for a peaceful, secure, and developed world. Corruption corrupts the rule of law. The public, private sectors and civil societies alike must fight corruption. We recommend a greater focus of the UN on anti-corruption and strengthening of the rule of law to achieve SDGs. Building of capacities among the state actors, the UN's officials and its specialized agencies and related organizations, the international organization, civil societies, and people in business organizations through education and training programs would go a long way in meeting these objectives. A global outreach and awareness program must enhance the involvement of the citizenry to reduce tolerance of corruption in all forms and make the rule of law a way of life. These recommendations do not take away the sheen from its spectacular work done by the UN. The UN General Assembly Special Session on Corruption in June 2021 is a welcome move in this direction.

NOTES

1. UN Docs. A/75/1, Declaration on the commemoration of the seventy-fifth anniversary of the United Nations Resolution, 28 September 2020.
2. UN doc. A/RES/60/1, World Summit Outcome, 24 October 2005.
3. Simon Chesterman, "An International Rule of Law?" *The American Journal of Comparative Law* 56, no 2 (2008): 331–361.
4. Jeremy Waldron, The Rule of Law, *The Stanford Encyclopaedia of Philosophy* (Summer 2020 Edition): (2020) accesses on March 10, 2021, https://stanford.io/3bLLffO.
5. Vienna Declaration and Programme of Action. Adopted by the World Conference on Human Rights in Vienna on 25 June 1993, https://bit.ly/39Zr3WG.
6. Chesterman, *An International Rule of Law?*, 345.
7. UN doc. S/2011/634, The rule of law and transitional justice in conflict and post-conflict societies: Report of the Secretary General, 2011, §§ 4–6.
8. Rachel Kleinfeld Belton, "Competing Definitions of the Rule of Law: Implications for Practitioners." *Carnegie Endowment for International Peace* (2005): 3–35.

9. Chesterman, *An International Rule of Law?*, 332.

10. UN doc. S/2004/616, The rule of law and transitional justice in conflict and post-conflict societies: Report of the Secretary General, 23 August 2004, § 4.

11. UN doc. A/70/206, Strengthening and coordinating United Nations rule of law activities: Report of the Secretary General, 27 July 2015, 11.

12. Belton, *Competing Definitions*, 3–35.

13. Brian Z. Tamanaha, "The History and Elements of the Rule of Law," *Singapore Journal of Legal Studies* (2012): 232–247.

14. Hans Koechler, "The Lockerbie Trial and the Rule of Law." *National Law School of India Review* 21, no 1 (2009): 149–162.

15. UN Docs. A/61/636 & S/2006/980, Uniting our strengths: Enhancing United Nations support for Rule of Law: Report of the Secretary General, 14 December 2006: §§ 41–42.

16. Chesterman, *An International Rule of Law?*, 355–356.

17. UN doc. A/70/206, Strengthening and coordinating rule of law activities, § 2.

18. UN doc. A/64/446, The rule of law at the national and international levels: Report of the Sixth Committee, 12 November 2009, 3.

19. Latin for Agreements must be kept–Refer to online Britannica at https://bit.ly/3zKgx1i

20. Chesterman, *An International Rule of Law?*, 357–360.

21. UN doc. A/61/636; S/2006/980, *Uniting Our Strengths*, § 1.

22. UN doc. S/2004/616, Transitional justice in conflict and post-conflict societies, § 41

23. Rwanda situation existed between 6 April and 15 July 1994.

24. UN doc. S/1994/1405, Preliminary report of the Independent Commission of Experts established in accordance with Security Council resolution 935 (1994), 9 December 1994.

25. UN doc. S/1994/1405, Preliminary report of the Independent Commission, § 121.

26. UN doc. S/1994/1405, *Preliminary Report*, § 121–122.

27. UN doc. S/1994/1405, *Preliminary Report*, § 120.

28. UN doc. S/1994/1405, *Preliminary Report*, § 126.

29. UN doc. S/1994/1405, *Preliminary Report*, § 128.

30. UN doc. S/1994/1405, *Preliminary Report*, §§ 130, 133.

31. UN doc. S/2004/616, Transitional justice in conflict and post-conflict societies, 16.

32. UN doc. S/RES/731, 21 January 1992, § 52.

33. UN doc. S/RES/883, 11 November 1993; UN doc. S/RES/1192, 27 August 1998.

34. Chesterman, *An International Rule of Law?* 347–348.

35. UN doc. S/2001/394, No exit without strategy: Security Council decision-making and the closure or transaction of United Nations Peacekeeping Operations. Report to the Security Council, April 20, 2001.

36. UN docs. A/61/636 & S/2006/980, Uniting our strengths, 12–13.

37. UN doc. S/2004/616, Transitional justice in conflict and post-conflict societies, 5.

38. Chesterman, "An International Rule of Law?"; Ralph Wilde and Nico Schrijver, "The complex role of the legal adviser when international organizations administer territory," Proceedings of the Annual Meeting, *American Society of International Law* 95 (2001): 251–261; Ralph Wilde, The United Nations as Government: The Tensions of an Ambivalent Role, Proceedings of the Annual Meeting, *American Society of International Law* 97 (2003): 212–215; Richard Caplan, *International Governance of War-Torn Territories: Rule and Reconstruction*, Oxford; Oxford University Press 2005.

39. Carolyn Bull, "No Entry Without Strategy: Building the Rule of Law under UN Transitional Administration," Tokyo: United Nations University Press 2008: 9.

40. Bull, *No Entry without Strategy*, 9.

41. Frank Upham, "Mythmaking in the rule of law orthodoxy," Research Report, Carnegie Endowment for International Peace, 2002: 8, accessed on March 5, 2021, https://bit.ly/35HeBbW.

42. Linn Hammergren, "Institutional Strengthening and Justice Reform," Center for Democracy and Governance, 1998, accessed on March 17, 2021, § 57, https://bit.ly/3d0MCrZ.

43. Aron, Leon, American Enterprise Institute, Russia Reinvents the Rule of Law, accessed on March 17, 2021, https://bit.ly/3ytTMhh.

44. UN doc. S/2004/616, Transitional justice in conflict and post-conflict societies, § 20.

45. UN doc. S/2013/341, Measuring the effectiveness of the support provided by the United Nations system for the promotion of the rule of law in conflict and post-conflict situations: Report of the Secretary General, 11 June 2013, § 11.

46. UN doc. S/2013/341, *Measuring*, § 63.

47. UN doc. S/2011/634, *The Rule of Law*, § 11.

48. UN doc. S/2011/634, *The Rule of Law*, §§ 8–18.

49. UN Women, A Global Study on the Implementation of the United Nations Security Council resolution 1325, 2015, 8–49, accessed on March 17, 2021, https://bit.ly/3tPNvJr.

50. UN doc. S/2011/634, *The Rule of Law*, §§ 7–8.

51. UN doc. S/2004/616, *Transitional Justice*, §§ 54–55.

52. UN doc. S/2011/634, *The Rule of Law*, § 8.

53. Purges involved wide-scale dismissal and disqualification based not on individual records but rather on party affiliation, political opinion, or association with a prior state institution.

54. UN doc. S/2004/616, *Transitional Justice*, §§ 52–53.

55. UN doc. S/2004/616, *Transitional Justice*, §§ 38–49.

56. UN doc. S/2004/616, *Transitional Justice*, § 39.

57. UN doc. S/1994/1405, Preliminary report of the Independent Commission of Experts established in accordance with Security Council resolution 935 (1994), §§ 135–138.

58. UN doc. S/2011/634, *The Rule of Law*, § 9.

59. UN doc. S/2013/341, *Measuring*, § 63.

60. UN doc. A/68/213, Strengthening and coordinating United Nations rule of law activities: Report of the Secretary General, 29 July 2013, § 52.

61. UN doc. S/2004/616, *Transitional Justice*, § 12.

62. UN doc. A/68/213, Strengthening and coordinating United Nations rule of law activities: Report of the Secretary General, § 12.

63. UN doc. S/2004/616, *Transitional Justice*, §§ 50–51.

64. UN doc. S/2004/616, *Transitional Justice*, § 11.

65. UN doc. A/58/592, Investigation into the fraudulent diversion of $4.3 million by a senior staff member of the reconstruction pillar of the UN Interim Administration Mission in Kosovo (UNMIK): 13 November 2003, § 2.

66. Report of the Office of Internal Oversight Services on the investigation conducted by the Investigations Tas Force into fraud and corruption allegations at Pristina Airport, 14 March 2006, §§ 1–39.

67. UN doc. A/60/720, Report of the Office of Internal Oversight Services on the investigation conducted by the Investigations Task Force into fraud and corruption allegations at Pristina Airport, 14 March 2006, §§ 8–46.

68. UN doc. A/62/169, Report of the Office of Internal Oversight Services on the comprehensive audit of the United Nations Interim Administration Mission in Kosovo mandate implementation, 18 April 2008, § 13.

69. UN doc. A/70/206, Strengthening and coordinating United Nations rule of law activities: Report of the Secretary General, 27 July 2015, § 65.

70. UN doc. S/2008/362, The United Nations in Kosovo: Report of the Secretary General, 15 July 2008, § 42.

71. UN doc. S/2011/634, *The Rule of Law*, § 11.

72. UN doc. S/2013/341, *Measuring*, § 39.

73. UN doc. A/RES/67/1, Declaration of the High-level Meeting of the General Assembly on the Rule of Law at the National and International Levels, 30 November 2012, § 4.

74. Chesterman, *An International Rule of Law?*, 351–361.

75. UN Security Council, The Deputy Secretary General's Remarks to Security Council on the promotion and strengthening of the rule of law in the maintenance of international peace and security, accessed on May 14, 2021, https://bit.ly/3fA3EO3.

76. Belton, *Competing*, 10.

77. Belton, *Competing*, 21.

78. UN doc. S/2011/634, *The Rule of Law*, 1–19.

79. Belton, *Competing*, 12.

80. Belton, *Competing*, 13.

81. Malanne A. Civic, Ralph Wilde, and Colette Rausch, "Restoring Rule of Law in Post-Conflict and Stabilization Operations: Respective Roles of Law and Politics," Proceedings of the Annual Meeting, *American Society of International Law* (2008): 323–324.

82. Civic, Wilde, and Rausch, "Restoring Rule of Law in Post-Conflict and Stabilization Operations: Respective Roles of Law and Politics," 326.

83. Thomas Carothers, "The Rule of Law Revival," *Foreign Affairs* 77, no. (1998): 95–106.

84. Brian Z. Tamanaha, "The History and Elements of the Rule of Law," *Singapore Journal of Legal Studies* (2012): 232–247.

85. UN Women, "A Global Study on the Implementation of the United Nations Security Council resolution 1325," 38.

86. UN doc. S/2004/616, *Transitional Justice*, §§ 50–51.

87. UN doc. S/2007/202, The situation concerning Western Sahara: Report of the Secretary General, 13 April 2007.

88. United Nations, United Nations Convention against Corruption (2004): Annex Page 5.

89. Alberto Ades, Rafael Di Tella, "The New Economics of Corruption: A Survey and some New Results," *Political Studies* 45 no. 3 (1997): 496–515; Mauro Paulo, Corruption and Growth, *Quarterly Journal of Economics* (1995): 381–712.

90. Stephanie Trapnell, Matthew Jenkin, Marie Chêne, "Monitoring Corruption and Anti-Corruption in the Sustainable Development Goals," Transparency International (2017)

91. Sustainable Development Solutions Network, Getting Started with the Sustainable Development Goals (2015), accessed on May 12, 2021, https://bit.ly/2QH8ssu.

92. UN Women, *A Global Study*, 4.

93. UN Women, *A Global Study*, 195.

94. Giovanni Tartaglia Polcini, "The Rule of Law as a Condition for Development Toward Sustainability," *The International Journal of Social Quality* 7, no. 2 (Summer 2017): 113–129.

95. Olivia Kokushubila Lwabukuna, International Rule of Law and Development, *Journal of Peacebuilding & Development* 11 no. 2 (2016): 89–94.

96. Trapnell, Jenkin and Chêne, "Monitoring Corruption and Anti-Corruption in the Sustainable Development Goals," 4–58.

97. Bianca Clausen, Aart Kraay, and Zsolt Nyiri, *openknowledge.worldbank.org*, accessed on May 2, 2021, https://bit.ly/3v80xmS.

98. Polcini, *The Rule of Law*, 132–134.

99. Polcini, *The Rule of Law*, 125–134.

100. UN doc. A/69/181, Report of the Secretary-General on Strengthening and coordinating United Nations rule of law activities, 24 July 2014.

101. Sustainable Development Solutions Network, "Getting Started," 6–7.

102. UN doc. A/68/213, Strengthening and coordinating United Nations rule of law activities: Report of the Secretary General, 29 July 2013.

103. Sophie Harman, David Williams, *Governing the World? Cases in Global Governance* (London-New York: Routledge, 2013), 69–76.

104. Sustainable Development Solutions Network, "Getting Started," 8

105. Mohamed Sami Ben Ali, Amira Gasmi, "Does ICT Diffusion Matter for Corruption? An Economic Development Perspective," *Telematics and Informatics* 34, no 8 (2017): 1445–1453.

106. Sustainable Development Solutions Network, "Getting Started," 8.

107. United Nations, "The Sustainable Development Goals Report," *Sustainable Development Goal Indicators* (2020), accessed on May 7, 2021, https://bit.ly/345f1YH.

108. Amanda Richardson, Stephanie Debere, Annette Jainter, Rukshana Nanayakkara, "Harnessing and Achieving the SDGs: Gendered Land Corruption and the Sustainable Development," *Transparency International*, accessed on May 4, 2021, https://bit.ly/3yy1BT1.

109. Trapnell, Jenkin and Chêne, *Monitoring*, 8–9.

110. United Nations, Financial Integrity for Sustainable Development: "Report of the High Level Panel on International Financial Accountability, Transparency and Integrity for Achieving the 2030 Agenda (2021), accessed on May 20, 2021, https://bit.ly/3ugRcYC.

BIBLIOGRAPHY

Ades, Alberto, and Rafael Di Tella. The New Economics of Corruption: A Survey and some New Results. *Political Studies* 45, no 3 (2008): 496–515.

Ali, Mohamed Sami Ben, and Amira Gasmi. "Does ICT Diffusion Matter for Corruption? An Economic Development Perspective." *Telematics and Informatics* 34, no 8 (2017): 1445–1453.

Aron, Leon. "American Enterprise Institute." Russia Reinvents the Rule of Law (March 2002). Accessed March 17, 2021. https://bit.ly/3ytTMhh.

Belton, Rachel Kleinfeld. "Competing Definitions of the Rule of Law: Implications for Practitioners." *Carnegie Endowment for International Peace* (2005): 3–35.

Berg. Louis-Alexandre, and Deval Desai. Background Paper: Overview on the Rule of Law and Sustainable Development for the Global Dialogue on Rule of Law and the Post-2015 Development Agenda. UNDP, 2013. Assessed on March 10, 2021. https://bit.ly/3qKjkTX

Bull, Carolyn. *No Entry Without Strategy: Building the Rule of Law under UN Transitional Administration*. Tokyo: United Nations University Press, 2008.

Burgerman, Susan D. "Building the Peace by Mandating Reform: United Nations-Mediated Human Rights Agreements in El Salvador and Guatemala." *Latin American Perspectives* 27, no. 3 (2000): 63–87.

Caplan, Richard. *International Governance of War-Torn Territories: Rule and Reconstruction*. Oxford: Oxford University Press, 2005.

Carothers, Thomas. "The Rule of Law Revival." *Foreign Affairs* 77, no. 2 (1998): 95–106.

Chesterman, Simon. "An International Rule of Law?" *The American Journal of Comparative Law* 56, no 2 (2008): 331–361.

Chesterman, Simon. *You, The People: The United Nations, Transitional Administration, and State-building*. Oxford: Oxford University Press, 2004.

Civic, Malanne A., Ralph Wilde, and Colette Rausch. "Restoring Rule of Law in Post-conflict and Stabilization Operations: Respective Roles of Law and Politics." *Proceedings of the Annual Meeting American Society of International Law* (2008): 319–327.

Clausen, Bianca, Aart Kraay, and Zsolt Nyiri. 2011. "openknowledge.worldbank.org." Published August 12, 2011. Accessed May 2, 2021. https://bit.ly/3v80xmS.

Hammergren, Linn. "Institutional Strengthening and Justice Reform." Center for Democracy and Governance (1998) August. Accessed March 17, 2021. https://bit.ly/3d0MCrZ.

Harman, Sophie, and David, Williams. *Governing the World?: Cases in Global Governance*. London-New York: Routledge, 2013.

Koechler, Hans. "The Lockerbie Trial and the Rule of Law." *National Law School of India Review* 21, no 1 (2009): 149–162.

Lwabukuna, Olivia Kokushubila. "International Rule of Law and Development." *Journal of Peacebuilding & Development* 11, no. 2 (2016): 89–94.

Paulo, Mauro. "Corruption and Growth." *Quarterly Journal of Economics* 110, no. 3 (August 1995): 681–712.

Polcini, Giovanni Tartaglia. 2017. "The Rule of Law as a Condition for Development Toward Sustainability." *The International Journal of Social Quality* 7, no. 2 (Summer 2017): 113–137.

Richardson, Amanda, Stephanie Debere, Annette Jainter, and Rukshana Nanayakkara. "Harnessing and Achieving the SDGs: Gendered Land Corruption and the Sustainable Development." Published 2018. Accessed March 5, 2021. https://bit.ly/3yy1BT1.

Sustainable Development Solutions Network. A Framework for Sustainable Development. Sustainable Development Solutions Network. Published December 19, 2012. Accessed May 12, 2021. https://bit.ly/3zMPDpe.

Sustainable Development Solutions Network. "Getting Started with the Sustainable Development Goals." A Guide for Stakeholders. Published December 15, 2015. Accessed May 12, 2021. https://bit.ly/2QH8ssu.

Tamanaha, Brian Z. "The History and Elements of the Rule of Law." *Singapore Journal of Legal Studies* (2012): 232–247.

Trapnell, Stephanie, Matthew Jenkin, and Marie Chêne. Monitoring Corruption and Anti-Corruption in the Sustainable Development Goals. Resource Guide, Transparency International, 2017. Accessed May 7, 2021. https://bit.ly/347aBRd.

UN doc. A/58/592. Investigation into the fraudulent diversion of $4.3 million by a senior staff member of the reconstruction pillar of the UN Interim Administration Mission in Kosovo (UNMIK). 13 November 2003.

UN doc. A/60/720. Report of the Office of Internal Oversight Services on the investigation conducted by the Investigations Task Force into fraud and corruption allegations at Pristina Airport. 14 March 2006.

UN doc. A/62/169. Report of the Office of Internal Oversight Services on the comprehensive audit of the United Nations Interim Administration Mission in Kosovo mandate implementation. 18 April 2008.

UN doc. A/68/213. Strengthening and coordinating United Nations rule of law activities: Report of the Secretary General. 29 July 2013.

UN doc. A/69/181. Report of the Secretary-General on Strengthening and coordinating United Nations rule of law activities. 24 July 2014.

UN doc. A/70/206. Strengthening and coordinating United Nations rule of law activities: Report of the Secretary General. 27 July 2015.

UN doc. A/74/139. Strengthening and coordinating United Nations rule of law activities: Report of the Secretary General. July 24 2014.

UN doc. A/RES/60/1. 2005 World Summit Outcome. 24 October 2005.

UN doc. A/RES/67/1. Declaration of the High-level Meeting of the General Assembly on the Rule of Law at the National and International Levels. 30 November 2012.

UN doc. S/1994/1405. Preliminary report of the Independent Commission of Experts established in accordance with Security Council resolution 935 (1994): 9 December 1994.

UN doc. S/2001/394. No exit without strategy: Security Council decision-making and the closure or transaction of United Nations Peacekeeping Operations. Report to the Security Council. 20 April, 2001.

UN doc. S/2004/616. The rule of law and transitional justice in conflict and post-conflict societies: Report of the Secretary-General. 23 August 2004.

UN doc. S/2007/202. The situation concerning Western Sahara: Report of the Secretary General. 13 April 2007.

UN doc. S/2008/362. The United Nations in Kosovo: Report of the Secretary General. 15 July 2008.

UN doc. S/2011/634. The rule of law and transitional justice in conflict and post-conflict societies: Report of the Secretary General. 12 October 2011.

UN doc. S/2013/341. Measuring the effectiveness of the support provided by the United Nations system for the promotion of the rule of law in conflict and post-conflict situations: Report of the Secretary-General. 11 June 2013.

UN doc. S/RES/1192. Lockerbie case. 27 August 1998.

UN doc. S/RES/731. 21 January 1992.

UN doc. S/RES/883. Libyan Arab Jamahiriya. 11 November 1993.

UN docs. A/61/636 & S/2006/980. Uniting our strengths: Enhancing United Nations support for Rule of Law: Report of the Secretary General. 14 December 2006.

UN docs. A/64/446. The rule of law at the national and international levels: Report of the Sixth Committee. 12 November 2009.

UN docs. A/75/1. Declaration on the commemoration of the seventy-fifth anniversary of the United Nations. 28 September 2020. https://bit.ly/3yDQzfk.

UN General Assembly. Strengthening and coordinating United Nations rule of law activities: Report of the Secretary General. July 20, 2016.

UN Security Council. Report Submitted to the UN Secretary General by Dr Enoch Dumbutshena and Prof Henry G Schermers on the Scottish Judicial System. December 18, 1997.

UN Security Council. "Resolution S/1999/378: Letter dated 5 April 1999 from the Secretary General addressed to the President of the Security Council."

UN Security Council. "The Deputy Secretary-General Remarks to Security Council on the promotion and strengthening of the rule of law in the maintenance of international peace and security." June 29, 2010. Accessed May 14, 2021. https://bit.ly/3fA3EO3.

UN Security Council. "Third special report of the Secretary-General on theUnited Nations Organization Mission in the Democratic Republic of the Congo." August 16, 2004.

UN Women. "A Global Study on the Implementation of the United Nations Security Council resolution 1325." New York: United Nations, 2015. Accessed March 17, 2021. https://bit.ly/3tPNvJr.

United Nations. "Financial Integrity For Sustainable Development: Report of the High Level Panel on International Financial Accountability, Transparency and Integrity for Achieving the 2030 Agenda." New York: United Nations, 2021. Accessed May 20, 2021. https://bit.ly/3ugRcYC.

United Nations Human Settlements Programme. "Tracking Progress towards Inclusive, Safe, Resilient and Sustainable Cities and Human Setttlements. Synthesis Report." Nairobi: United Nations, 2018. Accessed May 10, 2021. https://bit.ly/3fa4jqk.

United Nations. "Report on Strengthening and coordinating United Nations rule of law activities. Report of the Secretary-General." New York: United Nations, 2015.

United Nations. "The Sustainable Development Goals Report." Sustainable Development Goal indicators website. United Nations Statistics Division. Published 2020. Accessed May 7, 2021. https://bit.ly/345f1YH.

United Nations. "United Nations Convention against Corruption." Convention, New York: United Nations, 2004.

Upham, Frank. Mythmaking in The Rule of Law Orthodoxy. Research Report, Carnegie Endowment for International Peace, Published September 10, 2002. Accessed February 10, 2021. https://bit.ly/3yoioqO.

Vienna Declaration and Programme of Action. Adopted by the World Conference on Human Rights in Vienna on 25 June 1993. https://bit.ly/39Zr3WG.

Waldron, Jeremy. "The Rule of Law." In The Stanford Encyclopaedia of Philosophy (Summer 2020 Edition), ed. Edward N. Zalta. Accessed March 10, 2021.https://stanford.io/3bLLffO.

Wilde, Ralph and Schrijver, Nico. "The Complex Role of the Legal Adviser When International Organizations Administer Territory." *Proceedings of the Annual Meeting American Society of International Law* 95 (2001): 251–261.

Wilde, Ralph. "The United Nations as Government: The Tensions of an Ambivalent Role." *Proceedings of the Annual Meeting* 97 (2003): 212–215.

Chapter 2

The Rule of Law in the Voluntary Reviews of the Implementation of the United Nations 2030 Sustainable Development Agenda

Megan Capp

INTRODUCTION

Strengthening the rule of law is generally seen as fundamental in reducing violent conflict, protecting human, social, and political rights, and creating an environment conducive to peace and sustainable development.[1] The significance of the rule of law was recognized by the international community with the 2015 adoption of the United Nations *2030 Agenda for Sustainable Development*, and in particular, Sustainable Development Goal (SDG) 16, which seeks "the promotion of peaceful and inclusive societies for sustainable development, the provision of access to justice for all, and building effective, accountable institutions at all levels."[2]

Attempts by the international community to evaluate progress toward the *2030 Agenda for Sustainable Development* have produced a broad debate on how to measure progress toward SDG 16 and its associated targets relating to the rule of law. On July 6, 2017, the United Nations General Assembly adopted resolution A/RES/71/313 providing universal indicators for voluntary country-led review on each of the seventeen SDGs. This framework was based on the work of the Inter-Agency and Expert Group on SDG Indicators (IAEG-SDG) and the United Nations Statistical Commission, with the ultimate intention of further refining indicators for use at the national, regional, and global levels. With a focus on national ownership, it has additionally been recommended that context-specific measures be developed to supplement the existing SDG indicators. This recommendation recognizes that current indicators may not be suitable or applicable in all contexts, including in conflict-affected or post-conflict environments. This is particularly relevant for SDG 16 due to the complexity of the conceptualization of rule of law and rule of law reform.[3] More practically, existing indicators may be irrelevant in situations where the rule of law is notoriously weak and/or absent—including post-conflict situations.[4,5,6] In that regard, the work to further refine feasible measurement of SDG 16 continues through the IAEG-SDG, the United Nations Statistical Commission, Eurostat, and other regional authorities, as well as national statistical agencies.

Although there are many forms of rule of law reform, their tangible impact remains challenging to measure. For example, (1) while there has been improvement in the tools used for data collection, reliable rule of law data is often unavailable; (2) it often takes generations to see real change in the rule of law; (3) multiple actors and influencers are involved and it is difficult to distinguish between the impacts of their respective efforts; (4) justice and security sector reforms do not necessarily occur in a linear fashion; and (5) in circumstances where progress is ascertainable, attributing that progress to a particular entity's assistance can also be challenging.

Compounding the above challenges, attempting to measure the impact of rule of law and progress toward SDG 16 is particularly challenging in post-conflict environments due to the unique characteristics of these states. This presents an ironic state of affairs as post-conflict states are often most in need of rule of law monitoring, while simultaneously having the greatest challenges in implementing such a project. In these environments, the rule of law may be nonexistent or have minimal legitimacy for the population. This is where data to measure progress toward SDG 16 is most needed, yet least available.

Prior to elaborating on these challenges and how they impact the Voluntary National Review process toward SDG 16, it is imperative to understand the unique characteristics of the rule of law as it pertains to the 2030 Agenda and SDG 16.

UNDERSTANDING THE RULE OF LAW

The importance and relevance of the rule of law as a general concept is increasingly debated. Perspectives range from viewing the concept as a magical elixir ready to cure all of the world's challenges[7] to being essentially meaningless and irrelevant.[8]

The rule of law should not be conceived as a simplistic topic, nor as a transactional pact between state and citizen. Rather, the periphery "wins" that arise from strengthening the rule of law should be acknowledged. There is strong, though not undisputed, recognition that strengthening the rule of law creates

environments right for economic growth, the protection of the environment and vulnerable groups, and for sustainable development. A gap is that these considerations are often observed through the declaratory lens, with limited empirical evidence backing these suggestions.

A realistic view of the rule of law recognizes it holds high declaratory value, while also acknowledging that international codification of the rule of law has far outpaced the reality of rule of law protection, particularly for those who need it most—including in post-conflict environments. To add to this complexity, even though the rule of law is seen central to the international legal order, consensus has yet to be achieved on how to explicitly define it.

Prior to 2004, there was variance in the way the literature described the rule of law with some viewing the rule of law as a goal or a concept and others as tangible legal institutions.[9] The year 2004 marked a turning point when the term was first articulated by the United Nations secretary general in a report to the Security Council:

> It refers to a principle of governance in which all persons, institutions and entities, public and private, including the State itself, are accountable to laws that are publicly promulgated, equally enforced and independently adjudicated, and which are consistent with international human rights norms and standards. It requires, as well, measures to ensure adherence to the principles of supremacy of law, equality before the law, accountability to the law, fairness in the application of the law, separation of powers, participation in decision-making, legal certainty, avoidance of arbitrariness and procedural and legal transparency.[10]

Although this continues to be the most broadly used definition, it has yet to receive universal acceptance. It is a great contribution, rather, was to formalize the concept and set the stage for increasing the declaratory value of the rule of law in the international arena.[11] During the following year, in 2005, world leaders met for the World Summit. The resulting outcome document A/RES/60/1 identified the rule of law as a key thematic area demanding more attention while restating a universal commitment to the principles of the rule of law, at both the national and international levels. The rule of law was conceptualized as being central to a healthy international order and essential for sustainable development and the reduction of poverty. A/RES/60/1 increased the declaratory importance of the rule of law, however, member states at the World Summit failed to agree on a single operational definition. This was primarily attributed to concerns around sovereignty and national ownership.[12] In spite of these logistical challenges, the stage had been set for perhaps a significant resolution, A/RES/67/1, in which the rule of law is the standalone topic. Following the 2012 United Nations Conference on Sustainable Development, A/RES/67/1 declares the importance of adherence to rule of law principles as foundational for democracy, peace, and sustainable development. Despite the tremendous value ascribed to the rule of law, the concept was not captured under a unified definition.

A commitment to the rule of law was again reaffirmed in 2018 through the Global Compact for Safe, Orderly and Regular Migration. The resulting resolution, A/RES/73/195, declared that respect for the rule of law, due process, and access to justice are fundamental to all aspects of migration governance. In practical terms, this means that the state, public and private institutions, and persons themselves, are accountable to laws which are publicly promulgated, equally enforced and independently adjudicated, and in consistency with international law. The clarification provided in A/RES/73/195 significantly elevated the definition of the rule of law.

In 2021, arising from the Fourteenth United Nations Congress on Crime Prevention and Criminal Justice, A/CONF.234/L.6 was drafted. Although this document also does not provide a definition of the rule of law, it reaffirms the importance of the rule of law toward sustainable development and economic growth. Recognizing the increased complexity of addressing crime in a modern world, the draft document focuses heavily on cooperation—an ideal that was also stated in the previously mentioned resolutions, as well as formally in the SDGs (SDG 17).

While conceptualizations around the rule of law vary, it is important to note that no country has ever achieved the ideal of the "rule of law." Rather, the rule of law enables access to justice whose benchmarks move on as we approach them. Even in countries which typically score highly on rule of law assessments, justice remains on the horizon. Each country must address the constant and unique challenge of renewing and developing their institutions and norms to support rule of law progress. Implementation of the rule of law and, in particular, rule of law reform is inherently political and affects the balance of powers within a state.[13] The high aspirations of the rule of law can also, in practice, lead to conflicting values, confusion, and contradictory results at the local level.[14] Despite these conceptual challenges, the rule of law remains a central part of sustainable development and peacebuilding. Van Veen effectively sums up this dichotomy by stating, "few concepts are as vague and disputed, and yet as relevant and promising, as the 'Rule of Law.' "[15]

The declaratory value of the rule of law at the international levels can be thought to have two main purposes: aspiration for increased security,[16] and support for domestic debate on how best to achieve rule of law reform.[17] This brings up another interesting point of tension. Rule of law reform is generally supported by the international community, although the practicalities of how this reform is actually achieved are still debated.[18] While it is important to have a guiding framework to aspire to, declarations on the rule of law are not very useful unless they are followed by action. Action is not very useful unless it is followed by measurement to assess effectiveness and impact.

Parker and Upin articulate this relationship as follows:

> Implementation is what makes or breaks reforms, and the challenges associated with implementation are many: The human, fiscal or technical resources may be inadequate for the task at hand; training and support may be lacking; the strategy or selected program's goal is not a good fit for the need that exists; or the strategy or program is not implemented as it was designed and fails to achieve the anticipated outcomes. If there is no way to monitor implementation progress and measure outcomes, there is no way to know if the implementation is effective.[19]

As we grapple with the worldwide retreat of the rule of law, the most effective conceptualization must remain both aspirational *and* relevant to individual citizens. Despite the promise provided by the rule of law, the lack of consensus around the concept, and the challenge with measuring something yet to be fully defined, continues to be problematic. These challenges not only hinder buy-in of the concept but also significantly impacted the drafting process of the 2030 Agenda. This continues to have a lasting effect on the ability to effectively measure progress toward SDG 16, particularly where it is needed the most.[20]

To understand the challenges with measuring the rule of the law within the SDGs, it is important to recognize the path taken toward the 2030 Agenda, and the tangible lessons that were learned along the way.

THE PATH TO SDG 16

The 2000–2015 Millennium Development Goals (MDGs) were the first global framework to be adopted by the international community. Immediately following the MDGs, and being only the second global development framework to have ever existed, the SDGs, in both process and desired outcomes, were shaped by the MDG experience. This is particularly apparent concerning the relationships between the rule of law, justice, good governance and sustainable development, and the challenges with empirically measuring progress.

Focusing primarily on the reduction of poverty and increased living conditions, the rule of law (under the umbrella of human rights) was only briefly touched upon in the MDGs. The MDGs were widely criticized for their lack of focus on universal human rights,[21,22] and for portraying development as a narrow technical process of poverty alleviation.[23]

Reflections on the process view the failure of the MDGs to incorporate the rule of law as a crosscutting component of the agenda as a central theme. For example, the permanent representative of Pakistan stated, "one of the main lessons drawn from the implementation of the UN Millennium Development Goals has been the absence of synergy between the governance, Rule of Law and development."[24] Recognizing this gap, although with much debate, a stand-alone governance/rule of law goal—SDG 16—was adopted within the 2030 Agenda.

An essential lesson learned from the MDG experience was recognition of highly unequal national progress toward the goals, with conflict-affected countries achieving significantly less progress than other developing countries.[25] Along with unequal progress, measuring progress toward the goals proved extremely challenging for some countries. Global and regional progress toward the realization of the MDGs was assessed by the Inter-Agency Expert Group—MDG (IAEG-MDG), which consisted of international agencies, regional organization, and national statistical offices. Indicator and target selection was a top-down initiative and, according to a 2013 United Nations report, Lessons Learned from MDG Monitoring from a Statistical Perspective, the failure to consult with countries on targets and indicators was a primary cause of numerous inconsistencies and inadequacies with data collection. Additionally, many developing countries felt burdened and unsupported by developed countries in the efforts needed to meet the MDGs.[26]

Learning from these lessons, expectations regarding monitoring were revised for the SDGs with a stronger focus on national ownership—although this has not been without controversy.[27,28,29] The voluntary nature of reviews has been seen as minimizing their relevance as a tool for transformative change.[30] Using the example of the African Union's (AU) Agenda 2063 Mulligan (2015) highlights the challenges with committing to a global framework which may contradict an existing national agenda. In this example it is argued that the SDGs are relevant only in the context that they support the AU Agenda. Stewart (2015) expands this point arguing that targets and indicators determined at the global level are unable to account for the unique characteristics and national priorities of individual countries. With it being well established in the literature that the rule of law is best understood and reformed at the local level,[31] a remedy offered is for more context-specific and relevant national indicators to be developed. While this is a valid recommendation, it also does not account for the complexities with practical implementation. It further minimizes the fact that where rule of law data is most needed, it is least available.

The challenge remains that, even if appropriate national monitoring frameworks for measuring the rule of law are established, post-conflict settings are limited in their capacity to gather data, particularly toward SDG 16.

SDG 16 TARGETS AND INDICATORS

SDG 16 includes twelve targets which include both procedural and substantive components of the rule of law. The only target which explicitly mentioned the rule of law is target 16.3, which seeks to "promote the Rule of Law at the national and international levels and ensure equal access to justice for all." General characteristics of the rule of law, such as reduction of corruption (target 16.5), accountable institutions (target 16.6), and reduced violence and death rates (target 16.1) are interwoven throughout SDG 16. Recognizing the importance of collaboration and local ownership on strengthening and developing the rule of law, SDG 17 and SDG 4.7 are also of particular relevance to SDG 16, although the literature on this link is extremely lacking.

After much negotiation, the agreed-upon global measurement framework to measure progress toward target 16.3 included two indicators:

- Indicator 16.3.1—the proportion of victims of violence in the previous twelve months who reported their victimization to competent authorities or other officially recognized conflict resolution mechanisms.
- Indicator 16.3.2—unsentenced detainees as a proportion of overall prison population. The adoption of these two indicators to measure progress illustrates the complexity involved in attempting to express the rule of law in simple variables. These indicators alone offer a narrow view of criminal justice and do not account for the many diverse and varied components of the rule of law. Highlighting this, a 2016 expert meeting between the United Nations Development Programme (UNDP) and the Peace Research Institute of Oslo (PRIO) suggested that the two global indicators for 16.3, with their focus on prisons and violent victimization, are actually proxy measures of security service capacity and their relevance to the rule of law are restricted. It has also been suggested that the broadness of the target is not due to chance. Softening the language of "the Rule of Law" by including "access to justice" could be seen as a compromise for those member states strongly against the "rule of law" terminology. Although the specific indicators for SDG 16 are generally accepted as adequate in addressing their targets of interest,[32] there is also growing recognition that they do not fully capture the complex dimensions of rule of law. This was somewhat mitigated in 2020 when the UN IAEG-SDG included a third indicator to measure accessibility of formal or informal civil justice mechanisms.
- Indicator 16.3.3—proportion of those who experienced a legal problem in the last two years who could access appropriate information or expert help and were able to resolve the problem.

Greatly augmenting the initial two indicators, due to its person-centered focus and inclusion of informal justice mechanisms, the cluster of indicators remain vague. The vagueness of target 16.3 increases the challenges with attempting to measure progress toward it. The challenge in measuring SDG 16 and target 16.3 could hint at the lack of response toward this target in the Voluntary National Reviews, although this is not yet confirmed.

VOLUNTARY NATIONAL REVIEWS OF SDG 16

After the adoption of the 2030 Agenda in 2015, the member states of the United Nations committed to action on the 17 Sustainable Goals and their respective 169 targets. Not only was there the requirement to act, but also to engage in voluntary, country-led, transparent reviews. The results of such reviews are published through the Voluntary National Reviews ("VNRs"), which are guided by the UN Secretary-General's Voluntary Guidelines, recognized by the UN General Assembly in 2016 through A/79/684. The UN Department of Economic and Social Affairs offers a handbook to support countries in preparing their 2021 VNRs, with presentations happening during annual high-level political forum sessions. The 2030 Agenda explicitly states that all VNRs should be:

- voluntary and country-led;
- focused on universal, integrated, and interrelated goals and targets, including means of implementation;
- open, inclusive, participatory, and transparent for all people;
- people-centered, gender-sensitive, and respect, protect, and promote human rights, with a focus on the people who are the poorest, most vulnerable, and left furthest behind;
- built on existing platforms and processes, while taking into consideration emerging methodologies;
- rigorous and evidence based, informed by country-led evaluations and data that is high quality, accessible, timely, reliable and disaggregated by income, sex, age, race, ethnicity, migration status, disability and other geographic location and other characteristics relevant in the national context;
- longer-term orientation, and identify achievements, challenges, gaps and critical success factors;
- focused on stakeholder engagement/private sector involvement.

Despite these clear guidelines, a 2017 UNDP perception survey determined that countries awareness of both the VNR requirement, and in particular, how to engage in the VNR process was low.

Since 2016, 168 countries have presented 205 VNRs with 10 countries presenting their VNRs for the first time in 2021. Analysis of the available data shows that in 2020, forty-five countries presented VNRs on SDG 16. For target 16.3, forty-three countries presented data and demonstrated an increase of 8.23 percent toward progress, in comparison with the previous year. Countries were counted as producing a VNR toward SDG 16 if they simply referred to the topic, even when supporting data or the specific indicator was not explicitly discussed. This being said, it appears as, for the forty-five reporting countries, adherence to the guidelines in the 2030 Agenda was followed to some degree. For example, forty-three out of forty-five countries identify their process as inclusive and participatory—although the level of detail provided varied.[33]

In the 2020 Voluntary National Review Synthesis report, there is a designated section to address fragile countries, including those in conflict or post-conflict periods. Eight of these countries reported on their progress sharing a common message of aspiration toward realizing the rule of law as a precursor to sustainable peace. Only one country (Nigeria) discussed the challenges with data collection toward the SDGs during times of conflict. Although minimally mentioned in the report, this challenge with data collection must be emphasized.

An aspirational goal provides hope and direction, yet without the ability to effectively measure progress toward that goal it is essentially meaningless. We are on the threshold of clarifying our collective value of the rule of law as a tool for sustainable development. The existing research is telling us that this is the best tool we have toward economic prosperity for all, protecting the environment, and sustainable development. For all of the SDGs, and particularly for SDG 16, the voluntary national reports (VNRs) should not be dismissed as a superficial or token process, but rather one which supports transformative change toward a more equitable world.

While remaining grounded in the realities of our current world, the issue remains that where data on the rule of law and SDG 16 is most needed, it is the most challenging to collect. This is particularly true in environments where the rule of law is notoriously weak or absent—including in post-conflict settings. In order to articulate the importance of the rule of law as a tool for sustainable development in these settings it is important to understand their unique and dynamic nature.

CHARACTERISTICS OF POST-CONFLICT ENVIRONMENTS

The literature demonstrates that post-conflict settings are not homogenous. Rather, they vary geographically, regarding the history and nature of the conflict, and in the existence of governance and functioning structures. According to the academic literature and practitioner reports, post-conflict settings are generally characterized by the following:[34],[35]

- The reduced (or collapsed) capacity of the justice and security sectors due to damage of infrastructure;
- Lack of capacity and inadequate leadership or high levels of corruption;
- A diversion of funds from justice systems to the conflict;
- Segregation of bureaucracy along ethnic or religious lines;
- Mistrust toward the police and judiciary from the general population;
- The need to address past violations of human rights and atrocities;
- Departure of legal personnel from conflict-affected areas due to intimidation and fear;
- Possible militia formation;
- Disarmament, demobilization, and reintegration;
- Impunity;
- Impact of displaced populations;
- Increased disenfranchisement; and,
- General instability.

Post-conflict environments are characterized by criminal and civil offending occurring at higher rates in comparison with conflict-free states,[36] coupled with additional forms of offending, such as land and water violations.[37] The literature abounds with examples of groups who have been traditionally marginalized, such as women, being disproportionately impacted by conflict[38] and facing the effects of intersecting vulnerabilities if they also belong to a minority or otherwise precarious group.

An understudied area of great importance is the conflict that occurs between refugees and displaced persons during the repatriation process.[39],[40] Despite being one of the most vulnerable populations, and becoming so through conflict, the experiences of these groups deserve more attention in the literature. Another gap is understanding how customary justice mechanisms impact rule of law reform in post-conflict environments. Customary justice is often cited as making up 80 percent of the post-conflict reality[41]and is often the preferred mechanism,[42] although there may be concerns with their ability to provide justice in accordance with international human rights standards.[43] To fully understand how the rule of law is experienced through these customary mechanisms, it is necessary to measure their impact. While indicator 16.3.3 sets the stage to invite discussion on this topic, measuring how the rule of law is developed through these processes is still very much a work in progress[44] and one which should be given attention during the VNR process.

The aforementioned characteristics of the post-conflict reality dually impact the presence of the rule of law and the feasibility of implementing measurement processes to monitor rule of law progress.[45] Post-conflict environments remain unique as being the most in need of rule of law monitoring and reform, yet least likely to have the resources to implement this monitoring. Aside from these complexities, as with all member states, post-conflict environments are required to participate in the VNR process to monitor their progress toward the SDGs.

THE NATURE OF RULE OF LAW REFORM IN POST-CONFLICT ENVIRONMENTS

The SDG Voluntary National Review process requires member states to collect and report data on the SDGs and, in particular, target 16.3. While there is recognition that rule of law reform is extremely important in these environments, less attention is paid to the nuances with implementing a measurement process in a post-conflict setting.

There has been a promising shift in rule of law reform in post-conflict environments. There is growing recognition that the traditional top-down engagement with formal state institutions, while ignoring customary justice mechanisms, is largely ineffective.[46] Over the last decade or so, there has been an increase in bottom-up rule of law reform which highlights the reality of legal pluralism and includes customary systems.[47],[48] This approach recognizes that power and cultural norms are key components of the rule of law and supporting these components can strengthen the rebuilding of formal laws and institutions.[49]

Local participation, consultation, and ownership in rule of law reform are generally seen as essential in maintaining sustainability and effectiveness.[50],[51] This suggests that linking these reforms to a measurement process which leads to real decision-making capacities is much more likely to achieve buy-in than a process created and implemented by a third party. Despite the great potential of local ownership for sustainable rule of law reform, the challenge remains that the logistical capacity for post-conflict states to implement a monitoring process is severely diminished.

The Logistics of Measuring Rule of Law Reform in Post-Conflict Environments

A variety of factors contribute to the challenges post-conflict states may experience while trying to measure progress toward target 16.3, and the rule of law in general. In addition to the complex characteristics of post-conflict environments mentioned above, many national statistics offices are not equipped with the resources and necessary statistical capacity to measure rule of law.[52] The legal and administrative systems of a state are often most vulnerable to conflict.[53] This becomes particularly problematic when administrative data is required to measure the indicator, as the official buildings holding these administrative records may have been destroyed. Even if the buildings were not destroyed and administrative data did exist, in a post-conflict setting the quality is generally extremely poor.[54]

In addition to a general lack of infrastructure, there may be factors affecting a states willingness to measure rule of law reform. It may be precisely due to the lack of local capacity to manage their own justice needs that lead to the descent into conflict.[55] The government may also have been involved in the violence and conflict. This further complicates things as it reduces the trust and objectivity for indicators developed by the state.[56]

Many post-conflict states may also have cultural biases against measurement systems[57] creating tension between local ownership and international guidance. Some countries may not see the value in making decisions and guiding policy using statistics.[58] There may be strong skepticism around international data sources and concern that international data does not reflect national priorities.[59]

This highlights both the challenges of buy-in, and the limited capacity of post-conflict states to collect reliable administrative data. It is particularly problematic as two indicators for target 16.3 (16.3.1 and 16.3.2) rely on administrative data. In looking toward the most promising way to measure progress toward sustainable rule of law reform, particularly for target 16.3.3, an alternative for administrative data is perception data collected through surveys.

Opportunities for Perception-Based Surveys

Perception-based surveys offer an alternative or supplement to administrative data. This type of data holds value in its ability to stimulate public debate on measuring, and acting on, what is truly important for people. Although these data sources also have limitations, particularly in post-conflict settings, they remain the best option to capture information toward indicator 16.3.3.

Limitations in a post-conflict environment may include the (possibly state-controlled) media's influence on perceptions and the ability of surveys to capture the experiences of hard-to-reach vulnerable groups[60],[61] and challenges due to linguistic and cultural differences or sensitive issues.[62] For example, sexual and domestic violence victimization are not readily captured through surveys due to the sociocultural pressure not to report—with nonresponse being likely to go up in these situations.[63]

Additionally, subjective measures are generally prone to concerns of validity or bias.[64] There are also challenges with giving voice to inaccurate perceptions. For example, a country which has many citizens who are quick to criticize the government may report levels of corruption to be higher than they actually are. This has the negative consequence of weakening trust in institutions for citizens who initially had trust in the mechanism. Another aspect skewing the reliability of perception data, particularly relevant to post-conflict situations, is adaption or habituation.[65] This refers to the normalizing of one's living conditions and the subsequent diminished psychological or emotional response. There are also limited strategies on how to reach the most vulnerable in a post-conflict setting, particularly in a manner which does not further stigmatize.

These issues are not insurmountable; the American Bar Association[66] recommends the ideal situation as one which uses both objective and perceptive data sources to measure the quality and local legitimacy of justice mechanisms. It is clear that this will be particularly problematic for post-conflict environments to achieve. The cruel irony is that this is where measurement on rule of law is most needed, yet least accessible. Some measurement tools have been designed which support monitoring of the rule of law in post-conflict situations. These include the *UN Rule of Law Indicators*, the *UN Human Rights Indicators*, the *World Justice Project Rule of Law Index*, and the *Fragility Spectrum*. Although promising, these developments have yet to be given the attention they deserve in national monitoring of SDG 16 for post-conflict environments. The challenge remains that monitoring rule of law reform and progress toward SDG 16 is limited for post-conflict environments.

CONCLUSION

Though somewhat diluted in the 2030 Agenda and, in particular, the targets and indicators for SDG 16, the rule of law retains its aspirational declaratory value within the international legal order. Although continually evolving, and in general global decline, the rule of law remains our best option toward sustainable development and a more equitable future. The impact of periphery wins from rule of law reform, such as creating environments ripe for economic investment and protecting the environment, cannot be overlooked and deserve much more attention in future research. Another understudied area which may facilitate progress toward SDG 16 is understanding the link between cooperation and rule of law reform. Although cooperation is codified as an important component of rule of law development, there is a paucity of empirical evidence which focuses on this relationship.

The reality remains that the aspirational quality of the rule of law, while not to be understated, is virtually meaningless unless combined with tangible action. This action is of particular importance for the vulnerable groups who need rule of law protection the most. It remains that this action is also severely limited, unless it is accompanied by robust measurement and evaluation processes to assess impact. Much more attention needs to be paid to the challenges post-conflict environments face in collecting data on rule of law reform, especially during the VNR process. While there are some promising developments, including existing measurement tools, there is still a gap in understanding how best post-conflict environments can measure their progress toward SDG 16 and target 16.3. Literature on data collection methodologies do not often account for the unique characteristics of the post-conflict setting making this a uniquely understudied area.

The fact that increasing numbers of countries are reporting their progress toward target 16.3 through the VNRs is promising. The VNR process has tremendous value in both providing information on the targets, as well as providing insight into the measurement process. We must grasp this learning opportunity. It must be clear that rule of law reform and progress is not just about the VNRs and posturing public commitment to the SDGs. As the cornerstone of sustainable development, justice, protection for vulnerable groups, and economic growth, commitment to the rule of law remains our hope for sustainable peace. The current reality that those who need the protection of the rule of law the most have the least tools available to monitor it represents a fundamental injustice, and one which deserves much more attention among both academics and practitioners.

NOTES

1. Rachel Kleinfeld, Advancing the Rule of Law Abroad: Next Generation Reform Carnegie Endowment for International Peace, Washington DC, 2012.

2. General Assembly resolution 70/1, Transforming our world: the 2030 Agenda for sustainable development. A/RES/70/1 (25 September 2015).

3. Shane Chalmers, "The Mythology of International Rule-of-Law Promotion." *Law and Social Inquiry* 44, no. 4 (2019): 95–86.

4. Maurits Barendrecht, "Rule of Law, Measuring and Accountability: Problems to Be Solved Bottom Up." *Hague Journal on the Rule of Law* 3, no. 2 (2011): 281–304.

5. Institute for Economics and Peace. *Sustainable Development Goal 16–From Now To 2030: What Is Needed to Measure Goal 16.* (Institute for Economics and Peace, 2016)

6. United Nations Department of Peacekeeping Operations, *Rule of Law and Security Indicators to Measure Progress toward Sustainable Development Goal 16 in Conflict-Affected Societies* (New York: United Nations, 2015).

7. Kleinfeld, Advancing the Rule of Law Abroad.
8. Chalmers, *The Mythology*.
9. Rama Mani, *Beyond Retribution: Seeking Justice in the Shadows of War* (Cambridge, UK: Polity Press, 2002).
10. UN doc. S/2004/616, *The Rule of Law and Transitional Justice in Conflict and Post-Conflict Societies* (23 August 2004).
11. Noora Aranjarvi, "The Rule of Law in the 2030 Agenda." *Hague Journal on the Rule of Law* 10, no. 1(2018): 187–217.
12. Aranjarvi, "The Rule of Law."
13. Stéphane Jean, "Leadership and the Rule of Law in Conflict and Post-Conflict Societies: A Leadership Approach through the Sustainable Development Goals." *International Journal of Public Leadership* 15, no. 3 (2019): 130–36.
14. Kleinfeld, Advancing the Rule of Law Abroad.
15. Erwin van Veen, *A Shotgun Marriage: Political Contestation and the Rule of Law in Fragile Societies* (Clingendael: Netherlands Institute of International Relations 2017).
16. Naomi Johnstone, "What Context Matters? Rule of Law Programming in the Midst of Post-Conflict Insecurity." *Hague Journal on the Rule of Law* 9, no. 2 (2017): 337–71.
17. Erwin van Veen, *A Shotgun Marriage.*
18. Kleinfeld, Advancing the Rule of Law Abroad.
19. B. Pierce Parker and T. Upin, "So the Juvenile Justice Reform Legislation has Passed–now What?" *Corrections Today* 5, no. 6 (2016): 15–18.
20. Aranjarvi, "The Rule of Law."
21. Ved Nanda, "The Journey from the Millennium Development Goals to the Sustainable Development Goals." *Denver Journal of International Law and Policy* 44, no 3 (2016).
22. Inga Winkler and Carmel Williams, "The Sustainable Development Goals and Human Rights: A Critical Early Review." *International Journal of Human Rights* 21, no. 8 (2017): 1023–28.
23. Pieter Fourie, and Colleen O'Manique, "'It Sells, But It Does Not Fly': An Early Assessment of the 2030 Agenda for Sustainable Development." *Development* 59, nos. 3–4 (2016): 274–79.
24. Aranjarvi, "The Rule of Law."
25. Olga Mironenko, Paul L. Lucas, Natalia Tarasova, and Janos Zlinszky, "Sustainable Development Goals: Why Do We Need Them?" *Social Evolution & History* 14, no. 2 (2015): 176–90.
26. Kate Donald, and Sally-Anne Way, "Accountability for the Sustainable Development Goals: A Lost Opportunity?" *Ethics & International Affairs* 2 (2016): 201.
27. Gabriella Mulligan, "Sustainable Development Goals: Global or Not? Africa's Developmental Goals Seem to Have Two Competing Roadmaps." *African Business* (2015).
28. Frances Stewart, "The Sustainable Development Goals: A Comment." *Journal of Global Ethics* 11, no. 3 (2015): 288–93.

29. Fourie, *It Sells.*

30. Eivind Engebretsen, Kristin Heggen, and Ole P. Ottersen. "The Sustainable Development Goals: Ambiguities of Accountability." *The Lancet* 389, no 10067 (2017): 365.

31. Kleinfeld, *Advancing.*

32. Micheal Jandl, *Toward the Monitoring of Goal 16 of the United Nations' Sustainable Development Goals (SDGs)* (Helsinki: HEUNI, 2017).

33. United Nations Department of Economic and Social Affairs, *2020 Voluntary National Review Synthesis Report* (New York: United Nations, 2020).

34. Martin Edmonds, Greg Mills, and Terence McNamee, "Disarmament, Demobilization, and Reintegration and Local Ownership in the Great Lakes: The Experience of Rwanda, Burundi, and the Democratic Republic of Congo." *African Security* 2, no. 1 (2009): 29–58.

35. United Nations Development Program, *Programming for Justice: Access for All* (New York. United Nations, 2005).

36. Beatrice Pouligny, "UN Peace Operations, INGOs, NGOs, and Promoting the Rule of Law: Exploring the Intersection of International and Local Norms in Different Postwar Contexts." *Journal of Human Rights* 2, no. 3 (2003): 359–77.

37. Sandra Joireman., and Laura S. Meitzner Yoder, "A Long Time Gone: Post-Conflict Rural Property Restitution under Customary Law." *Development & Change* 47, no. 3: (2016): 563–85.

38. Michele Bachelet, "Increasing Women's Access to Justice in Post-conflict Societies." *UN Chronicle* 49, no. 4 (2012), bit.ly/3rZjoV.

39. Christopher Faulkner, and Samuel Schiffer, "Unwelcomed? The Effects of Statelessness on Involuntary Refugee Repatriation in Bangladesh and Myanmar." *Round Table* 108, no. 2 (2019): 145–58.

40. Stephanie Schwartz, "Home, Again: Refugee Return and Post-Conflict Violence in Burundi." *International Security* 44, no. 2 (2019): 110–45.

41. B. Baker and E. Scheye, "Access to Justice in a Post-conflict State: Donor-supported Multidimensional Peacekeeping in Southern Sudan." *International Peacekeeping* 16, no. 2 (2009): 171–85.

42. Tim Luccaro. *Customary Justice: An Introduction to Basic Concepts, Strengths, and Weaknesses* (International Network to Promote the Rule of Law, 2016).

43. Tanja Chopra, and Deborah Isser, "Access to Justice and Legal Pluralism in Fragile States: The Case of Women's Rights." *Hague Journal on the Rule of Law* 4, no. 2 (2012): 337–58.

44. Yvon Dandurand, *The United Nations Rule of Law Indicators: Mapping the Way Forward* (New York: United Nations Department of Peacekeeping Operations, 2015).

45. Vivienne O'Connor, *Mapping the Justice System and Legal Framework in a Conflict-Affected Country* (Washington, DC: International Network to Promote the Rule of Law (INPROL), 2015).

46. Barendrecht, *Rule of Law.*

47. Johnstone, *Why Context Matters.*

48. Craig Valters, Erwin Van Veen, & Lisa Denney, *Security Progress in Post-conflict Contexts: Between Liberal Peacebuilding and Elite Interests* (London: Overseas Development Institute, 2015).

49. Kleinfeld, *Advancing*.

50. Barendrecht, *Rule of Law*.

51. Linn Hammergreen, "Indices, Indicators and Statistics: A View from the Project Side as to Their Utility and Pitfalls." *Hague Journal on the Rule of Law* 3, no. 2 (2011): 305–16.

52. Institute for Economics and Peace, "Sustainable Development Goal 16."

53. Richard Sannerholm, "Legal, Judicial and Administrative Reforms in Post-conflict Societies: Beyond the Rule of Law Template." *Journal of Conflict and Security Law* 12, no. 1 (2007): 65–94.

54. Dandurand, *Rule of Law*.

55. Willem Oosterveld and Renaud Galand, "Justice Reform, Security Sector Reform and Local Ownership." *Hague Journal on the Rule of Law* 4, no. 1 (2012): 194–209.

56. Institute for Economics and Peace, "Sustainable Development Goal 16."

57. Cedric de Coning and Paul Romita, "Monitoring and Evaluation of Peace Operations." (New York: International Peace Institute, 2009).

58. Innocent Chukwuma and E. Ebai, *Promoting the Rule of Law through Evaluation and Performance Measurement in Nigeria: Challenges and Prospects* (Abuja: CLEEN Foundation, 2012).

59. Grace Morgan, "Traction on the Ground: From Better Data to Better Policy." *Hague Journal on the Rule of Law* 3, no. 2 (2011): 380–96.

60. Javier Herrera, Mireille Razafindrakoto, & Francois Roubaud, "Governance, Democracy and Poverty Reduction: Lessons Drawn from Household Surveys in Sub-Saharan Africa and Latin America." *International Statistical Review,* 75, no. 1 (2007): 70–95.

61. Laura Rodriguez Takeuchi and Sebastien Hine, *Asking People What They Think: Using Perceptions Data to Monitor the post-2015 Agenda* (London: Overseas Development Institute, 2015).

62. *Addressing Conflict and Violence from 2015. A Vision of Goals, Targets, and Indicators* (United Kingdom: Saferworld, 2013).

63. Rodriguez and Hine, *Asking People*.

64. Tom Ginsburg, "Pitfalls of Measuring the Rule of Law." *Hague Journal on the Rule of Law* 3, no. 2 (2011): 269–80.

65. Rodriguez and Hine, *Asking People*.

66. *American Bar Association, Access to Justice Assessment Tool* (Washington, DC: American Bar Association, 2012).

BIBLIOGRAPHY

Access to Justice Assessment Tool. Washington, DC, American Bar Association, 2012.

Addressing Conflict and Violence from 2015. *A Vision of Goals, Targets, and Indicators*. United Kingdom, Saferworld, 2013.

Arajärvi, Noora, "The Rule of Law in the 2030 Agenda," *Hague Journal on the Rule of Law* 10, no. 1 (2018): 187–217.

Bachelet Michele, "Increasing Women's Access to Justice in Post-conflict Societies," *UN Chronicle* 49, no. 4 (2012), bit.ly/3rZjoV.

Baker B. and Scheye E., "Access to Justice in a Post-conflict State: Donor-supported Multidimensional Peacekeeping in Southern Sudan," *International Peacekeeping* 16, no. 2 (2009): 171–185.

Barendrecht, Maurits, "Rule of Law, Measuring and Accountability: Problems to Be Solved Bottom Up," *Hague Journal on the Rule of Law* 3, no. 2 (2011): 281–304.

Chalmers, Shane, "The Mythology of International Rule-of-Law Promotion," *Law & Social Inquiry* 44, no. 4 (2019): 957–986.

Chopra, Tanja and Isser, Deborah, "Access to Justice and Legal Pluralism in Fragile States: The Case of Women's Rights," *Hague Journal on the Rule of Law* 4, no. 2 (2012): 337–358.

Chukwuma, Innocent and Ebai, E., *Promoting the Rule of Law through Evaluation and Performance Measurement in Nigeria: Challenges and Prospects.* Abuja: CLEEN Foundation, 2012.

Dandurand, Y. *The United Nations Rule of Law Indicators: Mapping the Way Forward.* New York, United Nations Department of Peacekeeping Operations, 2015.

de Coning, Cedric and Romita, Paul, *Monitoring and Evaluation of Peace Operations.* New York, International Peace Institute, 2009.

Donald, Kate and Way, Sally-Anne, "Accountability for the Sustainable Development Goals: A Lost Opportunity?" *Ethics & International Affairs* 30, no. 2 (2016): 201–213.

Edmonds, Martin, Mills Greg and McNamee Terence, "Disarmament, Demobilization, and Reintegration and Local Ownership in the Great Lakes: The Experience of Rwanda, Burundi, and the Democratic Republic of Congo," *African Security* 2, no. 1 (2009): 29–58.

Engebretsen, Eivind, Heggen Kristen, and Ottersen Ole P., "The Sustainable Development Goals: Ambiguities of Accountability," *The Lancet* 389, no 10067 (2017): 365.

Faulkner, Christopher and Schiffer, Samuel, "Unwelcomed? The Effects of Statelessness on Involuntary Refugee Repatriation in Bangladesh and Myanmar," *Round Table* 108, no. 2 (2019): 145–158.

Fourie, Pieter and O'Manique, Colleen, "'It Sells, But It Does Not Fly': An Early Assessment of the 2030 Agenda for Sustainable Development," *Development* 59, no.3/4 (2016): 274–279.

Ginsburg, Tim, "Pitfalls of Measuring the Rule of Law," *Hague Journal on the Rule of Law* 3, no. 2 (2011): 269–280.

Hammergreen, Linn, "Indices, Indicators and Statistics: A View from the Project Side as to Their Utility and Pitfalls," *Hague Journal on the Rule of Law* 3, no. 2 (2011): 305–316.

Herrera, Javier, Razafindrakoto Mireille and Roubaud Francois, "Governance, Democracy and Poverty Reduction: Lessons Drawn from Household Surveys in Sub-Saharan Africa and Latin America," *International Statistical Review* 75, no. 1(2007): 70–95.

Human Rights Indicators–A Guide to Measurement and Implementation. New York and Geneva, United Nations Office of the High Commissioner for Human Rights, 2012.

Jandl, Michael, Toward the Monitoring of Goal 16 of the United Nations' Sustainable Development Goals (SDGs) (Helsinki, HEUNI, 2017).

Jean, Stéphane, "Leadership and the Rule of Law in Conflict and Post-Conflict Societies: A Leadership Approach through the Sustainable Development Goals," *International Journal of Public Leadership* 15, no. 3 (2019): 130–136.

Johnstone, Naomi, "What Context Matters? Rule of Law Programming in the Midst of Post-Conflict Insecurity," *Hague Journal on the Rule of Law* 9, no. 2 (2017): 337–371.

Joireman, Sandra and Meitzner Yoder, Laura S., "A Long Time Gone: Post-Conflict Rural Property Restitution under Customary Law," *Development & Change* 47, no. 3 (2016): 563–585.

Kleinfeld, Rachel, *Advancing the Rule of Law Abroad. [Electronic Resource]: Next Generation Reform.* Carnegie Endowment for International Peace, Washington, DC, 2012.

Lessons learned from MDG Monitoring from a Statistical Perspective: Report of the Task Team on lessons learned from MDG monitoring of the IAEGMDG. United Nations, 2013.

Luccaro, Tim, *Customary Justice: An Introduction to Basic Concepts, Strengths, and Weaknesses.* New York, International Network to Promote the Rule of Law, 2016.

Mani, Rami, *Beyond Retribution: Seeking Justice in the Shadows of War.* Cambridge, UK, Polity Press, 2002.

Mironenko, Olga, Lucas, Paul, L., Tarasova, Natalia and Janos Zlinszky, "Sustainable Development Goals: Why Do We Need Them?" *Social Evolution & History* 14, no. 2 (2005): 176–190.

Morgan, Grace, "Traction on the Ground: From Better Data to Better Policy," *Hague Journal on the Rule of Law* 3, no. 2 (2011): 380–396.

Mulligan, Gabriella, "Sustainable Development Goals: Global or Not? Africa's Developmental Goals Seem to Have Two Competing Roadmaps," *African Business* (2015).

Nanda, Ved, "The Journey from the Millennium Development Goals to the Sustainable Development Goals," *Denver Journal of International Law and Policy* 44, no 3 (2016).

Note on the Fragility Spectrum. (G7+, 2013).

O'Connor, Vivienne, *Mapping the Justice System and Legal Framework in a Conflict-Affected Country*, (Washington DC, International Network to Promote the Rule of Law (INPROL), 2015).

Oosterveld, Willem and Galand, Renaud, "Justice Reform, Security Sector Reform and Local Ownership," *Hague Journal on the Rule of Law* 4, no. 1 (2012): 194–209.

Parker, Barbara and Upin, Tessa, "So the Juvenile Justice Reform Legislation Has Passed—Now What?" *Corrections Today* 3 (2006): 15.

Pouligny, Beatrice, "UN Peace Operations, INGOs, NGOs, and Promoting the Rule of Law: Exploring the Intersection of International and Local Norms in Different Postwar Contexts," *Journal of Human Rights* 2, no. 3 (2003): 359–377.

Programming for justice: Access for all. United Nations Development Program, 2005.

Report of the Conveners. (United Nations Development Program and Peace Research Institute of Oslo. UNDP/PRIO Expert meeting on measuring SDG 16: Targets 16.1 on peace, 16.3 on justice, 16.7 on inclusion and 16.10 on freedoms, 2016).

Rodriguez Takeuchi, Laura and Hine, *Asking People What They Think: Using Perceptions Data to Monitor the post-2015 Agenda*. London, Overseas Development Institute, 2015.

Rule of Law Index. Washington, DC, *World Justice Project*, 2009.

Sannerholm, Richard, "Legal, Judicial and Administrative Reforms in Post-conflict Societies: Beyond the Rule of Law Template," *Journal of Conflict and Security Law* 12, no. 1 (2007): 65–94.

Schwartz, Stephanie, "Home, Again: Refugee Return and Post-Conflict Violence in Burundi," *International Security* 44, no. 2 (2007): 110–145.

Stewart, Francis, "The Sustainable Development Goals: A Comment," *Journal of Global Ethics* 11, no. 3 (2015): 288–293.

Sustainable Development Goal 16—From now to 2030: what is needed to measure Goal 16. Institute for Economics and Peace, 2016.

UN doc. 2005 World Summit Outcome. UN Doc. A/RES/60/1. 16 September 2005.

UN doc. 2020 Voluntary National Review Synthesis Report. United Nations Department of Economic and Social Affairs, 2020.

UN doc. A/CONF.234/L.6. 17 February 2021 Draft Kyoto Declaration on Advancing Crime Prevention and Criminal Justice and the Rule of Law: Toward the Achievement of the 2030 Agenda for Sustainable Development.

UN doc. A/RES/66/288. The Future We Want. 27 July 2012.

UN doc. A/RES/70/1. Transforming Our World: The 2030 Agenda for Sustainable Development. 25 September 2015.

UN doc. A/RES/73/195. Global Compact for Safe, Orderly and Regular Migration. 19 December 2018.

UN doc. S/2004/616. The Rule of Law and Transitional Justice in Conflict and Post-Conflict Societies. 23 August 2004.

UN doc. A/RES/71/313. Work of the Statistical Commission pertaining to the 2030 Agenda for Sustainable Development. SEVENTY-FIRST SESSION. 6 July 2017.

UN doc. Rule of Law and Security Indicators to Measure Progress towards Sustainable Development Goal 16 in Conflict-Affected Societies. New York, United Nations Department of Peacekeeping Operations, 2015.

UN doc. Voluntary Common Reporting Guidelines for Voluntary National Reviews at the High-Level Political Forum for Sustainable Development (HLPF). New York, United Nations, 2020.

Valters, Craig, Van Veen Erwin & Denney, Lisa, *Security Progress in Post-conflict Contexts: Between Liberal Peacebuilding and Elite Interests*. London, Overseas Development Institute, 2015.

van Veen, Erwin, *A Shotgun Marriage: Political Contestation and the Rule of Law in Fragile Societies*. Clingendael: Netherlands Institute of International Relations, 2017.

Winkler, Inga and Williams, Carmel, "The Sustainable Development Goals and Human Rights: A Critical Early Review," *International Journal of Human Rights* 2, no. 8 (2017): 1023–1028.

Chapter 3

Power Politics versus the Rule of Law in Brazil

A Case Study

Eduardo Pinheiro Granzotto da Silva
and Newton Tavares Filho

THE RISE OF RIGHT-WING CONSERVATISM IN BRAZIL

In 2014, Brazilian officials began a criminal investigation that changed the layout of the country's political landscape. Officials initially investigated a chain of gas stations and car washes allegedly being used to launder funds obtained illegally from criminal organizations. The investigation focused on corruption-related crimes and money laundering and came to be known as "Operation Car Wash" (*Operação Lava-Jato*). Originating in Paraná, a state in southern Brazil, the operation reached national proportions in 2015, when it uncovered a significant corruption scheme. With strong support from the media and public opinion, Operation Car Wash became the largest anti-corruption and anti-money-laundering initiative in Brazil's history.[1]

The success of the investigation rocked Brazilian politics. Money changers, influential business executives, politicians from different parties, former directors of the state-run oil company (Petrobras), former ministers, a former president of the Chamber of Deputies, governors, and a prior president (Lula) were all arrested. As the operation reached the highest echelons of Brazilian politics, tensions grew between the branches of government. The executive branch was led by President Dilma Rousseff, President Lula's successor and a fellow member of the country's leftist Worker's Party (PT). PT had governed Brazil since 2003 and was at the center of the Operation Car Wash. With many members of Congress being revealed as targets of investigations, pressure grew in the Legislative Branch to weaken laws on white-collar crimes. Meanwhile, the judicial branch, mainly the Supreme Court, supported the Operation Car Wash investigations.

As a result of this tension between the branches, President Rousseff was removed from office in an impeachment trial initiated by Congress in 2016. With the economy in a recession, PT leaders involved in corruption scandals, and her difficulties in working with Congress, President Dilma's popularity fell rapidly. Members of Congress recognized these issues as an opportunity and, using the argument that her administration had engaged in a series of illegal public accounting and borrowing maneuvers to finance budget gaps known locally as *pedaladas fiscais*, voted to remove Dilma from office.[2]

Vice President Michel Temer assumed office, though his party, the centrist Brazilian Democratic Movement (MDB) party, was also being investigated in Operation Car Wash. In 2017, the federal prosecutor general levied two corruption charges against Temer as a result of the investigation, accusing him of crimes such as passive corruption, being a member of a criminal organization, and obstruction of justice. However, the Chamber of Deputies, which is responsible for authorizing a trial against the president for crimes of this nature, did not approve of an investigation into these charges while Temer was still in office; the Chamber's decision was clear show of force against Operation Car Wash, since many members of Congress were also being investigated.

It was in this context that Jair Bolsonaro began his campaign for president. In addition to the political tension generated by the corruption investigations, the economic recession, and resulting increases in unemployment and urban violence were taking their toll on citizens. These factors fed into feelings of anger and disappointment toward PT, which had governed the country for more than thirteen years. Citizens were expressing a widespread distrust in government institutions overall. In a survey performed shortly before the 2018 election, 68 percent of Brazilians reported having no trust in political parties; 67 percent reported having no trust in Congress, and 64 percent reported a lack of trust in the president.[3] Meanwhile, almost eight in ten Brazilians (78 percent) agreed with the statement that the armed forces represented the most trustworthy institution in the country.[4]

Bolsonaro seemed to represent everything that Brazilians wanted at that moment. He was a former military army captain, meaning he had strong ties to the armed forces, there were no formal accusations against him in Operation Car Wash, and he was a fierce critic of PT. Bolsonaro served in Congress for almost thirty years, but his lack of political loyalty (he had changed political parties eight times) gave many voters the impression that he was an anti-party figure and a political outsider. In addition, he promised to get the country back on track to economic growth, and he defended ideals such as law and order, patriotism, traditional customs, and Christian morality. His campaign slogan was "Brazil above everything; God above everyone."

Despite his political career marked by controversy, Bolsonaro won the run-off vote against a PT candidate in the 2018 presidential election and pulled the highest office in the country to right-wing conservatism. Using the argument that he was a necessary evil for restoring order in Brazil, the majority of the electorate chose to ignore his past, which he had made no effort to hide. His almost thirty years in the Chamber of Deputies were marked by homophobic, racist, sexist, nationalist, pro-gun, authoritarian, and anti-human-rights discourse typical of the far right.[5] For many, Bolsonaro's election would lead to a period of uncertainty regarding the rule of law in Brazil.

In this context, and from the perspective of constitutional law, this chapter will explore case studies that reveal the struggle between power politics and the rule of law in Brazil between 2018 and 2020, with a focus on three main topics: constitutionalism; the independence of the judiciary, the impartiality of both the legal profession and legal education; and the independence of mass media.

CONSTITUTIONALISM

Over the last few decades, several features of the 1988 constitutional regime have been determinant for a gradual reshaping of the rule of law and the separation of powers in Brazil. In particular, Brazil's recent constitutionalism expresses a paradox: while it has had a clear anti-authoritarian orientation, it has also generated tensions that today threaten to undermine the same democratic institutions it intended to safeguard. This section explores some of these traits.

The Constitution of 1988 marked the end of the military regime born with the coup of 1964. More than three decades later, the right-wing coalition in power today departs, in many ways, from the libertarian ideals that inspired the Constituent Assembly in 1987. The conservative wave that led to Bolsonaro's election in 2018 mobilizes an imaginary similar to that of the military coup of 1964, presenting itself as its successor.[6] Bolsonaro's victory also expresses the intense rejection of previous administrations,[7] after a period of economic crisis and political instability that resulted, in no small part, from the actions of judges and prosecutors engaged in fighting corruption.[8] In this regard, a central feature of the incumbent government is the promotion of conservative principles, inspired by autocratic tendencies.

A first element to consider is the present administration's disregard for the separation of powers. On this point, Bolsonaro and his entourage have been intensely antagonizing Congress, on the grounds that the legislative branch would be plagued by corrupt and archaic political practices. In the president's view, the so-called old politics would be a direct obstacle to popular sovereignty, as expressed in his election. Thus, the government's political agenda has often been stalled in the legislature due to the refusal to negotiate with traditional parties. The president's contentious stance inarguably "denied him a majority to pass any legislation and to prevent Congress undoing key administrative changes he implemented by provisional presidential order."[9] Conflicts with the judiciary also occurred, which will be addressed in the following section.

As for the distribution of federative powers, Bolsonaro clashed with local authorities, notably concerning the management of the public health crisis caused by COVID-19. Because of its denialist policies,[10] Bolsonaro was isolated and confronted by a broad political coalition that included no less than twenty-four of the twenty-seven governors of the federal states. The dispute was eventually taken to the Supreme Court. Ruling against the claims of the federal government, the Court affirmed the shared competence of federal, state, and municipal authorities to address the coronavirus pandemic, disallowing federal policies regarding the virus outbreak.

A second distinctive element of the present administration is the belittling, whether expressed or veiled, of democratic values, manifested in numerous statements of an autocratic nature. Still a candidate, Bolsonaro voiced his admiration for the military regime, declaring that this had been "a very good" period that would have prevented Brazil from succumbing to the influence of the Soviet order.[11] Once elected, the president praised key figures of the military regime, stating that Colonel Carlos Alberto Ustra, "an Army officer who was convicted of torture during the country's 1964–1985 military dictatorship, was a 'national hero.' "[12] The president also granted great prestige to the armed forces, filling several posts in his office with fellow military personnel. Bolsonaro thus seeks to show independence from the traditional political class, with whom he has always antagonized himself.[13]

The chief of state has also manifested support for public demonstrations against democracy. An example can be found in the rally that took place on April 19, 2020, in Brasília. In the midst of the coronavirus pandemic, Bolsonaro joined protesters waving banners to demand an end to social isolation, the reinstatement of dictatorial laws of the military regime, and the closure of the National Congress and the Supreme Court.[14]

Finally, a third issue is the contempt for fundamental rights. Bolsonaro made numerous homophobic statements, voicing his disapproval of citizens who are lesbian, gay, bisexual, or transsexual.[15] He also expressed open misogyny stating, for instance, that he would not rape a fellow Congresswoman simply because she did not deserve it[16] or mocking women as "idiots" and "tramps," unworthy of equal pay.[17] In addition, his many racist declarations generated vigorous criticism.[18]

State secularism was also challenged under Bolsonaro's administration. In 2019, the head of state asserted his intention to appoint a "terribly evangelical" minister to the Supreme Court.[19] At the beginning of his presidential term, Bolsonaro stated that he would make Judeo-Christian principles a priority of his government, also declaring that Brazilians were "God-fearing men."[20] The Minister of Women, Family and Human Rights, Damaris Alves, implemented controversial conservative policies, openly inspired by her evangelical confession.[21]

The present government's stance, as seen, has been to discredit the democratic regime currently in force in Brazil. This strategy culminated in the president's statement that he himself would embody the Constitution.[22] The impact of this strategy on the independence of the judiciary has been substantial and will be discussed in the next section.

THE INDEPENDENCE OF THE JUDICIARY, THE IMPARTIALITY OF THE LEGAL PROFESSION, AND UNIVERSITY LEGAL EDUCATION

One of the main features of the Bolsonaro administration has been the hostility vis-à-vis the judiciary, particularly the Supreme Court. This section highlights key tensions between these two branches of government and examines their repercussions on judicial independence.

While the Constitution of 1988 mainly reinstated an independent legislative branch as the primary seat of Brazilian democracy, it also considerably increased the powers of the judiciary. As acknowledged by Meyer,[23] "in transitional societies, judicial authorities gain more attention since they can work as institutional guarantors of the rules of the game." That was the case of Brazil in 1988: courts were appointed guardians of the newly restored rule of law, receiving broad competences to enforce the legal order, which had become democratic.[24]

Particularly, constitutional review was reinforced, and the Federal Supreme Court received broader powers to strike down unconstitutional legislation and public policies. Constitutional review of legislative omissions, a concept imported from Portugal, led the Court to eventually fill legislative voids left by Congress. In addition, newly expanded access to concentrated constitutional review gave civil society organizations a new power: they could now transfer to the Supreme Court conflicts unresolved within the legislative branch. The Court became, from then on, a major player in the resolution of political disputes.

The expansion of the judiciary's influence found theoretical support in the neoconstitutionalist doctrine, which blurs traditional boundaries between legislative and jurisdictional functions by emphasizing judicial power.[25] As a result of the adoption of neoconstitutionalist postulates, Brazilian courts became increasingly involved in matters that, until then, were considered to be the exclusive domain of the elected branches.

Altogether, the above factors contributed to an ever-increasing judicialization of politics, often bringing the courts to the forefront of the political scene. Not infrequently, there were frictions with the legislative and the executive, resulting in confrontations and corresponding reactions from the elected branches. In this regard, courts have been an important source of instability in Brazilian constitutionalism—which results from "anomalies in the exercise of powers by institutional actors inside the constitutional system."[26]

The ample powers and institutional guarantees accorded to the judiciary by the Constitution of 1988 have not been able to avoid increasingly severe clashes with the current administration. As reported by the *Financial Times*, ever since his inauguration, the chief of state "has stoked fears over the future of democracy with constant attacks on Congress, the courts, the press and civil society."[27] Bolsonaro's election carries an intrinsic paradox: While the presidential candidate presented himself as an anti-corruption champion, siding with judges in this combat, he also included the attack on judicial activism as a strong point in his government program. Driven by voters' acute rejection of the leftist Workers' Party, Bolsonaro benefited from the popularity of the fight against corruption led by judges and prosecutors, while vigorously opposing an alleged over-independence of the courts in performing their jurisdictional function. The tension is, therefore, permanent between the alleged aspiration to "moralize" political life and the explicit opposition to the very institutions that ensure the respect for the rule of law.

Bolsonaro deliberately abandoned institutional means to challenge judicial decisions, using, instead, legal disputes as a catalyst to induce belligerence against the Supreme Court and the justice system.[28] This hostility is shared by his close allies, such as three of his sons who are members of the federal and municipal legislative branches. As an illustration, *Reuters* reported in 2018 that "social media exploded over a video of comments made in July by [Representative] Eduardo Bolsonaro saying the top court could be forcibly disbanded by the Army if it stripped his father of an electoral victory."[29] In this sense, threats of breaking the constitutional order, in a harsh anti-establishment tone, have been commonplace in the present administration. This has occurred, notably, through the support for public mobilization against judicial activism and the Supreme Court, as mentioned above, or by attempts to meddle in criminal investigations, or, still, by efforts to undermine the authority of the Court.

In a striking episode, Justice Minister Sérgio Moro resigned in protest over an alleged attempt by Bolsonaro to meddle in federal and local police inquiries, to his own benefit. The president's malicious activities would have then exceeded the strict limits of the judiciary, to reach other institutions directly linked to the jurisdictional function. As reported by Deutsche Welle,[30] Moro alleged that "Bolsonaro had fired Mauricio Valeixo, the Federal Police head, to appoint a person who would illegally share reports with him." Moro also claimed that "Bolsonaro had tried to fire the head of police in the state of Rio de Janeiro, to protect his sons who are currently under investigation." The head of state dismissed the accusations as frivolous, calling Moro "vain and dishonest" and affirming he "didn't 'need permission' to fire anyone." The episode resulted in an inquiry, currently under way in the Supreme Court, which could result in accusations of fraudulent misrepresentation, obstruction of justice, and passive corruption against the president.[31]

Bolsonaro and his circle also made efforts to undermine the authority and legitimacy of the Supreme Court. An example can be found in the so-called hate cabinet, an "alleged clandestine network of bots, businessmen and bloggers is said by some lawmakers and Brazil's biggest newspaper to rain vitriol on all who oppose President Jair Bolsonaro."[32] The Court initiated its own inquiry, which seeks to determine whether the said cabinet has used fake news to topple opponents, institutions, and even democracy itself. Likewise, the use of fake news would possibly be behind the election of Bolsonaro in 2018, who would have benefited from a powerful misinformation campaign in social networks.[33]

Another episode illustrating the hostility before the Supreme Court occurred in 2017. In a lecture, General Hamilton Mourão, future vice president, argued that there could be a "constitutional" military intervention if the judiciary did not solve the country's political problems.[34] Mourão's statement was based on an interpretation of Article 142 of the Constitution, according to which the armed forces could exercise "moderating power" vis-à-vis constitutional powers. The controversy was brought to the Supreme Court's scrutiny in 2020. Justice Luiz Fux ruled that the command of the armed forces is a limited capacity, excluding any interpretation of article 142 that could legitimize military intervention. In response, Bolsonaro, Mourão, and the Minister of Defense, General Fernando Azevedo e Silva, stated in a note that the military forces were subject to the authority of the president of the Republic, and would not accept orders to seize power.[35]

The government also threatened outright disobedience to Supreme Court decisions. In the inquiry into Bolsonaro's alleged meddling in police investigations, his chief of staff for Institutional Security, General Augusto Heleno, declared there would be "unpredictable consequences" if the Court ordered the president to hand over his cell phone. For Heleno, the Court's order would constitute "an affront to the supreme authority of the executive branch and an unacceptable interference by another power in the private life of the President of the Republic and in the institutional security of the country."[36] The open menace sparked outrage in Brazilian political circles.

As seen, Bolsonaro employed multiple strategies to jeopardize judicial independence, seeking not only to intimidate the Supreme Court but also to evade criminal investigations. The Court's reaction could be seen, for instance, in a text message by Justice Celso de Mello, which was leaked to the press. For Mello, Brazil could become an "abject dictatorship" under Bolsonaro: "we must resist the destruction of the democratic order to avoid what happened in the Weimar Republic when Hitler, after he was elected by popular vote, did not hesitate to annul the Constitution and impose a totalitarian system in 1933."[37] Along the same lines, more than 600 jurists signed a manifesto entitled "*Basta*" ("Enough"), vehemently condemning the present administration.

Regarding the legal profession, the Brazilian regulatory framework complies with the United Nations standards, as stated in the Basic Principles on the Role of Lawyers, adopted by the Eighth United Nations Congress on the Prevention of Crime and the Treatment of Offenders in 1990 in Havana, and the United Nations Office of High Commissioner for Human Rights report by the special rapporteur on the independence of judges and lawyers, published on September 5, 2018. Lawyers enjoy ample legal protection in the performance of their professional activities. Even though Bolsonaro did not alter this legal regime, his relations with the Brazilian Bar Association (OAB) have been marked by innumerous contentious episodes.

The OAB has opposed several key policies of the Bolsonaro government, both in the courts and before public opinion. In March 2019, for instance, the OAB petitioned the United Nations regarding the anniversary celebrations of the 1964 "revolution," as directed by the president. According to the Bar Association, the president's refusal to recognize the military coup as such unduly sought to modify the historical narrative, thus violating the right to memory and truth, as well as international treaties signed by Brazil.[38]

The OAB has also considered petitioning Congress for the impeachment of Bolsonaro.[39] In addition, the OAB presented a public report vigorously questioning one of the government's most important bills, which contained sweeping anti-crime measures.[40] In yet another relevant episode, the OAB challenged before the Supreme Court the constitutionality of federal policies against COVID-19, requesting that the president be compelled to comply with WHO protocols.[41]

The Bolsonaro administration, in turn, has on several occasions acted against the interests of lawyers and the Bar Association itself. In 2019, the executive proposed a constitutional amendment seeking to dispense with membership in professional councils, such as the Bar Association.[42] This measure would greatly impair the supervisory and disciplinary powers over the legal profession, currently attributed to the OAB. The president also expressed his opposition to the mandatory Bar exam.[43]

Mr. Santa Cruz, president of the Bar Association, has not only questioned key federal policies, but also corroborated accusations made against the head of state. Bolsonaro, in turn, questioned the democratic character of the Bar Association's governance, criticizing the indirect election for the presidency of the organization.

Concerning legal education in Brazil, its impartiality has not suffered direct attacks from the current government. According to long-held statutes, each type of degree program in the country possesses its own national curricular guidelines established by the National Board of Education, an autonomous state agency. The latest resolution for law degree program curriculum guidelines was issued in December 2018 (Resolution No. 5 of December 17, 2018, from the Ministry of Education), days before Bolsonaro took office, and there have thus far been no efforts to change these guidelines.

However, there have been broader and more indirect threats to the independence of legal education. Bolsonaro began a crusade against public universities as soon as he took office. He argues that these universities are hubs for far-left political indoctrination and became obsessed with eradicating "cultural Marxism," "gender ideology," and "political correctness" from academic settings.[44] In these culture wars, his administration has employed strategies such as changing the practices used to select deans of federal public universities and declaring sudden budget cuts at public universities.

The issue of how federal university deans are selected has reached the Supreme Court. Federal Law No. 9.192, from December 21, 1995, established parameters for the nomination of university deans which, briefly, occurs as follows: (a) the academic community votes for its preferred candidates; (b) a list of the top three candidates (in terms of votes) is created; (c) the list is submitted to Brazil's president, who selects the winner. In the first two years of his term, however, Bolsonaro nominated some temporary or interim deans (more aligned with his government) who had not made it on the list or who had not been candidates at all.[45] In addition, the Bolsonaro administration tried to change the 1995 law on two occasions (Provisional Presidential Orders No. 914/2019 and 979/2020) but was blocked by Congress. The OAB took the debate to the Supreme Court and, in a preliminary decision in December 2020 (ADPF 759), the reporting justice determined that the president must select the deans from one of the top three candidates provided on the list out of respect for the law and the academic community.

The government has also cut funding for higher education. With no clear explanation, the Minister of Education announced cuts to public university funding in early 2019 as punishment for acts which the minister described as partisan manifestations and for "promoting disorder." Only after strikes and mass protests organized by unions and studies against the government was the money again approved.[46] For 2021, the government has submitted a budgetary bill to reduce the federal higher education budget,[47] a shortage which will hobble all public university operations, including law degree programs.

INDEPENDENCE OF MASS MEDIA

Despite solid constitutional protection, the independence of the mass media has been tested to its limits. This section intends to expose how President Bolsonaro ended up becoming the main author of attacks on journalists and the means of communication in general, putting in doubt the right to freedom of information in Brazil.

After more than two decades of a military dictatorship, the Brazilian Constitution of 1988 guaranteed independence of mass media. The military dictatorship, which lasted from 1964 to 1985, used censorship as one of its main tools against its opponents and journalists who provided critical, independent information were persecuted, tortured, and, in many cases, assassinated.[48] For this reason, the 1988 Constitution guaranteed the independence of mass media as one of the pillars of the country's new democracy.

However, this independence is still a challenge in practice. According to the NGO Reporters Without Borders (RSF), Brazil is considered to be violent against the press, with dozens of cases of threats against, aggression toward, and murders of journalists, reporters, radio announcers, and other media professionals in recent years.[49] Most of these cases have occurred in small towns and mid-sized cities in the Brazilian countryside when journalists covered or investigated cases of corruption or organized crime (Brasil–Um 2020).[50]

This hostility worsened after the 2018 presidential elections and the rise of right-wing conservatism into power. RSF reports that Bolsonaro's campaign was "marked by hate speech, disinformation, violence against journalists and contempt for human rights,"[51] and has "ushered in a particularly dark era" for Brazilian democracy and the country's freedom of the press.[52] The numbers of crimes against the press during Bolsonaro's time in office are startling. Attacks against journalists and the means of communication more generally increased 54 percent in 2019, according to the country's National Federation of Journalists (FENAJ).[53] Of the 208 cases reported in 2019, the president was the perpetrator in 121 (58 percent).[54] Between January and September 2020, the FENAJ recorded 299 attacks against journalism carried out by Bolsonaro, representing an average of almost one attack per day.[55] On a scale created by RSF, which monitors freedom of the press in 180 countries, Brazil has fallen since Bolsonaro took power.[56] Today, Brazil is in 107th place, lower than countries such as Burkina Faso (38th place), Botswana (39th place), and Sierra Leone (85th place).[57]

In addition to posting on social media, Bolsonaro typically greets and talks with supporters in front of his official residence during routine but informal morning meetings. It has been at this site that many journalists have been verbally assaulted. Cases representative of the president's methods include the day he was asked about his senator son's involvement in corruption and money-laundering schemes. Bolsonaro responded to the journalist by saying, "You look terribly like a homosexual."[58] On another occasion, he was asked whether he was attempting to interfere in the federal police's probe into his sons, and he told the journalist to "shut up."[59] In May 2020, after receiving verbal attacks and threats from some of the president's supporters, large media outlets decided to stop covering Bolsonaro's informal morning meetings at his residence as a security measure to protect their journalists.[60]

In addition to these verbal attacks, the government has tried to limit the right to information during the COVID-19 pandemic through a measure that was blocked by the Supreme Court. Brazilian Law No. 12.527, known as the Access to Information Act (LAI), regulates the provision of the Constitution that establishes the right of any citizen to receive information of interest to society from the government. The passing of the law in 2011 was a milestone for Brazil's political and administrative transparency, and it is with its backing that many journalists have been able to provide society with news. Early in the pandemic, however, the Bolsonaro administration issued Provisional Presidential Order No. 928/2020, which sought to alter the LAI by limiting the public's access to information provided by government agencies as part of the COVID-19 public health emergency. Professional journalist associations publicly declared themselves to be against the measure,[61] and the case made it to the country's Supreme Court. The Supreme Court judges suspended the measure, with the reporting justice arguing that the president's provisional order was an abuse of power (ADI 6351).

Besides the Supreme Court, other agents have sought to guarantee the independence of the mass media under the Bolsonaro administration. There have been at least ten requests for Bolsonaro's impeachment issued to the Chamber of Deputies in which the complainant has argued that the president has committed crimes of responsibility in his attacks on journalists and his restrictions on freedom of the press. Note that Brazilian Law No. 1.079 from April 10, 1950, provides citizens with the opportunity to initiate impeachment proceedings by formally reporting a president's crime of responsibility to the Chamber of Deputies. In one of the requests (No. 0014), a group of attorneys alleged that Bolsonaro violated the constitutional principle of impersonality by expressly asking businesses not to advertise with media outlets that criticized his administration, by excluding certain media outlets from public bidding processes, and by allowing for more government advertising funds to be provided to television networks that supported his government. These and all of the other impeachment requests are awaiting a ruling by the president of the Chamber of Deputies which is legally responsible for going forward with any impeachment proceedings.

CONCLUSION

When the Operation Car Wash investigations went national in scope in 2015, many Brazilians were jubilant over the possibility of justice against rampant corruption. With influential business executives and politicians being arrested in the largest corruption and money-laundering scheme in the history of the country, the feeling was that public institutions were working better than ever and that the law was finally being applied to everyone. For many, the rule of law was finally taking shape in the country. This feeling, however, gave way to a sentiment known to be dangerous to democracies: aversion to politics. Fed up with prior administrations and the countless reports of corruption involving political parties across the spectrum, many Brazilians began to seek a savior, or some kind of messiah who could combat corruption, moral degradation, and the old ways of politics at any cost. Brazil's 2018 election was marked by this context, which ushered in a president that embodied right-wing conservatism.

Since Bolsonaro took office, the struggle between politics and the rule of law has been constant, particularly in the case of constitutionalism, independence of the judiciary, independence of the legal profession, impartiality of university legal programs, and independence of the mass media. The right-wing coalition currently in power in Brazil has replaced the liberal ideals that inspired the country's 1988 Constitution with conservative tendencies and autocratic rule. Bolsonaro exhibits a clear disregard for the separation of powers, for democratic values, and for the fundamental rights established by the country's Constitution. Furthermore, the independence of the judiciary has been threatened by the president's numerous attempts to intimidate the Supreme Court and discredit it in a way that negatively affects public opinion of it. The free practice of law is still preserved; however, there is constant conflict between Bolsonaro and the Brazilian Bar Association (OAB). There have been no direct attempts to interfere in law degree programs, but the current administration has actively fought to hobble academic freedom and public universities. The independence of mass media has also been under significant attack, and the president has lodged frequent attacks against journalist and media outlets in general in recent years. The damage to the rule of law has not been greater only because the judicial branch, the legislative branch, and many people in civil society have resisted the executive branch's onslaughts.

NOTES

1. Jonathan Watts, "Operation car wash: Is this the biggest corruption scandal in history?" *The Guardian*, accessed June 1, 2021, https://bit.ly/34ztEUF.

2. "Brazil President Dilma Rousseff removed from office by Senate," *BBC*, accessed September 1, 2020, https://bbc.in/3vGByYj.

3. Datafolha Instituto de Pesquisa, "Partidos, Congresso e Presidência são instituições menos confiáveis do país," accessed June 15, 2021, https://bit.ly/3caeglM.

4. Datafolha Instituto de Pesquisa, "Partidos, Congresso e Presidência são instituições menos confiáveis do país."

5. Guardian Staff, "Who is Jair Bolsonaro? Brazil's far-right President in his own words," *The Guardian*, accessed August 29, 2021, https://bit.ly/2SQexmT.

6. Mariana Valente, "Freedom in brazil gradually eroded," *Deutsche Welle*, accessed August 18, 2021, https://bit.ly/3fBzBGN.

7. Philip Reeves, "Jair Bolsonaro, A polarizing figure, prepares to become Brazil's president," *NPR*, accessed August 31, 2021, https://n.pr/3pbyroP.

8. Murilo Gaspardo, "Brazil's elections and the defeat of political liberalism," *Global Policy,* accessed October 22, 2020, https://bit.ly/3pdIiui.

9. Tom Hennigan, "Brazil's political crisis deepens after Bolsonaro supporters protest," *The Irish Times*, accessed May 27, 2020, https://bit.ly/34FgLZ0.

10. Ernesto Londoño, Manuela Andreoni, and Letícia Casado, "Bolsonaro, isolated and defiant, dismisses coronavirus threat to Brazil," *The New York Times*, April 1, 2020, https://nyti.ms/3c9BhW5.

11. Philip Reeves, "Dictatorship was a 'very good' period, says Brazil's aspiring president," *NPR*, accessed July 30, 2021, https://n.pr/2 So. 0g75L.

12. Reuters Staff, "Brazil's Bolsonaro extols convicted torturer as a 'national hero'," *Reuters*, accessed August 8, 2019, https://reut.rs/3pbuYGP.

13. Anthony Boadle, "Brazil's Bolsonaro militarizes his inner cabinet," *Reuters*, accessed February 23, 2021, https://reut.rs/3g1lVUz.

14. Tom Phillips, "Brazilian President Jair Bolsonaro denounced for joining pro-dictatorship rally," *The Guardian*, accessed April 20, 2021a, https://bit.ly/3fFxt0L.

15. Mariana Simões, "Brazil's polarizing new president, Jair Bolsonaro, in his own words," *The New York Times*, August 28, 2018, https://nyti.ms/34 A. 1VDl.

16. Simões, "Brazil's polarizing new president, Jair Bolsonaro, in his own words."

17. Tom Phillips, "'Stop this disaster': Brazilian women mobilize against 'misogynist' far-right Bolsonaro," *The Guardian*, accessed September 21, 2021, https://bit.ly/3wIfoVs.

18. Tom Phillips, "Jair Bolsonaro's racist comment sparks outrage from indigenous groups," *The Guardian*, accessed January 24, 2021, https://bit.ly/3i5LFSo.

19. Ricardo Brito, "Brazil's Bolsonaro hopes to appoint evangelical minister to supreme court," *Reuters*, accessed August 6, 2021, https://reut.rs/34zwRDw.

20. George Thomas, "'We are god-fearing men': Brazil's president a friend to trump and biblical values," *CBN News*, accessed March 20, 2021, https://bit.ly/3ignBvY.

21. Ernesto Londoño and Letícia Casado, "Brazil under bolsonaro has message for teenagers: Save sex for marriage," *The New York Times*, January 27, 2021, https://nyti.ms/3pm1BSh.

22. Bryan Harris and Andres Schipani, "Brazil's top judges take stand against Bolsonaro," *Financial Times*, accessed June 4, 2020, https://on.ft.com/3wIeFUe.

23. Emilio P. N. Meyer, "Judges and courts destabilizing constitutionalism: The Brazilian judiciary branch's political and authoritarian character," *German Law Journal* 19, no. 4 (2018): 759, https://doi.org/10.1017/S2071832200022860.

24. Rogerio B. Arantes, "Constitutionalism, the Expansion of Justice and the Judicialization of Politics in Brazil," in *The Judicialization of Politics in Latin America*, ed. Rachel Sieder, Line Schjolden, and Alan Angell (New York: Palgrave Macmillan, 2005), 231.

25. Ezequiel Gonzalez-Ocantos, "Courts in Latin American POLITICS," *Oxford Research Encyclopedia of Politics* (2019): 1–21, https://doi.org/10.1093/acrefore/9780190228637.013.1680.

26. Meyer, "Judges and Courts Destabilizing Constitutionalism."

27. Watts, "Operation car wash: Is this the biggest corruption scandal in history?"

28. Thomas Bustamante and Emilio P. N. Meyer, "Judicial responses to Bolsonarism: The leading role of the federal supreme court," *Verfassungsblog on Matters Constitutional* (blog), *Verfassungsblog,* June 20, 2021, https://bit.ly/34CubVM.

29. Anthony Boadle, "Brazil's right-wing candidate scolds son for threat to shut top court," *Reuters*, accessed October 22, 2018, https://reut.rs/2SJQuGk.

30. Deutsche Welle, "Brazil: Bolsonaro 'expects' supreme court to drop investigation into police meddling," accessed May 26, 2020, https://bit.ly/3fYTzdv.

31. Tom Phillips, "Jair Bolsonaro faces inquiry into claims of meddling with police," *The Guardian*, accessed April 28, 2021, https://bit.ly/3vItGFE.

32. Andrew Rosati and Mario S. Lima, "In hunt for 'office of hate,' Brazil's supreme court closes in," *Bloomberg*, accessed June 22, 2021, https://bloom.bg/34DPQNs.

33. Tai Nalon, "Opinion: Did WhatsApp help bolsonaro win the brazilian presidency?" *The Washington Post*, accessed August 1, 2021, https://wapo.st/3uKqGHo.

34. Bustamante and Meyer, "Judicial responses to Bolsonarism."

35. Augusto Fernandes, "Bolsonaro: Forças Armadas não aceitam tentativas de tomada de Poder," *Correio Braziliense*, accessed June 12, 2021, https://bit.ly/2SQcuzd.

36. "Brésil: demande de saisie du téléphone de Bolsonaro, le gouvernement furieux," *Le Figaro*, accessed May 22, 2021, https://bit.ly/3fUX4li.

37. Anthony Boadle and Ricardo Brito, "Bolsonaro joins rally against Brazil's top court; judge warns democracy at risk," *Reuters*, accessed May 31, 2020, https://reut.rs/3pbRwqA.

38. Fabián Salvioli, "UN Human Rights Office of the High Commissioner," *United Nations Human Rights Office of the High Commissioner*, accessed March 29, 2019, https://bit.ly/2RZrjiU.

39. Edson Sardinha, "Conselho da OAB vai votar pedido de impeachment de Bolsonaro," *Congresso Em Foco*, accessed June 4, 2021, https://bit.ly/3wQK0Ey.

40. Felipe S. Cruz and Juliano Breda, *Análise do Projeto de Lei Anticrime: OAB Nacional* (Brasília: Ordem dos Advogados do Brasil and Conselho Federal, 2019), https://bit.ly/3wMWJYx.

41. Danilo Vital, "Conduta de Bolsonaro que descumpre protocolo da OMS é inconstitucional, diz OAB," *Consultor Jurídico*, accessed March 31, 2021, https://bit.ly/3fFttxn.

42. Janary Júnior, "Proposta do governo Bolsonaro desobriga inscrição em conselho profissional," *Câmara dos Deputados*, accessed August 6, 2021, https://bit.ly/3g2J88O.

43. "Bolsonaro diz que não acha justo exame da OAB para exercer advocacia," *CNN Brasil*, accessed May 29, 2021, https://bit.ly/3wG5YtI.

44. Katy Watson, "How Brazil's culture wars are being waged in classrooms," *BBC*, accessed May 7, 2021, https://bbc.in/34AX2cS.

45. Ana C. Moreno, "Governo interveio em 6 de 12 nomeações de reitores de universidades federais até agosto," *G1-Globo*, accessed August 31, 2021, https://glo.bo/3wPqN5S.

46. Tom Phillips, "Students protest across Brazil over Jair Bolsonaro's sweeping cuts to education," *The Guardian*, accessed May 30, 2021, https://bit.ly/2Rhj0ik.

47. "Projeto de Lei de Diretrizes Orçamentária (PLDO)," *Ministério da Economia*, accessed April 28, 2021, https://bit.ly/3fFxyBB.

48. Cristina Burack, "Brazil charges 6 ex-military dictatorship agents in journalist's murder," *Deutsche Welle*, accessed March 18, 2021, https://bit.ly/3vCOCxE.

49. Reporteres Sem Fronteiras, "Brasil: Um clima de ódio e desconfiança alimentado pelo presidente Bolsonaro," accessed June 6, 2021, https://bit.ly/3cabKvQ.

50. Reporteres Sem Fronteiras, "Brasil: Um clima de ódio e desconfiança alimentado pelo presidente Bolsonaro."

51. Reporteres Sem Fronteiras, *Brasil.*

52. Reporteres Sem Fronteiras, *Brasil.*

53. Federação Nacional de Jornalistas (FENAJ), V*iolência contra Jornalistas e Liberdade de Imprensa no Brasil–Relatório 2019* (Brasília: FENAJ, 2020), https://bit.ly/3fHwtsQ.

54. FENAJ, V*iolência contra Jornalistas e Liberdade de Imprensa no Brasil - Relatório 2019.*

55. "Em nove meses, Bolsonaro cometeu 299 ataques ao jornalismo," *Federação Nacional de Jornalistas (FENAJ)*, accessed October 14, 2021, https://bit.ly/3peMidN.

56. "Classificação Mundial da Liberdade da Imprensa 2020," *Repórteres sem Fronteira*, accessed June 6, 2021, https://bit.ly/3i9338F.

57. "Classificação Mundial da Liberdade da Imprensa 2020."

58. Dom Phillips and Tom Phillips, "Brazil: Bolsonaro in homophobic outburst as corruption scandal swirls," *The Guardian*, accessed August 20, 2021, https://bit.ly/3vN0cGM.

59. Ricardo D. Coletta, "Bolsonaro tells reporters to shut up, attacks Folha and denies interference with federal police," *Folha De S. Paulo*, accessed May 6, 2021, https://bit.ly/2SKN9H1.

60. Reuters Staff, "Brazilian media boycott Bolsonaro residence due to harassment," *Reuters*, accessed May 26, 2021, https://reut.rs/3g2gi8t.

61. "Só venceremos a pandemia com transparência," *Associação Brasileira de Jornalistas Investigativos (ABRAJI)*, accessed March 24, 2021, https://bit.ly/3fCnHN0.

BIBLIOGRAPHY

Arantes, Rogerio B. "Constitutionalism, the Expansion of Justice and the Judicialization of Politics in Brazil." In *The Judicialization of Politics in Latin America*, edited by Rachel Sieder, Line Schjolden, and Alan Angell, 231–62. New York: Palgrave Macmillan, 2005.

Associação Brasileira de Jornalistas Investigativos (ABRAJI). "Só venceremos a pandemia com transparência." Accessed March 24, 2021. https://bit.ly/3fCnHN0.

BBC. "Brazil President Dilma Rousseff removed from office by Senate." Accessed September 1, 2020. https://bbc.in/3vGByYj.

Boadle, Anthony, and Ricardo Brito. "Bolsonaro joins rally against Brazil's top court; judge warns democracy at risk." *Reuters*. Accessed May 31, 2020. https://reut.rs/3pbRwqA.

Boadle, Anthony. "Brazil's Bolsonaro militarizes his inner cabinet." *Reuters*. Accessed February 23, 2021. https://reut.rs/3g1lVUz.

Boadle, Anthony. "Brazil's right-wing candidate scolds son for threat to shut top court." *Reuters*. Accessed October 22, 2018. https://reut.rs/2SJQuGk.

Brito, Ricardo. "Brazil's Bolsonaro hopes to appoint evangelical minister to supreme court." *Reuters*. Accessed August 6, 2021. https://reut.rs/34zwRDw.

Burack, Cristina. "Brazil charges 6 ex-military dictatorship agents in journalist's murder." *Deutsche Welle*. Accessed March 18, 2021. https://bit.ly/3vCOCxE.

Bustamante, Thomas, and Emilio P. N. Meyer. "Judicial Responses to Bolsonarism: The Leading Role of the Federal Supreme Court." *Verfassungsblog on Matters Constitutional* (blog). *Verfassungsblog,* June 20, 2020. https://bit.ly/34CubVM.

CNN Brasil. "Bolsonaro diz que não acha justo exame da OAB para exercer advocacia." Accessed May 29, 2021. https://bit.ly/3wG5YtI.

Coletta, Ricardo D. "Bolsonaro Tells Reporters to Shut Up, Attacks Folha and Denies Interference with Federal Police." *Folha De S. Paulo*. Accessed May 6, 2021. https://bit.ly/2SKN9H1.

Cruz, Felipe S., and Juliano Breda. *Análise do Projeto de Lei Anticrime: OAB Nacional*. Brasilia: Ordem dos Advogados do Brasil and Conselho Federal, 2019. https://bit.ly/3wMWJYx.

Datafolha Instituto de Pesquisa. "Partidos, Congresso e Presidência são instituições menos confiáveis do país." Accessed June 15, 2021. https://bit.ly/3caeglM.

Deutsche Welle. "Brazil: Bolsonaro 'expects' Supreme Court to drop investigation into police meddling." Accessed May 26, 2020. https://bit.ly/3fYTzdv.

Federação Nacional de Jornalistas (FENAJ). "Em nove meses, Bolsonaro cometeu 299 ataques ao jornalismo." Accessed October 14, 2020. https://bit.ly/3peMidN.

Federação Nacional de Jornalistas (FENAJ). *Violência contra Jornalistas e Liberdade de Imprensa no Brasil – Relatório 2019*. Brasilia: FENAJ, 2020. https://bit.ly/3fHwtsQ.

Fernandes, Augusto. "Bolsonaro: Forças Armadas não aceitam tentativas de tomada de Poder." Correio Braziliense. Accessed June 12, 2021. https://bit.ly/2SQcuzd.

Gaspardo, Murilo. "Brazil's Elections and The Defeat of Political Liberalism." *Global Policy*. Accessed October 22, 2020. https://bit.ly/3pdIiui.

Gonzalez-Ocantos, Ezequiel. "Courts in Latin American Politics." *Oxford Research Encyclopedia of Politics* (2019): 1–21. https://doi.org/10.1093/acrefore/9780190228637.013.1680.

Guardian Staff. "Who is Jair Bolsonaro? Brazil's far-right president in his own words." *The Guardian*. Accessed October 29, 2018. https://bit.ly/2SQexmT.

Harris, Bryan, and Andres Schipani. "Brazil's top judges take stand against Bolsonaro." *Financial Times*. Accessed June 4, 2020. https://on.ft.com/3wIeFUe.

Hennigan, Tom. "Brazil's political crisis deepens after Bolsonaro supporters protest." *The Irish Times*. Accessed May 27, 2020. https://bit.ly/34FgLZ0.

Júnior, Janary. "Proposta do governo Bolsonaro desobriga inscrição em conselho profissional." *Câmara dos Deputados*. Accessed August 6, 2021. https://bit.ly/3g2J88O.

Le Figaro. "Brésil: demande de saisie du téléphone de Bolsonaro, le gouvernement furieux." Accessed May 22, 2021. https://bit.ly/3fUX4li.

Londoño, Ernesto, and Letícia Casado. "Brazil Under Bolsonaro has message for teenagers: Save sex for marriage." *The New York Times*. January 27, 2020. https://nyti.ms/3pm1BSh.

Londoño, Ernesto, Manuela Andreoni, and Letícia Casado. "Bolsonaro, isolated and defiant, dismisses coronavirus threat to Brazil." *The New York Times*. April 1, 2020. https://nyti.ms/3c9BhW5.

Lynch, Christian E. C., and Jorge Chaloub. "The 1988 Brazilian Constitution and the Political Regimes: An Outline of Intellectual History (1972–2019)." *Journal of Constitutional History* 40, no. II (2020): 259–75. https://bit.ly/3uAvejy.

Meyer, Emilio P. N. "Judges and Courts Destabilizing Constitutionalism: The Brazilian Judiciary Branch's Political and Authoritarian Character." *German Law Journal* 19, no. 4 (2018): 727–68. https://doi.org/10.1017/S2071832200022860.

Ministério da Economia. "Projeto de Lei de Diretrizes Orçamentária (PLDO)." Accessed April 28, 2021. https://bit.ly/3fFxyBB.

Moreno, Ana C. "Governo interveio em 6 de 12 nomeações de reitores de universidades federais até agosto." *G1-Globo*. Accessed August 31, 2021. https://glo.bo/3wPqN5S.

Nalon, Tai. "Opinion: Did WhatsApp Help Bolsonaro Win the Brazilian Presidency?" *The Washington Post*. Accessed August 1, 2021. https://wapo.st/3uKqGHo.

Phillips, Dom, and Tom Phillips. "Brazil: Bolsonaro in homophobic outburst as corruption scandal swirls." *The Guardian*. Accessed December 20, 2019. https://bit.ly/3vN0cGM.

Phillips, Tom. "'Stop this disaster': Brazilian women mobilize against 'misogynist' far-right Bolsonaro." *The Guardian*. Accessed September 21, 2018. https://bit.ly/3wIfoVs.

Phillips, Tom. "Brazilian president Jair Bolsonaro denounced for joining pro-dictatorship rally." *The Guardian*. Accessed April 20, 2021a. https://bit.ly/3fFxt0L.

Phillips, Tom. "Jair Bolsonaro's racist comment sparks outrage from indigenous groups." *The Guardian*. Accessed January 24, 2021b. https://bit.ly/3i5LFSo.

Phillips, Tom. "Jair Bolsonaro faces inquiry into claims of meddling with police." *The Guardian*. Accessed April 28, 2021c. https://bit.ly/3vItGFE.

Phillips, Tom. "Students protest across Brazil over Jair Bolsonaro's sweeping cuts to education" *The Guardian*. Accessed May 30, 2019. https://bit.ly/2Rhj0ik.

Reeves, Philip. "Dictatorship Was A 'Very Good' Period, Says Brazil's Aspiring President." NPR. Accessed July 30, 2018a. https://n.pr/2S0g75L.

Reeves, Philip. "Jair Bolsonaro, a polarizing figure, prepares to become Brazil's president." NPR. Accessed December 31, 2018b. https://n.pr/3pbyroP.

Repórteres sem Fronteira. "Classificação Mundial da Liberdade da Imprensa 2020." Accessed June 6, 2021. https://bit.ly/3i9338F.

Repórteres Sem Fronteiras. "Brasil: Um clima de ódio e desconfiança alimentado pelo presidente Bolsonaro." Accessed June 6, 2021. https://bit.ly/3cabKvQ.

Reuters Staff. "Brazilian media boycott Bolsonaro residence due to harassment." *Reuters*. Accessed May 26, 2020. https://reut.rs/3g2gi8t.

Reuters Staff. "Brazil's Bolsonaro extols convicted torturer as a 'national hero'." *Reuters*. Accessed August 8, 2019. https://reut.rs/3pbuYGP.

Rosati, Andrew, and Mario S. Lima. "In Hunt for 'Office of Hate,' Brazil's Supreme Court Closes In." *Bloomberg*. Accessed June 22, 2021. https://bloom.bg/34DPQNs.

Salvioli, Fabián. "UN Human Rights Office of the High Commissioner." United Nations Human Rights Office of the High Commissioner. Accessed March 29, 2019. https://bit.ly/2RZrjiU.

Sardinha, Edson. "Conselho da OAB vai votar pedido de impeachment de Bolsonaro." Congresso Em Foco. Accessed June 4, 2020. https://bit.ly/3wQK0Ey.

Simões, Mariana. "Brazil's Polarizing New President, Jair Bolsonaro, in His Own Words." *The New York Times*. October 28, 2018. https://nyti.ms/34A1VDl.

Thomas, George. "'We Are God-Fearing Men': Brazil's President a Friend to Trump and Biblical Values." *CBN News*. Accessed March 20, 2021. https://bit.ly/3ignBvY.

Valente, Mariana. "Freedom in Brazil gradually eroded." *Deutsche Welle*. Accessed August 18, 2021. https://bit.ly/3fBzBGN.

Vital, Danilo. "Conduta de Bolsonaro que descumpre protocolo da OMS é inconstitucional, diz OAB." *Consultor Jurídico*. Accessed March 31, 2021. https://bit.ly/3fFttxn.

Watson, Katy. "How Brazil's culture wars are being waged in classrooms." *BBC*. Accessed May 7, 2021. https://bbc.in/34AX2cS.

Watts, Jonathan. "Operation car wash: Is this the biggest corruption scandal in history?" *The Guardian*. Accessed June 1, 2021. https://bit.ly/34ztEUF.

Chapter 4

Power Politics versus the Rule of Law in India

A Case Study

Murugesan Srinivasan and Varsha Vijayan

As evident from the writings of several scholars across the world, *power politics* is an international construct. It has been a frequently discussed theme throughout Professor Schwarzenberger's—a well-known legal scholar—postwar studies. According to him, international law has become "merely power politics in disguise." The key to his entire analysis is that power is the determining factor for the formation of international hierarchies of nations, which are divided into world powers, middle powers, and small states.[1] Another renowned scholar, Professor Julius Stone, has stated that illusory choice between power politics and the world community does in fact deprive all human beings of any constructive role, however small in the struggle for peace. In light of the above, several scholars have expressed that an alternative to power politics should exist in the international sphere if the world community is to survive.[2] The "rule of law" is the real alternative to power politics as it is one of the most important political ideals and one of the arrays of ideals constitutive of modern political morality. Moreover, societal prospects for wealth, freedom, and many other goods are affected by the depth and sustainability of the commitment to be governed by the "rule of law." It also serves to channel decision-making in attractive ways to make decisions more predictable and also increase the chances for fair administration of public power in a basically just society.[3] In India, the power derived from politics and political institutions is more colossal than the power derived from other sources that include bureaucracy, police, judiciary, and so on. Operationally, in the Indian context, power politics may be understood as to how politics is used as a powerful tool to attain power. But politics and political institutions are influenced by several factors including caste and religion. With this opinion in mind, the authors of this chapter confront Indian realities such as caste, religion, caste, and communal politics that affect the implementation of the rule of law. The authors also attempt to demonstrate how these factors, the legal institutions, and legal provisions and, last but not least, perpetual inequality make the rule of law a paper ideal. Hence, the practice of the rule of law in the Indian context is influenced by the prevailing sociopolitical conditions.

UNDERSTANDING THE RULE OF LAW

We need to understand the concept of "law" before we can understand the "rule of law." The purpose of this part of the chapter is to understand the rule of law both as a concept and as an array of principles from the viewpoints of various international institutions, scholars, and others.

In simple terms, the "rule of law" is a complex phrase, and the word "law" is only one of its components. But this suggestion appears to be misleading since one cannot grasp the concept of "law" without, at the same time, understanding the values comprised in "rule of law." However, this does not mean that one must understand the concept of "rule of law" first and then go on to conceptualize law itself. Instead, one should try to understand both the "rule of law" and the concept of "law" as a package and not as a separable component of the other.[4]

The United Nations which came into existence in 1945, since the explicit reference to the rule of law in the Universal Declaration of Human Rights, has clearly been guided by the rule of law. After more than seven decades, the contemporary society has brought before us various challenges and opportunities that emerged due to a complex political, social, and economic transformation. Such challenges and opportunities require the collective response. It must be guided by the rule of law. It is also considered the foundation of both friendly and equitable relations between countries and also the foundation of fair societies. From the point of view of the United Nations system as a principle of governance, the rule of law entails that all persons, both public and private institutions, the state and other entities, are accountable to publicly promulgated laws. The rule of law also ensures that the laws are equally enforced and independently adjudicated. For the United Nations system, the rule of law also requires initiatives so as to ensure adherence to various principles such as the supremacy of the law, equality before the law, accountability to the law, fairness while applying the law, separation of powers and so on. The rule of law also forms the necessary base to international peace and security, and it is at the core to protect people's rights and their fundamental freedom.[5]

In the last few decades, scholars and academics also have extensively discussed and written on the concepts of rule of law and its need and significance. It is not practically possible, due to space constraints, to give the features of all those writings and works. However, the works of a few established and renowned legal scholars, who have elucidated the role of rule of law in the contemporary society, are briefly presented here.

In the introduction to his book on "Rule of Law" in America, Professor Ronald A. Cass (a well-known legal scholar in the United States of America) stated that some fundamental choices set the pattern for the society, and commitment to be governed by the rule of law is one among such fundamental choices. Societal prospects for wealth, freedom, and many other goods are affected by the depth and sustainability of the commitment to be governed by the rule of law. He further stated that the rule of law serves to channel decision-making in attractive ways to make decisions more predictable and to increase the chances for fair administration of public power in a basically just society. On the contrary, in a society that lacks basic requisites of justice, the rule of law does not play a clear role.[6] Another renowned scholar, who has written extensively on the rule of law, is Professor Jeremy Waldron (a professor of legal and political philosophy, currently working at New York School of Law). One of his essays on "The Concept and Rule of Law" published in the year 2008 is a comprehensive one. According to him, in the contemporary society, the "rule of law" is one of the most important political ideals and is one of the arrays of ideals constitutive of modern political morality. The "rule of law" is considered a crucial ideal because it is the one that is appropriately invoked whenever any government of any country tried to get away by arbitrary and oppressive action or sometimes by sidestepping the norms and procedures laid down in their laws or constitutional provisions. The other examples of the abuses of the rule of law include: interfering with the courts, imprisoning someone without legal justification, detaining individuals without any safeguards of due process, manipulating the constitutional provisions for partisan advantage, and so on.[7]

Thus, the "rule of law" is not simply a concept and is not a mere set of ideals but it forms the foundation for a just and fair society. The rule of law has been in public discourse for centuries; it has been an important ideal in the political tradition for millennia. Therefore, to comprehend and evaluate modern understandings of rule of law, it will be interesting and worthwhile to grasp its historical heritage. Such heritage of arguments begins with Aristotle (c. 350 BC). The argument about rule of law also proceeds with medieval theorists like Sir John Fortescue (1471). The argument further goes on through the early modern period in the work of Sir John Locke (1689), James Harrington (1656), and (oddly enough) Niccolò Machiavelli (1517). In Europe, in the writings of Montesquieu (1748), in American Constitutionalism, in the Federalist Papers; in the writings of A. V. Dicey (1885) and F. A. Hayek (1944, 1960 and 1973), and so on in Britain; and in the writings of Lon Fuller (1964) and others in America.[8] However, in the Indian context both as a concept and a guiding principle, the "rule of law" has evolved alongside India's movement for freedom from the British. As the "rule of law" has been in public discourse in different places at different times, India too has a distinct history in this discourse.

RULE OF LAW AS AN IDEOLOGICAL FACET OF THE INDIAN NATIONAL MOVEMENT

Rule of law both as a concept and as a principle encompassing various ideals such as human rights, civil liberties, freedom of speech, evolved over centuries. Though certain features of rule of law are common across space and time, certain other features are unique to certain places, regions, countries and certain times. In the Indian context, the evolution of rule of law both as a concept and as a principle had been a part of the Indian National Movement. It is imperative to understand how do the ideals of rule of law—human rights, civil liberty, freedom of speech—were very much part of the ideology of the Indian National Movement. Several of such ideals were crystallized and incorporated in the form of the Articles of Constitution of India, after India's independence.

The Indian National Movement was considered the product of the central contradiction between the interest of the Indian people and colonialism. The leadership of the Indian National Movement had a clear, scientific, and firm understanding of colonialism. That is, the leadership understood that British were using political control to subordinate both the Indian economy and the Indian society to the needs of the British economy and the British society.

As in any mass movement, ideology plays a crucial role. The firm anti-colonial basis of the movement was also very important. Unlike normal politics, active participation in a mass movement involves immense sacrifice, and it cannot simply take place on the basis of sense of being exploited or being poor. Such mass movement requires a very firm ideological commitment. Hence, it was the scientific anti-colonial ideology of the Indian National Movement that became the prime-mover in its anti-imperialistic struggle. Interestingly, along with these anti-colonial perspectives, there were also certain other ideological elements that constituted a social, economic, and political vision of the movement. The vision was that of capitalist independent economic development and a secular, republican, democratic, civil libertarian political order based on the principles of social equality. Notably, the above vision remained unquestioned throughout the Indian National Movement except the controversy on the capitalist character of economic order that was seriously questioned after the 1920s.[9]

The ideological development of the Indian National Movement that occurred during the entire period between the 1880s and 1940s was based on the firm anti-imperialism and on a program of socioeconomic reform. The Indian National Movement was also fully committed to parliamentary democracy and civil liberties. Since the foundation of the Indian National Congress, the nationalists and various other mass organizations were organized along democratic lines. Further, they fought for freedom of press, freedom of speech, freedom of association, and other civil liberties.[10]

CONSTITUTIONAL LAW OF INDIA AND THE RULE OF LAW

The Constituent Assembly was elected and held its first sitting on December 9, 1946, and reassembled on August 14, 1947, as a sovereign Constituent Assembly for the Dominion of India. The historic Objective Resolution of Jawaharlal Nehru greatly inspired the shaping of the Constitution. One of the important resolutions is: the Constitution shall guarantee and secure to all the people of India, social, economic, and political justice. The Constitution shall also guarantee equality of status, equality of opportunity, and equality before law. Further, the Constitution shall guarantee freedom of thought, freedom of expression, freedom of belief, freedom of faith, freedom of worship, freedom of vocation, freedom of association and action (subject to law and public morality). While commenting on the Objective Resolution, Jawaharlal Nehru said that the resolution was something more than a resolution—"It is a declaration, a firm resolve, a pledge, an undertaking and for all of us a dedication." The ideal included in the above Objective Resolution is reflected in the Preamble to the Constitution. The Preamble summarizes the aim and objects of the Constitution.[11]

The framers of the Constitution of India had adopted fundamental rights to safeguard individual liberty and to ensure social, economic, and political justice for every member of the community. The Constitution of India has included a number of fundamental rights in Part III of the Constitution, including the right to equality. According to Article 14 (one of the fundamental rights) of the Constitution—"The State shall not deny to any person equality before the law or the equal protection of the laws within the territory of India."[12] The concept of equality and equal protection of laws encompasses social and economic justice in a political democracy. Further, the principle of equality is a basic feature of the Constitution of India and is the essence of democracy. The Supreme Court in *Dalmia Cement vs. Union of India*[13] was of the view that the doctrine of equality before the law is a necessary corollary to the concept of the rule of law. Protection of life and personal liberty are also ensured by the Constitution through Article 21, which provides that "no person shall be deprived of his life or personal liberty except according to the procedure established by law."[14] The Supreme Court in its judgments (e.g., *Maneka vs. Union of India*)[15] held that right to life as laid down in Article 21 means something more than survival or more than animal existence. It would include the right to live with human dignity. It would also include all those aspects that go to make a man's life meaningful, complete, and worth living. Further, the principle of rule of law and due process are closely linked with human rights protection.[16]

INDEPENDENCE OF JUDICIARY AND THE RULE OF LAW

The literature on independence of judiciary is extensive and reflected in academic writings. A former professor at the University of Delhi, M. P. Singh, citing several works (e.g., Philip S. Anderson, 1998) has underscored the importance of an independent judiciary. For a free and constitutional democracy, an independent judiciary is necessary since it ensures the rule of law and realization of human rights.[17] The starting and principal point of the concept of the independence of judiciary is clearly the doctrine of the separation of powers. Achieving independence of judiciary secures liberty by preventing the concentration of power in one person or body; it also places restraints on the executive and legislative. Further, the doctrine of separation of powers ensures that the exercise of judicial power is unhindered by the other two branches. Hence, the independence of judiciary signifies that the judiciary as an institution is independent of the other institutions, namely the executive and the legislative, but does not imply independence of judges in the exercise of functions.[18]

Thus, an independent judiciary requires the complete freedom of every individual judge from the controls of all organs of the state. Besides, the independence of the individual judges and the collective independence of the judiciary as a body are visibly different from each other, and they together constitute judicial independence. An independent and impartial judiciary is indispensable for any democratic institution. To ensure such an independent and impartial judiciary, several factors such as the appointment of judges, their tenure, their relationship with other agencies of the government, independence of judiciary from influence and interference from executive and legislative must be considered.[19]

The highest judiciary namely the Supreme Court of India and the High Courts of various states have significantly contributed to upholding the constitutional rights and the principles. A development of Public Interest Litigation is one such latest contribution by the Supreme Court. The court has ruled that some persons, due to poverty or disability, are unable to approach the court for enforcement of their fundamental rights. Judicial redress is sought by such disadvantaged individuals when they suffer any legal injury or legal wrong; any person or any member of the public acting bona fide can maintain an action for judicial redress. As a result of such development, the underprivileged and the downtrodden have secured access to court through the agency of a public-spirited individual or an organization.[20]

In 1981, the Supreme Court of India in Francis Coralie *Mullin vs the Administrator, Union Territory of Delhi and Ors.* declared that "right to life" is not limited only to the protection of limbs or faculty but it includes the "right to live" with human dignity and all that goes along with it, including the right to the basic necessities of life and function as that constitutes the bare minimum expression of the human self.[21] This contribution made by the Supreme Court of India in the development of human rights jurisprudence has an extremely special significance in developing world countries. The Indian judiciary particularly the Supreme Court of India has upheld the rule of law and preserved our constitutional values. However, one cannot brush aside the public disillusionment and lack of confidence in the judiciary. To ensure that the judiciary is able to command respect in the eyes of the people, several reforms need to be done. For instance, just like how Constitution provides for the composition and powers of executive and legislative, it should also provide for the composition and powers of the judiciary. The Constitution may also provide for the composition of the courts and their jurisdiction and the appointment, terms of office and tenure of the judges.[22]

Sudhanshu Ranjan, a TV journalist while commenting on the Indian judiciary, said that "there is nothing Indian about Indian judiciary." He stated that there is an absence of anything indigenous including the language, the apparel, and the mode of addressing judges of the higher judiciary. As stated earlier, all necessary efforts should be made by the elected to ensure the functional independence of judiciary so that judges can decide cases without fear of consequences which will, in turn, ensure the rule of law.[23]

FACTORS CONTRIBUTING TOWARDS THE RULE OF LAW TO REMAIN JUST AN IDEAL

The principle of rule of law is a popularly understood concept across the globe; particularly, it is closely associated with the Constitution of England. However, in India, the doctrine of equality before law is a corollary to the principle of rule of law. In simple terms, the doctrine of equality before law is a declaration of equality of all persons, within the territory of India, thereby implying the absence of any privilege in favor of any individual. It also means that no man is above the law of the land.

The ground reality in India is that the rule of law exists only on paper and does not often exist in practice. There are several factors responsible for this grim situation. It may also be noted that when the principle of rule of law or doctrine of equality before the law became the constitutional principle in India, both legal institutions and the institutions of governance were established to practice the principles of the rule of law. In other words, mechanisms to realize the abstract principles were created, yet the rule of law does not always exist in practice. The authors of the present chapter have attempted to examine the predominant factors that contribute toward the rule of law to remain most often as a mere ideal. The two predominant factors that contribute to the rule of law to often exist only on paper are caste and religion; caste politics and communal politics. Besides the above factors, the authors have also discussed on how certain legal institutions and provisions are antithetical to the principles of rule of law.

Caste and Caste Politics

The caste system in India is disparate from the social systems in other countries. This system denies the rights of man and appears to be an obstacle to the economic progress of millions of people. Caste is considered as an aberration, and several authors have more often tried to explain the caste system as an anomaly than understand it as an institution. One of the features of modern society is equality but equality is the most immediately opposed to the caste system.[24]

Professor Lloyd Rudolph and Professor Suzzane Hobor Rudolph—Padma Bhushan awardees and well-known political scientists during the 1960s—published an article on "The Political Role of India's Caste Associations." The authors threw light on the role of caste associations in creating political awareness. According to them, caste provides channels of communication on the basis of leadership and organization which enable those people still immersed in the traditional society and culture to beat the technical political illiteracy. If the political illiteracy is not transcended, it would handicap their ability to participate in the democratic politics. Caste associations in the form of "Sabhas" and "Sangams" were involved in these kinds of political activity. Though caste associations were visible in the mid-nineteenth century, they have proliferated in number and strength only during the early part of the twentieth century. Such associations became increasingly visible after independence. They drew a parallel between the voluntary associations/volunteer groups or interest groups familiar to European and American politics to that of caste associations in India.[25]

In modern India, to demonstrate how caste, as a political construct, has evolved, the origin and growth of *Bahujan Samaj* Party (BSP) in Uttar Pradesh is a typical example. The BSP has its origins in the 1970s under Kanshi Ram (Mayawati's mentor) as initially the "Backward and Minority Classes Federation" and later the "Dalit Shoshit Samaj Sangharsh Samiti." Also, initially, the BSP as a party was identified with Dalits and lower castes, which later (in 2007) had more upper castes. In 2007, the BSP won 206 out of 403 seats in the Assembly by distributing several seats to upper castes. And unlike its predecessors like the Scheduled Caste Federation and later the "Republican Party of India," which was formed by B. R. Ambedkar, the BSP has captured the Dalit vote. In post-independence politics, several factors have contributed to the persistence and consolidation of caste identities, including the Indian state's policy on caste. For instance, the implementation of Mandal Commission Report in 1990 triggered a large-scale and violent change in the caste equation in Indian politics, particularly in the Hindi-speaking parts of North India. Mandal Commission recommended reservations for 400 castes that were identified as Other Backward Classes. On top of it, the implementation of Mandal Report incentivized and encouraged caste and vote bank politics. In fact, following the implementation of Mandal Commission Report, several political parties were formed. Of those, the two most prominent leaders who emerged during the post-Mandal period were Mulayam Singh Yadav, who founded Samajwadi Party in 1992 (subsequently he became the chief minister of Uttar Pradesh in 1994), and Lalu Prasad Yadav, who formed Rashtriya Janata Dal in 1997 (who subsequently became the chief minister of Bihar). These two leaders used the post-Mandal phase to advance their party as well as the interest of their communities, namely Yadavs. The politics of these two leaders were good examples of how dominant castes were able to get benefits out of reservation policies and state patronage. Further, caste seems to be very much alive in Indian politics. It is also true that caste is not the only factor that influences when people vote, especially when there is more than one candidate of the same caste contesting in the same constituency. Other issues like food prices, drinking water, unemployment, also increasingly influence a majority of voters. No one can be certain what goes through the mind of a voter in making electoral choices.

However, it is a matter of fact that the political parties and the state treat caste as a crucial mobilization.[26]

Further, many sociologists and political scientists demonstrated how the Indian politics is inseparable from caste. Professor Christophe Jaffrelot has traced the history of various national and regional political parties across India. According to him, many of the regional parties are associated with a single caste and/or a religious community. Partially, some state units of national parties also have such association. This development has taken place because of the reason that states themselves are often identified with a few *Jatis*. This may be also due to the redrawing of the map of India on linguistic lines in the 1950s. The demand for linguistic states was primarily spelled out in cultural terms but it mostly was articulated by the dominant caste, which had spread throughout the area of one vernacular language. After the redrawing of state boundaries, these dominant castes tended to align themselves with one party.[27]

While analyzing the electoral outcome of 2009, authors like Yogendra Yadav and Suhas Palshikar have specifically examined the role of caste or community at both micro and macro levels. According to them, caste or community continued to be the primary building block of political affiliation at the micro-level. However, the politics of building a macro-political coalition based on these blocks suffered a setback. Therefore, they inferred that the politics of social identity has reached a point of saturation. Such saturation is evident from the roadblocks hit by some regional parties such as the Rashtriya Janata Dal (RJD) in Bihar and Samajwadi Party in Uttar Pradesh, Pattali Makkal Katchi in Tamil Nadu and the BSP in Uttar Pradesh. These parties, which depended on one single caste for the bulk of their votes, have found little scope for any enlargement of their votes. They also found that secondary alliances built by them (e.g., with Muslims by RJD and with Brahmins by BSP) proved short lived. But this does not mean that caste or community does not matter for voting anymore. It does not also mean that all sections of society reached a point of saturation in their political mobilization.[28]

Equality is a critical feature of the rule of law. In this context, it is not only interesting but also worthwhile to present Rousseau's "Discourse on Inequality" since he was considered a rebel against inequality. In the above text, Rousseau's chief merit is to distinguish between natural inequality and moral inequality. Moral inequality results from natural inequality for social ends.[29] The inequality created by the caste system of India is a form of moral inequality and not of natural inequality. "Essays on the Caste System" written by Célestin Bouglé (1958) demonstrates how the caste system perpetuates inequality. According to him, the caste system divides the entire society into enormous number of hereditary groups, which are different from one another and connected together by three characteristics, namely (i) separation in matters of marriage and contact; (ii) division of labor (either in theory or by tradition), each group having a profession from which their members deviate only within certain limits; and (iii) hierarchy, which ranks the hereditary groups as relatively superior or inferior to one another. These are considered as the main and apparent characteristics of the caste system in India.[30] All these characteristics are against the principle of equality. Equality is the principal feature of rule of law. The authors of this chapter have made some efforts to examine the caste system in the context of the rule of law. The authors also strongly believe that as long as the caste system prevails, inequality would continue to exist. Further, the caste system is considered a moral inequality, and the existing political system and politics are surrounded and covered completely by caste. Rajni Kothari, a well-known political scientist in the Introduction to his famous work *Caste in Indian Politics* stated that "It is not politics that gets caste-ridden, it is caste that gets politicized."[31]

As long as caste is politicized and politicized consciously for both mobilization and for votes, the caste system would continue to exist. As a result, inequality, an essential feature of the caste system, would persist. The foundation of rule of law is equality, which is immediately opposed to the caste system. Therefore, the rule of law and caste system cannot coexist.

Religion and Communal Politics

Other predominant factors are religion and communal politics. The authors of the chapter have examined the impact of dividing and mobilizing people on religious lines and how religion is used as a powerful tool in advancing the political powers of some parties. Though the Indian Constitution has declared that India is a secular state, the present political regime in power is subverting the spirit of secular state and secularism.

According to Western theorists, secularism means the strict disestablishment of religion from state. In other words, secularism denotes strict exclusion of religion from all state affairs for the sake of promoting the religious liberty and equal citizenship of all people.[32] Unlike the West-centric model of secularism, secularism has been defined in India not as neutrality toward all religions but as equal respect for all religions.[33] This view is in consonance with the Constitution of India.

Indian Constitution has declared India a secular state, which means that state protects all religions equally, and it also means that state does not uphold any religion as state religion. In 1976, by the Constitution (42nd Amendment) Act, the secular objective of the state has been expressed specifically by inserting the word "secular" in the Preamble. The framers of the Constitution adopted Articles 25 to 28 to further secularism. In fact, secularism was very much embedded in constitutional philosophy. The secular component in the

Indian Constitution was further strengthened in *Bommai vs. Union of India.*[34] In a nutshell, it can be said that the Indian Constitution guarantees to each individual, freedom to profess or practice and propagate religion and assures strict impartiality on the part of the state and its institutions toward all religions.[35] However, some political scientists have critically looked at constitutional guarantees and assurances. For instance, Godrej observed that though the Indian Constitution implies the strict separation of state and religion, it recognizes the rights of religious minorities. The Constitution also commits the state to provide aid to educational institutions established and administered by religious minority communities and so on.[36] These criticisms are also the version of Hindu Nationalism. As a result, there has been a reemergence of a sociopolitical hegemony privileging the Hindu majority. Along with these, there have been instances of mass religious violence. Also, a desire to reassert the rights of the upper-caste Hindus followed by rising anxiety about the rights of minorities like Muslims, Christians and lower-caste Hindus.[37]

The trend for the past three decades indicates that India is moving toward Hindu Nationalism. The Indian National Congress remained the predominant party in power for nearly half a century. No other political party could gain enough power to challenge the Indian National Congress until the Bhartiya Janata Party (BJP) became a predominant party. From 1947 to 2002, the Indian National Congress held the majority of seats in Parliament, with exceptions of 1977–1979 and 1996–1999 (when the Bhartiya Janata Party/BJP gained the majority of votes). As the BJP's central philosophy centers on Hindu Nationalism, its increasing popularity was no coincidental but occurred alongside increasing tensions between Hindus and Muslims over nearly three decades. In 1990s, a key event that precipitated tensions throughout the country was the demolition of Babri Masjid. This event marked a critical turning point in Hindu-Muslim relationship in India. Following the demolition, riots broke out in Mumbai for several months, which eventually resulted in the death of approximately 2,000 people, primarily Muslims. As the city of Mumbai was recovering from the riots, it experienced the worst terrorist attack in 50 years of history, which led to the death of 257 persons and left over 1,000 injured. The series of bomb blasts were believed to be coordinated by Muslims in the criminal underworld. As a result of these attacks, the *Vishwa Hindu Parishad* and *Shiv Sena* (Hindu Militant Group) rose in popularity to fight to what they believed to be a "growing assault" on Hindu values.[38]

The BJP won the majority of seats in the Parliament in the first general elections that took place since (the elections took place in 1996) 1993 riots. Hindu nationalism became the main platform for BJP, especially they pushed for the banning of cow slaughter as well as reclaiming Kashmir as fully Indian.[39] In the state of Gujarat, Narendra Modi became the chief minister in 2001. He became an inspirational figure to many Hindus. He was groomed by Rashtriya Swayamsevak Sangh (RSS)—an ultraconservative Hindu organization devoted to preserving and restoring Hindu identity in India, especially through the establishment of Hindu state. In 2002, Modi became prominent at the national and international level after the Gujarat riots. In Gujarat, the Hindu pilgrims were returning from Ayodhya by a train, which was attacked and burned by a mob of 1,000–2,000 villagers, who were believed to be Muslims. Sixty pilgrims died in the attack. As a result of this train attack, wide-scale riots took place in Gujarat. Over 2,000 people (majority Muslims) were killed in the riots. Nearly 150,000 people were displaced and ended up in refugee camps. The response of the government and Narendra Modi to these riots was condemned. Many organizations and scholars claimed that BJP was also complicit in the riots. Narendra Modi's role in the riots was a matter of controversy. However, it did not tarnish his reputation in the eyes of BJP. In 2013, BJP named him as the candidate for prime minister of India. In the 2014 elections, Narendra Modi and BJP went on to win an overwhelming majority in the Parliament gaining 166 seats, while Indian National Congress lost 162 seats. Overall, the BJP won 282 seats in the 543-member Parliament. Thereafter, the saffronization of India has been well underway. After independence, Jawaharlal Nehru's commitment to secularism made him give a declaration that India could be a peaceful, multireligious state. Now, with the increasing popularity and the success of the Indian nationalistic party, the secular values of India are at stake.[40]

During the last three decades, communal politics and political mobilization based on religion have been steadily increasing. Such politics have also helped political parties to attain political power both at the all-India level and also in several states. Therefore, we believe that dividing people on religious lines and sometimes, unleashing violence on religious minorities would continue to be used as a tool to advance their political agenda. In June 2021, Washington, DC-based Pew Research Center released a report "Religion in India: Tolerance and Segregation." Several critical articles were written on the report. According to such articles, there is a growing influence of Hindutva politics on India's social fabric.[41]

As India is a multireligious society and the Indian Constitution is committed to secularism, political mobilization on religious lines is against the interests of people belonging to various religions. In the words of Justice Govind Mathur, the then-chief justice of Allahabad High Court, the concept of equality is a treasure in a multiclass society like India. He further stated that communalism, casteism, and so on are an antithesis to our constitutional ideals.[42] These constitutional ideals also include the doctrine of equality before law, which is a necessary corollary to the rule of law. The authors of the present chapter are of the opinion that communal politics and communalism as a whole are antithetical to the principles of rule of law.

Provisions in the Procedural Laws vis-à-vis Rule of Law

The expression of rule of law has in it a large set of ideals including the human rights of the suspects and the accused. A. V. Dicey, a well-known English political philosopher, in one of his classic books titled *Introduction to Study of the Law of the Constitution* has explained the "rule of law," its nature, and its general applications. He said the supremacy of the rule of law is a characteristic of the English Constitution. This one expression (supremacy of rule of law) includes at least three distinct but related conceptions. Firstly, this expression means that no man is punishable or no man can be lawfully made to suffer in body or goods except for a well-defined violation of law established in the ordinary legal manner before the ordinary courts of the land.[43] The essence of the above is also reflected in the provisions of the Indian Constitution and the procedural law of India. Accused in a trial derive certain fundamental rights enshrined in the Constitution of India. However, it appears that the Constitution of India does not explicitly enshrine certain important rights of an accused. For example, the right to be represented by a lawyer, the right to be confronted with charges, the right to cross-examine the witness, and the non-admissibility of extra-judicial confessions are some of the rights of accused person, which are provided in the procedural law, namely, the Code of Criminal Procedure, 1973. Moreover, much before the Constitution was drafted and came into force, certain procedural rights were already provided in then the Code of Criminal Procedure, 1898 and Indian Evidence Act, 1872 (IEA). The procedural rights of the accused provided in the CrPC continued to exist even though the CrPC was revamped in 1973. In other words, none of the rights of an accused in a criminal trial have been taken away. Despite these constitutional guarantees and procedural rights under the CrPC, the violation of rights of accused manifests in several forms. There have been a significant number of cases of custodial violence and deaths in India. The intervention of the higher judiciary has by and large mitigated the sufferings of the victims of custodial violence and deaths. To secure their rights, the Supreme Court of India took earnest efforts to put an end to custodial torture and deaths. In 1997, in *the D. K. Basu v. the State of West Bengal*, the Supreme Court of India issued certain guidelines to adhere to while arresting a suspect or an accused.[44] The ground reality seems to be different, where most of the directions of the Supreme Court have not been strictly followed.[45] As a result, several cases of custodial deaths have been reported. According to the National Crime Records Bureau, 581 custodial deaths have occurred over a seven-year period between 2014 and 2020.[46]

RIGHT TO FREEDOM OF EXPRESSION

In the contemporary world, the issue of free speech is a widely debated issue. There have been many discussions and debates on the limitations placed upon free speech. That is, every society places some limits on the exercise of free speech. Interestingly, the American literary critic Stanley Fish (1994) said that there is no such thing as free speech. He said that "free speech" is a term used to focus the attention of people on a particular form of interaction. The phrase "free speech" is not meant to suggest that speech should never be limited. Free speech, according to Fish, is not an independent value but a political price.[47] In line with the ideas of Stanley Fish, in 1998, Alan Haworth suggested that right to freedom of speech is not something we have or something we own the same manner as we possess our arms or legs. Four decades ago, Alexander and Horton (1984) noted that speech contains several or varied activities such as speaking, writing, singing, acting, burning flags, shouting at street corners, advertising, threats, slander and so on. Some of these forms of communication are more important than others. Therefore, they require different levels of protection.[48]

Part III of the Indian Constitution deals with fundamental rights. There are six sets of fundamental rights including right to freedom. According to Article 19, all citizens of India shall have the right to freedom of expression; the right to assemble peaceably and without arms; the right to form associations and unions, and so on. In 1951, in the first constitutional amendment, certain additional clauses were incorporated (subclause 2 and 3). Article 19(2) states that nothing in subclause (a) of clause (1) (All citizens shall have the right to freedom of speech and expression; to assemble peaceably and without arms; to form associations/ union etc.) shall affect the operation of any existing law or shall prevent the state from making any law, in so far as such law imposes reasonable restrictions on the exercise of the right conferred by subclause (a) in the interests of sovereignty and integrity of India; in the interests of security of the state; in the interest of friendly relations with foreign states; in the interests of public order, decency or morality or in relation to contempt of any court, or in relation to defamation or incitement to an offense.[49]

Ever since the Constitutional Law of India came into force, and particularly after the First Amendment in 1951 with additional clauses, specifically clause (2), jurists, legal scholars, and activists have been deliberating on the phrase "reasonable restrictions." In the history of such never-ending discourse and deliberations over the reasonable restrictions imposed on freedom of speech, the Supreme Court of India in the *Kedar Nath v. State of Bihar* made certain noteworthy observations.[50] As provided by Article 19(2) of the Constitution, the state shall make new laws to place reasonable restrictions on the freedom of speech and expression. However, interestingly, Indian Penal Code, 1860 (IPC), which was enacted several decades before the Constitution came into force, has a provision imposing restrictions on the freedom of speech and expression. That is, Section 124(A) (inserted by Amendment Act of 1870) makes sedition an offense. According to 124(A) of the Indian Penal Code, whoever by words, either spoken or written or other forms like signs, visible representations or otherwise whoever brings or attempts to bring into hatred or contempt or whoever excites or attempts to excite disaffection toward the government established by law shall be punished with imprisonment for life or any shorter period to which fine may be added or imprisonment which may extend up to three years to which fine may be added or shall be punished with fine. Several issues emanate from the above constitutional provisions and also from the provisions of the penal code: (i) right to freedom of speech and expression is guaranteed through Article 19(1) of the Constitution of India; (ii) Article 19(2) places reasonable restrictions by the state on the right to freedom of speech and expression; (iii) Section 124(A) provides for punishment for individuals, who, by words or by signs, brings or attempts to bring hatred or to excite disaffection toward the government—both the latent and manifest content of this section signal that government established by law is beyond criticism, and the expression "disaffection" includes disloyalty and all feelings of enmity; (iv) another important point of contention here is that all these words and phrases such as "hatred," "contempt," "disaffection," "disloyalty," and "feelings of enmity" are abstract in nature. These terms are qualitative in nature and, hence, it is left to the discretion of judiciary to define, redefine, or interpret. Consequently, a large number of cases tried under this section end in acquittal. For instance, from 2016 to 2020, the total number of persons arrested on charges of sedition was 472. Of these chargesheets submitted against 336 persons, the number of cases disposed of by police was 228. Of the 425 (i.e., cases pending prior to 2016 and the total number of cases during 2016 to 2020) cases that went for trial between 2016 and 2020, trials were completed in only 58 cases. Only twelve individuals were convicted over the period of five years (2016 to 2020).[51] In light of the above, certain clear inferences can be made. The conviction rate is negligibly low. The prosecution has failed to prove charges on those who were arrested under Section 124(A). It may simply be due to the reason that persons were arrested under 124(A) without any prima facie.

Recently, legal scholars have been advocating either to scrap or repeal section 124(A) from the lawbook. The discourse and discussion on scrapping or repealing is not a recent development but it occupied an important part of the discussion in the context of democracy both during the pre-independence era and in the immediate post-independence period. The main point of argument is that the scope of 124(A) is too broad to be compatible with free speech in a democracy. A state where a citizen is not afraid to criticize the government and the citizens can peacefully voice their dissent is one of the crucial indicators of a true democracy. By extension, freedom of expression is not only a fundamental human right but one of the most important political rights vested with the citizenry. Any undemocratic curb placed on freedom of expression is a breach of the principles of rule of law.

While carefully examining the content of section 124(A), one can easily understand that whoever either excites or attempts to excite disaffection against the government, it can be construed as an offense. The freedom to criticize government is generally thought to be more important than other forms of freedom of speech. According to Alexander and Horton (1984), the government is the servant of the people, and they should not be allowed to censor them. They further argue that the main reason for justifying free speech or political speech is important because it allows the public to exercise an important value, namely, democracy. If people's defense of speech is crucial to a well-functioning democracy and any legislation that goes against this or undermines this goal is irrelevant.[52]

Many scholars (e.g., Bhatia, 2016) have commented that the sedition provision in the Indian Penal Law (124(A) of IPC) is considered a colonial era survival in an independent Indian polity. Section 124(A) was used by the British to contain and repress the freedom struggle, its retention in independent India to restrict free speech and political dissent must still be viewed as an anomaly.[53] Another law that is considered by many scholars and activists as an anti-rights law is the Unlawful Activities (Prevention) Act, 1967. This law allows the state to designate an individual as a terrorist without trial and to imprison them almost indefinitely. Several known activists were imprisoned using the provisions of UAPA. In August 2018, Sudha Bharadwaj (a lawyer and an activist) was arrested under the provisions of UAPA; her bail application was rejected three times and still, she has only recently been released on bail. She spent several years defending the rights of the workers in Chhattisgarh. Another tragic case was the detention of 83-year-old Jesuit Priest, Father Stan Swamy, who was detained under the provisions of UAPA by the National Investigation Agency. Most unfortunately, very recently, he died while in judicial custody. Both Sudha Bharadwaj and Father Stan Swamy were accused of supporting the banned Communist Party of India (Maoist). The above is a classic case, which demonstrates how the principles of rule of law have been violated. Through the provisions of UAPA, a state is empowered to arrest and imprison people for a long period. The arrest and detention for a long period without establishing the guilt through the established procedures itself is a punishment.[54]

The doctrine of equality before the law, which is a corollary to the principle of rule of law, is an important human rights principle in India. Equality before the law can be ensured only by the provisions of the Constitution or the laws. The institutional framework created for the said purpose should also be congruent to the principles of rule of law. Further, the laws that are passed for some specific purposes should not contravene the principles enshrined in the Constitution including the principle of equality. However, the above discourse exposes the existence of incongruence between the letter and spirit of the Constitution; and the provisions of the laws, the legal institutions created thereto. Therefore, the authors feel that most often the ideal of rule of law or equality before law remains only as an ideal.

FREEDOM OF ACADEMIA AND MEDIA: PREREQUISITES FOR THE RULE OF LAW

In the history of India, even before the freedom from British rule in 1947, academia particularly students actively participated in the struggle for independence of India. The legacy continued even after independence; the educational campuses of India have always been politically active with the backing of the constitutional guarantee of freedom of expression. However, during the last few years, academic freedom has weakened as the intimidation of professors, students, and educational institutions over political and religious issues has increased. There have been instances where Akhil Bhartiya Vidyarthi Parishad (ABVP), the student wing of the Hindu nationalist organization RSS, has used violent tactics on campuses of various parts of the country. There have also been instances where the activists of ABVP unleashed attacks on students and professors. Speakers or experts who are known to be critical of the ruling government have also been targeted.[55] To cite a few instances in 2016, the former students of Jawaharlal Nehru University (JNU), New Delhi, Kanhaiya Kumar, Umar Khalid, Anirban Bhattacharya, and seven others were arrested on charges of sedition (124A IPC); voluntarily causing hurt (323 IPC); using as genuine, a forged document or electronic record (471 IPC); unlawful assembly (143 IPC); rioting (147 IPC), and criminal conspiracy (120B IPC).[56] In December 2019, the students of two universities, Jamia Millia Islamia and Aligarh Muslim University, were brutally targeted for protesting against the Citizenship (Amendment) Act, 2019. In January 2020, the JNU campus was vandalized by masked ABVP students. Students and faculty were beaten up by them despite the presence of police close to the university. This incident took place after months of protests against fee hikes. In addition to these campus incidents of attacks and arrests, students and faculty have also been arrested or suspended for social media posts.[57]

India has various types of universities/institutions (public and private, central and state, and so on). As the kinds of regulatory structures and even legal guarantees vary depending upon the nature of universities/institutions, critical discussions that would involve questions of academic freedom also significantly vary. Any private college or university—profit and professional-oriented ventures run by local business families—are unlikely to encourage academic freedom. Given this situation, academic freedom—freedom of students and teachers—to critically think, discuss, and express their views is at stake. Various constitutional provisions such as Articles 14, 15, and 16 could be invoked to defend academic freedom. Articles 14, 15, and 16 to provide the right for equality, prohibit discrimination, and ensure equality of opportunity in matters of public employment could be invoked to realize academic freedom.[58] The ground reality is that academic freedom has been compromised at various educational institutions. Academic freedom protects the right to freedom of opinion and the right to expression, which are important elements of democracy, which, in turn, is essential for ensuring the rule of law in society.

The legislative, the executive, the judiciary and the press are the four pillars of democracy. Of these, the judiciary and the media are the best instruments to keep power in check. These institutions also protect the rights of the common people. However, in the recent past, two main noticeable changes have been taking place: (1) media's credibility is being questioned due to the way the facts are being presented,[59] (2) the private media are diverse and vigorous. On the one hand, there is a close relationship among politicians, business executives, and lobbyists; on the other hand, leading media personalities and owners of outlets have dented public confidence in the media.[60] Despite such shortcomings, the media has also done yeoman services. But, of late, there is a consistent effort to curtail the freedom of media particularly after 2014.[61] State authorities have used national security, defamation, sedition, and hate speech laws as well as contempt of court charges to curb critical voices in the media.[62] Recently, the top newspaper and TV media companies in India filed a petition in the Madras High Court seeking an order to declare the Information Technology (Intermediary Guidelines and Digital Media Ethics Code) Rules, 2021, ultra vires of the Constitution, and also they sought an order from the court to declare it as void and infringement of Article 14, Article 19(1)(a) and Article 19(1)(g) of the Constitution. They argued that the new rules opened the door to suppressing freedom of speech and independence of news media in the country.[63] Another incident that has been in news recently is Pegasus spyware. That is, a group of news publications has reported that a spyware known as Pegasus has been used to spy on politicians, activists, and journalists in several countries. It was also reported that at least forty journalists, cabinet ministers, and holders of constitutional positions were subjected to surveillance in India. Though there have been legal provisions which provide for intercepting a message or a class of messages and for surveillance of telephonic conversations, the Supreme Court of India has, on more than one occasion, put restrictions on such surveillance.[64] In 2017, the Supreme Court of India (*Justice K. S. Puttaswamy (Retd.) vs. Union of India*) has reiterated the need for oversight of surveillance. It was observed by the Court that the right to privacy cannot be violated without a just, fair, and reasonable law. It also has to fulfill the test of proportionality: (a) existence of a law; (b) must serve a legitimate state aim; (c) proportionality, that is, proportional to the need for surveillance. Therefore, any government action in this regard should carefully and meticulously be carried out without impinging on the right to privacy.[65] The extent of realization of the rule of law also depends on upholding or strengthening the pillars of democracy, including media, which is one of the main pillars of democracy.

In this chapter, the authors have attempted to demonstrate certain factors such as caste, religion, caste, and communal politics; legal institutions and legal provisions that contribute to holding the rule of law just as an ideal. The authors have specifically underlined the role of caste and caste politics in perpetuating inequality. Hence, any deliberation on the rule of law in the Indian context ought to be in the light of the prevailing sociopolitical conditions. Moreover, the authors are of the view that power politics, that is, the power derived from politics and political institutions, are enormous. As the politics and political institutions are the tools to attain such colossal power, the individuals who are at the helm of affairs of politics and political institutions use all means and methods—caste, religion, caste, and communal politics—to attain political power. In a nutshell, the rule of law would remain as an ideal as long as power politics continues, for it is antithetical to the rule of law.

NOTES

1. Robert A. Friedlander, "Power Politics and the Rule of Law: Professor Schwarzenberger Reconsidered," *DePaul Law Review* 24, no. 4 (Summer 1975): 837, https://bit.ly/2WkpHme.

2. Julius Stone, "Legal Controls of International Conflict," quoted in Robert A. Friedlander "Power Politics and the Rule of Law: Professor Schwarzenberger Reconsidered," in *DePaul Law Review* 24, no. 4 (Summer 1975): 839.

3. Ronald A. Cass, *The Rule of Law in America* (Baltimore: Johns Hopkins University Press, 2003), xi–xii.

4. Jeremy Waldron, "The Concept and the Rule of Law," *Georgia Law Review* 43, no. 1 (Fall 2008): 3, https://bit.ly/3o6D70C.

5. United Nations and the Rule of Law, "What is the Rule of Law," United Nations and the Rule of Law, accessed June 2, 2021, https://bit.ly/3odDKFt.

6. Cass, *The Rule of Law in America*, xi–xii.

7. Waldron, "The Concept and the Rule of Law," 5.

8. Jeremy Waldron, "The Rule of Law," in *The Stanford Encyclopaedia of Philosophy,* ed. Edward N. Zalta (Metaphysics Research Lab, Stanford University, 2020), https://stanford.io/3m7rZOx.

9. Bipan Chandra et al., *India's Struggle for Independence: Revised and Updated,* (Gurgaon: Penguin Books, 2016): 518–519.

10. Bipan Chandra, "Struggle for the Ideological Transformation of the National Congress in the 1930s," *Social Scientist* 14, no. 8/9 (August–September 1986): 18–19, https://doi.org/10.2307/3517433.

11. Durga Das Basu, *Introduction to the Constitution of India,* 23rd ed. (Gurgaon: LexisNexis, 2018), 19–20.

12. Indian Constitution. art. XIV.

13. Dalmia Cement (Bharat) Ltd. v. Union of India, 10 SCC 104 (1996).

14. Indian Constitution. art. XIX.

15. Maneka Gandhi v. Union of India, AIR 1978 SC 597 (1978).

16. Basu, *Introduction to the Constitution of India*, 93–123.

17. Philip S. Anderson, "Judicial Independence and Accountability," quoted in M. P. Singh, "Securing the Independence of the Judiciary—The Indian Experience," in *Indiana International & Comparative Law Review* 10, no. 2 (2000): 245.

18. M. P. Singh, "Securing the Independence of the Judiciary–The Indian Experience," in *Indiana International & Comparative Law Review* 10, no. 2 (2000): 247, https://doi.org/10.18060/17703.

19. Shimone Shetreet, "Judicial Independence: New Conceptual Dimensions and Challenges," in *Judicial Independence: The Contemporary Debate*, ed. Shimone Shetreet, Jules Deschenes (Dordrecht-Boston-Lancaster: Nijhoff, 1985), 590.

20. Soli J. Sorabjee, "Role of the Judiciary: Boon or Bane?," *India International Centre Quarterly* 38, no. 3/4 (Winter 2011–Spring 2011): 137, https://bit.ly/3AQQTIc.

21. Francis Caralie Mullin v. The Administrator, Union Territory of Delhi & Ors. AIR 746, 1981 SCR 516 (1981).

22. Singh, "Securing the Independence of the Judiciary—The Indian Experience," 249.

23. Sudhanshu Ranjan, "Media and Judiciary: Revitalization of Democracy," *Journal of the Indian Law Institute* 57, no. 3 (July-September 2015): 420, https://www.jstor.org/stable/44782789.

24. Louis Dumonte, *Homo Hierarchicus: The Caste System and Its Implications,* trans. Mark Sainsbury, Louis Dumonte and Basia Gulati (1970, New Delhi: Oxford University Press, 1999), 1, 11.

25. Lloyd Irving Rudolph and Susanne Hober Rudolph, "The Political Role of India's Caste Associations," *Pacific Affairs* 33, no. 1 (March 1960): 5–6, https://doi.org/10.2307/2753645.

26. Runojoy Sen, "The Persistence of Caste in Indian Politics," *Pacific Affairs* 85, no. 2 (June 2012): 363–369, https://doi.org/10.5509/2012852363.

27. Christophe Jaffrelot, "The Caste based mosaic of Indian politics," *Seminar*, May 2012, https://bit.ly/3ALOej9.

28. Yogendra Yadav and Suhas Palshikar, "Between Fortuna and Virtu: Explaining the Congress' ambiguous victory in 2009," *Economic and Political Weekly* 44, no. 39 (October 2009): 38. https://bit.ly/3sAwgg4.

29. Jean-Jacques Rousseau, "Discourse on the origin of inequality," quoted in Louis Dumont, *Homo Hierarchicus: The Caste System and Its Implications*, trans. Mark Sainsbury, Louis Dumonte and Basia Gulati (1970, New Delhi: Oxford University Press, 1999), 12.

30. Célestin Charles Alfred Bouglé "Essays on the Caste System," quoted in Louis Dumont, *Homo Hierarchicus: The Caste System and Its Implications*, trans. Mark Sainsbury, Louis Dumonte and Basia Gulati (1970, New Delhi: Oxford University Press, 1999), 21.

31. Rajni Kothari, "Introduction: Caste in Indian Politics," in *Caste in Indian Politics*, ed. Rajni Kothari (1970, reprint, Hyderabad: Orient Longman, 2004), 20.

32. Andrew Davison, *Secularism and Revivalism in Turkey: A Hermeneutic Reconsideration* and Madan, *Modern Myths, Locked Minds* quoted in Farah Godrej, "Secularism in India: A 'Gandhian' Approach," in *Multiculturalism in the British Commonwealth: Comparative perspectives on theory and practice*, ed. Richard T. Ashcroft and Mark Bevir (Oakland: University of California Press, 2019), 157.

33. Farah Godrej, "Secularism in India: A 'Gandhian' Approach," in *Multiculturalism in the British Commonwealth: Comparative Perspectives on Theory and Practice*, ed. Richard T. Ashcroft and Mark Bevir (Oakland: University of California Press, 2019), 157.

34. S. R. Bommai v. Union of India, AIR 1994 SC 1918 (1994).

35. Basu, *Introduction to the Constitution of India*, 28, 132.

36. Godrej, "Secularism in India: A 'Gandhian' Approach," 157.

37. Sudipta Kaviraj, "Languages of Secularity," *Economic and Political Weekly* 48, no. 50 (December 2013), https://bit.ly/3z8KdEm.

38. Andrea Malji, "The Rise of Hindu Nationalism and its Regional and Global Ramifications," *Education about Asia* 23, no. 1 (Spring 2018): 41, https://bit.ly/2UBKi4t.

39. Ranbir Vohra, *The Making of India: A Political History*, 3rd ed. (New York: Routledge, 2013): 305.

40. Malji, "The Rise of Hindu Nationalism and its Regional and Global Ramifications," 42–43.

41. Shaikh Mujibur Rehman, "The Many Shades of Intolerance," *The Hindu*, August 13, 2021, https://bit.ly/3z8wduj.

42. Omar Rashid, "Communalism, Casteism, regionalism antithesis to constitutional ideals," *The Hindu*, April 15, 2020, https://bit.ly/3mmZxcT.

43. A. V. Dicey, *Introduction the study of the Law of the Constitution*, 9th ed. (Indianapolis: LibertyClassics, 1982).

44. D. K. Basu v. State of West Bengal, AIR 1997 SC610 (1997).

45. Alok Prasanna Kumar, "Criminal Laws and Civil Rights," *Economic and Political Weekly* 53, no. 42 (October 2018, https://bit.ly/3kd4cLZ.

46. National Crime Records Bureau, "Crime in India," (New Delhi: Ministry of Home Affairs, Government of India, 2014–2020).

47. Stanley Eugene Fish, *There Is No Such Thing as Free Speech and It's A Good Thing, Too* (New York: Oxford University Press, 1994), 220.

48. Lawrence Alexander and Paul Horton, "The Impossibility of a Free Speech Principle," quoted in David van Mill "Freedom of Speech" in *The Stanford Encyclopedia of Philosophy,* ed. Edward N. Zalta (Metaphysics Research Lab, Stanford, CA: Stanford University, 2021).

49. Basu, *Introduction to the Constitution of India*, 112.

50. Kedar Nath Singh v. State of Bihar, AIR 1962 SC1955 (1962).

51. National Crime Records Bureau, "Crime in India," (New Delhi: Ministry of Home Affairs, Government of India, 2016–2020).

52. Lawrence Alexander and Paul Horton, "The Impossibility of a Free Speech Principle," *Northwestern University Law Review* 78, no. 5 (1984): 1324.

53. Gautam Bhatia, *Offend, Shock or Disturb: Free Speech under the Indian Constitution,* 1st ed. (New Delhi: Oxford University Press, 2016): 64.

54. Supriya Chaudhuri, "Thought–Crimes: Dissent, Disaffection and Intellectual Labour in Contemporary India," *Postcolonial Studies* 24, no. 1 (January 2021): 20. https://doi.org/10.1080/13688790.2021.1882076.

55. Sarah Repucci, ed., *Freedom in the World 2020* (New York: Freedom House, 2020), 528.

56. "JNU Sedition Case: Umar Khalid, Kanhaiya Kumar, other accused appear in Court," *The Wire,* March 16, 2021, https://bit.ly/3i7 F. 5de.

57. Nandini Sundar, Gowhar Fazili, "Academic Freedom in India," *The India Forum,* September 4, 2020, 1, https://bit.ly/3ocRJvi.

58. Sundar, "Academic Freedom in India," 3.

59. Ranjan, "Media and Judiciary: Revitalization of Democracy," 416.

60. Repucci, ed., *Freedom in the World 2020,* 527.

61. Ranjan, "Media and Judiciary: Revitalization of Democracy," 418.

62. Repucci, ed., *Freedom in the World 2020,* 527.

63. M. K. Venu, "Invoking free speech violations over new IT rules, big media finally goes to court," *The Wire,* June 25, 2021, https://bit.ly/3kN4fzL.

64. P. J. George, "Explained: Pegasus and the laws on surveillance in India," *The Hindu,* July 25, 2021, https://bit.ly/2Y1mpF6.

65. Justice K. S. Puttaswamy v. Union of India, AIR 10 SCC 1 (2017).

BIBLIOGRAPHY

Alexander, Lawrence, and Paul Horton. "The Impossibility of a Free Speech Principle." *Northwestern University Law Review* 78, no. 5 (1984): 1319–57.

Basu, Durga Das. *Introduction to the Constitution of India.* 23rd ed. Gurgaon: LexisNexis, 2018.

Bhatia, Gautam. *Offend, Shock, or Disturb: Free Speech under the Indian Constitution*. First edition. New Delhi: Oxford University Press, 2016.

Bouglé, Célestin Charles Alfred. *Essays on the Caste System*. trans. David Francis Pocock. Cambridge University Press, 1971.

Cass, Ronald A. *The Rule of Law in America*. Baltimore: Johns Hopkins University Press, 2003.

Chandra, Bipan. "Struggle for the Ideological Transformation of the National Congress in the 1930s." *Social Scientist* 14, no. 8/9 (1986): 18–39. https://doi.org/10.2307/3517433.

Chandra, Bipan, Mridula Mukherjee, Aditya Mukherjee, Kandiyur Narayana Panikkar, and Sucheta Mahajan. *India's Struggle for Independence: Revised and Updated*. Gurgaon: Penguin Books, 2016.

Chaudhuri, Supriya. "Thought-Crimes: Dissent, Disaffection and Intellectual Labour in Contemporary India." *Postcolonial Studies* 24, no. 1 (January 2021): 16–23. https://doi.org/10.1080/13688790.2021.1882076.

Davison, Andrew. *Secularism and Revivalism in Turkey: A Hermeneutic Reconsideration*. Yale Studies in Hermeneutics. New Haven: Yale University Press, 1998.

Dicey, A. V. *Introduction to the Study of the Law of the Constitution*. Indianapolis: Liberty Classics, 1982.

Dumonte, Louis. *Homo Hierarchicus: The Caste System and Its Implications*. Trans. Mark Sainsbury, Louis Dumont, and Basia Gulati. Complete Revised English edition. 1970. Reprint, New Delhi: Oxford University Press, 1999.

Fish, Stanley Eugene. *There's No Such Thing as Free Speech, and It's a Good Thing, Too*. New York: Oxford University Press, 1994.

Friedlander, Robert A. "Power Politics and the Rule of Law: Professor Schwarzenberger Reconsidered." *DePaul Law Review* 24, no. 4 (Summer 1975): 836–851.

George, P. J. "Explained: Pegasus and the laws on surveillance in India." *The Hindu*, July 25, 2021. https://bit.ly/2Y1mpF6.

Godrej, Farah. "Secularism in India: A 'Gandhian' Approach." In *Multiculturalism in the British Commonwealth: Comparative Perspectives on Theory and Practice*, ed. Richard T. Ashcroft and Mark Bevir, 150–66. Oakland: University of California Press, 2019.

Haworth, Alan. *Free Speech*. London: Routledge, 1998.

Jaffrelot, Christophe. "The caste based mosaic of Indian politics." *Seminar*, May 2012. https://www.india-seminar.com/2012/633/633_christophe_jaffrelot.htm.

"JNU Sedition Case: Umar Khalid, Kanhaiya Kumar, other accused appear in Court." *The Wire*. March 16, 2021. https://bit.ly/3i7F5de.

Kaviraj, Sudipta. "Languages of Secularity." *Economic and Political Weekly* 48, no. 50 (December 2013): 93–102.

Kothari, Rajni. "Introduction: Caste in Indian Politics." In *Caste in Indian Politics*, ed. Rajni Kothari, 3–26. 1970. Reprint, Hyderabad: Orient Longman, 2004.

Kumar, Alok Prasanna. "Criminal Laws and Civil Rights." *Economic and Political Weekly* 53, no. 42 (October 2018): 10–11.

Madan, T. N. *Modern Myths, Locked Minds: Secularism and Fundamentalism in India*. 2nd ed. New York: Oxford University Press, 2009.

Malji, Andrea. "The Rise of Hindu Nationalism and Its Regional and Global Ramifications." *Education about Asia* 23, no. 1 (Spring 2018): 39–43.

Mill, David van. "Freedom of Speech." In *The Stanford Encyclopedia of Philosophy*, ed. Edward N. Zalta, Spring 2021. Metaphysics Research Lab, Stanford University, 2021. https://plato.stanford.edu/archives/spr2021/entries/freedom-speech/.

National Crime Records Bureau. "Crime in India." New Delhi: Ministry of Home Affairs, Government of India, 2014, 2015, 2016, 2017, 2018 and 2019.

Ranjan, Sudhanshu. "Media and Judiciary: Revitalization of Democracy." *Journal of the Indian Law Institute* 57, no. 3 (July-September 2015): 414–425. https://www.jstor.org/stable/44782789.

Rashid, Omar. "Communalism, Casteism, Regionalism Antithesis to Constitutional Ideals." *The Hindu*, April 15, 2020, https://bit.ly/3mmZxcT.

Rehman, Shaikh Mujibur. "The Many Shades of Intolerance." *The Hindu*, August 13, 2021. https://bit.ly/3z8wduj.

Repucci, Sarah. ed., *Freedom in the World 2020*. New York: Freedom House, 2020.

Rousseau, Jean-Jacques. *Discourse on the Origin of Inequality*. Oxford University Press, 1999.

Rudolph, Lloyd Irving, and Susanne Hoeber Rudolph. "The Political Role of India's Caste Associations." *Pacific Affairs* 33, no. 1 (March 1960): 5–22. https://doi.org/10.2307/2753645.

Sen, Ronojoy. "The Persistence of Caste in Indian Politics." *Pacific Affairs* 85, no. 2 (June 2012): 363–69. https://doi.org/10.5509/2012852363.

Shetreet, Shimone. "Judicial Independence: New Conceptual Dimensions and Challenges." In *Judicial Independence: The Contemporary Debate*, ed. Shimone Shetreet and Jules Deschenes. Dordrecht-Boston-Lancaster: Nijhoff, 1985.

Singh, M. P. "Securing the Independence of the Judiciary—The Indian Experience." *Indiana International & Comparative Law Review* 10, no. 2 (2000): 247. https://doi.org/10.18060/17703.

Sorabjee, Soli J. "Role of the Judiciary: Boon or Bane?" *India International Centre Quarterly* 38, no. 3/4 (Winter 2011–Spring 2011): 130–140. https://bit.ly/3AQQTIc.

Sundar, Nandini., Gowhar Fazili, "Academic Freedom in India." *The India Forum*, September 4, 2020. https://bit.ly/3ocRJvi.

United Nations and the Rule of Law. "What is the rule of law." Accessed June 2, 2021. https://www.un.org/ruleoflaw/what-is-the-rule-of-law/.

Venu, M. K. "Invoking free speech violations over new IT rules, Big Media finally goes to court." *The Wire*, June 25, 2021. https://bit.ly/3kN4fzL.

Vohra, Ranbir. *The Making of India: A Political History*. 3rd ed. New York: Routledge, 2013.

Waldron Jeremy. "The Concept and the Rule of Law." *Georgia Law Review, University of Georgia Law* 43, no. 1 (Fall 2008). https://bit.ly/3scuQrS.

Waldron, Jeremy. "The Rule of Law." In *The Stanford Encyclopedia of Philosophy*, ed. Edward N. Zalta, Summer 2020. Metaphysics Research Lab, Stanford University, 2020. https://plato.stanford.edu/archives/sum2020/entries/rule-of-law/.

Yadav, Yogendra, and Suhas Palshikar. "Between Fortuna and Virtu: Explaining the Congress' Ambiguous Victory in 2009." *Economic and Political Weekly* 44, no. 39 (October 2009): 33–46.

Chapter 5

Power Politics versus the Rule of Law in the United States

A Case Study

Cora True-Frost

The limits of the Constitution and system of law in the United States have been tested by the previous US administration's open embrace of power over the rule of law.[1] Even before the notorious Capitol riots of January 6, 2021, American legal scholars warned of the imperiled impartiality of law and proposed various reforms of core domestic institutions such as the Supreme Court[2] and Congress.[3] This chapter's argument is straightforward: the United States has been alerted to the potential lasting damage that existing legal gaps may have on the balance between justice and impunity in the future. Legal reforms to the executive-media relationship and the pardon power are necessary to foreclose the possibility of these abuses in the future, and to forestall some aspects of the erosion of the separation of powers.

Jeremy Waldron has argued, "while the Rule of Law is a multi-faceted ideal, most conceptions of this ideal, . . . give central place to the requirement that people in positions of authority should exercise their power within a constraining framework of public norms."[4] In this chapter, I argue that the abuse of norms and aggressive use of litigation by the former US executive necessitates reforms to ensure that democracy and rule of law will be protected in the United States. Consistent with this book's other case studies, I focus on two key examples for strengthening the rule of law against power politics, the need to (1) close loopholes enabling much of the recent executive's abuse of the freedom of the press, and (2) place constraints on the president's pardon power. Many other threats to democracy have increased in recent years. For example, money, an easy proxy for power in the absence of law, abounds in elections in the United States; income stratification is rapidly increasing; and concerns about "fake news" and social media preoccupy both political parties in the United States, raising difficult questions for both constitutional and statutory speech law. These foci are necessary, but alone they will not be sufficient to achieve the admittedly amorphous goals of protecting democracy and the rule of law from the assaults of unadulterated political power in the United States. Although intimately related to the balance between law and power, those important topics must remain beyond the scope of this chapter. In closing I note that as a matter of policy, in its efforts to promote rule of law internationally, the United States should proceed with a new sense of humility, or as Thomas Carothers calls it, "mutuality."[5]

Astute readers will have recognized that the two central rule of law reforms discussed here apply to the Executive Branch and more specifically to the office of the president, and as such are focused on preventing abuses of power by future presidents of the United States. According to the Constitution, a chief executive's duty is to "take care that the laws be faithfully executed," and to "Commission all the Officers of the United States."[6] No law explicitly forbids the US president from withholding his tax returns, refusing members of the press access to White House press briefings, "weaponizing" the office of legal counsel by treating the office as his own private litigator, or even, somewhat remarkably, from pardoning himself.

In recent years, since the embrace of the unitary executive theory by the Supreme Court of the United States in 2000, legal scholars have recommended reforms to this branch.[7] Tracing the history of the take care clause, Professors Lieb, Kent, and Shugerman[8] argue that its history undermines imperial claims about the powers of the presidency. Analogously, David Driesen details the erosion of American democracy by way of the increasingly powerful chief executive, and the multiple ways that the unitary executive theory has consolidated power in this office.[9] In the wake of the previous president's moves to push control even further, Professors Goldsmith and Bauer recommend wide-ranging reforms to the office of the president itself, including, for example, limiting the president's ability to intimidate the press, and preventing the misuse of the pardon power.[10]

The chapter begins with a brief discussion of the term "rule of law" in the context of US law and policy, and then turns to exploring the legal gaps that subject the independence of the press to executive influence. It next turns to concerns about impartiality of the law raised by prosecutorial interference and the legally unconstrained use of the presidential power to pardon. It also touches on the ways that the independence of the judiciary in the United States has been affected but has also provided a critical backstop to democracy. For comparison to the other case studies in this volume, the chapter briefly offers insights into recent concerns regarding the independence of the judiciary and legal academia in the United States. The chapter closes with reflections on implications of this discussion for future US efforts to promote and export rule of law.

THE EROSION OF THE RULE OF LAW IN THE UNITED STATES AND THE VOLATILITY OF NORMS IN AUTOCRATS' HANDS

There are many difficulties in defining rule of law. Chief among these difficulties is that many proponents of "rule of law" use the phrase as a synonym for their particular policy preferences. Indeed, even among countries that all claim to observe "rule of law," variations abound in what is deemed as necessary to rule of law.

For purposes of this necessarily brief chapter, however, "rule of law" may be adequately captured by the following ideals, antithetical to Machiavelli's emphasis on power. "All persons and authorities within the state, whether public or private, should be bound by and entitled to the benefit of laws publicly made, taking effect in the future and publicly administered in the courts.[11]" "[Rule of Law is] a principle under which all persons, institutions, and entities are accountable to laws that are publicly promulgated, equally enforced, independently adjudicated, and consistent with international human rights principles."[12]

It is rare that a single ruler can be held solely responsible for the success of their efforts to dismantle the rule of law and human rights. Indeed, in the case of the United States, as well as some of the other cases in this book, the chief executive enjoyed both significant popular support and legislators' acquiescence. Closely examining the democratic decline in Hungary, Turkey, and Poland, and analogizing the situation in the United States to those declines, however, David Driesen argues that democratic decline is exacerbated by the strengthening of the office of the president through judicial concession to laws that enable presidential emergency powers. He adds that judicial permission to increase presidential control of the administrative functions of the state has also been a contributing factor to democratic decline.[13] In the United States, the current state of rule of law was fueled in part by what Fred Schwartz and Aziz Huq have called the "monarchist claims of executive power" of the Bush administration. Schwartz and Huq argue that "executive unilateralism not only undermines the delicate balance of our Constitution, but also lessens our human liberties and hurts vital counterterrorism campaigns."[14] The Obama administration, too, stretched its executive power, for example, by engaging forces in Iraq and Libya without congressional authorization. To do so, the Obama administration adopted the broadest definition to date of the "the national interest" for the president's unilateral use of war powers.[15] Over time, rule of law in the United States has expanded to accommodate the "unitary executive," with the judiciary eventually embracing this conception. As the next sections elaborate, however, the most recent administration stretched the idea of a unitary, powerful, president (including a "right to do whatever I want as President,"[16]) continued the pattern of consolidating power in the executive to unprecedented extremes in many domains.

While the Trump administration's threats and actions have exposed many weak points in the legal edifice of American democracy, many of these vulnerable points result not only from the gradual erosion of separation of powers and the strength of the executive, but also this particular officeholder's bold, even outrageous, refusal to follow norms that had been observed reliably by previous presidents.[17] Such norms exist between the realms of law and power—in the realm of institutional practice, decency, and morality.

Correspondingly, a central problem implicated in striking the appropriate balance between rule of law and politics is that many authoritarian-leaning or populist[18] leaders' most outrageous actions or threatened actions may not, strictly speaking, violate the law, even as they turn rule of law on its head. That is, they raise the question whether more law is required or simply different laws. Indeed, authoritarian and populist leaders have often pursued what Kim Lane Scheppele has aptly termed "autocratic legalism" in many countries around the world,[19] changing laws or disregarding norms rather than openly breaking the law. "Constitutional hardball" is played using aggressive tactics and transcending constitutional customary norms to achieve a desired goal.[20] In a divisive political climate, the type that autocrats nurture and which has been sweeping the globe,[21] hardball is frequently played by courts, by legislators, and by the executive.[22] Interpreting executive authority in a way that claims to comply with the law, even as it stretches beyond any earlier precedent, autocrats claim to be acting according to the rule of law.

In the United States, a political change of administration may temporarily correct the balance toward procedural protections and respect for norms, elevating rule of law slightly over power. However, the January 6 Capitol riots arguably demonstrate the effects of the erosion of democracy and just how high the stakes are in the United States today. Below, the chapter recommends embracing legal reforms to prevent future encroachments, focusing on the independence of the press vis-à-vis the president and the abuse of the pardon power.

FROM NORM TO LAW: THE FREEDOM OF THE PRESS

The First Amendment of the Constitution protects the press, and the United States has a notoriously high threshold for what constitutes illegal speech.[23]

No law forbids a president from calling the press "slime," "garbage," or "the enemy of the people," as the previous president has done. Nor does any law forbid the president from using his personal social media account to attack journalists.[24] Law cannot, and arguably should not, compel the executive and the press to be amiable and cooperative at all times; a critical function of the press is to hold government accountable and to inform the people, including about government secrets.

But the level of invective against the press not only by the previous president, but also his appointees, was unprecedented. Describing the breadth and intensity of President Trump's actions against the press, including "through rhetoric, restricted access, retaliation, and the apparent launching of smear campaigns by the President's political supporters,"[25] legal scholars have characterized President Trump as waging war on the press.

Numerous presidents before Donald Trump have had strained, hostile relationships with the press. No law requires the president to hold press conferences but press conferences have been the norm in the United States. As for the rhetoric of the president, the United Street has always been an outlier among democracies in its willingness to tolerate so-called low-value speech, setting the bar high for illegal or abusive speech.[26] The Court's broad interpretation of the First Amendment makes a legal response to executive intimidation of the press challenging, but not impossible. One of the tactics of autocrats is to divide the people and make extreme claims, refusing to credit diverging viewpoints.[27] The closure of local news providers continued in the United States over the last five years and fueled in part by the rhetoric of the president, distrust of media increased. Indeed, in the last year of the Trump administration, Reporters without Borders reported that the freedom of the press in the United States had worsened considerably, with "nearly 400 journalists assaulted and more than 130 detained—unprecedented numbers according to the U.S. Press Freedom Tracker."[28]

What law constrains a US president from retaliating against members of the press who paint him or his policies in an unflattering light? As long as some process is followed, the president has broad discretion about which press units receive White House passes to attend press conferences, or as the previous president called them, press briefings. In the Jim Acosta CNN incident in the United States CNN successfully sued to restore correspondent Acosta's White House press credentials after the White House summarily pulled them. According to the DC District Court, Acosta was entitled to procedural protections before his existing pass was revoked and the circumstances of the revocation had been very erratic.[29] In this case, the judiciary played an important role in checking the chief executive's attempt to exercise power without process.

As the White House will likely retain authority to grant or deny a journalist pass in the near term, however, little reform aside from the formalization of process will materialize in the realm of press access to the White House. This is concerning for the US system of rule of law, for which an independent press is necessary, as corporate media coverage has become increasingly polarized in the market for fast news, and there is the real possibility that only partisan news outlets will be granted access to the White House while others will be denied access to information.[30]

Some protection against groundless revocation of press passes may be offered by increased procedural protections (or, in the hands of an autocrat, such procedures may simply lead to the issuance of far fewer passes with frequent expiration, thus subjecting the press once again to the authority of the president), but the worry about retaliation against the press extends beyond granting access to the White House. Reported instances of retaliation include interference with business interests and intimidation using the administrative branches of the government. For example, President Trump made no attempt to hide his animus for Jeff Bezos, the owner of the *Washington Post*, who also owns Amazon. After tweeting that he had "stated [his] concerns with Amazon long before the Election,"[31] and that "it is reported that the U.S. Post Office will lose $1.50 on average for each package it delivers for Amazon,"[32] Amazon's share price declined markedly after this executive attention.[33] The president also allegedly used his administrative control to interfere with the award of a Department of Defense contract with Amazon. While the Inspector General of the Department of Defense did not find evidence of interference by the White House in the contract award process, the report also said that the White House did not allow open access to witnesses.[34] A federal judge allowed Amazon's bias claim against the administration related to the interference with the Joint Enterprise Defense Infrastructure (JEDI) contract[35] to proceed.[36] Now reports are coming to light regarding the Justice Department's subpoenaing of journalists reporting on the White House in supposed leak investigations.[37]

In short, as the United States looks to the future of its democracy, further consolidation of the power of the executive against the independence of administrative agencies (such as the Department of Justice and the Postal Service) could permit a president to use licensing and market pressure to control opposing media.[38]

Fortunately, it is possible to use law to respond to some retaliation against the press by the president. The Inspector General Act of 1978 allows inspectors to conduct audits and investigations to detect fraud and abuse. Professors Goldsmith and Bauer propose amending this Act to define "abuse" to encompass "official acts" intended to harass or intimidate news media organizations or journalists. They elaborate that by limiting the amendment to official acts,

Executive Branch officials' rhetoric would be left to the political process. An administration's attempts to, for example, put pressure on the postal service to double rates applicable to a particular political opponent, whose press coverage was unfavorable to the president,[39] would be subject to review for abuse and fraud. Of course, as this chapter has highlighted, a legal response alone is not sufficient, as even such an amendment to the Inspector General Act is subject to possible political interference, and thus will require legal authorities and politicians to respect norms and not to abuse the potential the amendment to the Act would provide.

IMPARTIALITY OF THE LAW: PROSECUTORIAL INTERFERENCE, SEEKING FAVORS, AND THE PARDON POWER

Not only has the free press been diminished and smeared by the Executive Branch in the United States, with a concomitant diminution in public debate, but the growing strength of the executive over time has permitted greater consolidation of power unchecked by law. It is a core characteristic of autocracy to use government power to punish foes and to protect friends, which of course violates the definition of rule of law, "the principle under which all persons, institutions, and entities are accountable to laws that are publicly promulgated, equally enforced, independently adjudicated, and consistent with international human rights principles."[40]

This section explores select instances of prosecutorial interference by the executive and explains how the president's violation of the norm of prosecutorial independence, together with abuse of the pardon power, endangers judicial independence. In closing, it focuses on possible legal reforms to the president's pardon power, a power granted in the Pardon Clausein Article II of the Constitution, which does not provide the grounds or requirements for its exercise. The few legal constraints on the very broad pardon power are court-imposed; while pardon powers are common throughout various democracies, the United States is unique in the breadth of its reliance on the pardon power.[41] The pardon power is intended to provide an escape hatch from rule of law, and the clause itself offers little guidance about the situations in which it should be used. Historically, presidents have used pardons to help individual circumstances in which the law, as applied, might be too severe or fail to account for illness or infirmity.[42] In addition, past presidents have used the pardon power as a transitional justice and public policy tool. For example, President Obama commuted 1,715 sentences of federal inmates convicted of nonviolent crimes to address over-incarceration in the United States.

While judicial and constitutional constraints on the pardon power are scant, over time, the pardon process has become more formalized. Eventually the attorney general acquired the task of reviewing pardon applications, and now the Department of Justice has a formal role in the process.[43] The involvement of the Justice Department has offered a buffer between those seeking presidential pardon and the officeholder themselves.[44] Presidents have observed the general norm that they should give reasons for granting pardons. When past presidents have issued pardons by avoiding the Justice Department process or in circumstances that appear uncomfortably close to a quid pro quo, questions have been raised.[45] Yet, no previous president has been so willing to break from the norms,[46] issuing numerous pardons with no accompanying legal rationale and in circumstances that very strongly seem for his own benefit as has President Trump.[47]

The previous officeholder's predilection for aggressive litigation and weaponizing the law, including by making clear that he has the power to forgive the application of the law, even going so far as to say he could pardon himself, may well be an anomaly. But to strengthen rule of law in times such as we see described repeatedly in this book, the US government would be wise to take any steps possible to protect against vulnerabilities President Trump exposed.

President Trump was certainly not the first president to issue controversial pardons. However, he is the first president to threaten to pardon himself, and legal scholars agree that the breadth and scope of his use of the pardon power to forgive friends was unprecedented. A sample of these vulnerabilities related to the pardon power is next, followed by some possible legal reforms to avoid future trouble. The president almost never used the official attorney process in the Justice Department for the pardons he granted. Some previous presidents had avoided the process on occasion, but President Trump did so in at least thirty-one of thirty-six pardons available according to public records.[48] He also announced pardons on Twitter without even venturing to offer a legal justification. Rather he asserted that a particular beneficiary was a "patriot" "worthy" of a pardon, for example, in the case of Sheriff Joe Arpaio, or simply that "he was treated unfairly" about conservative pundit Dinesh D'Souza for illegally contributing to Senate campaigns. In pardoning former Illinois governor Ron Blagojevich for extortion, then-president Trump said Blagojevich had been prosecuted by the "same people—Comey, Fitzpatrick, the same group"[49] as those whom he saw as persecuting him. The president also applied the pardon power for his own personal interest, as when he commuted the sentence of Roger Stone. Stone had refused to testify against the president regarding conversations they had about WikiLeaks related to the campaign interference being investigated by the FBI director, James Comey, whom President Trump later fired. Fitzpatrick was Comey's attorney after he was fired by the president.[50]

No law explicitly requires a losing candidate to recognize his defeat, but until recently, norms regarding the rule of law and faithful execution of the laws, which of course includes election law, have sufficed to ensure that the losing candidate concedes.[51] Yet, using his personal Twitter account to subvert official White House communications channels, President Trump repeatedly attacked the legitimacy of the 2020 presidential election. Indeed, he signaled his intention to assert power over legal process early on, when, in late March and early April 2016, then-candidate Trump pulled out of a Republican Party pledge which would have guaranteed his support of the party's nominee in the 2016 election. When asked in a primary debate why he would not continue to abide by his pledge, Trump aired a grudge and responded that "I have been treated very unfairly."[52] In October 2016, at the last presidential debate before the November election, Trump "refused to commit to accepting the election result if he loses."[53] Later on January 6, 2021, Donald Trump distinguished his presidency from all other American presidents by refusing to concede his election defeat,[54] and by encouraging his supporters to "stop the steal," because "you'll never take back our country with weakness. You have to show strength, and you have to be strong."[55]

Trump's supporters' subsequent actions to "stop the steal" are now infamous. For our purposes in this section on the pardon, it is worth noting that the first of the more than 460 federal defendants[56] in the Capitol riots cases to be identified beseeched the president to use his pardon power to relieve them of responsibility.[57] But during the two weeks between January 6 and the end of his presidency,[58] President Trump in fact refrained from pardoning the supporters who trespassed and violently entered the Capitol. Also, although President Trump had tweeted that he had an "Absolute right to PARDON myself,"[59] and made other references to the permissibility of the unprecedented practice of self-pardoning, he ultimately refrained from doing so. Notwithstanding his restraint in those regards, in the last week of his presidency, consistent with his previous practice described above, he pardoned 143 people (in a combination of both commutations and pardons), including many of his helpmates, such as his former chief strategist and longtime ally Steve Bannon and his former top fundraiser Elliott Broidy, both of whom were charged with financial crimes related to Donald Trump's campaign. He also pardoned family and friends of his supporters, for example, Albert J. Pirro, Jr., the ex-husband of Fox News host and longtime Trump ally Jeanine Pirro, who had been sentenced for bribery and campaign finance crimes.[60]

For US lawyers concerned about the integrity of rule of law, President Trump's threats and his Capitol supporters' entreaties for pardon, as well as President Trump's disregard for pardon norms and his willingness to interfere with prosecutorial independence, should nevertheless serve as a warning and be met with legal limits against future presidents' use of the pardon power. To avoid further interference by presidents with the legal system and to promote integrity in the chief executive office, Congress and the judiciary should clarify the scope of existing laws and their possible application to the pardon power as well as enacting legislation to prevent presidential self-pardon.

As constitutional amendments are very difficult to adopt in the best of times, and these times are deeply divided, there is little likelihood of success of a constitutional amendment.

Here I sketch a few possible solutions (short of constitutional amendments) offered by legal scholars regarding the admittedly open-ended pardon power to correct the balance between rule of law and power in the United States after its recent flagrant stretching beyond previously known limits.

In lieu of a constitutional amendment, Congress can enact statutory reform or clarify existing statutes to make it clear that law does apply to the pardon power, and to curb its most flagrant abuses.[61] For example, presidents can be charged with a crime if using the pardon power for personal gain. Professors Goldsmith and Bauer compellingly suggest that the federal anti-bribery statute, 18 U.S.C. § 201, is suitable for this purpose, so long as the judiciary accepts the argument that the president is a "public official" covered by the statute. Indeed, Congress could clarify that the restriction on public officials receiving bribes "in return for being influenced in the performance of an official act" covers seeking a presidential pardon. Applying this statute to the pardon power would thus reach instances of outright quid pro quo agreements to pardon in exchange for political contributions, while still leaving traditional applications of the pardon power untouched. Pressing such charges, and announcing that they are viable charges now, would serve as a warning that even with the concessions to politics that the pardon power is intended to accommodate, it does have hard and fast limits.

In addition, obstruction of justice, codified at 18 USC § 1503, can be applied to a pardon offered in exchange for the recipient's false or misleading testimony in a judicial or other official proceeding.[62] Finally, Congress can enact a law to make clear that self-pardon is not authorized by Article II and a president's attempt to pardon himself has no force and effect. As with any of these congressional initiatives, however, they rely on the willingness of the political legislative body to protect and promote the rule of law. As the chapter analyzes in closing, the United States has long been a protector and promoter of rule of law around the world. The question these suggestions for congressional reforms beg is whether US legislators are willing to do so at home.

INDEPENDENCE OF THE JUDICIARY

Case studies in this book have related various governments' recent successes in curtailing the independence of the judiciary. This chapter has related the ways that the former president was unique in his willingness to "weaponize" the law and use it aggressively. Thankfully, in the United States, the judiciary frequently struck down Executive Branch actions and proposed legislation to hand the president defeats. For example, during the previous administration, the Trump administration lost 83 percent of its administrative law challenges.[63]

In contrast to many of the other countries in this book, in the United States, judges are granted lifelong tenure,[64] which thus substantially divests judges from political control, though of course those seeking political appointment to a higher office may be more sensitive to political influence. Still, the judiciary is by no means secure from the influence of politics, as majorities on the Supreme Court, where the nine justices enjoy lifelong appointment, can approve sweeping changes to the law. In terms of raw numbers, of past presidents, Republican president Reagan appointed the most judges to the federal judiciary, including four Supreme Court Justices. In his two terms in office, President Obama appointed just 2 Supreme Court Justices and 329 federal court judges. As a single-term president, President Trump still succeeded in appointing three justices to the Supreme Court and 242 judges to federal courts.[65]

The president was not able to have such a significant and lasting impact on the Supreme Court, and thus on the rule of law in the United States, without the assistance of raw, unprecedented and illegitimate power plays by his party in Congress. Another characteristic of authoritarian rule is that it refuses to compromise with other powerholders, or to consider minority opinion.[66] Specifically, when Reagan-appointed Justice Scalia died in March 2016, the last year of President Obama's administration, President Obama nominated Merrick Garland to succeed him. Merrick Garland is a centrist who has been called "essentially the model, neutral judge."[67]

According to the Constitution, the president's nomination is subject to consideration of the Senate and a vote approval, but no law requires the Senate Majority Leader to schedule the consideration within a certain number of days. Abusing norms of respect and collegiality, Republican majority leader Mitch McConnell refused to submit Garland's nomination to the Senate for consideration. This marked the first time since the Civil War of the 1800s that a nominee whose nomination had not been withdrawn had failed to receive consideration for an open seat on the Court.[68] This permitted President Obama's successor, Donald Trump, to nominate a Justice to fill the vacancy on January 31, 2017, soon after assuming office.[69] The confirmation of Garland would have given Democratic appointees a majority on the Supreme Court for the first time since the 1970 confirmation of Justice Blackmun.[70]

THE INDEPENDENCE OF LEGAL ACADEMIA

This book's case studies have described numerous instances of legal attempts to control or even purge legal academia, yet another tactic of power-craving autocracies. The US marketplace for legal education may appear to place legal academia largely beyond the influence of the government, at least more so than countries where higher education is considered a public good with heavy government involvement. As a practical matter, it may appear irrelevant whether the president respects academia or not. Indeed, President Trump, unlike President Obama, who was a law professor, never expressed respect for legal academia. Indeed, in President Trump's "America First" speech to the United Nations General Assembly, he went so far as to imply that universities and the professors working in them represent a threat to the US progress.[71] In addition, the Trump administration later worked to use academia as an important part of its strategy against foreign policy foes such as China, described Chinese researchers and students as threats to the United States.[72]

But students and universities both rely on government funding to fuel the marketplace. And indeed, this funding was targeted by the previous administration. In the final weeks of the previous administration, the president issued an executive order directing that no federal funding be provided to universities adopting diversity, equity, and inclusion policies.[73] While later overturned by the Biden administration,[74] this attack on diversity, equity, and inclusion policies continues to be a hot political topic with implications for discrimination, affirmative action, and many other policies. As discussed below, another executive order regarding international criminal law and International Criminal Court swept into its gambit dual-nationality legal academics working in this area and potentially subjected them to sanctions. The unilateral reversal by executive order of the government's policies and laws relating to diversity, equity, inclusion, and the sanctioning of those working with the International Criminal Court, like many of the other threats described here, demonstrated a vulnerability for universities, including law schools.

INTERNATIONAL IMPLICATIONS: US EFFORTS TO EXPORT THE RULE OF LAW

In conclusion, the previous administration's focus on dismantling and discrediting international institutions and the media and rewarding friends and punishing foes has left enduring effects that are worth considering in relation to the US significant investment in the export of rule of law programs globally. The US current era of rule of law development assistance began in the 1990s, after the fall of the Soviet Union and the transition of formerly Communist countries to new forms of government.[75] According to the Congressional Research Service, the United States spends over $2 billion annually for "democracy promotion activities" which include "support for good governance (characterized by participation, transparency, accountability, effectiveness, and equity), rule of law, and promotion of human rights."[76]

Regardless of its particular political leadership, the US historical relationship with international human rights law and international criminal law has been complex; "American exceptionalism" aptly captures the dynamic.[77] For example, even as the United States has famously and zealously promoted and exported international human rights law globally after World War II, advocating its embrace and observation by other countries, the United States has simultaneously refused to ratify six of the ten core human rights treaties.[78] Yet, of the four treaties to which the United States is party, fully half cover international criminal law and thus overlap with the subject-matter jurisdiction of the International Criminal Court; those being the Convention against Torture and Other Cruel, Inhuman or Degrading Treatment or Punishment (CAT),[79] and the Convention on the Prevention and Punishment of the Crime of Genocide.[80]

But the United States, like its fellow UN Security Council members, China and Russia, continues to object to an independent international institution applying international criminal law to its military[81] even though the Rome Statute permits the UN Security Council to delay proceedings before the International Criminal Court.[82] The United States controversially innovated so-called Article 98 agreements to encourage bilateral partners to exempt American service members from the jurisdiction of the International Criminal Court (ICC). The Obama administration signaled a willingness to cooperate with the ICC,[83] however, and assisted the ICC in various ways short of actual, formal collaboration. By contrast, the Trump administration defied even the exceptionalist norms of modern American international law in its disregard for the rule of law, for example, by using the pardon power over the objections of the highest levels of US military leadership, to pardon American soldiers. The Trump administration pardoned seven accused war criminals, four of whom were already convicted, overriding the verdicts of military tribunals and the objections of military commanders, thus signaling that international criminal law does not bind the United States.[84] In addition, the Trump administration took, unprecedented in any country in the world, shocking unilateral executive action and sanctioned the International Criminal Court Prosecutor and staff, even potentially sanctioning law professors with dual citizenship who work on ICC matters.[85] Though it is beyond the scope of this chapter to explore this issue further, the populist Trump administration's rejection of international cooperation and withdrawal from international organizations such as the World Health Organization and the United Nations Educational, Scientific and Cultural Organization, arguably sheds light on the central theme of this book, that is the assent of power politics at the expense of the rule of law and democracy[86] around the globe.

How does the US domestic embrace of rule of law interrelate with its international policy? Renowned proponents of the export of rule of law have said that although the state of democracy in the United States is at an "all-time low," with course corrections and humility, the United States might be able to legitimately continue to promote rule of law, assuming it makes its own domestic reforms.[87] In the global world we live in today, the United States must continue to engage internationally, the analysis above suggests that it should do so under a new model—one of mutual learning rather than "exporting."[88]

Going forward, rather than styling itself as the standard-bearer for rule of law, the United States should be learning from other countries, like those covered in this book, about their own diminishing domestic rule of law and move forward with "chastened experience and humility."[89]

In summary, as law is an anthropological project and not a naturally observable phenomenon, the reforms above will require agreement and collaboration between legislators intent on increasing the strength of rule of law, as a good in itself, even if the result may be temporary loss of some power for some subset of them. Few people living in the world's endangered democracies today would intentionally prefer an autocracy or monarchy, even one which conforms to their own policy preferences. To the extent that Machiavelli's writings founded modern political science, and the study of the political world as it is rather than a sought-after-but-unobtained ideal, and Montesquieu's writings gave shape to the noble goals of separation of powers and civil rights, today, both modern political science theories and legal theories of democracy embrace as necessary the rule of law and separation of powers. Recent events in now-fragile democracies worldwide, including in the United States, underscore the necessity of maintaining separation of powers and rule of law as a counterbalance to pure power.

ACKNOWLEDGMENT

Thanks to Chris Day, David Driesen, Lauryn Gouldin, and Chris Ramsdell for helpful comments. For excellent research assistance, thanks to Madeline Cittadino, Caleb Geiger, Justin Lange, Tiffany Love, and Matt McCartin.

NOTES

1. See generally Bob Bauer and Jack Goldsmith, *After Trump: Reconstructing the Presidency* (Washington, DC: Lawfare Press, 2020).

2. See, e.g. Daniel Epps and Ganesh Sitaraman, "How to Save the Supreme Court," *Yale Law Journal* 129, no. 1 (October 2019): 148–207; Michael J. Klarman,

"The Degradation of American Democracy–and the Court+," *Harvard Law Review* 134 (November 2020): 1–263 (examines the degradation of American democracy and canvasses the Supreme Court's contribution to such degradation.); Joshua Braver, "Court-Packing: An American Tradition?" *Boston College Law Review* 61 (November 2020): 2747–2808 (Court-packing, manipulating the number of Supreme Court seats to alter the ideological balance of the Court, has been done seven times in American history but is still nearly novel and would pose unprecedented dangers if utilized today.); Stephen M. Feldman, "Court-Packing Time? Supreme Court Legitimacy and Positivity Theory," *Buffalo Law Review* 68 (December 2020): 1519–1559 (suggesting that court-packing is unlikely to weaken the American people's support for the Court as a judicial institution because of positivity theory.); Joshua P. Zoffer and David Singh Grewal, "The Counter-Majoritarian Difficulty of a Minoritarian Judiciary," *California Law Review Online* 11 (October 2020): 437–62 (Increasing numbers of minoritarian and super-minoritarian judges will start to resemble the "juristocracy" that critics have long alleged, instead of a third branch of government that serves the people.)

3. Scholars in many disciplines have engaged the topic, including Steven Levitzky and Daniel Ziblatt, *How Democracies Die* (New York: Crown, 2018); Tom Ginsburg and Aziz Z. Huq, *How to Save a Constitutional Democracy* (Chicago: University of Chicago Press, 2018); Carolyn Shapiro, "Democracy, Federalism, and the Guarantee Clause," *Arizona Law Review* 62 (2020): 183–240 (The Guarantee Clause of the Constitution allows, and requires, Congress to address antidemocratic state-level practices.); David Landau and Rosalind Dixon, "Abusive Judicial Review: Courts Against Democracy," *University of California Davis Law Review* 53 (February 2020): 1313–1387 (Courts around the world have legitimated antidemocratic laws and practices, and this shows that it is not uncommon for judges to issue decisions that intentionally attack the core of electoral democracy.)

4. Jeremy Waldron, "The Concept and the Rule of Law," *Georgia Law Review* 43, no. 1 (2008): 1, 6.

5. Thomas Carothers and Frances Z. Brown, "The Chastened Power" (March 10, 2021), (American Purpose).

6. U.S. Const. art. 2 sec. 3

7. See e.g. David M. Driesen, *The Specter of Dictatorship* (Stanford University Press, 2021): 125 (citing Elena Kagan "Presidential Administration"); Kathryn A. Watts, "Controlling Presidential Control," *Michigan Law Review* 114 (2016) 83–745.

8. Andrew Kent, Ethan Leib, and Jed Shugerman, "Faithful Execution and Article II." *Harvard Law Review* 321 (2019): 2111. They argue it requires of the executive: (1) diligent, careful, good faith, and impartial execution of law or office; (2) a duty not to misuse an office's funds and or take unauthorized profits; and (3) a duty not to act ultra vires, beyond the scope of one's office.

9. David Driesen, *The Specter of Dictatorship* (Redwood City: Stanford University Press, 2021): 122–26.

10. Bauer and Goldsmith, *After Trump*, Part I. In addition, they recommend reforms to eliminate financial conflicts of interest, make tax disclosure a requirement and regarding the relationship between the Office of the President and the

other branches of government, such as Congress and the administrative branch. Specifically, presidential control over nuclear weapons and the use of military force should wisely be constrained by requiring Congressional approval, as well as by altering many aspects of the executive's power over the core "rule of law" organization in the U.S., the Justice Department, as well as over senior Executive Branch positions. *See also*, David M. Driesen, "The Political Remedies Doctrine," *SSRN*, published November 16, 2020, https://bit.ly/3xY2IKz.

11. Tom Bingham, *The Rule of Law* (London: Penguin, 2011): 3.

12. United States Courts, "Overview–Rule of Law," accessed June 15, 2021, https://bit.ly/3ss5O8g.

13. Driesen, *The Specter of Dictatorship*, at 95–96.

14. Frederick A. O. Schwartz, Jr., and Aziz Z. Huq, *Unchecked and Unbalanced: Presidential Power in a Time of Terror* (New York City: The New Press, 2008).

15. Bauer and Goldsmith, *After Trump*, 285.

16. Jane Chong, "Donald Trump's Strange and Dangerous 'Absolute Rights' Idea," The Atlantic, February 29, 2020, https://bit.ly/3ASFW8B.

17. Bauer and Goldsmith, *After Trump,* 21.

18. Although populism has many different and often contested meanings, here I adopt the "ideational approach" to defining populism, purporting to employ an exclusionary notion of the people—the real people, as opposed to disfavored groups that are unworthy and purports to rule on behalf of the real people whose will should not be constrained. Gerald L. Neuman, *Human Rights in a Time of Populism: Challenges and Responses* (Cambridge: Cambridge University Press, 2020).

19. Kim Lane Scheppele, "Autocratic Legalism," *University of Chicago Law Review* 85, no. 2 (March 2018): 545–84. (David Landau, 2013 "The set of formal rules found in constitutions is proving to be a mere parchment barrier against authoritarian and quasi-authoritarian regimes.")

20. Mark Tushnet, "Constitutional Hardball." *John Marshall Law Review* 27 (2004): 523–53.

21. Tom Ginsburg and Aziz Z. Huq, *How to Save a Constitutional Democracy* (Chicago: The University of Chicago Press, 2018).

22. Driesen, *The Specter of Dictatorship*, 97.

23. U.S. Const. amend. I.

24. Internal governance at social media companies is, at present, the strongest tool for norm-setting. *See* Kate Klonick, "Inside the Making of Facebook's Supreme Court," *The New Yorker*, February 12, 2021, https://bit.ly/2W8Qhyp.

25. Bauer and Goldsmith, *After Trump*, 101. *See also*, Jonathan Peters, "The Modern Fight for Media Freedom in the United States." *First Amendment Law Review* 18 (2020): 71 (Trump has posted more than 1,300 tweets critical of the press since declaring his candidacy in 2015 and is waging "an illiberal and rhetorical campaign against the press as an institution.").

26. Frederick Schauer, "The Exceptional First Amendment," in *American Exceptionalism and Human Rights*, ed. Michael Ignatieff (Princeton: Princeton University Press, 2009).

27. *See* Kim Lane Scheppele, "Autocratic Legalism." *The University of Chicago Law Review* 85 (2018): 568–69 ("They develop a constitution-making process

justified in the name of the majority, without including any views of the minority, and voila! A new constitutional order is born.").

28. "United States: Despite Improvements, Troubling Vital Signs for Press Freedom Persist," https://rsf.org/en/united-states (Reporters Without Borders) (ranking the United States as having the 45th most free press of 180 countries. According to RSF, "Trump himself vilified bona fide news outfits as 'fake news' and qualified award-winning journalists as the 'enemy of the people,' feeding the type of threatening behavior, including violence and the destruction of equipment, that journalists faced during the uprising against the U.S. Capitol Building on 6 January 2021. As dozens of alleged insurrectionists face serious jail time for federal crimes, the erosion of trust in the American media and unchecked conspiracy theories that continue to flourish online will require a concerted effort by all—the public sector and private companies alike—to ensure that press freedom in the U.S. runs more than just skin deep.").

29. *Karem v. Trump*, 404 F.Supp.3d 203 (D.C. 2019).

30. JP Perry, "Defamation and the First Amendment: Protecting Free Speech While Promoting Accountability Under Trump," *CUNY Law Review* 21 (2018): 259.

31. Trump, Donald. Twitter Post. March 29, 2018, 7:57 a.m. EST, https://bit.ly/3gefJJF.

32. Trump, Donald. Twitter Post. March 31, 2018. 8:45 a.m. EST, https://bit.ly/3AUZPf4.

33. Bloomberg, "President Trump is Tweeting About Amazon Again—and its Stock Price is Falling," *Fortune*, April 2, 2018,. https://bit.ly/3AQqud5.

34. Daniel Seiden, "Amazon Didn't Waive Trump Bias Claim in $10B JEDI Contract Case," Bloomberg Law, April 30, 2021, https://bit.ly/3AQA13R (Microsoft and the DOJ were unable to demonstrate that Amazon waived its bias claim under the standard articulated in *Blue & Gold Fleet LP v. United States*.); Lauren Brier, "COFC Denies DOJ/Microsoft Motion to Dismiss Amazon JEDI Protest," *PilieroMazza PLLC*, May 6, 2021, https://bit.ly/37ViACK (U.S. Court of Federal Claims issued a sealed decision denying the Department of Justice and Microsoft's motions to dismiss Amazon's bid protest of the JEDI contract.); Robert Burns, "Pentagon Reconsidering Huge JEDI Cloud-Computing Contract," *AP News*, May 10, 2021, https://bit.ly/3gfhZjT (Pentagon reconsidered how to make a shift to cloud computing in response to legal challenges to the JEDI contract).

35. The JEDI contract was to allow the Department of Defense to acquire cloud services solutions that would be "accessible to the entirety of the Department that [could] support Unclassified, Secret, and Top Secret requirements." See Heidi M. Peters, "The Department of Defense's JEDI Cloud Program," *Congressional Research Service* (August 2, 2019): 1.

36. Jared Serbu, "Court keeps Amazon's JEDI challenge intact, dealing blow to DoD, Microsoft," *Federal News Network*, April 28, 2021, https://bit.ly/3gbllo2.

37. Mailyn Fidler, "Justice Department Subpoenas Journalists' Phone Records," Reporters Committee for Freedom of the Press, May 17, 2021, https://bit.ly/3iWPJnZ (Justice Department seized the records of journalists as part of a leak investigation); Associated Press in Washington, "US Department of Justice will no longer obtain

reporters' phone records," The Guardian, June 5, 2021, https://bit.ly/3z02yU2 (The Department of Justice announced that it would no longer secretly obtain members of the press' phone records during leak investigations.); Eric Lichtblau, "Trump's DOJ Was Wrong to Seize My Phone Records," *The Intercept*, June 8, 2021, https://bit.ly/3CXSM7q (Journalist states that he and three other *New York Times* reporters were the target of subpoenas for their phone records over an 8,000-word story they did on the FBI's role in the 2016 election, including its dual investigations into Hillary Clinton's emails and the Trump campaign's possible ties to Russia.); Chas Danner, "Trump DOJ's Secret Subpoenas and Data Seizures: What We Know," Intelligencer, June 16, 2021, https://nym.ag/3iWcKYc (The Department of https://nym.ag/3iWcKYc. Justice seized phone and email records of multiple journalists, congressional Democrats, and one of Trump's top lawyers, to identify government officials who may have leaked damaging or embarrassing information about President Trump to the press.); Bruce D. Brown, "Why did the Trump DOJ secretly seize phone records from *Post* journalists?," *Columbia Journalism Review*, May 12, 2021, https://bit.ly/2UwZT5s (Department of Justice delayed telling journalists or media outlets that it had seized records until after it had already seized the records, contrary to advance notice of toll-records requests per the Department of Justice's internal guidelines.)

38. Driesen, *The Specter of Dictatorship*, 131.

39. Sydney Ember, "To Trump, It's the 'Amazon Washington Post.' To Its Editor, That's Baloney," *New York Times*, April 2, 2018, https://nyti.ms/3iWlyx9.

40. "What is the Rule of Law," United Nations and the Rule of Law, Accessed June 15, 2021, https://bit.ly/3sqgDrs.

41. Andrew Novak, *Comparative Executive Clemency: The Constitutional Pardon Power and the Prerogative of Mercy in Global Perspective* (Boca Raton: CRC Press, 2016) ("Most countries tend not to use the pardon for political or self-serving purposes as frequently as the U.S. presidents have been seen to, even before Trump, although Trump has pushed further than others in that direction.")

42. See Bauer and Goldsmith, *After Trump*, 114.

43. See Bauer and Goldsmith, *After Trump*, 115.

44. See Bauer and Goldsmith, *After Trump*, 116.

45. See Bauer and Goldsmith, *After Trump*, 116. Controversial uses of the Pardon by past presidents included those involved in the Iran-Contra Affair, Clinton's use of Pardons, Bush and Libby.

46. Bauer and Goldsmith, *After Trump*, 111.

47. See Bauer and Goldsmith, *After Trump*, 120; Yuliya Talmazan, Rachel Elbaum, and Sara Mhaidli, "Full List of Trump's Last-Minute Pardons and Commuted Sentences," *NBC News*, Jan. 20, 2021, https://nbcnews.to/3yZlvX8.

48. Bauer and Goldsmith, *After Trump*, 121.

49. Bauer and Goldsmith, *After Trump*, 122–24.

50. Bauer and Goldsmith, *After Trump*, 124.

51. The separate but related issue of election interference by foreign powers is beyond the scope of this chapter, see Jens David Ohlin, *Election Interference: International Law and the Future of Democracy* (Cambridge: Cambridge University Press, 2020).

52. Brian Bennett, "Trump Refuses to Rule Out Third Party Run if He Loses GOP Nomination," *Los Angeles Times*, April 3, 2016, https://lat.ms/3gcu5KP.

53. "U.S. Presidential Debate: Trump Won't Commit to Accept Election Result," *BBC News*, Oct. 20, 2016, https://bbc.in/3m9sVDz.

54. That is not to say, though, that there is not historical precedent for at least initial reluctance to concede. Indeed, in 1916, Republican presidential nominee Charles Evans Hughes took nearly two weeks to congratulate President Woodrow Wilson on his reelection to a second term. Additionally, then-Vice President Al Gore's retracted concession in the 2000 presidential election is widely known. Ewan Palmer, "First Presidential Concession in 1896 Started Tradition Lasting More than 120 Years," *Newsweek*, Nov. 9, 2020, https://bit.ly/3y3TPza; Matt Smith, "Gore Retracts Concession as Florida Eyes Recount in Presidential Race," *CNN*, Nov. 8, 2000, https://cnn.it/3sqjoJk.

55. "Donald Trump Speech 'Save America' Rally Transcript January 6," Rev, Jan.6, 2021,. https://bit.ly/3gcXbti.

56. A common charge against these defendants is, 40 U.S.C § 5104 (e)(2)(D), which makes it a crime to (D) utter loud, threatening, or abusive language, or engage in disorderly or disruptive conduct, at any place in the Grounds or in any of the Capitol Buildings with the intent to impede, disrupt, or disturb the orderly conduct of a session of Congress or either House of Congress, or the orderly conduct in that building of a hearing before, or any deliberations of, a committee of Congress or either House of Congress. This seems the most likely challenge as most other charges have been related to actual acts of violence, carrying weapons, or aiding and abetting someone doing so. "Capitol Hill Siege." Program on extremism. George Washington University, June 26, 2021, https://extremism.gwu.edu/Capitol-Hill-Cases.

57. Many argued that they were following superior orders, apparently attempting to resuscitate a long-ago discredited defense in international criminal law. Rosalind S. Helderman, Spencer S. Hsu, and Rachel Weiner, "'Trump Said to Do So': Accounts of Rioters Who Say the President Spurred Them to Rush the Capitol Could Be Pivotal Testimony," *Washington Post*, January 16, 2021, https://wapo.st/37TMnfc.; Jenna Ryan in interview with CBS News, "I would like a pardon from the President of the United States . . . I think that we all deserve a pardon. I'm facing a prison sentence. I think that I do not deserve that." Ashley Collman, "A Texas Real-Estate Agent Who Flew on a Private Jet to Join the Capitol Riot Has Asked Trump for a Pardon, Saying She Was Only Following His Orders," *Business Insider*, January 18, 2021, https://bit.ly/3mdowzB. Adam Newbold, a retired U.S. Navy SEAL, to ABC News, said, "I would like to express to you just a cry for clemency, as you understand that my life now has been absolutely turned upside-down." James Gordon Meek and Catherine Sanz, "'I Am Not a Terrorist': Retired Navy SEAL Speaks after Capitol Siege," *ABC News*, January 13, 2021, https://abcn.ws/3CRERjj.

58. Talman, Elbaum, and Mhaidli, "Full List of Trump's Last-Minute Pardons and Commuted Sentences."

59. Bauer and Goldsmith, *After Trump*, 120.

60. Talmazan, Elbaum, and Mhaidli, "Full List of Trump's Last-Minute Pardons and Commuted Sentences."

61. Bauer and Goldsmith, *After Trump*, 125.

62. Bauer and Goldsmith, *After Trump*, 128.

63. Driesen, *The Specter of Dictatorship*, 125.

64. U.S. Const. art. III, § 1.

65. Bauer and Goldsmith, *After Trump*. John Gramlich, "How Trump compares with other recent presidents in appointing federal judges." *Pew Research Center*, Jan. 13, 2021. https://pewrsr.ch/3fu4snT.

66. David Landau, "Abusive Constitutionalism," *U.C. Davis Law Review* 47 (2013): 199.

67. JoLissa Jones, "Merrick Garland and the Stalemate Senate: Does the Senate Owe Nominees A Vote?" *Thurgood Marshall Law Review Online* 42 (2018): 6.

68. JoLissa Jones, "Merrick Garland and the Stalemate Senate: Does the Senate Owe Nominees A Vote?"

69. Michael J. Gerhardt and Richard W. Painter, "Majority Rule and the Future of Judicial Selection," *Wisconsin Law Review* 2 (2017): 266–67.

70. Benjamin Pomerance, "Inside a House Divided: Recent Alliances on the United States Supreme Court," *Albany Law Review* 81, no. 2 (2017): 364.

71. "President Trump United Nations General Assembly Address," C-Span, September 24, 2019https://bit.ly/3xXn8mP. ["A permanent political class is openly disdainful, dismissive, and defiant of the will of the people. A faceless bureaucracy operates in secret and weakens democratic rule. Media and academic institutions push flat-out assaults on our histories, traditions, and values."]

72. Kenneth Hammond, "Trump Administration weaponizing academia," Asia Times, September 8, 2020, https://bit.ly/3mdUHi8. ["In a series of measures over recent months the [United States] government has been putting pressure on universities and other educational institutions to suppress academic freedom and inhibit intellectual exchanges and research by Chinese scholars and their American colleagues."] It bears mentioning that the Obama administration had some similar policies.

73. "Executive Order 13950 of September 22, 2020, Combating Race and Sex Stereotyping." *Code of Federal Regulations*, title 85 (2020): 60683–60689. https://www.federalregister.gov/documents/2020/09/28/2020-21534/combating-race-and-sex-stereotyping.

74. "Executive Order 13985 of January 20, 2021, Advancing Racial Equity and Support for Underserved Communities through the Federal Government." *Code of Federal Regulations*, title 86 (2021): 7009–7013. https://www.federalregister.gov/documents/2021/01/25/2021-01753/advancing-racial-equity-and-support-for-underserved-communities-through-the-federal-government.f.

75. Cynthia Alkon, "The Flawed U.S. Approach to Rule of Law Development," *Penn State Law Review* 117, no. 3 (2013): 797–867, 805.

76. Marian L. Lawson and Susan B. Epstein. *Democracy Promotion: An Objective of U.S. Foreign Assistance* (Washington, DC: Congressional Research Service, 2019): 1.

77. Harold Hongju Koh, "On American Exceptionalism," *Stanford Law Review* 55 (2003): 1479; but see also, Jed Rubenfeld, "Unilateralism and Constitutionalism," *New York University Law Review* 79, no. 6 (December 2004): 1971. The United States was an avid supporter of the application of international criminal law against its enemies in the wake of war in the Nuremberg Trials, and

later in the UN Security Council's ad hoc establishment of tribunals applying international criminal law.

78. The United States is the only democracy not to ratify CEDAW. Liane Schalatek, "CEDAW and the USA: When Belief in Exceptionalism Becomes Exemptionalism," Heinrich Boll Stiftung, the Green Political Foundation, December 10, 2019, https://bit.ly/3xVIv88. The United States is the only country not to ratify CRC. Sarah Mehta, "There's Only One Country That Hasn't Ratified the Convention on Children's Rights: US," ACLU, November 20, 2015, https://bit.ly/2W64WKH. The United States has also not ratified ICESCR. "Human Rights & the U.S.: How Has the United States Handled Human Rights Issues in the Past & Today?." The Advocates for Human Rights, https://bit.ly/3gcqzjE.

79. United Nations, G.A. Res. 39/46, Convention against Torture and Other Cruel, Inhuman or Degrading Treatment or Punishment (Jun. 26, 1987).

80. United Nations, G.A. Res. 260 A (III), Convention on the Prevention and Punishment of the Crime of Genocide (Jan. 12, 1951), 1–4.

81. During the Rome Statute negotiations, the U.S. famously lobbied to ensure that the UN Security Council maintained sole power over ICC prosecutions, and the U.S. never embraced the independent Prosecutor under the so-called Singapore Compromise. Cora True-Frost, "The International Civil Servant: How the First Prosecutor Engaged the U. N. Security Council," in *The First Global Prosecutor: Promise and Constraints*, eds. Martha Minow and Alex Whiting (Ann Arbor: University of Michigan Press, 2015), 251–84.

82. "Rome Statute of the International Criminal Court" (1998), art. 16.

83. Megan A. Fairlie, "The United States and the International Criminal Court Post-Bush: A Beautiful Courtship but an Unlikely Marriage," *Berkeley Journal of International Law* 29 (2011): 528–75 ("In the wake of senior members of the Obama administration both praising the ICC and lamenting the fact that the United States is not a part of the Court, the United States was represented at the annual meeting of the ICC's Assembly of States Parties–for the first time ever–in late 2009."); *see also* Stephen Eliot Smith, "Definitely Maybe: The Outlook for U.S. Relations with the International Criminal Court During the Obama administration," *Florida Journal of International Law* 22, no. 2 (August 2010): 155–87 ("Thus, although the policy of official American hostility toward the ICC may have come to an end, the advent of the Obama administration does not automatically mean that U.S. membership in the court will be embraced.")

84. Colleen Flaherty, "Diversity Work, Interrupted," *Inside Higher Ed*, Oct. 7, 2020, https://bit.ly/3sqTiWy.

85. Executive Order 13928, Blocking Property of Certain Persons Associated with the International Criminal Court, of June 11, 2020, https://www.federalregister.gov/documents/2020/06/15/2020-12953/blocking-property-of-certain-persons-associated-with-the-international-criminal-court; Mary Ellen Cagnassola, "Outgoing ICC Prosecutor Fatou Bensouda Says Trump Crossed a 'Red Line' with Sanctions against Her," *Newsweek*, June 14, 2021, https://www.newsweek.com/outgoing-icc-prosecutor-fatou-bensouda-says-trump-crossed-red-line-sanctions-against-her-1600538.

86. "Freedom in the World 2021: United States," Freedom House, https://bit.ly/3yYEKA5. "However, in recent years its democratic institutions have suffered erosion, as reflected in partisan pressure on the electoral process, bias and dysfunction in

the criminal justice system, harmful policies on immigration and asylum seekers, and growing disparities in wealth, economic opportunity, and political influence."

87. Carothers and Brown, "The Chastened Power."
88. Carothers and Brown, "The Chastened Power."
89. Carothers and Brown, "The Chastened Power."

BIBLIOGRAPHY

Alkon, Cynthia. "The Flawed U.S. Approach to Rule of Law Development." *Penn State Law Review* 117, no. 3 (2013): 797–872.

Associated Press in Washington. "US Department of Justice Will No Longer Obtain Reporters' Phone Records." *The Guardian*. Published June 5, 2021. https://bit.ly/3z02yU2.

Bauer, Bob, and Jack Goldsmith. *After Trump: Reconstructing the Presidency*. Washington, DC: Lawfare Press, 2020.

Bennett, Brian. "Trump Refuses to Rule Out Third Party Run if he Loses GOP Nomination." *Los Angeles Times*. Published April 3, 2016. https://lat.ms/3y81soh.

Bingham, Tom. *The Rule of Law*. London: Penguin, 2011.

Bloomberg. "President Trump is Tweeting about Amazon Again–and Its Stock Price is Falling." *Fortune*. Published April 2, 2018. https://bit.ly/3AQqud5.

Braver, Joshua. "Court-Packing: An American Tradition?" *Boston College Law Review* 61 (November 2020): 2747–2808.

Brier, Lauren. "COFC Denies DOJ/Microsoft Motion to Dismiss Amazon JEDI Protest." *PilieroMazza PLLC*. Published May 6, 2021. https://bit.ly/37ViACK.

Brown, Bruce D. "Why Did Trump DOJ Secretly Seize Phone Records from *Post* Journalists?" *Columbia Journalism Review*. Published May 12, 2021. https://bit.ly/3sF0Vcl.

Burns, Robert. "Pentagon Reconsidering Huge JEDI Cloud-Computing Contract." *AP News*. Published May 10, 2021. https://bit.ly/3gbc27A.

Cagnassola, Mary Ellen. "Outgoing ICC Prosecutor Fatou Bensouda Says Trump Crossed a 'Red Line' with Sanctions Against Her." *Newsweek*. Published June 14, 2021. https://bit.ly/3AOdogz.

"Capitol Hill Siege." Program on Extremism. George Washington University. Published June 26, 2021. https://bit.ly/3884 P. 41.

Carothers, Thomas and Frances Z. Brown. "The Chastened Power." *American Purpose*. Published March 10, 2021. https://bit.ly/3xWFnc5.

Chong, Jane. "Donald Trump's Strange and Dangerous 'Absolute Rights' Idea." *The Atlantic*. Published February 29, 2020, https://bit.ly/3sF1vqx.

Collman, Ashley. "A Texas Real-Estate Agent Who Flew on a Private Jet to Join the Capitol Riot has Asked Trump for a Pardon, Saying She Was Only Following His Orders." *Business Insider*. Published January 18, 2021. https://bit.ly/3sF1KBX.

Danner, Chas. "Trump's DOJ Secret Subpoenas and Data Seizures: What We Know." Published June 16, 2021. https://nym.ag/3z1MLUP.

"Donald Trump Speech 'Save America' Rally Transcript January 6." Rev. Published January 6, 2021. https://bit.ly/3gcXbti.

Driesen, David M. "The Political Remedies Doctrine." SSRN. Published November 16, 2020. https://bit.ly/3xY2IKz.

Driesen, David M. *The Specter of Dictatorship*. Redwood City: Stanford University Press, 2021.

Ember, Sydney. "To Trump, It's the 'Amazon Washington Post.' To Its Editor, That's Baloney." *New York Times*. Published April 2, 2018. https://nyti.ms/3iWlyx9.

Epps, Daniel, and Ganesh Sitaraman. "How to Save the Supreme Court." *Yale Law Journal* 129, no. 1 (October 2019): 148–207.

Exec. Order No. 13928, 85 Fed. Reg. 36,139 (Jun. 11, 2020). https://bit.ly/3me2bC2.

Exec. Order No. 13950, 85 Fed. Reg. 60,683 (Sept. 22, 2020). https://bit.ly/3m9QZWU.

Exec. Order No. 13985, 86 Fed. Reg. 7,009 (Jan. 20, 2021). https://bit.ly/3CVp82H.

Fairlie, Megan A. "The United States and the International Criminal Court Post-Bush: A Beautiful Courtship but an Unlikely Marriage." *Berkeley Journal of International Law* 29, no. 2 (December 2011): 528–76.

Feldman, Stephen M. "Court-Packing Time? Supreme Court Legitimacy and Positivity Theory." *Buffalo Law Review* 68 (December 2020): 1519–1559.

Fidler, Mailyn. "Justice Department Subpoenas Journalists' Phone Records." *Reporters Committee for Freedom of the Press*. Published May 17, 2021. https://bit.ly/3gdc7Yv.

Flaherty, Colleen. "Diversity Work, Interrupted." Inside Higher Ed. Published October 7, 2020. https://bit.ly/3yZAWP5.

"Freedom in the World 2021: United States." *Freedom House*. Accessed June 15, 2021, https://bit.ly/37VkJi2.

Gerhardt, Michael J., and Richard W. Painter. "Majority Rule and the Future of Judicial Selection." *Wisconsin Law Review* 2 (2017): 263–84.

Ginsburg, Tom, and Aziz Z. Huq. *How to Save a Constitutional Democracy*. Chicago: University of Chicago Press, 2018.

Gramlich, John. "How Trump compares with other recent presidents in appointing federal judges." *Pew Research Center*, Jan. 13, 2021. https://pewrsr.ch/3fu4snT.

Hammond, Kenneth. "Trump Administration Weaponizing Academia." *Asia Times*. Published September 8, 2020. https://bit.ly/3mdUHi8.

Helderman, Rosalind S., Spencer S. Hsu, and Rachel Weiner. "'Trump Said to Do So': Accounts of Rioters Who Say the President Spurred Them to Rush the Capital Could Be Pivotal Testimony." *Washington Post*. Published January 16, 2021,

"Human Rights & the U.S.: How Has the United States Handled Human Rights Issues in the Past & Today?" *The Advocates for Human Rights*. https://wapo.st/3CXCoDW.

Jones, JoLissa. "Merrick Garland and the Stalemate Senate: Does the Senate Owe Nominees a Vote?" *Thurgood Marshall Law Review Online* 42, no. 3 (2018): 1–22.

Karem v. Trump, 404 F.Supp.3d 203 (D.C. 2019).

Kent, Andrew, Ethan Leib, and Jed Shugerman. "Faithful Execution and Article II." *Harvard Law Review* 132, no. 8 (June 2019): 2111–2192.

Klarman, Michael J. "The Degradation of American Democracy–and the Court+." *Harvard Law Review* 134 (November2020): 1–263.

Klonick, Kate. "Inside the Making of Facebook's Supreme Court." *The New Yorker.* Published February 12, 2021. https://bit.ly/2W8Qhyp.

Koh, Harold Hongju. "On American Exceptionalism." *Stanford Law Review* 55 (2003): 1479–1527.

Landau, David. "Abusive Constitutionalism." *U.C. Davis Law Review*, 47 (2013): 189–260.

Landau, David, and Rosalind Dixon. "Abusive Judicial Review: Courts against Democracy." *University of California Davis Law Review* 53 (2020): 1313–1387.

Lawrence, Marian L., and Susan B. Epstein. *Democracy Promotion: An Objective of U.S. Foreign Assistance.* Washington, DC: Congressional Research Service, 2019.

Levitzky, Steven, and Daniel Ziblatt. *How Democracies Die.* New York: Crown, 2018.

Lichtblau, Eric. "Trump's DOJ Was Wrong to Seize My Phone Records." *The Intercept.* Published June 8, 2021. https://bit.ly/3gd8jql.

Meek, James Gordon, and Catherine Sanz. "'I Am Not a Terrorist': Retired Navy SEAL Speaks After Capitol Siege." *ABC News.* Published January 13, 2021. https://abcn.ws/3xXRHsr.

Mehta, Sarah. "There's Only One Country That Hasn't Ratified the Convention on Children's Rights: US." *ACLU.* Published November 20, 2015. https://bit.ly/3iUVMcz.

Neuman, Gerald L. *Human Rights in a Time of Populism: Challenges and Responses.* Cambridge: Cambridge University Press, 2020.

Novak, Andrew. *Comparative Executive Clemency: The Constitutional Pardon Power and the Prerogative of Mercy in Global Perspective.* Boca Raton: CRC Press, 2016.

Ohlin, Jens David. *Election Interference: International Law and the Future of Democracy.* Cambridge: Cambridge University Press, 2020.

Palmer, Ewan. "First Presidential Concession in 1896 Started Tradition Lasting More than 120 Years." *Newsweek.* Published November 9, 2020. https://bit.ly/3CXhRiF.

Perry, JP. "Defamation and the First Amendment: Protecting Free Speech While Promoting Accountability under Trump." *CUNY Law Review* 21 (2018): 259–84.

Peters, Heidi M. "The Department of Defense's JEDI Cloud Program." *Congressional Research Service* (August 2, 2019): 1–20.

Peters, Jonathan. "The Modern Fight for Media Freedom in the United States." *First Amendment Law Review* 18 (2020): 60–93.

Pomerance, Benjamin. "Inside a House Divided: Recent Alliances on the United States Supreme Court." *Albany Law Review* 81 no. 2 (2017): 361–437.

"President Trump United Nations General Assembly Address." *C-Span.* Published September 24, 2019. https://bit.ly/3gfbgql.

"Rome Statute of the International Criminal Court, art. 16" International Criminal Court. Published 1998, https://bit.ly/3m7SOng.

Rubenfeld, Jed. "Unilateralism and Constitutionalism." *New York University Law Review* 79, no. 6 (Deecember 2004): 1971–2028.

Schalatek, Liane. "CEDAW and the USA: When Belief in Exceptionalism Becomes Exemptionalism." Heinrich Boll Stiftung, *The Green Political Foundation*. Published December 10, 2019. https://bit.ly/3y1TtJ8.

Schauer, Frederick. "The Exceptional First Amendment." In *American Exceptionalism and Human Rights*, edited by Michael Ignatieff, 29–56. Princeton: Princeton University Press, 2009.

Scheppele, Kim Lane. "Autocratic Legalism." *University of Chicago Law Review* 85, no. 2 (March 2018): 545–84.

Schwartz Jr., Frederick A. O., and Aziz Z. Huq. *Unchecked and Unbalanced: Presidential Power in a Time of Terror*. New York City: The New Press, 2008.

Seiden, Daniel. "Amazon Didn't Waive Trump Bias Claim in $10B JEDI Contract Case." *Bloomberg Law*. Published April 30, 2021. https://bit.ly/3AQA13R.

Serbu, Jared. "Court Keeps Amazon's JEDI Challenge Intact, Dealing Blow to DoD, Microsoft." *Federal News Network*. Published April 28, 2021. https://bit.ly/3gbllo2.

Shapiro, Carolyn. "Democracy, Federalism, and the Guarantee Clause." *Arizona Law Review* 62 (2020): 183–240.

Smith, Matt. "Gore Retracts Concession as Florida Eyes Recount in Presidential Race." *CNN*. Published November 8, 2000, https://cnn.it/2Xxr1Cl.

Smith, Stephen Eliot. "Definitely Maybe: The Outlook for U.S. Relations With the International Criminal Court During the Obama Administration." *Florida Journal of International Law* no. 2 (August 2010): 155–89.

Talmazan, Yuliya, Rachel Elbaum, and Sara Mhaidli. "Full List of Trump's Last-Minute Pardons and Commuted Sentences." *NBC News*. Published January 20, 2021. https://nbcnews.to/3yZlvX8.

True-Frost, Cora. "The International Civil Servant: How the First Prosecutor Engaged the U.N. Security Council." In *The First Global Prosecutor: Promise and Constraints*, edited by Marthow Miniow and Alex Whiting, 251–84. Ann Arbor: University of Michigan Press, 2015.

Trump, Donald. Twitter Post. March 29, 2018, 7:57 a.m. EST. https://bit.ly/3gefJJF.

Trump, Donald. Twitter Post. March 31, 2018. 8:45 a.m. EST. https://bit.ly/3swpB6v.

Tushnet, Mark. "Constitutional Hardball." *John Marshall Law Review* 27 (2004): 523–53.

United Nations. G.A. Res. 39/46. "Convention against Torture and Other Cruel, Inhuman or Degrading Treatment or Punishment." (June 26, 1987).

United Nations. G.A. Res. 260 A (III). "Convention on the Prevention and Punishment of the Crime of Genocide." (Jan. 12, 1951).

United States Courts. "Overview–Rule of Law." Accessed June 15, 2021, https://www.uscourts.gov/educational-resources/educational-activities/overview-rule-law.

"United States: Despite Improvements, Troubling Vital Signs for Press Freedom Persist." Reporters Without Borders. Accessed July 12, 2021, https://rsf.org/en/united-states.

U.S. Const. amend. I.

U.S. Const. art. 2 sec. 3.

U.S. Const. art. 3 sec. 1.

"US Presidential Debate: Trump Won't Commit to Accept Election Result." *BBC News*. Published October 20, 2016. https://bbc.in/3sqiJrs.

Waldron, Jeremy. "The Concept and the Rule of Law." *Georgia Law Review* 43, no. 1 (2008): 1–54.

Watts, Kathryn A. "Controlling Presidential Control." *Michigan Law Review* 114 (2016): 683–745.

"What is the Rule of Law." United Nations and the Rule of Law. Accessed June 15, 2021. https://bit.ly/3sqgDrs.

Zoffer, Joshua P. and David Singh Grewal. "The Counter-Majoritarian Difficulty of a Minoritarian Judiciary." *California Law Review Online* 11 (2020): 437–62.

Chapter 6

Power Politics versus the Rule of Law in Turkey

A Case Study

Şerife Ceren Uysal

INTRODUCTION

In the second half of 2016, Turkey experienced a coup d'état attempt. As people were observing military vehicles occupy the streets, they saw the state-owned TV station being on-air overtaken by armed forces, and the announcement stating that the army had seized control was also broadcast live. At the end of the day, many citizens lost their lives, and many more got injured. Despite all the unanswered questions regarding this coup attempt, one must acknowledge that the events were quite alarming and triggering for a large part of the society as Turkey had faced coups before. Moreover, even during civil administration periods when the army was not in control, people systematically and continuously felt the crippling impact military tutelage had on the democratic mechanisms.

On July 20, 2016, immediately after the attempted coup, a three-month State of Emergency (SoE) was declared. The SoE was subsequently extended seven times without interruption. Finally, it was officially lifted on July 19, 2018. Repercussions of this two-year period were quite heavy for large segments of the society and the effects are still noticeable today.

Under the SoE, thirty-seven Statutory Decrees (*kanun hükmünde kararname*—KHK after its acronym in Turkish) were issued in total, and all the regulations covered by these decrees were later accepted as laws. As Human Rights Watch underlined this strategy both normalized the unconventional and caused the procedures that should have been limited to SoE to become permanent even after SoE was lifted.[1]

During this two-year SoE period, over 100,000 public officials, including judges and prosecutors, were dismissed from duty, and banned from working in public service thereafter. Meanwhile, their passports were canceled as well. Many students were expelled from educational institutions. By the end of the first year of the SoE, the estimated number of people arrested in connection with the coup attempt was over 50,000.[2] Between July 2016 and March 2018, the number of people who were subjected to the pre-detention was 228,137. Within just the first year of the SoE, nearly 4,000 judges and prosecutors went under criminal investigation and approximately 3,000 were arrested.[3] According to the report data, Human Rights Watch (HRW)[4] published in 2019, the number of lawyers who were prosecuted was 1,546. At the time of HRW's report,[5] 274 of these lawyers had been convicted and 598 had been remanded in custody for varying periods. An array of 2,761 institutions, including newspapers, TV channels, associations, foundations, and even private commercial companies were shut down by the KHKs.[6] Another practice which became permanent was the arrest of elected members of the parliament who opposed the government. Furthermore, the state-appointed trustees in place of many elected mayors and their deputies.

In short, Turkey endured an SoE period that lasted for two years and this period included a constitutional amendment with questionable legitimacy in many ways. Additionally, as an unequivocal result of conducts which did not confirm with the relevant SoE legislation in force at the time, the country entered a phase during which this regime became institutionalized and normalized. This process is still ongoing with all its hardships.

Naturally, it is an indisputable fact that the SoE declaration points to a critical moment for Turkey. However, when mentioning an institutionalized and systematic series of violations, it becomes apparent that it is just not the two-year period between 2016 and 2018 but the periods before and after as well. Associating Turkey's increasing authoritarianism only with the SoE declaration would mean ignoring the ongoing violations of the rule of law principles and, with it, prevent us from fully comprehending the deepening anti-democratic practices. The matter is regarding a repressive regime being established that is diverging further away from the rule of law principle and becoming more institutionalized with each passing day. It is evident that this process did not begin with the SoE declaration, nor end with the lifting of the SoE.

TRANSFERRING THE LEGISLATIVE POWER TO THE EXECUTIVE AND THE ABSENCE OF JUDICIAL REVIEW: KHK REGIME

The legal basis for the SoE in 2016 mainly consisted of the applicable articles of the Constitution of the Republic of Turkey and the State of Emergency

Act. Article 120 of the Constitution, which was still in effect at the time, stated that:

> In the event of serious indications of widespread acts of violence aimed at the destruction of the free democratic order established by the Constitution or of fundamental rights and freedoms, or serious deterioration of public order because of acts of violence, the Council of Ministers, meeting under the chairmanship of the President of the Republic, after consultation with the National Security Council, may declare a state of emergency in one or more regions or throughout the country for a period not exceeding six months.[7]

On the other hand, Article 15 of the Constitution[8] regulates that during an SoE, exercising fundamental rights and freedoms may be limited if obligations under international law are not violated. In conformity with the European Convention on Human Rights in the second paragraph the article further restricts these limitations. It specifies the inviolable fundamental rights and principles such as the right to life, freedom of thought, freedom of expression, and presumption of innocence. In other words, Article 15 of the Constitution defines the circumstances under which the fundamental rights and freedoms may be limited and clearly restricts the boundaries of these limitations.

Article 121 of the Constitution,[9] which was in force at the time, complements these two articles. This article carries the biggest fundamental importance. It determines and demarcates the extraordinary powers granted to the executive by the SoE that was inevitably declared due to compelling reasons. The significance of this article emanates from the fact that it authorizes the executive to issue a decree during the SoE. However, there is no doubt that the same article dictates that the statutory decrees issued during an SoE needs to be related to the threat that caused the SoE. The problem with the two-year SoE in Turkey and ruling by decrees during this phase stems from this point onwards. It is known that the grounds for declaring an SoE was the coup attempt that took place on July 15, 2016. As this was the reason, the scope of these emergency decrees should have also been limited to the failed coup attempt. Even though it is not explicitly specified in the Constitution, it is also clear that these emergency decrees should have had a temporal limit by the literal interpretation of the law. This is because the executive's authority to issue statutory decrees is meant to be used to protect the public interest and to eliminate said threat when there is a threat against the public order. However, when we examine the contents of the statutory decrees issued in Turkey during this two-year period, we see that their consequences do not align with this purpose.

As mentioned, the decrees issued during this two-year period covered a wide range of matters and all became a law afterwards. These decrees cover a multitude of subjects such as these: dismissal of more than a 100,000 public officials; permanent closure of many associations, foundations, private companies, and media organizations; expulsion of many students from educational facilities. Nevertheless, this is not the full extent of the subjects of these decrees. Few of the examples are particularly striking. For instance, the Decree no. KHK/668 allowed the placement of contract teachers without a preliminary exam. Decree no. KHK/671 amended the retirement age of the faculty members and also changed some of the regular practice of criminal procedure law, such as probation periods and conditional release requirements. As an even more striking example, Decree no. KHK/676 made extensive changes to the right of defense, limiting the number of defense counsel allowed inside the courtroom per defendant to three and introducing limitations for attorney-client meetings at the prison facilities. The same decree also authorized Ministry of Interior to establish offices abroad. Moreover, this decree is the source of another authority transfer that is still causing political tension today: handing the power to appoint university rectors to the president. Decree no. KHK/680 provided which institution would be handling vehicle registrations while Decree no. KHK/684 regulated the payment requirements for prepaid house sale contracts, Decree no. KHK/687 was related to winter tire regulations and finally Decree no. KHK/690 provided some fundamental regulations and banned wedding reality shows on the side.[10]

As seen from these examples, many of the subjects ranging from wedding reality shows to winter tire practices, prepaid house sale contracts to permanently amending fundamental laws such as the Criminal Code and the Civil Code covered by these regulations had nothing to do with the cause of the SoE. As such, the executive branch has replaced the legislature for two full years, demonstrating a very broad regulation conduct that did not correspond to the main limitation criteria of the Article 121 of the Constitution: "being related to the SoE."

The problem only deepens when these decrees are evaluated within the scope of the separation of powers. On the one hand, the wide array of topics these decrees cover implies that the executive has usurped the authorities of the legislature. On the other hand, considering that the decrees governing matters such as dismissal from the public service or closure of associations and similar institutions were issued on the grounds of membership or affiliation with a terrorist organization, we see that the essence of these actions also extend to the judiciary's area of authority.[11] These actions constitute a clear violation of the presumption of innocence principle while bearing the same legal consequences as a judicial decision. This all points to a KHK regime where all authority is gathered within the executive instead of a separation of powers. The constitutional amendments of 2017 only intensified this problem, more or less replacing the executive with the president.

No judicial review could be carried out regarding these power extorting regulations, which were in clear violation of the Constitution at the time of their issuance. Even though the members of the opposition parties in the parliament applied to the constitutional court (AYM) to ensure judicial review against these decrees which were fully enacted later, the constitutional court ruled that it does not have the authority to inspect the constitutionality of the statutory decrees in terms of form and substance.[12]

Constitutional court referred to Article 148 of the Constitution[13] while explaining the basis of their judgment. Indeed, when the relevant article is subjected to a literal interpretation, we would need to conclude that the court's decision of lack of jurisdiction was appropriate. This is because the first paragraph of Article 148 states that decrees issued during an SoE or war shall not be brought before the constitutional court alleging their unconstitutionality as to form or substance. Nonetheless, due to this decision of the constitutional court, these regulations, which were issued on a much wider scope than what was determined by the Constitution and in a way to regulate the ordinary matters during an extraordinary period, were deprived of judicial review. However, the judicial precedent of the constitutional court dated January 10, 1991,[14] aimed to prevent the overreach of powers that are likely to occur during an extraordinary period—in other words, the abuse of the SoE powers. The precedent states that "*the Constitutional Court cannot be bound by the name of the text brought up for review*" and considered itself authorized to examine the decrees of the relevant period, thus implying that this prohibition of review shall only apply to the decrees that were issued in accordance with Article 121 of the Constitution. In the aftermath of the constitutional court reversing this precedent and declaring that the court lacks the power to review this matter, Turkish legal order has witnessed many laws that include regulations that overreach their authority with questionable legitimacy.

CONSTITUTIONAL AMENDMENT DURING THE SOE AND THE QUESTION OF LEGITIMACY

Constitution of the Republic of Turkey was radically amended on April 16, 2017, during the SoE and after a highly controversial referendum. Essentially, the 1982 Constitution in effect was also initially drafted after a military coup, and 110 of the 177 Articles of the Constitution had already been amended following referendum before 2017. However, considering the political, legal, and societal circumstances, the 2017 referendum took place under the referendum process is clearly different from all the previous ones. The relevant constitutional amendment came with a question of legitimacy due to the contents, political circumstances, and methods.[15]

Constitutionalism is the assurance that the government will stay within the rule of law principles.[16] In other words, constitutions exist not to ensure the survival of the rulers of a state, but to ensure the fundamental rights and freedoms of the people against a powerful institution like the state. Exactly for this reason, the method adopted during constitutional amendments is not a mere legal technicality discussion. On the contrary, the discussion is regarding legitimacy that should be considered directly in relation to the rule of law.

Regarding the possible methods adopted for constitutional amendments and the risks they contain, "the Venice Commission"—a subsidiary expert advisory body of the Council of Europe—makes important observations in their report dated December 11–12, 2009:

1. That the rules on constitutional change are too rigid. The procedural and/ or substantial rules are too strict, creating a lock-in, cementing unsuitable procedures of governance, blocking necessary change. This means too tight confinements on democratic development, and disenfranchisement of the majority that wants reform.
2. That the rules on constitutional change are too flexible. The procedural and/or substantial rules are too lax, creating instability, lack of predictability and conflict. Democratic procedures, core values and minority interests are not sufficiently protected. The issue of constitutional reform becomes in itself a subject of continuous political debate, and the political actors spend time arguing this instead of getting on with the business of governing within the existing framework.[17]

The report further states that "The constitutional amendment procedures should be drafted in a clear and simple manner, and applied in an open, transparent and democratic way."[18] According to *the Venice Commission*, an amendment process that allows the public and other institutions to participate in discussions is essential for constitutional legitimacy. In this sense, the controversy regarding transparency and democratic participation is clearly not just about the lawmaking process itself.[19] Report especially emphasizes that all political forces and civil community should contribute to reaching a consensus together, while freedom of expression and information should be protected definitively. These highlights are of utmost importance in terms of what Turkey went through.

The first and foremost issue with the legitimacy of the constitutional amendment process in Turkey is that these amendments happened during an SoE. At the time of these amendments, large segments of the public were already in deep fear and concern due to the arbitrariness and lack of legal certainty that deepened with the SoE. According to the data provided by the Ministry of Justice, 2,579 people were prosecuted for insulting the president in 2016 and 5,150 in 2017, the first year 883 individuals were convicted of these charges and 2,099 in the second year. Additionally, 1,128 academics from the Academics for Peace were charged with making terrorist propaganda after collectively signing a petition in support of peace. Four of these academics were kept in pretrial detention and after declaration of the SoE, almost all of them had to stand criminal trial in severe criminal courts.[20] As reported by the Ministry of Internal Affairs, out of the 102 municipalities that Peoples' Democratic Party (HDP) had won, ninety-four were placed in government conservatorship.[21] It would be unrealistic to expect these political and judicial circumstances to not instill a serious sense of fear and mistrust in the majority of the public. Constitutional amendment is a process that requires participatory discussion broad enough to include public consensus and critical thinking. Thus, making it impossible to take place in such a fearful atmosphere.

Tensions of this period also reflected on the parliament. Members of the parliament had quarrels, some of which that led to fistfights. Incidentally, the bill for the amendment was put to open ballot instead of the secret ballot system that is specified in the law. As eleven members of the party were in pretrial detention under terrorism charges at the time of voting, members of HDP, a party that represents over 10 percent of the population, could not take place in the discussions or the voting process.

After the decision to hold a referendum, the preparations regarding this matter were directly affected by the political atmosphere of the time as well. The limitations on meetings and protests due to the SoE, resulted in a blockage of all democratic channels the dissenting groups could use to voice their requests.[22] The government and the president conducted a huge "yes" campaign directly using the parliament's budget. On the other hand, the "no" campaign, which should have been nothing out of the ordinary for a democratic society, took place with limited funds and under a threat of arrests every step of the way. On many occasions, the president directly emphasized that "asking people to vote no or voting no" would be tantamount to terrorism.[23]

On March 10–11, 2017, the Venice Commission issued a report on the constitutional amendment in Turkey. This report raised concern over the risks of amending the Constitution while the SoE was still ongoing. The official statement provided in response by the Republic of the Turkey Ministry of Justice expressed that this report "*carries no authority or credibility for Turkey*" and accused the Venice Commission for supporting the "no" campaign and not being impartial.[24]

In sum, Turkey had quite a tense pre-referendum period, and the legitimacy debate shadowed over the amendments right before the voting. Even without the SoE conditions, it is obvious that we cannot consider this constitutional amendment legitimate: An amendment solely carried out via political party representatives that took place after a process that does not allow the people to express their demands or voice their concerns but instead just poses a "yes" or "no" question; a process that is closed to discussions and contributions of different ethnicities, religions, and sects living in the same country; a process that even excludes the experts on the subject.[25]

Day of the referendum was also controversial. The International Referendum Observation Mission noted multiple accounts of violation in their report.[26] The same report remarks that the Supreme Board of Election's (YSK) to "consider unstamped ballots as valid" was against the law.[27] Indeed, the decision no. 560 by YSK[28] did raise serious questions as it could not be appealed. The legitimacy crisis only got deeper when this decision and close election results were assessed together; the amendment passed merely with 51.41 percent yes and 48.59 percent no votes. Since the number of votes counted valid per the decision of YSK—which is still null and void under the current legislation—is unknown, it is impossible to accurately determine how it affected the election results.

Even if a constitutional amendment that included the most democratic regulations took place using the methods and under the kind of political atmosphere described above, its legitimacy and legality would still be subject to controversy. However, in this specific Turkey example, the constitutional amendment directly damaged the separation of powers and changed the form of the government; hence even more care and attention are required to conduct these discussions.

The referendum only amended eighteen articles, some of which had minimal impact. However, some amendments led to a radical change in the government of Turkey. For example, the impartiality requirement for the president previously regulated under Article 101 was excluded from the Constitution. The president of the Republic no longer has to sever their relations with their party after being elected. Therefore, it was not surprising to see President Recep Tayyip Erdogan rejoin his Justice and Development Party (AKP) right after this amendment, after which he was elected to be the party chair. Before this amendment, the president was already known to violate his impartiality obligation under the Constitution on many occasions. For instance, on June 7, 2015, the president had organized election rallies in favor of AKP before the parliamentary elections. This way, the relevant amendment legalized the president's violations of the Constitution.

However, the most significant amendment was regarding the appointment of members of Council of Judges and Prosecutors (HSK), which implies a direct interference to the judicial mechanism by the executive. The number of full members of the council was decreased to thirteen from the previous twenty-two. Before the amendment, the president could appoint four out of the twenty-two members (excluding the minister of justice and the undersecretary). The other members of the council were appointed by different organizations in the judicial mechanism. After the amendment, the structure of the council was determined as follows: two out of the thirteen members will be the minister of justice and undersecretary to the minister of justice, four members will be directly appointed by the president and the remaining members will be appointed by the parliament. Realizing that the minister of justice and the president belong to the same political party, this regulation may mean that six members out of thirteen will be appointed directly by the ruling party. Considering the ruling party also holds an overwhelming majority of the seats in the parliament which will be appointing the remaining seven members, the council of judges and prosecutors has become an organization that is almost fully appointed by the ruling party. Since the council's duties include essential procedures such as admission, appointment, transfer, promotion, suspension, and dismissal of judges and prosecutors, determining the members of this council is almost equal to determining all matters regarding the judicial process. Furthermore, the council decisions are final except for the cases of discharge from the profession. In short, the amendments tie the appointment of the judicial mechanism to the executive and legislature, and since the ruling party holds the majority of the legislative power, the resulting council's independence is controversial.

Of course, these two examples are not the only changes. The new constitution allows the president to declare SoE and issue emergency decrees. Additionally, on the condition that presidential election is also renewed, powers such as the authority to renew parliamentary elections and budget preparation were also transferred to the president. Under these circumstances, we cannot say Turkey established a conventional presidential system; however, the parliament has been significantly neutralized while the president has been given extensive authority that could cover the scope of the legislature and determine the judicial mechanism. It can be argued that Turkey has established a regime that does not confirm with the fundamental principles of the separation of powers. There is practically no answer on how to limit the authority of the single person who holds all the powers, or more importantly how to supervise their actions.

THE INQUIRY COMMISSION ON THE SOE MEASURES AS A MECHANISM THAT TOOK OVER JUDICIAL POWER

In order to better understand the state of Turkish judiciary and to comprehend the consequences of diverging from separation of powers, one should mention the Inquiry Commission on the SoE Measures (the Commission).

On October 5, 2018, the Commission disclosed that a total of 125,678 people had been dismissed from public service during the SoE as per decree laws. The affected parties were not allowed the right of defense during the conduct of these actions. The justification stated for the dismissal or closure decisions (regarding the person or institution) is as follows: "membership, connection, affiliation, cooperation or contact with terrorist organizations or structures/entities or groups established by the National Security Council as engaging in activities against the national security of the State."[29]

This created a deepening judiciary review crisis from the first day of conducting these decisions. Administrative courts rejected the applications regarding the dismissal decisions since these were based on decrees with force of law which are within the scope of legislative acts, so there was no administrative action for the court to review. The Court of State (*Danıştay*), which is the higher administrative court, also rejected all applications based on lack of jurisdiction and further stated that the administrative courts should have jurisdiction over these disputes. As a result, thousands of citizens directly affected by the consequences of the decrees were left with no domestic remedies against these unilateral decisions. During this period, there was an influx of applications to the constitutional court and European Court of Human Rights (ECtHR); however, both courts rejected the applications because domestic remedies were not exhausted.

Due to decree laws causing very serious cases of unjust treatment, along with the legal ambiguity regarding the judicial remedy, both Council of Europe and Venice Commission have asked the government to take the necessary steps and advised Turkey to set up a special committee that could examine the dismissal decisions in particular. However, in the same assessment Venice Commission underlined that these steps should be taken "without prejudice to the power of the Constitutional Court to assess the constitutionality of the emergency decree laws." Following these discussions, Decree no. KHK/685 titled "Law On Establishment Of The Inquiry Commission On The State Of Emergency Measures" was published on January 23, 2017.[30] The Commission's scope of duty is limited to individuals dismissed from public service, students expelled, and institutions shut down per the decree laws.

The Commission has quite a unique structure and, as the name implies, is not designed to be a judicial mechanism but was rather planned as an administrative remedy and preliminary examination mechanism. Nevertheless, to carry out its duty, the Commission must examine whether the applicant has any relation or contact with a terrorist organization and then accept or reject their request for reinstatement. In other words, even though the Commission is only a preliminary assessment step and not a judicial unit, it is equipped with the authority (and duty) to make an evaluation regarding criminal law.[31]

This naturally raises an important question on the independence and impartiality of the Commission. Although some jurists have argued that as an administrative mechanism, independence, and impartiality is not a necessity, the Commission's function makes this subject worthwhile to discuss.[32]

In fact, the Venice Commission had specially emphasized the independency and impartiality criteria as they were advising Turkish government to set up a Commission: "This body should be independent, impartial and be given sufficient powers to restore the *status quo ante*, and/or, where appropriate, to provide adequate compensation. The law should enable for subsequent judicial review of decisions of this ad hoc body."

The decree that established the commission was the first sign that this structure would not be in conformity with the advice of Venice Commission. Article 1/2 regulates the composition of the Commission and provides that out of the seven members, three will be appointed by the prime minister, one by the minister of justice, one by minister of internal affairs, and the remaining two by council of judges and prosecutors. In other words, the institutions that appoint the members of the Commission are the same institutions which issue the decree laws that the Commission will be examining.[33] The regulation regarding the guarantees and rights of members of the Commission is another question mark.[34] According to Article 4 of the decree, members of the Commission can only be relieved from duty if there is an administrative investigation being initiated or permitted by the prime ministry on the grounds that they have a connection with a terrorist organization or similar structures. Therefore, it is doubtful whether the members have secure positions in the conventional sense or not.

The Commission started accepting applications six months after the day its foundation decree was published in the Official Gazette. Frankly, this means that public officials dismissed from duty right after the SoE declaration were completely deprived of a judicial remedy for nearly an entire year. On top of that, the 2020 Activity Report published on February 5, 2021, leaves no doubt that the Commission was not an efficient measure. The reports include the following information:

> The number of the applications filed before the Commission is 126,630 as of 31 December 2020. Regarding the number of the decisions (a total of 112,310 applications, 13,170 of which are acceptance decisions and 99,140 of which are rejection decisions) issued as of 31 December 2020 the number of the pending applications is 14,320.[35]

As the numbers reveal, by October, 28, 2021 the Commission has only approved 11.87 percent of the applications. The data should be interpreted as follows: despite the SoE being lifted, 78.29 percent of the people dismissed in that period are continuing the legal process before first- and second-degree administrative courts today, and 11.30 percent still does not have access to the judicial remedy. After seeing this mechanism in practice for three years, it would be safe to say the Commission has proved ineffective and only delays the judicial remedy applications, while deepening the aggrievement in the current condition.

CONCLUSION

In its opinion entitled "The Rule of Law Checklist" dated March 16, 2016, the Venice Commission describes the fundamental characteristic of a state governed by rule of law as follows: "The notion of the Rule of Law requires a system of certain and foreseeable law, where everyone has the right to be treated by all decision-makers with dignity, equality, and rationality and in accordance with the laws, and to have the opportunity to challenge decisions before independent and impartial courts through fair procedures."[36]

The same document expresses that a consensus on the essential aspects of rule of law could be reached, stressing that these principles are not just formal but substantive and material as well:

> These core elements are: (1) Legality, including a transparent, accountable, and democratic process for enacting law; (2) Legal certainty; (3) Prohibition of arbitrariness; (4) Access to justice before independent and impartial courts, including judicial review of administrative acts; (5) Respect for human rights; and (6) Non-discrimination and equality before the law.[37]

As outlined briefly above, it is not possible to claim that these elements were inherent properties of Turkish legal system during or after the SoE. Both the legal system that was altered by the decree laws which were enacted and the constitutional amendment that took place during the SoE reveal that it is not possible to speak of a democratic lawmaking process. Also, there are serious ongoing issues regarding access to justice and accountability, as we can see from the lack of judicial review against these decrees.

The recently enacted Law to Suppress Financing of Weapons of Mass Destruction Proliferation[38] clearly shows that the lawmaking style of passing omnibus bills is hindering the principle of transparency. A law that should only have been regarding the spread of weapons of mass destruction, as its name suggests, includes highly anti-democratic regulations regarding the nongovernmental organizations' fields of work. Moreover, the same law amends Law on Associations, creating a legal gateway that enables immediate closure of the NGOs operating in Turkey even if they are not established or based in Turkey.

Legal certainty and prohibition of arbitrariness are two of Turkey's most crucial issues. Part of the problem is caused by the uncertainty regarding legal regulations on specific crimes. Especially Article 220/6-7 and Article 314 of Turkish Penal Code (TPC) are the prime examples of how legal uncertainty reflects on criminal proceedings, especially considering how wide their scope of application is. Although in many judgments, ECtHR has expressed that these articles violate the legal certainty principle, we observe that the practice is getting worse rather than trying to fix this problem, which is a hindrance to the rule of law. For example, in a judgment (no: 41226/09) regarding TPC 220/6, ECtHR provides the following statements:

> As to the foreseeability requirement, the Court notes at the outset that the text of Article 220 § 6 of the Criminal Code tied the status of membership of an illegal organization to the mere fact of a person having acted "on behalf" of that organization, without the prosecution having to prove the material elements of actual membership. Furthermore, the wording of Article 220 § 6 of the Criminal Code did not itself define the meaning of the expression "on behalf of an illegal organization."[39]

An important criterion of legal certainty and prohibition of arbitrariness is foreseeability. As it is mentioned in *Demirtaş v. Turkey*[40] judgment according to the ECtHR:

> One of the requirements flowing from the expression "prescribed by law" is foreseeability. In the Court's view, a norm cannot be regarded as a "law" within the meaning of Article 10 § 2 of the Convention unless it is formulated with sufficient precision to enable people to regulate their conduct; they must be able—if need be with appropriate advice—to foresee, to a degree that is reasonable in the circumstances, the consequences which a given action may entail.[41]

In the same judgment, ECtHR defines foreseeability as "quality of the law implies that domestic law must be sufficiently foreseeable in its terms to give individuals an adequate indication as to the circumstances in which and the conditions on which the authorities are entitled to resort to measures affecting their rights under the Convention."[42]

Besides these elements, the principle of legal certainty and prohibition of arbitration also show that a legal order, which prevents arbitrary interference with the rights and does not protect expansion of crimes by comparison or interpretation, is also fundamental to rule of law. In this context, when we examine the increasing trend of arrests in Turkey, and the crime types used as a premise for the arrest warrants, a deep crisis is revealed. At the beginning of 2021, many of the students who attended the peaceful protests as a reaction to the president appointing a rector to Boğaziçi University from outside the institution were arrested on charges of violating the Law on Meetings and Demonstrations. Likewise, some citizens have been arrested for defending LGBTIQ+ rights (Lesbian, Gay, Bisexual, Trans, Intersex and Queer) on social media on the grounds of provoking the public to hatred and hostility. However, Article 100/3 of Turkish Code of Criminal Procedure provides a *numerus clausus* list of the crimes that are grounds for arrest, and the reasons included in these examples are light crimes that are not included in this provision.

In order to comprehend the severity of the situation, we must mention mass prosecution of lawyers in Turkey as well. Hundreds of lawyers in Turkey are in pretrial detention because of their professional activities. The trial of Progressive Lawyers Association (ÇHD), which is being closely followed by the international law community and has been subject to many legal opinions and reports,[43] is only one example of an obvious violation of the right to a fair trial and arbitrariness. The report prepared by various legal institutions, bar associations, and the Council of Bars and Law Societies of Europe contains multiple instances of violation of the right to a fair trial including double jeopardy, equality of arms principle, and right of defense. Many of the lawyers that are on trial have been on remand for over three years, with their applications waiting for constitutional court examination. Some of these lawyers had to leave the country in fear of arbitrary arrest and detention. Two of the lawyers on trial, Ebru Timtik and Aytaç Ünsal, after exhausting all legal remedies available, went on a hunger strike in January 2020. They wanted to publicize the increasing violations of the right to a fair trial, hoping to get the government to take concrete steps. Despite the persistent call for action by international law community, Turkish government did nothing to address this situation and consequently Ebru Timtik, a young lawyer, lost her life after months of hunger strike. Soon after Timtik's death, Aytaç Ünsal was temporarily discharged by the Court of Cassation due to health problems, and he ended the hunger strike after his release. However, he was rearrested while undergoing treatment and is still in prison today, unable to access his doctors due to pandemic measures.

Freedom of expression has been completely abolished along with its variations under special protection, thus creating a vicious cycle within the social sphere. There are lawyers facing trials and risk of imprisonment because of a petition for review they wrote or a defense speech they gave in the courtroom. The judicial environment is not equipped to put a stop to these practices within legal framework. As with the ÇHD example above, the judges who do not meet the expectations of the government regarding cases of political importance may be exiled to various places within Turkey. The extensive censorship practice that withholds this information from the public only intensifies the problem. Journalists face long-term convictions and heavy financial consequences for trying to ignore the censorship and do their jobs.

The academia is also in a miserable state. Universities have lost their autonomous structure and the scientific output has been severely interrupted because of the political conditions directly interfering with academic freedom and the dismissals during the SoE which affected 6,055 academics. Turkish prisons might have the highest intellectual density in the world: journalists, members of the parliament, over 50,000 students, lawyers, judges, and prosecutors are currently behind bars.

The pattern ECtHR has underlined in the *Demirtas v. Turkey* decision that was previously mentioned summarizes of Turkey's status regarding the rule of law:

> The Court attaches considerable weight to the observations of the intervening third parties, and in particular the Commissioner for Human Rights, who stated that national laws were increasingly being used to silence dissenting voices. The Court therefore considers that the decisions on the applicant's initial and continued pretrial detention are not an isolated example. On the contrary, they seem to follow a certain pattern.[44]

If Turkey cannot change this pattern even ECtHR spotted, it will not be possible to speak of a state governed by the rule of law. Respectively, this would mean that the futures of large segments of the society will be left to arbitrariness with no legal safeguards. Considering the current circumstances of academia and the education system, it is possible to predict that the present damage will only deepen at this rate, and for many years to come, we will continue to feel the traces and repercussions of this damage. In the light of above assessments and information, one must break free from the illusion that Turkey is governed by rule of law. Over the years, Turkey has lost the fundamental characteristics of a democracy upholding the rule of law. Today what we need is to be able to discuss how to initiate the inevitable rebuilding process to ensure Turkey is governed by rule of law again.

NOTES

1. "Turkey: Normalizing the State of Emergency," *Human Rights Watch*, accessed February 20, 2017, https://bit.ly/3opKqyx.

2. Zeynep Altiok, "Ohal Bilancosu Hak Ihlalleri Raporu," [Reports on State of Emergency Related Violations], *Republican People`s Party,* accessed February 20, 2021, https://bit.ly/2QwgRim.

3. "Justice Suspended: Access to Justice and the State of Emergency in Turkey," 2018, *International Commission of Jurists*, accessed February 20, 2021, https://bit.ly/2Qwfbp4.

4. "Lawyers on Trial: Abusive Prosecutions and Erosion of Fair Trial Rights in Turkey," *Human Rights Watch*, accessed February 20, 2021, https://bit.ly/3orMqGt.

5. Human Rights Watch, "Lawyers on Trial."

6. "The Inquiry Commission on the State of Emergency Measures, The Inquiry Commission on the State of Emergency Measures Activity Report 2018," The Inquiry Commission on the State of Emergency, accessed February 20, 2021, https://bit.ly/2SXIYb4.

7. Constitution of the Republic of Turkey, § 120, repealed on April 16, 2017; Act No. 6771.

8. Constitution of the Republic of Turkey, § 15, amended on April 16, 2017; Act No. 6771.

9. Constitution of the Republic of Turkey, § 121, repealed on April 16, 2017; Act No. 6771.

10. Venice Commission, Opinion No: 865/2016 and Opinion No: 872/2016.

11. Dincer Demirkent, Kerem Altiparmak, and Murat Sevinc, "Atipik KHK'ler ve Daimi Hukuksuzluk: Artik Yasalari Idare mi Iptal Edecek," [Atypical KHKs and Permanent: Will the administrative cancel the laws yet?], *Insan Haklari Ortak Platformu,* accessed February 27, 2021. https://bit.ly/3yfaBg1.

12. The Turkish Constitutional Court Judgment, October 12, 2016, Case No. 2016/166, Decision No. 2016/159.

13. Constitution of the Republic of Turkey, § 148, amended on September 12, 2010; Act No. 5982, and on April 16, 2017; Act No. 6771.

14. The Turkish Constitutional Court Judgment, January 10, 1991, Case No. 1990/25, Decision No. 1991/1.

15. Şerife Ceren Uysal, "Constitutional Amendments in Turkey: The Problem of Legitimacy and the Constitutional Dictatorship," *Juridikum* 03/2017 (2017): 393–404.

16. Uysal, "Constitutional Amendments," 402–3.

17. Venice Commission, Study no. 469 / 2008: 4.

18. Venice Commission, Study no. 469 / 2008: 40.

19. Venice Commission, Study no. 469 / 2008: 5.

20. Serdar Tekin, "Üniversitenin Olaganüstü Hali: Akademik Ortamin Tahribati Üzerine Bir Inceleme," [State of Emergency of University: A Review of the Destruction of the Academic Environment] *Türkiye Insan Haklari Vakfi* [Turkey's Human Rights Foundation], accessed March 3, 2021, https://bit.ly/3va0MxC.

21. "Belediyelerdeki Kayyum Sistemi ve Mevcut Durum Raporu," [Trustee System in the Municaplities and Report on the Current Situation], *Republic of Turkey Ministry of Interior*, accessed March 3, 2021, https://bit.ly/3uXYwcZ.

22. "BM İnsan Hakları Komiseri: Toplu gözaltı, ihraç ve OHAL'in uzatılmasından kaygılıyız" [The Un Human Rights Commissioner: We are concerned about mass detention, dismissals and extension of the State of Emergency], accessed March 3, 2021, https://bbc.in/2RXoxuh.

23. Uysal, "Constitutional Amendments," 402–3.
24. "Republic of Turkey Ministry of Justice, Press Statement," accessed March 5, 2021, https://bit.ly/2RiwZEB.
25. Uysal, "Constitutional Amendments," 401.
26. "International Referendum Observation Mission Republic of Turkey, Constitutional Referendum Statement of Preliminary Findings and Conclusions," *OSCE*, accessed March 5, 2021, https://bit.ly/3fuEqQO.
27. OSCE, "Preliminary Findings."
28. Supreme Electoral Council, Decision No: 560, Date: 16.04.2017.
29. "The Inquiry Commission on the State of Emergency Measures, The Inquiry Commission on the State of Emergency Measures Activity Report 2020," *The Inquiry Commission on the State of Emergency*, accessed February 20, 2021, https://bit.ly/3u19uwW.
30. Law On Establishment Of The Inquiry Commission On The State Of Emergency Measures, Decree no. KHK/685, 23 January 2017.
31. Kerem Altiparmak, "Is the State of Emergency Inquiry Commission, Established by Emergency Decree 685, an Effective Remedy?," *Human Rights Joint Platform*, accessed March 6, 2021, https://bit.ly/2SQdCTy.
32. Philip Leach, Sanya Karakas, and Serife Ceren Uysal, "Access to Justice in Turkey? A Review of the State of Emergency Inquiry Commission," *Turkey Litigation Support Project,* accessed March 6, 2021, https://bit.ly/3hufls6.
33. Leach, Karakas, Uysal, "Access to Justice."
34. Altiparmak, "Effective Remedy?".
35. The Inquiry Commission, Activity Report 2020.
36. Venice Commission, Study no. 711/2013: 15.
37. Venice Commission, Study no. 711/2013: 18.
38. Republic of Turkey, Law No. 7262 on the Suppression of the Financing of Weapons of Mass Destruction Proliferation.
39. ECtHR, Işırık v. Turkey, Application No: 41226/09, 14.11.2017.
40. ECtHR, *Demirtaş v. Turkey*, Application No: 14305/17, 22.12.2020.
41. ECtHR, No: 14305/17.
42. ECtHR, No: 14305/17.
43. "Fact-finding mission on CHD's trials Breach of Fair Trial, Independence of the Judiciary and Principles on the Role of Lawyers," accessed March 6, 2021, https://bit.ly/2RvtD0O.
44. ECtHR, No: 14305/17.

BIBLIOGRAPHY

Altiok, Zeynep. "Ohal Bilancosu Hak Ihlalleri Raporu," [Reports on State of Emergency Related Violations], *Republican People's Party,* accessed February 20, 2021, https://bit.ly/2QwgRim.

Altiparmak, Kerem., Dincer Demirkent, and Murat Sevinc, "Atipik KHK'ler ve Daimi Hukuksuzluk: Artik Yasalari Idare mi Iptal Edecek," [Atypical KHKs and

Permanent: Will the administrative cancel the laws yet?], *Insan Haklari Ortak Platformu,* accessed February 27, 2021. https://bit.ly/3yfaBg1.

Altiparmak, Kerem. "Is the State of Emergency Inquiry Commission, Established by Emergency Decree 685, an Effective Remedy?," *Human Rights Joint Platform,* accessed March 6, 2021, https://bit.ly/2SQdCTy.

"Belediyelerdeki Kayyum Sistemi ve Mevcut Durum Raporu," [Trustee System in the Municaplities and Report on the Current Situation], Republic of Turkey Ministry of Interior, accessed March 3, 2021, https://bit.ly/3uXYwcZ.

"BM İnsan Hakları Komiseri: Toplu gözaltı, ihraç ve OHAL'in uzatılmasından kaygılıyız" [The Un Human Rights Commissioner: We are concerned about mass detention, dismissals and extension of the State of Emergency], accessed March 3, 2021, https://bbc.in/2RXoxuh.

Constitutional Court Judgment, January 10, 1991, Case No. 1990/25, Decision No. 1991/1.

Constitutional Court Judgment, October 12, 2016, Case No. 2016/166 Decision No. 2016/159.

Constitution of the Republic of Turkey, § 120, repealed on April 16, 2017; Act No. 6771.

Constitution of the Republic of Turkey, § 15, amended on April 16, 2017; Act No. 6771.

Constitution of the Republic of Turkey, § 121, repealed on April 16, 2017; Act No. 6771.

Constitution of the Republic of Turkey, § 148, amended on September 12, 2010; Act No. 5982, and on April 16, 2017; Act No. 6771.

ECtHR, Işırık v. Turkey, Application No: 41226/09, 14.11.2017.

"Fact-finding mission on CHD's trials Breach of Fair Trial, Independence of the Judiciary and Principles on the Role of Lawyers," accessed March 6, 2021, https://bit.ly/2RvtD0O.

"International Referendum Observation Mission Republic of Turkey, Constitutional Referendum Statement of Preliminary Findings and Conclusions," *OSCE*, accessed March 5, 2021, https://bit.ly/3fuEqQO.

"Justice Suspended: Access to Justice and the State of Emergency in Turkey," 2018, International Commission of Jurists, accessed February 20, 2021, https://bit.ly/2Qwfbp4.

Karakas, Sanya., Leach, Philip, and Serife Ceren Uysal, "Access to Justice in Turkey? A Review of the State of Emergency Inquiry Commission," *Turkey Litigation Support Project,* accessed March 6, 2021, https://bit.ly/3hufls6.

"Lawyers on Trial: Abusive Prosecutions and Erosion of Fair Trial Rights in Turkey," *Human Rights Watch*, accessed February 20, 2021, https://bit.ly/3orMqGt.

Republic of Turkey, Law No. 7262 on the Suppression of the Financing of Weapons of Mass Destruction Proliferation.

"Republic of Turkey Ministry of Justice, Press Statement," accessed March 5, 2021, https://bit.ly/2RiwZEB.

Supreme Electoral Council, Decision No: 560, Date: 16.04.2017.

"The Inquiry Commission on the State of Emergency Measures, The Inquiry Commission on the State of Emergency Measures Activity Report 2018," *The Inquiry Commission on the State of Emergency*, accessed February 20, 2021, https://bit.ly/2SXIYb4.

"The Inquiry Commission on the State of Emergency Measures, The Inquiry Commission on the State of Emergency Measures Activity Report 2020," *The Inquiry Commission on the State of Emergency*, accessed February 20, 2021, https://bit.ly/3u19uwW.

Tekin, Serdar. "Üniversitenin Olaganüstü Hali: Akademik Ortamin Tahribati Üzerine Bir Inceleme," [State of Emergency of University: A Review of the Destruction of the Academic Environment] *Türkiye Insan Haklari Vakfi* [Turkey's Human Rights Foundation], accessed March 3, 2021, https://bit.ly/3va0MxC.

"Turkey: Normalizing the State of Emergency," *Human Rights Watch*, accessed February 20, 2017, https://bit.ly/3opKqyx.

Turkish Code of Criminal Procedure, § 100/3.

Uysal, Serife Ceren. "Constitutional Amendments in Turkey: The Problem of Legitimacy and the Constitutional Dictatorship," *Juridikum* 03 (2017): 393–404.

Venice Commission, Opinion No: 865/2016.

Venice Commission, Opinion No: 872/2016.

Venice Commission, Study No. 469 / 2008: 4.

Venice Commission, Study No. 469 / 2008: 5.

Venice Commission, Study No. 469 / 2008: 40.

Venice Commission, Study No. 711/2013: 15.

Venice Commission, Study No. 711/2013: 18.

Chapter 7

Power Politics versus the Rule of Law in Hungary

A Case Study

Bernadette Somody

INTRODUCTION

Constitutionalism means limited public power in order to secure citizens' freedom.[1] Judiciary, universities, media—all of them, even if in different roles and ways, serve as the guarantee of freedom. Thus, their independent or autonomous status is crucial for constitutionalism. The ideas of constitutionalism—the rule of law, democracy, fundamental rights—are embodied in the Constitution that is a political but also a legally binding document limiting the government.[2]

In Hungary, however, more than a decade ago, the government gained a two-thirds majority in the parliament; apart from a short period, it has managed to keep it since the elections of 2010. Having a supermajority in the Hungarian Parliament puts the government in an extraordinary position where it can shape even the constitutional limitations of its own operation. The qualified majority lost its function as the protector of the minority interests against the governing majority's unilateral decisions. The latter is able to amend the Constitution and even to pass a new one[3] as it happened in 2011—the new Fundamental Law of Hungary entered into force in 2012. The two-thirds majority is sufficient to pass and amend so-called cardinal acts,[4] among others the ones on judiciary and the Constitutional Court as well as on the freedom of the press and the media. Since 2010, the governing majority has been in the position to elect the members and the president of the Constitutional Court, the chief justice of the Supreme Court (the president of the Curia) and the head of the judicial administration (the president of the National Office for the Judiciary).[5] The legal safeguards of the Constitution, and furthermore, the content of the Constitution (Fundamental Law) itself, became up to the government. The Constitution shifted from the limit on everyday party politics to its instrument.[6]

For reasons of length constraints, I cannot offer a comprehensive picture about the status of constitutionalism and the rule of law in Hungary nor the previous process that led to it,[7] not even in regard to only the judiciary, universities or the media. Instead, I will highlight some indicators from the field of constitutional law and the contrast between the constitutional situation before and after 2010.

JUDICIAL INDEPENDENCE

Judiciary's role in securing freedom is prominent since it has to guarantee the autonomy of universities and the freedom of media as well. Universities are the safeguard of freedom of science and education; there is no democracy without free media. Judiciary is intended to guarantee the freedom of speech, press, education and science, and also the status of the entities that make up the institutional framework of exercising these rights. These freedoms, along with other fundamental rights, are recognized in constitutions. Constitutions are legally binding documents that have supremacy in the legal system. The essence of the constitutional recognition of rights and freedoms is giving them a legal nature, in other words, legal enforceability, namely before courts.[8]

Courts should have independent status; in lack of independence, they cannot perform their constitutional function. Obviously, one cannot control the other, that is, the judiciary cannot control the government if the former is dependent on the latter. The Hungarian Constitutional Court (HCC) stated the importance of judicial independence at the very beginning of its operation. The text of the previous Constitution, adopted in 1989 and being in force until 2011, did not contain the principle of the division of powers;[9] however, according to the settled caselaw of the HCC, it derives from the rule of law enshrined in the Constitution. The constitutional content of the division of powers reflects the form of government of Hungary, where the government depends on the parliament's political confidence. The main characteristic of parliamentary systems is the political unity between the executive and the majority in the legislature. However, the concentration of powers does not require the strict separation of the executive and the legislature; their political link can be balanced by control institutions granted with independent status. In the concept of the division of powers, the HCC distinguished between political and neutral branches of power. While the legislature and the executive are of political nature since they are driven by the political will of the majority, the judiciary and the Constitutional Court are constant and neutral, and they should be separated from the political influence of the majority. For the HCC, the most crucial problem of the division of powers was the intervention of political branches into the operation of the neutral ones. The constitutional guarantees have to focus on the independence of the judiciary, including the ordinary courts and the Constitutional Court.[10]

Right from the government getting supermajority in parliament in 2010, the main concerns surrounded the status and competences of the Constitutional Court and the independence of ordinary courts. By 2015, even according to moderate critics, the Constitutional Court was alive but severely impaired.[11] The crucial factor was the composition of the Constitutional Court. Already in 2010, the two-third governing majority amended the Constitution and changed the composition of the parliamentary committee responsible for the nomination of the justices of the Constitutional Court who are elected by the mentioned qualified majority. Until 2010, the candidates were nominated by a parliamentary committee in which each faction had one representative; after that, the committee's composition reflected the proportions of the parliamentary groups. While the previous manner of nomination required a compromise between the ruling parties and the opposition, according to the new regulation, the governing majority could solely nominate and elect its own people to the Constitutional Court. Some months later, the supermajority applied the technique of "court packing," and increased the number of justices from eleven to fifteen which enabled them to elect five new judges. As Zoltán Szente's empirical research proved in 2016, there is an extremely strong correlation between the voting behavior of the judges and the political standpoints of their nominating parties; the judges support the political parties that nominated them. He also pointed out that the nine new judges elected since 2010, a solid majority in the Constitutional Court by 2016, was chosen by the governing majority.[12]

As for the ordinary courts, the judicial administration proved to be the key question.[13] In 2012, the government introduced a new model of court administration. As the Venice Commission emphasized, the Hungarian model, that is a unique system of judicial administration, which exists in no other European country, threatened the independence of the judiciary.[14] In response to the early criticisms, the Hungarian government amended certain elements of the regulation; however, the essence of the system of the administration of courts (i.e., the concentration of powers in the hands of one person, the president of the National Office for the Judiciary, who is the head of the judicial administration) has remained the same. Many legal scholars argue that the conceptual problems have not been eliminated.[15]

The new model of judicial administration affected the mandate of the chief justice, the court executives in office, and the appointment of judges.[16] The president of the National Office for the judiciary is elected by a supermajority in the parliament; thus, in 2011, the support of the governing parties was sufficient for her appointment. At the same time, in a plea for the transformation of the system of judicial administration and the separation of the office of the head of central administration and that of the chief justice, the six-year mandate of the former president of the Supreme Court was prematurely ended after two years. The measure implemented by the new Fundamental Law of Hungary and its transitional provisions generated serious constitutional criticism at both the national and European levels since it violated the guarantee of security of tenure, which is a key element of the judiciary's independence.[17] In 2014, the European Court of Human Rights (ECtHR) concluded that there had been a violation of the European Convention on Human Rights. The case was referred to the Grand Chamber, which also held that Hungary violated the right of access to a court and the freedom of expression of the former president of the Hungarian Supreme Court. The Strasbourg Court found that the early removal of the former president of the Supreme Court had been due to his publicly expressed criticism of the government policy on judicial reform when he held the said position, underlining that the fear of sanction, such as losing judicial office, could have a "chilling effect" on the exercise of freedom of expression and risked discouraging judges from making critical remarks about public institutions or policies. The ECtHR also found that the chief justice's access to the court had been impeded, not by express legislative exclusion but by the fact that the premature termination of his mandate had been written into the new Hungarian Constitution (the Fundamental Law of Hungary) itself and was, therefore, not subject to any form of judicial review.[18]

The court administration was also significantly influenced by the introduction of a new mandatory retirement age for judges, lowered by the Fundamental Law of Hungary from 70 to 62 years effective January 1, 2012. In 2012, this measure affected the most senior 10 percent of the judiciary (over 270 out of approximately 2,900 judges), mostly judges holding higher judicial positions, including several court executives. The main criticism was that this way, many judicial leaders could be replaced with judges appointed by the new court administrative leadership. The rapid change in court executives served the government's political interests and threatened the judiciary's independence.[19]

In July 2012, the Constitutional Court of Hungary found that the related provisions of the cardinal act on the legal status of judges were unconstitutional and, therefore, annulled them with a retroactive force, taking effect on January 1, 2012.[20] Despite the retroactive annulment, the decision of the Constitutional Court did not form sufficient legal grounds for the direct reinstitution of the terminated service relationships of the discharged judges.[21]

In November 2012, the European Court of Justice ruled that the forced early retirement of judges, although not for reasons relating to the judiciary's independence, was incompatible with EU law.[22] In 2013, an amendment to the regulation on the judiciary permitted the previously retired judges to return to work; however, few returned to their original administrative positions. The judges who were already forced to retire could apply to be reinstated to their normal judicial service. However, former court executives could not be reinstated to their previous positions unless the positions had not been filled in the meantime. Moreover, those who did not request reinstatement were entitled to lump-sum compensation, and many chose this option. All in all, despite the decisions of the national and the European forums, the result was the replacement of the majority of former court executives.

The new appointment procedure for judges also raised concerns. According to the Fundamental Law, judges are appointed by the president of the Republic. The proposal for appointment, on the grounds of inviting applications for vacant judge positions, falls under the competence of the president of the National Office for the Judiciary (NOJ). This proved to be one of the main problematic powers of the position because the president of the NOJ was not bound by the proposal of the council of judges who were assessing applications for judicial positions and interviewing applicants. The relevant act[23] stated that the president of the NOJ might decide to deviate from the shortlist and propose the second or the third candidate on the list to fill the post. Since the act stipulated no conditions or criteria under which the president of the NOJ was allowed to deviate from the order of the shortlist, this seemed to be a full discretionary power of the president of the NOJ, which was also criticized by the Venice Commission.[24]

In 2012, the government amended the regulation that assigned a decisive role to the National Council of Justice (NCJ), a body of judicial self-government consisting of judges elected by their peers. According to the new rules, the NCJ is granted the right to veto the decision of the president of the NOJ if he or she intends to hire the applicant ranked second or third for the position in question. On the other hand, the president of the NOJ is entitled to declare the call for applications unsuccessful (e.g., when he or she changes the ranking, but it is not approved by the NCJ). The president of the NOJ is not obliged to provide reasons for doing so. This way, he or she can prevent the first-ranked candidate from being appointed.[25]

The governing majority's pressure on the independence of the judiciary has never lessened. In 2018, after securing its two-thirds majority in the parliament in the general parliamentary elections for the third time, the governing majority passed the Seventh Amendment to the Fundamental Law of Hungary. This constitutional amendment established the High Administrative Court, which had significance from the perspective of judicial independence since it transferred administrative justice from the ordinary judiciary to special courts administered partly by the minister of justice. According to the relevant act, the administration of the administrative courts would have been separated from ordinary administration performed by the president of the NOJ, and the minister of justice, so the executive power would have been granted strong administrative powers. He or she would have had competences in the appointment and removal of judges, appointed court executives and decided budgetary questions.[26] However, the separate administrative courts remained only in theory since a year later, the Eighth Amendment to the Fundamental Law canceled its establishment. Nevertheless, the reorganization of the administrative justice led to the automatic termination of the office of the heads of former first instance administrative courts. Despite the fact that in 2019, the government, urged by the European Union and other international institutions, suspended, and later canceled, the introduction of the separate administrative court system, the constitutional court[27] stated the constitutionality of the ministerial administration. It turned down the petition of opposition members of parliament claiming the violation of judicial independence.[28]

One of the most recent developments is the annulment of the incompatibility between the appointment for being a judge and a member of the Constitutional Court. On the one hand, an ordinary court judge can become a member of the Constitutional Court for the time of their mandate and then return to the judiciary. On the other hand, a member of the Constitutional Court is entitled to be appointed as an ordinary court judge upon their request; after the termination of their mandate, they automatically become judges at the Curia (the Supreme Court). The latter does not require the otherwise obligatory application procedure. In 2020, eight members of the Constitutional Court were appointed as judges, more of them without any judicial experience, including the one who was elected to the new president of the Curia some months later. His election as the chief justice needed the application of another recent piece of legislation, according to which the experience gained as a Constitutional Court judge should be calculated as an ordinary court judge's service relationship.

During the past decade, judicial independence has been under continuous political attacks. The means of the latter were rather simple and obvious. The government majority has had the two-thirds majority since 2010, which is sufficient to amend the Fundamental Law, to pass cardinal acts and this way to reorganize the structure of the institutions, to change the composition of the Constitutional Court or the system of court administration. This majority is also enough to elect persons to offices intended to be independent, and this way to directly influence who are the people who perform the control over the government.

THE FREEDOM OF THE MEDIA

The freedom of the media and the pluralistic media system is the essential guarantee of democracy. As the HCC[29] stated already in the early 1990s, the purpose of the constitutional freedom of the press and the media regulation is to develop and maintain democratic public opinion about public affairs. In public discourse, there is a place for all kinds of opinions regardless of their value and truth content; it is possible to disclose and access all relevant information and opinions.[30]

The media also was among the first targets of the governing majority after 2010. The new media regulation was adopted already in 2010, before the adoption of the new Fundamental Law and the related new cardinal acts. As Gábor Polyák emphasized after the first years of the new media regulation, it entailed risks to the freedom of the media. The risks were mainly not of a direct hindrance on the operation of the media but the chilling effect on editorial offices and the manipulation of citizens with one-sided information.[31]

The realization of the risks strongly depends on the independence of institutions responsible for overseeing private and public media[32] and the courts securing constitutional protection of media freedom. The Constitutional Court—getting more and more influenced by the government—had a decisive role in shaping the content of the freedom of the press in a restrictive way.[33] The Media Council, that can influence the media market through its competences related to the frequency tenders and the approval of media market mergers, should be an independent body within the National Media and Infocommunications Authority.[34] However, the supermajority of the ruling party in the parliament was sufficient to pass and amend the media laws which also secures that the ruling-party delegates should hold a majority in the Media Council under all kinds of circumstances.[35] Actually, since 2010, the Media Council has consisted of members nominated by the ruling parties. As a result of the new media laws, the public media system became a highly centralized system where there is space for political influence on the content of public media itself.[36] At the same time, business people with strong political ties own the market leaders of all media sectors, and due to the so-called soft censorship, critical opinions, and independent media outlets are disappearing.[37]

UNIVERSITY AUTONOMY

The autonomy of universities is an integral part of the freedom of education and scientific research since the democratic transition. As the Constitutional Court stated, the universities' autonomy is the realization and fundamental safeguard of these constitutional freedoms.[38] The autonomy of universities gained constitutional protection in the practice of the constitutional court.

The autonomy has different aspects, such as scientific, educational, organizational, and financial autonomy. On the one hand, these aspects are interrelated, and the scientific and educational autonomy requires the competences to decide on organizational and financial issues. On the other hand, the state as the maintainer of universities may have a legitimate interest in their efficient operation which may justify its role in financial and organizational decision-making.[39]

In 2013, while the institutions of higher educations preserved their sovereignty as regards the contents and methods of research and teaching, the Fourth Amendment to the Fundamental Law entitled the government to determine the universities' financial structure and monitor their financial management, which practically ceased the financial aspect of autonomy.[40] On this basis, the state introduced the institutions of chancellor and consistorium essentially appointed by the government, which directly restricted the universities' financial autonomy; however, in an indirect way, their competences also intruded into the scientific and education sovereignty.[41]

Since 2019, the most heated topic has been the so-called model change in Hungarian higher education. The transformation of the model of universities' operation means the transformation of their legal status into a foundation, from the public into a kind of private university. The state will continue to finance the universities changing their model but in a contractual framework and not from the central budget. The new maintainer, that is, the members of the board of trustees, are firstly appointed by the government, and it is granted broader competences while the senate has less significant powers in comparison to public universities. That is considered as a further reduction in university autonomy.

CONCLUSIONS

Autonomous entities, autonomous state institutions, as well as the nongovernmental sphere serve as fundamental safeguards of freedom and limit the government. The judiciary and the constitutional courts, the independent media, and the universities' autonomy are indispensable elements of the set of constitutional guarantees.

In the past decade, the governing majority carried out several constitutional and legal changes that allowed it to control the independent and autonomous institutions.[42] The government took note only legal measures and the legal measures aimed at not only the status of these entities.

The scenarios were different. The independent judiciary and Constitutional Court are the constitutional institutional safeguards of other's independence as well. Their status was affected by measures of the most legal nature. The free media and the pluralistic media market are the essential conditions of democracy, so no wonder that the freedom of the media was also one of the first subjects of regulation, along with judicial independence. However, unlike the courts, the media market mainly was affected by governmental measures beyond the legal regulation. At the same time, the significance of independence and the lack of its legal guarantees are shown when the institutions intended to be independent do not secure proper protection. The autonomy of universities may be considered as a more controversial constitutional issue regarding its different (scientific, educational, organizational, financial) aspects. Nevertheless, the gradual reduction of autonomy is beyond doubts.

The picture is more complex than the legal aspects of the independent status. The focus of the article can be explained by the fact that in lack of independence, the control over the government, the precondition of constitutionalism, is illusory.

NOTES

1. András Sajó and Renáta Uitz, *The Constitution of Freedom: An Introduction to Legal Constitutionalism* (Oxford: Oxford University Press, 2017), 6.
2. Sajó and Uitz, *The Constitution of Freedom: An Introduction to Legal Constitutionalism*, 13.
3. Formally, the two-thirds majority in Parliament can act as a constituent and constitution-amending power even if theoretically they are distinct from the legislative power. According to Article S) (2) of the Fundamental Law of Hungary, for the adoption of a Fundamental Law or for the amendment of the Fundamental Law, the votes of two-thirds of the Members of the National Assembly shall be required. There are no further criteria or restrictions.
4. According to Article T) (4) of the Fundamental Law of Hungary, Cardinal Acts are Acts, the adoption and amendment of which requires the votes of two-thirds of the Members of the National Assembly present.
5. Zoltán Pozsár-Szentmiklósy, "Supermajority in Parliamentary Systems–A Concept of Substantive Legislative Supermajority: Lessons from Hungary," *Hungarian Journal of Legal Studies* 58, no. 3(2017): 282, 286–89.
6. Pál Sonnevend, András Jakab and Lóránt Csink, "The Constitution as an Instrument of Everyday Party Politics: The Basic Law of Hungary," in *Constitutional Crisis in the European Constitutional Area: Theory, Law and Politics in Hungary and Romania*, ed. Armin von Bogdandy and Pál Sonnevend (London: Hart/Beck, 2015), 33–34.

7. See András Jakab and Eszter Bodnár, "The Rule of Law, democracy, and human rights in Hungary. Tendencies from 1989 until 2019," in *Rule of Law, Common Values, and Illiberal Constitutionalism. Poland and Hungary within the European Union*, ed. Tímea Drinóczi and Agnieszka Bień-Kacała (Abingdon: Routledge, 2020).

8. Sajó and Uitz, *The Constitution of Freedom: An Introduction to Legal Constitutionalism*, 23–24, 397.

9. Since 2012, Article C) (1) of the Fundamental Law has expressly declared that "the functioning of the Hungarian State shall be based on the principle of the division of powers."

10. Decision of 38/1993. (VI. 11.) AB.

11. Sonnevend, Jakab and Csink, "The Constitution as an Instrument of Everyday Party Politics: The Basic Law of Hungary," 88.

12. Zoltán Szente, "The Political Orientation of the Members of the Hungarian Constitutional Court between 2010 and 2014," *Constitutional Studies* 1, no. 1 (2016): 131.

13. Bernadette Somody, "Theme with Variations: Lessons from the Recent History of Judicial Administration in Hungary," in *Current Challenges in Court Administration*, ed. Piotr Mikuli (The Hague: Eleven International Publishing, 2017).

14. Venice Commission, "Opinion on Act CLXII of 2011 on the Legal Status and Remuneration of Judges and Act CLXI of 2011 on the Organization and Administration of Courts of Hungary," adopted by the Venice Commission at its 90th Plenary Session (Venice, 16-17 March 2012), CDL-AD(2012)001, para. 117.

15. Following the legislative amendments, the Venice Commission examined the new regulation on the issues addressed in the Opinion of the Venice Commission of March 2012. See Venice Commission, "Opinion on the Cardinal Acts on the Judiciary regarding the points that were amended following the Adoption of Opinion CDL-AD(2012) 001 on Hungary," adopted by the Venice Commission at its 92nd Plenary Session (Venice, 12–13 October 2012), CDL-AD(2012)020.

16. For a broader analysis including further issues see Somody, "Theme with Variations: Lessons from the Recent History of Judicial Administration in Hungary," 159–67.; Sonnevend, Jakab and Csink, "The Constitution as an Instrument of Everyday Party Politics: The Basic Law of Hungary," 98–107.

17. Venice Commission, "Opinion on Act CLXII of 2011 on the Legal Status and Remuneration of Judges and Act CLXI of 2011 on the Organization and Administration of Courts of Hungary," §§ 111–15.

18. Baka v. Hungary App. No. 20261/12 (ECtHR, 27 May 2014) and Baka v. Hungary App. No. 20261/12 (ECtHR, 23 June 2016).

19. Mátyás Bencze and Attila Badó, "A magyar bírósági rendszer hatékonyságát és az ítélkezés színvonalát befolyásoló strukturális és személyi feltételek," in *A magyar jogrendszer állapota*, ed. András Jakab and György Gajduschek (Budapest: MTA Társadalomtudományi Kutatóközpont, 2016), 437–38.

20. Decision 33/2012. (VII. 17.) AB, §§ 105–6.

21. For more details and a critical analysis, see Kim Lane Scheppele, "How to Evade the Constitution: The Hungarian Constitutional Court's Decision on Judicial Retirement Age, Part I-II.," *VerfassungsBlog*, August 9, 2012.

22. Case C-286/12, European Commission v. Hungary [2012] ECR 687.
23. Act CLXII of 2011.
24. Venice Commission, "Opinion on Act CLXII of 2011 on the Legal Status and Remuneration of Judges and Act CLXI of 2011 on the Organization and Administration of Courts of Hungary," § 58.
25. The new rules were criticized by the Venice Commission. See Venice Commission, "Opinion on the Cardinal Acts on the Judiciary regarding the points that were amended following the Adoption of Opinion CDL-AD(2012) 001 on Hungary,"§§ 44 and 93.7–93.9.
26. Eszter Bodnár, Fruzsina Gárdos-Orosz and Zoltán Pozsár-Szentmiklósy, "Hungary," in *2018 Global Review of Constitutional Law*, Richard Albert, David Landau, Pietro Faraguna and Simon Drugda, eds. (I·CONnect-Clough Center, 2019), 138–39.
27. Decision 22/2019. (VII. 5.) AB.
28. Eszter Bodnár, Fruzsina Gárdos-Orosz and Zoltán Pozsár-Szentmiklósy, "Hungary," in *2019 Global Review of Constitutional Law*, ed. Richard Albert, David Landau, Pietro Faraguna and Simon Drugda (I·CONnect-Clough Center, 2020), 167–69.
29. Decisions 30/1992. (V. 26.) and 37/1992. (VI. 10.) AB.
30. Gábor Polyák, "Context, Rules and Praxis of the New Hungarian Media Laws. How Does the Media Law Affect the Structure and Functioning of Publicity?," in *Constitutional Crisis in the European Constitutional Area: Theory, Law and Politics in Hungary and Romania*, ed. Armin von Bogdandy and Pál Sonnevend (London: Hart/Beck, 2015), 128.
31. Gábor Polyák, "Context, Rules and Praxis of the New Hungarian Media Laws. How Does the Media Law Affect the Structure and Functioning of Publicity?," 133.
32. Gábor Polyák, "Media in Hungary: Three Pillars of an Illiberal Democracy," in *Public Service Broadcasting and Media Systems in Troubled European Democracies*, ed. by Eva Połońska and Charlie Beckett (Palgrave Macmillan, 2019), 283.
33. Gábor Polyák, "Context, Rules and Praxis of the New Hungarian Media Laws. How Does the Media Law Affect the Structure and Functioning of Publicity?," 127, 132.
34. Gábor Polyák, "Media in Hungary: Three Pillars of an Illiberal Democracy," 287.
35. Gábor Polyák, "Context, Rules and Praxis of the New Hungarian Media Laws. How Does the Media Law Affect the Structure and Functioning of Publicity?," 141.
36. Gábor Polyák, "Media in Hungary: Three Pillars of an Illiberal Democracy," 287–88.
37. Gábor Polyák, "Media in Hungary: Three Pillars of an Illiberal Democracy," 282, 289.
38. Decisions 40/1995. (VI. 15.) and 41/2005. (X. 27.) AB.
39. While others argue that efficient management requires autonomy. See Zoltán Rónay, "Az autonómia újraértelmezése vagy eltörlése, avagy tendenciák és javaslatok a felsőoktatás rendszerszintű válságának idején," *Pro Futuro* 6, no. 2 (2016): 173.
40. Marianna Nagy, "Egyetemi autonómia közigazgatási jogi nézőpontból–avagy a kristálytükör meghasadt?," *Közjogi Szemle* 10, no. 2 (2017): 19.

41. Rónay, "Az autonómia újraértelmezése vagy eltörlése, avagy tendenciák és javaslatok a felsőoktatás rendszerszintű válságának idején," 176–77.

42. Bodnár, Gárdos-Orosz and Pozsár-Szentmiklósy, "Hungary," (2019), 167.

BIBLIOGRAPHY

Act CLXII of 2011 (Hungary).

Baka v. Hungary App. No. 20261/12 (ECtHR, 27 May 2014).

Baka v. Hungary App. No. 20261/12 (ECtHR, 23 June 2016).

Bencze, Mátyás and Attila Badó. "A magyar bírósági rendszer hatékonyságát és az ítélkezés színvonalát befolyásoló strukturális és személyi feltételek," in A magyar jogrendszer állapota, András Jakab and György Gajduschek, eds, 415–41. Budapest: MTA Társadalomtudományi Kutatóközpont, 2016.

Bodnár, Eszter, Fruzsina Gárdos-Orosz and Zoltán Pozsár-Szentmiklósy. "Hungary," in *2018 Global Review of Constitutional Law*, Richard Albert, David Landau, Pietro Faraguna and Simon Drugda, eds,138–42. I·CONnect-Clough Center, 2019.

Bodnár, Eszter, Fruzsina Gárdos-Orosz and Zoltán Pozsár-Szentmiklósy. "Hungary," in *2019 Global Review of Constitutional Law*, Richard Albert, David Landau, Pietro Faraguna and Simon Drugda, eds, 167–171. I·CONnect-Clough Center, 2020.

Case C-286/12, European Commission v. Hungary [2012] ECR 687.

Decision 30/1992. (V. 26.) AB.

Decision 37/1992. (VI. 10.) AB.

Decision 38/1993. (VI. 11.) AB.

Decision 40/1995. (VI. 15.) AB.

Decision 41/2005. (X. 27.) AB.

Decision 33/2012. (VII. 17.) AB.

Decision 22/2019. (VII. 5.) AB.

Fundamental Law of Hungary (25 April 2011).

Jakab, András and Eszter Bodnár. "The Rule of Law, democracy, and human rights in Hungary. Tendencies from 1989 until 2019," in *Rule of Law, Common Values, and Illiberal Constitutionalism. Poland and Hungary within the European Union*, Tímea Drinóczi and Agnieszka Bień-Kacała, eds, 105–20. Abingdon: Routledge, 2020.

Nagy, Marianna. "Egyetemi autonómia közigazgatási jogi nézőpontból–avagy a kristálytükör meghasadt?" *Közjogi Szemle* 10, no. 2 (2017): 17–20.

Polyák, Gábor. "Context, Rules and Praxis of the New Hungarian Media Laws. How Does the Media Law Affect the Structure and Functioning of Publicity?" In *Constitutional Crisis in the European Constitutional Area: Theory, Law and Politics in Hungary and Romania*, Armin von Bogdandy and Pál Sonnevend, eds, 125–50. London: Hart/Beck, 2015.

Polyák Gábor. "Media in Hungary: Three Pillars of an Illiberal Democracy," in *Public Service Broadcasting and Media Systems in Troubled European Democracies*, Eva Połońska and Charlie Beckett, eds, 279–303. Palgrave Macmillan, 2019.

Pozsár-Szentmiklósy, Zoltán. "Supermajority in Parliamentary Systems–A Concept of Substantive Legislative Supermajority: Lessons from Hungary." *Hungarian Journal of Legal Studies* 58, no. 3 (2017): 281–90.

Rónay, Zoltán. "Az autonómia újraértelmezése vagy eltörlése, avagy tendenciák és javaslatok a felsőoktatás rendszerszintű válságának idején." *Pro Futuro* 6, no. 2 (2016): 170–80.

Sajó, András and Renáta Uitz. *The Constitution of Freedom: An Introduction to Legal Constitutionalism.* Oxford: Oxford University Press, 2017.

Scheppele, Kim Lane. "How to Evade the Constitution: The Hungarian Constitutional Court's Decision on Judicial Retirement Age, Part I-II." *VerfassungsBlog*, August 9, 2012.

Somody, Bernadette. "Theme with Variations: Lessons from the Recent History of Judicial Administration in Hungary," in *Current Challenges in Court Administration*, by Piotr Mikuli, eds., 143–68. The Hague: Eleven International Publishing, 2017.

Sonnevend, Pál, András Jakab, and Lóránt Csink. "The Constitution as an Instrument of Everyday Party Politics: The Basic Law of Hungary," in *Constitutional Crisis in the European Constitutional Area: Theory, Law and Politics in Hungary and Romania*, Armin von Bogdandy and Pál Sonnevend, eds., 33–109. London: Hart/ Beck, 2015.

Szente, Zoltán. "The Political Orientation of the Members of the Hungarian Constitutional Court between 2010 and 2014." *Constitutional Studies* 1, no. 1 (2016): 123–49.

Venice Commission. "Opinion on Act CLXII of 2011 on the Legal Status and Remuneration of Judges and Act CLXI of 2011 on the Organization and Administration of Courts of Hungary," adopted by the Venice Commission at its 90th Plenary Session (Venice, 16–17 March 2012), CDL-AD(2012)001.

Venice Commission. "Opinion on the Cardinal Acts on the Judiciary regarding the points that were amended following the Adoption of Opinion CDL-AD(2012) 001 on Hungary," adopted by the Venice Commission at its 92nd Plenary Session (Venice, 12–13 October 2012), CDL-AD(2012)020.

Chapter 8

The Rule of Law and the European Union in Challenging Times

Rita Haverkamp*

INTRODUCTION

The rule of law is one of constitutive pillars of the European Union (EU) and guarantees its functioning. Recently, the rule of law, in conjunction with other fundamental values, namely democracy and human rights, has increasingly come under attack in several member states.[1] The most prominent examples have been the developments in Hungary since 2010 and in Poland since the end of 2015. In December 2017, the European Commission requested the council to initiate the early warning system—the sanction system of Article 7 (1) of the Treaty on European Union (TEU)—against Poland in order to prevent the risk of a serious violation of fundamental EU values.[2] Regarding Hungary, the European Parliament issued the same request to the council nine months later in September 2018.[3]

Because of these setbacks, which one can also witness in other member states such as Bulgaria and Romania, the rule of law has gained more legal and political attention in the EU.[4] When compared globally, numerous member states are acknowledged for their high standards and are at the top of the rankings for the rule of law. According to the Rule of Law Index 2020, among the top ten are seven member states (1 Denmark, 3 Finland, 4 Sweden, 5 the Netherlands, 6 Germany, 8 Austria, and 10 Estonia); Poland is in rank 28 and Hungary in rank 60 out of a total of 128 countries.[5] Hungary is thus the weakest performer among the member states included in the Rule of Law Index—the closest is Bulgaria in rank 53. Besides this, Freedom House observed that Poland declined from a consolidated democracy to a semi-consolidated democracy and Hungary to a transitional/hybrid regime in 2020.

*My special thanks go to my assistant Ms. Franca Langlet for her support.

This nongovernmental organization (NGO) emphasized that "Hungary's decline has been the most precipitous ever tracked in Nations in Transit; it was one of the three democratic frontrunners as of 2005, but in 2020 it became the first country to descend by two regime categories and leave the group of democracies entirely."[6]

The Union Rule of Law is enshrined in Article 2 TEU as one of several fundamental values. The Preamble of the EU Charter of Fundamental Rights (EUCFR) refers to this fundamental value as a founding principle of the Union. In those instances where the rule of law is violated, Article 7 TEU contains a complex enforcement mechanism and Article 258 TEU an infringement procedure. Yet, both threats seem to have a small influence on member states that violate fundamental values. While the sanction system of Article 7 TEU is difficult to enforce on member states due to the homogeneity clause, applicant states of the EU are closely scrutinized to ensure that they adhere to the Union's values.[7] This difference might also harm the credibility of the Union regarding third states when it comes to upholding the fundamental values as pronounced in Articles 3 and 21 TEU.[8]

Although Article 2 TEU mentions the rule of law, no definition of the fundamental value can be found in the treaties. Therefore, the conceptual understanding of the rule of law will be explored first. This will be done *inter alia* by an analysis of the rule of law developed in the relevant case law of the European Court of Human Rights (ECtHR) and the European Court of Justice (ECJ). Afterwards, the recent backsliding of the rule of law will be discussed including the latest developments in European countries, using Poland and partly Hungary as examples, and also considering the COVID-19 pandemic.

CONTOURS OF THE UNION RULE OF LAW

Even if the Union Rule of Law is ubiquitous, no legal definition exists in the treaties and its legal system "lacks a commonly agreed concept."[9] Rather, the fundamental value is described as a "conceptual puzzle"[10] because the conceptions vary in meaning and content. The roots of these differences lie in conceptual and philosophical distinctions between the major European legal traditions. While the doctrine of the German *Rechtsstaat* and the French *État de droit* reflect continental thinking with emphasis on written rules either in the constitution or in acts of the parliament, the Anglo-Saxon approach is based on the judge-made common law.[11] Furthermore, the notion is not defined in the law of the three countries mentioned: The German Basic Law (*Grundgesetz*) only contains the rule of law in three Articles (Arts 16 (2), 23 (1), 28 (1) Basic Law) without defining it; encompassing constitutional or statuary documents in United Kingdom and French positive law do not include a definition either.[12] Consequently, different ideas and traditions of the rule of law can be observed in the member states.[13] This raises the question of the contours and content of the Union Rule of Law. Before going into this in more detail, the discourse on a thin or thick concept will be outlined.

About Thinner and Thicker Concepts of the Rule of Law

In legal theory, the distinction between formal (thin) and substantive (thick) concepts has been long established.[14] This differentiation is not to be understood as two conflicting poles, but as a continuum from thinner to thicker formulations. Tamanaha makes a distinction between formal theories from thinnest to thin and substantive ones from thick to thickest;[15] he also stresses that "the formal versions have substantive implications and the substantive versions incorporate formal requirements."[16] In raw terms, formal conceptions are rule-based with a focus on legality and substantive conceptions refer to the content of the law.

The thinnest formal version is known as "rule by law" that authorizes and serves as an instrument of the government.[17] But even thinner theories are prone to authoritarian regimes because exclusion and segregation can be legally justified without substantive elements.[18] In this sense, pure formal legality is characterized as prospective, general, clear, and certain, as "the law . . . *must be capable of guiding the behavior of its subjects* (emphasis in the text)."[19] While according to this understanding, the rule of law improves individual autonomy, disagreement exists with regard to the equality requirement and the rule of law as a moral good.[20] Although some argue that equality prevents arbitrary laws, most followers reject this argument due to the substantive substance of arbitrary.[21] Therefore, they prefer the notion of equality before the law without further distinctions (e.g., race, religion, status).[22] The debate on the morality of formal legality concerns the obligation of citizens to obey the government that adheres to the rule of law when respective laws are morally enhanced and considered as fair and just.[23] Against this the objection stands that the rule of law in a formal sense as merely instrumental:[24] "the law has a specific virtue which is morally neutral in being neutral as to the end to which the instrument is put."[25] Compromising views recognize both a moral good as well as a possible exploitation of autocracy: on the one hand, a predictable and clear law furthers the citizens' dignity, and on the other hand authoritarian regimes have the power to enact whatever laws they please, consistent with the formal rule of law.[26] This is different when democracy is attached to formal legality. According to Habermas, modern law "[a]s *positive* or *codified* law (emphasis in the text) . . . calls for a political legislator, where the legitimacy of legislation is accounted for by a democratic procedure that secures the autonomy of the citizens. Citizens are politically autonomous only if they can view themselves jointly as authors of the laws to which they are subject as individual addressees."[27] Related to this is the question of the nature of the consent. A unanimous requirement is highly problematic "for it enables one person to hold the rest hostage, blocking initiatives that might benefit the collective or extracting disproportionate rewards as the price of securing the holdout's assent."[28] Tamanaha also points out the threat to the rule of law with regard to democracy "[that] may serve as the means by which an organized cabal or subgroup in society seizes the reins of government power, then utilizes the law to advance its particular agenda, while claiming the legitimacy conferred by democracy."[29]

The substantive conceptions have in common that they all include the elements of the formal rule of law. Individual rights shape thick versions of the rule of law. Dworkin states "that citizens have moral rights and duties with respect to one another, and political rights against the state as a whole. It insists that these moral and political rights be recognized in positive law, so that they may be enforced *upon the demand of individual citizens* (emphasis in the text) through courts or other juridical institutions of the familiar type, so far as this is practicable."[30] However, leaving disputed issues to the judiciary is viewed as worrying due to its power to balance individual rights against democratic principles and society's views.[31] Subjectivity cannot be dismissed in the case of contentious questions that have the potential to separate society. In order to achieve a balance, especially in supreme and constitutional courts, it is important to appoint judges of as many different political affiliations as possible.[32] Otherwise, politicizing the judiciary erodes trust in its credibility as an independent legal body.[33] A thicker formulation of the rule of law consists of the triad democracy, individual rights, and formal legality.[34] This understanding is expressed in the Declaration of the 1990 Copenhagen Meeting of the Conference on the Human Dimension of the Conference on Security and Co-operation in Europe. Representatives of thirty-five European countries, including Canada, the former Soviet Union and the USA, declared that "the rule of law does not mean merely a formal legality which assures regularity and consistency in the achievement and enforcement of democratic order, but justice based on the recognition and full acceptance of the supreme value of the human personality and guaranteed by institutions providing a framework for its fullest expression" and that "democracy is an inherent element of the rule of law."[35] Its functioning requires a watchful public that not only stands up for individual rights but also for democracy, a long-standing legal tradition that upholds the integrity of the law, and, crucially, a government that embraces these fundamental principles.[36] The thickest version of the rule of law complements social welfare conceptions.[37]

Regarding the legal traditions in Europe, the dominant concepts of the rule of law are the English *Rule of Law*,[38] the French *Ėtat de droit*[39] and the German *Rechtsstaat*.[40] They all "concern the problem of imposing effective limits on the exercise of public authority in order to safeguard the rights and liberties of the citizen. Their precise definition depends on the prevailing concept of law and of public authority which are themselves subject to change."[41] A formal understanding of the rule of law prevailed in all legal systems until World War II. The appalling experiences brought about a turn to substantive concepts based on the constitution, which is manifested particularly in the German Basic Law adopted in 1949. Despite the differences between the three concepts, the rule of law has become a constituent legal principle of constitutional value not only in the countries mentioned, but also in all EU member states. They also have in common that the legislator has refrained from defining the term except of the Spanish Constitution; therefore, its content and its core are still discussed.[42] Pech emphasizes

> that most if not all constitutions or courts in Europe [. . .] view the formal and substantive components of the rule of law as interdependent and not mutually exclusive. Indeed, the formal and procedural components of the rule of law in liberal and democratic European polities (proportionality, non-retroactivity, access to courts, fundamental rights protection, etc.) are supposed to serve the substantive values (human dignity, individual autonomy, social justice, etc.) upon which these societies are founded.[43]

These considerations concerning formal and substantial versions reveal how difficult it is to grasp the rule of law, as the concept is "an exceedingly elusive notion"[44] highly intertwined with its context and purpose.[45] This raises questions of how the Union's concept is to be classified, what functions the rule of law serves and how this fundamental value relates to the member states. Pech gets to the heart of the matter by noting,

> even if a similar meaning can be outlined, the scope of application and normative impact of the rule of law at the EU level could nevertheless legitimately differ from the one it has in the Member States if only because of the specific constitutional arrangements of this complex supranational polity. It would be therefore surprising if the rule of law were to fulfill entirely the same functions it does at the national level.[46]

THE RULE OF LAW IN THE COUNCIL OF EUROPE AND THE EU

To address the issues raised, the role of the Council of Europe and the case law of the ECtHR will first be described, followed by the development of the Union's Rule of Law and the case law of the ECJ.

Legal Framework of the Council of Europe

Originally, the ten founding members created the Council of Europe—which today includes forty-seven member states—in 1949 as the supranational good conscience in the struggle to guarantee human rights, democracy, and the rule of law.[47] Consequently, the Statute of the Council of Europe refers to the rule of law in its preamble: "Reaffirming their devotion to the spiritual and moral values which are the common heritage of their peoples and the true source of individual freedom, political liberty and the rule of law, principles which form the basis of all genuine democracy."[48] Membership is dependent on adherence to the rule of law[49] and thus accession as a member[50] or associated member.[51] In the event of a serious violation of the rule of law, the Committee of Ministers may suspend or even exclude the member state concerned from the council.[52] In contrast, the 1957 Treaty of Rome, which established the former European Economic Community created a common market to work toward political integration and economic growth and was not explicitly tied to the rule of law in its early years.[53]

Since its foundation, the Council of Europe has referred to the rule of law in major political and legal documents, above all the European Convention on Human Rights (ECHR). The Preamble of the Convention calls the fundamental value a "common heritage" and several articles in the convention reflect different elements of the rule of law: for example, right to liberty and security (Article 5), right to a fair trial (Article 6), no punishment without law (Article 7), and right to an effective remedy (Article 13). Further, noteworthy, Council of Europe documents emphasize the rule of law in the 1993 Vienna Declaration, the 1997 Strasbourg Declaration, and the 2005 Warsaw Declaration. In the Warsaw Declaration, the heads of state and government committed "to strengthening the rule of law throughout the continent, building on the standard setting potential of the Council of Europe and on its contribution to the development of international law" and highlighted "the role of an independent and efficient judiciary in the member states in this respect."[54] The latter elaborates on the Recommendation CM/Rec(2010)12 of the Committee of Ministers to member states on judges: independence, efficiency, and responsibilities.

Although the rule of law receives the utmost attention within the Council of Europe, the manifold documents do not offer a definition. Nevertheless, various bodies and monitoring mechanisms provide insight into what the Council of Europe means by the rule of law divided into the three topics "Justice," "Common standards and policies" and "Threats to the Rule of Law." Among these sources are, for example, the Commission for the Efficiency of Justice (CEPEJ) and the Consultative Council of European Judges (CCJE), the Group for democracy through Law (Venice Commission) and the European

Committee on Legal Co-operation (CDCJ) as well as the Group of States against Corruption (GRECO) and the Pompidou Group (Drug abuse and illicit trafficking).

The Venice Commission is probably the most famous, as the advisory body of the Council of Europe has shaped the contours and the scope of the rule of law in recent years.[55] In its "Report on the Rule of Law," the Commission proposed a functional non-exhaustive definition of the principle following the former British judge Lord Tom Bingham.[56] The definition is based on six formal and substantive main elements of the rule of law: "(1) Legality, including a transparent, accountable and democratic process for enacting law; (2) Legal certainty; (3) Prohibition of arbitrariness; (4) Access to justice before independent and impartial courts, including judicial review of administrative acts; (5) Respect for human rights; (6) Non-discrimination and equality before law."[57] The commission favors a thick meaning because of "the risks of a purely formalistic concept of the Rule of Law, merely requiring that any action of a public official be authorized by law. 'Rule by Law' or 'Rule by the Law,' or even 'Law by Rules' are distorted interpretations of the Rule of Law."[58] In 2016, the commission introduced its operational and practical checklist on the rule of law that "is neither exhaustive nor final: it aims to cover the core elements of the Rule of Law."[59]

The checklist focuses on five elements of the rule of law and does not include "Respect for human rights" as a distinct element. The commission, however, emphasized the impact of human rights for all elements of the principle: "The Rule of Law would just be an empty shell without permitting access to human rights. [. . .] While recognizing that the Rule of Law can only be fully realized in an environment that protects human rights, the checklist will expressly deal with human rights only when they are linked to specific aspects to the Rule of Law."[60]

The ECtHR has repeatedly addressed the concept of the rule of law and its various aspects but has not yet defined the notion.[61] In its first judgment referring to the rule of law, *Golder v. the United Kingdom*, in 1975, the court stated that the principle is not "a merely 'more or less rhetorical reference,' devoid of relevance for those interpreting the Convention," rather the signatory governments had a "profound belief in the rule of law."[62] Shortly thereafter, the Court stressed, "the notion of the rule of law from which the whole Convention draws its inspiration"[63] is "inherent in all the Articles of the Convention."[64] There is a plethora of case law on diverse aspects of the rule of law, but the Court does not systematically relate the principle to the human rights concerned.[65] In several judgments, the Court referred to the rule of law as "one of the fundamental principles of a democratic society"[66] and thus the principle is inherently tied to democracy.

In the landmark case *Stafford v. the United Kingdom*, the Grand Chamber stated with regard to the separation of powers that the far-reaching powers of the secretary of state to decide on the punitive elements of a criminal sentence "has become increasingly difficult to reconcile with the notion of separation of powers between the executive and the judiciary, a notion which has assumed growing importance in the case law of the Court."[67] The Court places considerable emphasis on the separation of powers in the selection and appointment of judges, as the process must be independent of undue pressure and interference.[68]

In *Baka v. Hungary*,[69] the applicant's right of access to a court was violated in light of international and Council of Europe instruments, case law and bodies, which attach to procedural fairness in cases relating to the removal and dismissal of judges. In addition to the right of access to a court,[70] the right to a fair trial[71] and an effective remedy[72] are repeatedly relevant in case law. The landmark case *Assanidze v. Georgia* touches on the independence of the judiciary. The Court laid down that the rule of law and the notion of a fair trial "preclude any interference by the legislature with the administration of justice designed to influence the judicial determination of the dispute. [. . .] Consequently, the Court would be extremely concerned if the legislation or practice of a Contracting Party were to empower a nonjudicial authority, no matter how legitimate, to interfere in court proceedings or to call judicial findings into question."[73] Furthermore, legal certainty has assumed increasing importance in the case law.[74] In *The Sunday Times v. the United Kingdom*, the Court means by "prescribed by law":

> [f]irstly, the law must be adequately accessible: The citizen must be able to have an indication that is adequate in the circumstances of the legal rules applicable to a given case. Secondly, a norm cannot be regarded as a "law" unless it is formulated with sufficient precision to enable the citizen to regulate his conduct: he must be able—if need be with appropriate advice—to foresee, to a degree that is reasonable in the circumstances, the consequences which a given action may entail.[75]

Recently, the Grand Chamber "gave an important ruling that may have wide-reaching implications for the ongoing attempts to curb the rule of law backsliding in Poland and other countries."[76] In *Guðmundur Andri Ástráðsson v. Iceland*, the Court found that the judicial appointment procedure is also part of the right to a tribunal established by law. To determine its violation, a three-step test is required entailing "(1) a *manifest* breach (2) of a *fundamental* rule of the appointment procedure and (3) whether allegations were effectively reviewed and redressed by the domestic courts in a Convention-compliant manner (emphasis in the text)."[77] Consequently, grave irregularities during the appointment procedure impair the very essence of this right.[78] To conclude, the jurisprudence on the rule of law "provides important guidance on the content of the principle."[79]

In *Reczkowicz v. Poland*, the ECtHR stated a violation of the right to fair a trial under Article 6 ECHR with respect to the newly created Polish Disciplinary Chamber in July 2021. According to the Court, "the procedure for appointing judges had been unduly influenced by the legislative and executive powers. That amounted to a fundamental irregularity that adversely affected the whole process and compromised the legitimacy of the Disciplinary Chamber of the Supreme Court, which had examined the applicant's case."[80]

RULE OF LAW IN THE EU

Since 2007, the Memorandum of Understanding has governed the cooperation between the Council of Europe and the EU. Under the heading "Rule of law, legal-cooperation and addressing new challenges," both organizations express their effort "to establish common standards thus promoting a Europe without dividing lines, without prejudice to their autonomy of decision"[81] and to cooperate stronger to achieve coherence between Union law and the standards of Council of Europe conventions.[82] The case law of the Court on the rule of law has left its mark on the Union as well as the functional approach of the Venice Commission[83] that is recognized as "one of the few more widely accepted conceptual frameworks for rule of law in Europe"[84] and reflected in the 2014 Communication from the European Commission on "A new EU Framework to strengthen the Rule of Law."

The Development of the Union Rule of Law

While the Rule of Law has been a prominent element in the preamble of the Statute of the Council of Europe, from the beginning, the then treaties of European Community of Coal and Steel and European Economic Community did not refer to the notion.[85] However, in the early 1960s, the first president of the European Commission, Walter Hallstein, coined the concept of a "community based on law" (*Rechtsgemeinschaft*)[86] to illustrate the constitutional character of the treaties.[87] In 1973, the Declaration on European Identity called the rule of law one of the fundamental elements of the European identity.[88] Against this background, the ECJ described the European Community in its seminal judgment *Les Verts v. Parliament* as "a Community based on the rule of law, inasmuch as neither its Member States nor its institutions can avoid a review of the question whether the measures adopted by them are in conformity with the basic constitutional charter, the Treaty."[89]

Only in 1992 was the rule of law incorporated as a principle in the Maastricht Treaty into EU primary law and its enshrinement happened in the context of the post–Cold War era.[90] The preamble of the treaty confirms *inter alia* the member states' commitment to the rule of law, although initially, this was mainly symbolic.[91] The 1997 Amsterdam Treaty had a greater impact: The drafters of the TEU described the rule of law as one of the EU's foundational principles which are common to the member states[92] and introduced, for the first time, a sanctioning mechanism[93] in the event of a serious and persistent breach by a member state; the 2001 Nice Treaty added a preventive mechanism. Furthermore, in the light of the enlargement process and the 1993 Copenhagen Criteria, candidate states are obliged to adhere to the principles in which the Union is rooted.[94] In the 2007 Treaty of Lisbon, the terminology shifted from principles to values along with a broadening of values—also for candidate countries—in Article 2 TEU: that means "[t]he Union is founded on the values of respect for human dignity, freedom, democracy, equality, the rule of law and respect for human rights, including the rights of persons belonging to minorities. These values are common to the Member States in a society in which pluralism, non-discrimination, tolerance, justice, solidarity and equality between women and men prevail." However, the shift in vocabulary is not consistent in the treaties, as the rule of law is still labeled as a principle in the Preamble of the EUCFR.[95] Additionally, the Union's external relations and policies "shall be guided by the principles which have inspired its own creation, development, and enlargement, and which it seeks to advance in the wider world: [. . .] the rule of law."[96] Also, the jurisdiction of the ECJ has also been expanded in various respects.[97]

As a result of the "rule of law backsliding,"[98] the commission adopted the Rule of Law Framework in 2014,[99] known as the "*pre*-Article 7 procedure (emphasis in the text),"[100] to prevent upcoming threats and, in the same year, the Council announced its Annual Rule of Law Dialogue.[101] The EU's rule of law toolbox has been combined with instruments to monitor and enhance the fundamental value in an accelerated and uncoordinated manner from 2012 onward, but it has not proven to be very successful in the member states at risk so far.[102] Launched in 2013, the EU Justice Scoreboard belongs to the Union's Rule of Law toolbox to assess the independence, quality, and efficiency of national justice systems.[103] The Justice Scoreboard's overall conclusion, while noting steady progress in most member states, refers somewhat elusively to threats to judicial independence in some national justice systems.[104] In 2016, the Commission activated the Rule of Law Framework for the first time in relation to Poland due to a lack of compliance with binding judgments of the Polish Constitutional Tribunal and the adoption of measures by the Polish legislature to destabilize its functioning.[105] While the Polish government remained unimpressed, the commission set the preventive mechanism[106] in motion for

the first time in 2017.[107] In 2018, the European Parliament initially triggered the preventive mechanism against Hungary addressing a serious and persistent breach of judicial independence, freedom of expression, and the rights of minorities, as well as the situation for migrants and refugees, and corruption.[108] Since 2018, the European Semester has also been increasingly involved in commenting frankly on rule of law developments in member states.[109] In 2019, the commission set up a new Rule of Law Review Cycle to monitor the situation in the member states.[110] The objectives include publishing an annual Rule of Law Report summarizing the situation in the member states and providing a synthesis of developments in the member states and in the EU in order to inform the dialogue with and within the European Parliament and the council.[111] Its first edition was issued in 2020.[112] The European Public Prosecutor's Office with one European Prosecutor from each of the twenty-two participating member states became operational in 2021 and has the competence to investigate, prosecute, and bring to judgment crimes against the EU budget (e.g., fraud, corruption) in order to protect the financial interests of the EU.[113] Despite this increased activity, the rule of law continues to erode in some member states and reluctance to intervene has come under criticism.[114]

The Concept of Union Rule of Law

The evolution of the Union Rule of Law demonstrates fragments of the concept, which will be explored in more depth now. The rule of law has a normative character[115] as the value is enshrined in Article 2 TEU: "The Union is founded on the values of respect for human dignity, freedom, democracy, equality, the rule of law and respect for human rights, including the rights of persons belonging to minorities. These values are common to the Member States in a society in which pluralism, non-discrimination, tolerance, justice, solidarity and equality between women and men prevail." The legally binding nature is underlined by the associated Articles of the TEU: Article 3 para 1 with the aim of promoting the EU's values and in Article 13 para 1 within an institutional framework, the legal binding of the EU institutions and the member states by the treaty objectives in Article 4 para 3 as well as the sanctioning procedure in Article 7 and the accession procedure in Article 49. Article 2 TEU is often understood as a "homogeneity clause,"[116] which "applies both vertically between the Union level and the Member States' level and horizontally among the Member States themselves."[117]

Multiple references to the rule of law in primary and secondary EU law highlight its significance and its manifoldness. Still, no conclusive definition of its fundamental values is laid down in the treaties. As a result, the rule of law "remains an elusive concept, impossible to define and hard to frame as a manageable and operational concept."[118]

So far, the Commission has not been able to refute the criticism, although it attempted to shed light on the core meaning and scope of the Union Rule of Law with the 2014 Communication regarding the newly established Rule of Law Framework[119] and the 2019 Communication and its further development .[120] The 2014 Communication includes a core meaning of the rule of law as a common EU value in accordance with Article 2 TEU.[121] With regard to the purpose, the commission drew not only on the case law of the ECJ and the ECtHR but also on documents by the Council of Europe and in particular on the expertise of the Venice Commission.[122] According to the commission, the rule of law comprises legality, legal certainty, prohibition of arbitrariness of the executive powers, independent and impartial courts, and effective judicial review including respect for fundamental rights and equality before the law.[123] This definition represents a non-exhaustive list of legal subprinciples[124] but applies to all member states "in spite of the different national identities and legal systems and traditions that the Union is bound to respect."[125] The 2019 Communication explicitly added the principle of separation of powers to this list, probably due to the post-2014 case law of the ECJ and the Commission's assessment of the situation in Poland.[126] The Commission understands the rule of law as a "constitutional principle with both formal and substantive components [. . .] intrinsically linked to respect for democracy and for fundamental rights."[127] Thus, the Union Rule of Law is a thick concept just as the member states. Critics bristle at this broad approach and call the Union Rule of Law a "conceptual puzzle."[128] This view is not upheld because it is in fact up to the EU institutions, in particular the ECJ, to define the term and apply the various key concepts and fundamental principles.[129] The following takes a closer look at the jurisprudence of the ECJ.

The Court of Justice of the EU

Since its groundbreaking ruling *Les Verts v. Parliament* has explicated the principles of the Union Rule of Law in its case law by deducing tangible legal rules.[130] The Commission recognizes the pivotal role of the ECJ: "recent case law of the Court of Justice of the EU has made an indispensable contribution to strengthening the rule of law, reaffirming the Union as a community of values."[131] In its extensive body of judgments, the Court has derived substantive rules from the principles of legality,[132] legal certainty,[133] confidence in the stability of a legal situation,[134] the protection of legitimate expectations,[135] and proportionality[136] and has identified various procedural guarantees as crucial elements of the rule of law; examples are the rights to a fair trial,[137] be heard,[138] of defense,[139] of access to the file,[140] and the obligation to state reasons.[141],[142] The Court's concept of the rule of law includes both formal and substantive components inherently associated with the other fundamental values such as democracy and fundamental rights.[143]

Just at the very outset of the twenty-first century, the ECJ was occupied with rule of law issues that were labeled as the "war on terror" and concerned the Union institutions.[144] The 2008 landmark judgment *Kadi and Al Barakaat v. Council & Commission* refers to the UN Security Council's 1267 sanctions regime with respect to the fundamental rights as protected by the Union legal order, "in a community based on the rule of law."[145] According to the Grand Chamber, "the rights of defense, in particular the right to be heard, and the right to effective judicial review of those rights, were patently not respected."[146] In light of the constitutional principles, the ECJ demanded effective judicial protection against restrictive measures, even if an international agreement contains an obligation to implement them.[147] Further cases on effective judicial protection are in particular associated with the EUCFR.[148] The case law on the rule of law as such addresses more general issues, especially the interrelation between legislative discretion and judicial scrutiny.[149] The ECJ acknowledges the broad discretion of the Union legislator concerning political, economic, and social matters as well as complex assessments and evaluations based on objective criteria appropriate to the legislator's aim.[150] With respect to the principle of proportionality, a violation is only assumed if the adopted measure is obviously unsuitable to achieve the objective envisaged by the institutions.[151] However, the Union legislature's discretion is narrowed when fundamental rights are affected. In the 2014 judgment, *Digital Rights Ireland and Seitlinger and Others v. Ireland*, the Grand Chamber ruled that the Data Retention Directive 2006/24 is invalid as a disproportionate measure regarding "the protection of personal data in light of the fundamental right to respect for private life and the extent and seriousness of the interference with that right."[152]

Meanwhile, a rich body of case law has emerged on rule of law violations in the member states.[153] In recent years, the ECJ has gained public attention with its rulings on Hungary and Poland. In 2012, the Commission launched two infringement procedures regarding Hungary. The first decision in 2012 concerned the forced early retirement of judges (see Somody in this volume).[154] According to the second judgment *Commission v. Hungary* in 2014, Hungary did not meet its obligations under the Data Protection Directive 95/46 because the data protection supervisor was removed from office in an act of disregard for legally established safeguards, thus jeopardizing its independence.[155]

In 2018, the ruling *Associação Sindical dos Juizes Portugueses v. Tribunal de Contas*[156] became groundbreaking regarding deficiencies in the rule of law in member states, in particular regarding the protection of judicial independence and the irremovability of judges.[157] The ECJ emphasized the substantive dimension of Article 2 TEU as the hard core of the Union law that is enforceable based on Article 19 TEU.[158] Since then, the ECJ has been kept busy with different issues concerning the rule of law in Hungary and Poland. In 2018, the commission initiated three further infringement procedures against Hungary concerning the NGO law, the Higher Education Law ("*Lex* CEU"), and the asylum procedures ("Stop Soros package"). In 2020, the Grand Chamber stated that the Hungarian law requiring nongovernmental organizations to disclose foreign funding is unlawful.[159] According to the Court, the NGO law "introduced discriminatory and unjustified restrictions [that are appropriate] to create a generalized climate of distrust vis-à-vis the associations and foundations at issue" and violates the rights of the NGOs concerned and their funders to respect for private and family life, to the protection of personal data, and to freedom of association.[160] In the same year, the Grand Chamber declared that Hungary failed to comply with the national treatment commitments under the General Agreement on Trade in Services and infringed the rights to academic freedom, and to the freedom to found higher education institutions as well as to conduct a business.[161] This not only strengthens academic freedom in member states but also clarifies for the first time that the jurisdiction of the Court is not precluded by the World Trade Organization's own dispute settlement system in an infringement procedure against a member state.[162] At the end of 2020, the Grand Chamber condemned Hungary for not fulfilling its obligations under Union law in respect of procedures for granting international protection and returning third-country nationals staying illegally.[163]

The experience with irreversible breaches of the rule of law in Hungary led the ECJ to order interim measures in three cases concerning Poland to ensure respect for the rule of law:[164] (1) threat of periodic penalty payment if the protected forest continues to be logged,[165] (2) suspending the application of the Polish provisions to the lowering of the retirement age of Supreme Court judges,[166] and (3) suspending the activities of the so-called disciplinary chamber as regards disciplinary cases concerning judges.[167] The *Associação Sindical dos Juizes Portugueses v. Tribunal de Contas* ruling influenced the judgment on the *Independence of the Polish Supreme Court* in 2018.[168] In contrast to the *Retirement Age* decision against Hungary based on age discrimination, the Grand Chamber invoked Article 19 TEU for the first time and declared the incompatibility of the Polish reform to lower the retirement age with the provision.[169] In 2018, the Polish Supreme Court asked the ECJ *inter alia* whether the new disciplinary chamber could be considered independent (in light of Articles 2 and 19 (1) (subpara 2) TEU, Article 267 TFEU, Article 47 of the EUCFRghts) and if not whether the Supreme Court may decide. In *A.K. and Others v. Sąd Najwyższy*,[170] the Grand Chamber left the scrutiny to the national court by giving criteria for assessing the judicial independence. If a court has jurisdiction but cannot be regarded as independent or impartial under Union law (especially Article 47 of the EUCFR), "another court before which such a case is brought has the obligation [. . .] to disapply that provision of national law, so that that case may be determined by a court which meets those requirements."[171] In a further judgment in *A.B. and Others v. Krajowa Rada Sądownictwa and Others*[172] in 2021, the Grand Chamber found that the successive amendments of the Polish Law on the National Council of the Judiciary are liable to infringe Union law due to the effect of removing effective judicial review. However, the referring Polish court has the task of ruling whether the procedure of appointing judges to the Polish Supreme Court offers sufficient guarantees of independence.[173] The referring court repealed the resolutions of the Council which recommended to the President of the Republic the questioned nominations, but his appointments the court ruled valid.[174] Furthermore, there have been more cases affecting the rule of law concerning Hungary and Poland (see under Rule of Law crisis in Poland and Hungary).[175]

Recently, the ECJ jurisprudence on member states where the rule of law is particularly at risk has received much attention. Even though the Treaty of Lisbon has strengthened the Union's fundamental values, significant backsliding regarding the rule of law can be observed in several member states. As a guardian of the foundational values, the ECJ discovered "the potential of Article 2 TEU, in conjunction with Article 19(1) TEU, for ensuring respect for the rule of law in the EU legal order."[176] In this sense, Article 19 TEU serves as "a rescue path through which the EU judicial branch can defend the effective judicial protection by independent courts as the undisputable core of the European rule of law."[177]

BACKSLIDING REGARDING THE RULE OF LAW IN RECENT YEARS

Yet, the ECJ is not in a position to save the rule of law in member states that are at risk. Rather, it depends on the interaction of the EU institutions. Above all, the ECJ judgments lag behind real life, as the example of the case *Lex* CEU shows: The ruling arrived too late, as the Central European University had already left Hungary and settled in Vienna.[178] In the EU, it was long taken for granted that member states largely adhered to the fundamental values rule of law, human rights, and democracy. The commission has met the slow but continuing processes of de-democratization in member states with hesitation and a certain helplessness in dealing with serious breaches of Article 2 TEU values. The reluctance to activate the sanction mechanism of Article 7

TEU is rooted in legal and political considerations, which are linked to the unfortunate experience with the political quarantine of the Austrian right-wing populist party in government ("Haider Affair") in 1999:[179] The wise men report found no violations and recommended the lifting of sanctions.[180] According to Scheppele and Pech, "[t]he Austrian case clearly haunted the Commission when it could have, but did not, take effective action to stop rule of law backsliding in Hungary."[181] The increasing backsliding regarding the rule of law has given rise to serious concerns, not only in Hungary and Poland, but also in other member states (e.g., Malta, Slovakia). Rule of law backsliding is understood as "the process through which elected public authorities deliberately implement governmental blueprints which aim to systematically weaken, annihilate or capture internal checks on power with the view of dismantling the liberal democratic state and entrenching the long-term rule of the dominant party."[182]

Rule of Law Framework

While the newer member states Bulgaria and Romania have been subject to a specific monitoring mechanism including benchmarks regarding their judicial systems since their accession, this has not been the case with Hungary and Poland. In contrast to the Austrian case, both Hungary and Poland have systematically violated the Article 2 TEU values over the past years. On the advice of the wise men's report,[183] the 2003 Nice Treaty added a preventive arm (para 1) to the Article 7 TEU sanctioning mechanism (para 2). In the event of certain rule of law concerns, which constitute a violation of a specific provision of EU law, the Commission may initiate infringement procedures under Article 258 TFEU.[184] In situations outside the scope of EU law, the preventive mechanism in Article 7(1) TEU may be activated when the values set out in Article 2 TEU are at a "clear risk of a serious breach" (para 1) and the sanction mechanism in Article 7(2) TEU when they are at a "serious and persistent breach" (para 2) by a member state. Consequently, the thresholds to start the mechanisms of Article 7 TEU are high and function as a last resort.[185]

In view of noticeable threats to fundamental values in several member states, the former President of the Commission Barroso found deficiencies in the protection of fundamental values in the EU: "We need a better developed set of instruments, not just the alternative between the 'soft power' of political persuasion and the 'nuclear option' of Article 7 of the Treaty."[186] In 2014, the commission intended to close the gap with its Rule of Law Framework and complemented Article 7 TEU with a "preventive-preventive process"[187] in order to prevent the emerging of a systemic threat to the rule of law in a member state.[188] Current examples of a systemic threat include the independence of judiciary and the separation of powers.[189] The commission activates the so-called pre-Article 7 procedure when national "rule of law safeguards" do not seem capable to counter effectively the threats. The pre-Article 7 procedure consists of a three-staged process of dialogue with a member state: the stages are the Commission assessment, the Commission recommendation and a follow-up to the recommendation.[190] The first stage refers to gathering and analyzing the relevant information, also by seeking external expertise (e.g., Venice Commission), in particular a comparative analysis of other member states. If the Commission identifies a systemic threat to the rule of law, it will prepare a "rule of law opinion" and give the member state concerned the opportunity to respond. In the event that the second stage is required, the member state will receive a "rule of law recommendation" to take steps for improving the situation within a fixed time period. The last stage includes monitoring the progress in the member state. If the follow-up given by the member state turns out to be unfavorable, the question of whether to activate one of the mechanisms of Article 7 TEU arises for the Commission. During the whole process, the European Parliament and the Council will be provided with information about the development of the dialogue.

The Rule of Law Framework can be called a "decisional communication":[191] "[t]he rules set forth in the RLF [Rule of Law Framework] communication can be interpreted as a measure to eliminate uncertainty of law resulting from the incompleteness of rules specified in Article 7 with regard to the triggering of the mechanism of RLF."[192] In a pre-Article 7 procedure, the Commissions' recommendations are not classified as binding legal acts, but their nonfulfillment gives considerable grounds for triggering the mechanism of Article 7 TEU.[193] The Commission first activated its RLF regarding Poland in January 2016. The dialogue lasted until December 2017 and its outcome consisted of one opinion and four recommendations by the Commission.[194] When the dialogue did not achieve the hoped-for effect, the Commission triggered the preventive mechanism of Article 7 (1) TEU in December 2017.[195] Besides the Commission, the European Parliament or one-third of the member states are authorized to activate the preventive procedure of Article 7(1) TEU.

Shortly after Poland, the European Parliament activated the preventive procedure under Article 7(1) TEU regarding Hungary in September 2018.[196] However, the sanction mechanism of Article 7(2) TEU has not been triggered by the Commission or one-third of the member states for as long as it has existed.

Harsh criticism has long been expressed regarding the Commission's reluctance to act against member states, most prominently Hungary and Poland, which continually violate the rule of law and dismantle democracy in a systemic way.[197] Back in 2018, Scheppele and Pech already considered both countries to be "well beyond the 'risk of breach' in the case of Poland and are already well into the territory where the rule of law has nearly vanished.

In Hungary, the rule of law has disappeared."[198] The ranking of Hungary and Poland in the Rule-of-Law Index 2020 proves them right: Poland weakened to a semi-consolidated democracy and Hungary to a transitional/hybrid regime that cannot be called a democracy any longer.[199] In the April 2019 Communication on "Further Strengthening the Rule of Law Framework," the Commission wants to reinforce the rule of law in the three pillars "promotion" of a shared rule of law culture, "prevention" through cooperation and "response" to breaches at the Union level.[200] Under the pillar "prevention," the Commission announced its new annual Rule of Law Circle to monitor the situation in the member states in the follow-up July 2019 Communication.[201] The next year the Commission published its first "2020 Rule of Law Report."[202] The report is another instrument in the EU's rule of law toolbox such as the EU Justice Scoreboard and the European Semester.[203]

Rule of Law Crisis in Poland and Hungary

The first Rule of Law Report provides insights into the development of the rule of law situation based on the justice system, the anti-corruption framework, media pluralism, and other institutional checks and balances in twenty-seven member states.[204] Although the report contains disturbing deficiencies in the rule of law in several member states (e.g., Bulgaria, Slovakia),[205] the focus is on the even more disconcerting development in Poland and partly Hungary (see Somody in this volume).[206] In July 2021, the second Rule of Law Report stated a further intensification of the issues raised in the first Rule of Law Report.[207]

In Hungary, the overwhelming majority achieved by the center-right party Fidesz (the Federation of Young Democrats–Hungarian Civic Alliance) in the 2010 election, which has ruled since then, the change to an "illiberal" democracy has accelerated.[208] The party, under its Prime Minister Viktor Orbán, has altered the political landscape largely in its favor. In order to remain in power, the party established new posts, with their supporters supervising the media and the judiciary.[209] Furthermore, Fidesz strived to position itself in the center of society with an ethno-nationalist agenda and, in parallel, to build a powerful system of (financial) favoritism for its followers.[210] Since coming to power, the prime minister has stringently pursued the path to an authoritarian system. Accordingly, the first Rule of Law Report concerning Hungary raises significant concerns about the rule of law.[211] In addition to several attacks on the judicial independence, the anti-corruption framework has serious shortcomings with regard to independent control mechanisms due to tight interconnections between politics and certain national businesses that facilitate corruption: "[w]hen serious allegations arise, there is a systemic lack of determined action to investigate and prosecute corruption cases involving high-level officials or their immediate circle."[212] In this context, media pluralism and independence[213] and other checks and balances are under attack: Independent institutions are being weakened and civil society is being exposed to increasing pressure; one example is that authorities are now able to challenge final court decisions before the constitutional court.[214]

Since October 2015, the governing party PiS (Law and Justice) has severely damaged the rule of law in Poland.[215] PiS has begun to neutralize the Constitutional Tribunal because it "has the power to conduct a judicial review of the constitutionality of norms."[216] The dispute about the legality of the election of judges escalated to the point that the then president refused to publish the verdicts of the Tribunal and to swear in judges, elected before PiS took over the government.[217] PiS not only succeeded in gaining control of the tribunal, but also in introducing a "further mechanism for destroying the autonomy of the courts, including extraordinary complaints, the new structure of the Supreme Court and last but not least, disciplinary proceedings."[218] Despite the Article 7(1) TEU procedure and interim measures by the ECJ, the rule of law situation is still worsening in Poland: the so-called "muzzle law" is considered a legislative reaction to the ECJ 2019 judgment.[219] The Venice Commission notes that the "muzzle law" "diminish[es] judicial independence and put[s] Polish judges into the impossible situation of having to face disciplinary proceedings for decisions required by the ECtHR, the law of the EU and other international instruments."[220] The Rule of Law Report also expresses serious concerns about the justice reforms since 2015, affecting all courts and the prosecution service and, thus, threatening judicial independence.[221] The double role as minister of justice and prosecutor general opens the door to political influence and corruption.[222] The Central Anti-Corruption Bureau is subordinated to the executive and, therefore, vulnerable to corruption.[223] Judicial independence is still at risk and the introduced measure to prevent corruption and to promote the integrity of persons in top legislative and executive functions remains dissatisfactory.[224] Media pluralism and independence have weakened due to the politically influenced appointment procedures for the National Broadcasting Council and the new National Media Council, which at present appoints and dismisses the management and supervisory boards of the Polish Television, Radio and Press Agency.[225] In August 2021, the Polish Parliament (*Sejm*) passed a media reform bill that bans ownership of TV and radio broad casting companies from outside the EU. Under the guise of preventing influence from non-EU countries, the bill is directed against the still independent TVN owned by a US-based media group (*Lex* TVN) and threatens fundamentally the freedom of press.[226] The opposition-held Senate will probably reject the bill, then PiS will depend on an absolute majority in the Parliament to overcome the Senate decision.[227] The Commission questions the independency of the National Regulatory

Authority (NRA), the Office of Electronic Communications (UKE), and decided to refer the case to the ECJ in September 2021.[228]

Other components of the system of checks and balances affect the rule of law, such as fast-track legislation with limited consultation of stakeholders or opportunities for the opposition to participate.[229] Furthermore, governing politicians attack critical representatives of civil society and of professional association of judges and prosecutors.[230]

Undeterred by the ongoing infringement proceedings, the ongoing Article 7 (1) TEU procedure, and ECJ judgments on unlawful reforms in both countries, Hungary and Poland continue to dismantle the rule of law. In May 2021, nearly one year after the ECJ ruling on the unlawfulness of the foreign funding NGO law, the Hungarian Parliament repealed the *Lex*NGO from 2017 by replacing it with a new bill threatening the work of NGOs. The new law requires the State Audit Office (ÁSZ) to conduct and publish annual financial audits of NGOs and discriminates specific NGOs which are exempt in case of religious, sport, and national organizations.[231]

Furthermore, the Commission renewed its call on Hungary to inform the commission of actions taken concerning the issues raised in the formal letter of notice concerning the new asylum legislation of October 2020 that was introduced in response to the COVID-19 pandemic and setting out that non-EU nationals are required to first make a declaration of intent expressing their intent to apply for asylum at a Hungarian embassy outside the EU.[232] The Commission regards this new legislation as a violation of the Asylum Procedures Directive (Directive 2013/32/EU) interpreted in light of the EUCFR.[233] Eventually, the Commission indicated to revert to monetary means—that is, suspension of EU funds—concerning Hungary to force Hungary to address major rule of law concerns.[234]

Poland is reacting in a similar way. After the ECJ ruling on the unlawfulness of the disciplinary chamber, the even more restrictive "muzzle law" entered into force in February 2020.[235] Early in 2021, the Commission launched an infringement procedure against the "muzzle law" to safeguard the independence of judges in Poland back in April 2020.[236] On March 31, 2021, the Commission referred Poland to the ECJ regarding the law on the judiciary (tightened "muzzle law") of December 2019 and asked for interim measures.[237] On July 15, 2021, the ECJ decided upon the "muzzle law" regarding the disciplinary regime for Polish judges. The Court upheld all complaints made by the Commission and concluded its incompatibility with EU law.[238] Then the Commission set a deadline of August 16, 2021, for the Polish government to act. In light of the threat of financial sanctions and of losing EU money for its COVID-19 recovery plan, the Polish government informed the European Commission on time to dissolve the disciplinary chamber; at the same time, it announced its intention to ensure disciplining of judges breaking the law or otherwise abusing the law by continuing its judicial reforms.[239] Consequently, the Commission considered Poland's failure to comply with the Court's interim measures order and asked the ECJ to impose daily fines on the country to ensure compliance on September 7, 2021.[240] Concurrently, the Commission decided to send a letter of formal notice (Article 260 (2) TFEU) to Poland, for not abiding by the ECJ judgment on the "muzzle law."[241]

In 2020, another struggle unfolded regarding the replacement of the Polish Ombudsman at the end of his term: after the rejection of five candidates by the PiS majority in the chamber, a great majority in the Polish Parliament (*Sejm*) finally approved Professor Marcin Wiącek in July 2021, who was confirmed later on by the Senate.[242] The urgency of the election was accelerated by a Constitutional Court ruling in April 2021 declaring the extension of the previous Ombudsman Bodnar, who was widely recognized for his commitment to the rule of law, incompatible with the Constitution and giving him three months to leave.[243] Due to a motion from the new Ombudsman, the Polish Constitutional Tribunal postponed its verdict on whether the Polish constitution or European treaties have priority.[244] The Ombudsman complained about the partiality of one judge, who has been very critical of the EU through his engagement in judicial reforms in opposition to the EU.

These developments make it abundantly clear that the Polish government is continuing to seek the confrontation with the EU. In late March 2021, the Polish prime minister particularly set the escalation spiral in motion and filed a motion at Poland's Constitutional Court questioning the primacy of EU law over Poland's supreme law.[245] Meanwhile, requests of the Commission to withdraw the motion[246] as well as the order of the deputy head of the ECJ issued to suspend the application of national provisions relating in particular to the powers of the disciplinary chamber of the Supreme Court remained unsuccessful.[247] After four adjournments Poland's Constitutional Curt found key European treaty norms (Art. 1 and 19 (1) TEU), incompatible with Poland's Constitution on October 7, 2021.[248] In contrast to the Polish Constitutional Tribunal, the German Federal Constitutional Court has never questioned the fundamental primacy of EU law.[249] One day before the Polish constitutional court's ruling, the ECJ questioned again the judicial independence by declaring a transfer of a Kraków district judge critical of the government as "null and void" as the decision at last instance was made by a judge appointed "in clear breach of fundamental rules concerning the establishment and functioning of the judicial system concerned."[250] In light of the Polish Constitutional Court's decision denying primacy of EU law, the question is at hand what significance the rulings of the ECJ will still have in Poland. The same applies to the Commission, especially in view of a potentially financial response. Apart from this, the Polish government is able to delay the entry into force of the ruling due to its discretion; according to Polish law, decisions of the Polish Constitutional Court only come into force when the Polish government officially publishes them.

Despite this, the Commission initiated legal actions against Poland and Hungary for violating principal rights of LGBT (Lesbian, Gay, Binary and Transsexual) people.[251] In view of the progressing negative developments, a résumé is resigned: "[d]espite ten years of EU attempts at reining in Rule of Law violations and even as backsliding Member States have lost cases at the Court of Justice, illiberal regimes inside the EU have become more consolidated: the EU has been losing through winning."[252] Besides this, the COVID-19 pandemic is further exacerbating the situation.

Rule of Law under Pressure during the COVID-19 Pandemic

In spring 2020, the Hungarian government declared a state of danger pursuant to the constitutional provisions.[253] As the governmental decree did not prescribe a time limit, the state of danger ended with another governmental decree in June 2020.[254] In its Interim Report, the Venice Commission suggests abstaining from declarations or measures without a specific time limit if a regular review of the development is not guaranteed.[255] As such, in November 2020, the Hungarian parliament voted for an extension of the state of danger for a time period of ninety days[256] and, in February 2021, Prime Minister Orbán called on lawmakers for a further extension of ninety days.[257]

In April 2020, the Council of Europe was already offering a toolkit for member states for dealing with the COVID-19 sanitary crisis regarding democracy, the rule of law and human rights.[258] Pursuant to Article 15 of the ECHR, contracting states derogate in times of emergency from their obligation to secure certain rights and freedoms under the ECHR in a temporary, limited, and supervised manner. Notifications under Article 15 of the ECHR have been sent by the EU member states Estonia, Latvia, and Romania.[259] According to the ECtHR, contracting states have a wide margin of discretion "to determine whether that life is threatened by a public 'emergency' and, if so, how far it is necessary to go in attempting to overcome the emergency."[260] Following on from this, the Venice Commission defines a state of emergency as "a—temporary—situation in which exceptional powers are granted to the executive and exceptional rules apply in response to and with a view to overcoming an extraordinary situation posing a fundamental threat to a country."[261] The "precautionary principle" guides the application of emergency measures *inter alia* in light of the rule of law by considering the general conditions necessity, proportionality, and temporariness.[262] Concerning the distribution of powers, "the executive may, temporarily, exercise certain powers that would be otherwise reserved to the legislative. The exercise has to have a clear and prospective legal basis."[263] Nevertheless, parliamentary oversight, judicial review and monitoring by the media must be guaranteed not only to control the declaration and prolongation of the state of emergency, but also the activation and application of emergency powers and measures.[264]

The first Rule of Law Report also includes the burdens on the member states and calls the COVID-19 crisis "a real-life stress test for the resilience of national systems in times of crisis,"[265] particularly with regard to the checks and balances, the media and civil society as well as the justice system.[266] Consequently, the Commission has monitored the rule of law in a public emergency with its emergency measures.[267] Although in Hungary a decree was only in force for around two weeks in March, the government suspended the functioning of the courts, except for certain urgent cases, for an undefined period of time and changed, subsequently, the procedural laws to facilitate the operation of the justice system during the "state of danger."[268] The Hungarian Civil Liberties Union observed further "systemic obstruction of the work of the independent media."[269] In particular, the Commission is worried about the new offense "spreading false information" on COVID-19, which threatens legal certainty and the freedom of expression.[270] In Poland, the state of epidemic raises concerns about the impact of certain emergency measures with regard to specific state authorities, such as the Office of Electronic Communications, which caused infringement proceedings by the Cmmission.[271] The Venice Commission emphasizes that "even the state of emergency is regulated by law, albeit through a more flexible legal regime."[272]

As the situation in Hungary and Poland has deteriorated further in 2020, the question was raised of how more adherence to the rule of law could be accomplished among the member states. That is why, the European Council suggested "a regime of conditionality" during the negotiations about the seven-year Multiannual Financial Framework and the new EU COVID-19 Recovery Fund (Next Generation EU) in July 2020.[273] In mid-November 2020, Hungary and Poland refused to adopt the September 2020 compromise proposal due to the clause of conditionality linked to the compliance with the rule of law.[274] On December 16, 2020, a compromise was reached by the European Council and the European Parliament on a general regime of conditionality for the protection of the Union budget, applicable from January 1, 2021.[275] Pursuant to the Regulation, the Commission can initiate the procedure when reasonable grounds are found that breaches of the rule of law in a member state affect or seriously risk affecting the sound financial management of the EU budget or the protection of the financial interests of the EU.[276] Its adoption was accompanied by an "interpretative declaration" by the European Council,[277] which aroused strong objections due to its potential to delay the implementation of the mechanism.[278] Point 2 (c) of the declaration meets with the gravest misgivings. Contrary to the declaration, the legally binding regulation refers neither to "guidelines" and to a "methodology for carrying out the Regulation's assessment" which the Commission intends to create nor to an action for annulment of the regulation which would postpone the finalization of the guidelines until after the ECJ judgment. The European Parliament resolution, however, states that "the applicability, purpose and scope of the Rule of Law Regulation is clearly defined in the legal text of the said Regulation" and that "the European Council shall not exercise legislative functions."[279] As expected, Hungary and Poland launched a legal challenge against the conditionality mechanism at the ECJ on March 11, 2021. In a plenary debate, many members of the European Parliament spoke in favor of activating the conditionality mechanism and the parliament adopted a resolution on March 25, 2021, warning the Commission to apply the mechanism, which is applicable since January 1, 2021. If the Commission fails to fulfill its obligation and does not take suitable actions necessary to defend European financial interests and its values, the parliament "will consider this to constitute a failure to act and subsequently shall take action under Article 265 of the TFEU against the Commission."[280] This step is based on the Commission insisting to develop guidelines to which the application of the regulation shall be subject to. Hence, the parliament stresses that such guidelines not only delay its application but bear the potential to "undermine the intention of the co-legislators."[281] However, the Commission decided to adhere to the decision of developing guidelines first, which the European Parliament "[d]eeply regrets."[282]

CONCLUSION

The rule of law is a complex fundamental principle that is praised all over the world.[283] This seeming unanimity is due to the wide range of conceptions from thin to thick.[284] In Europe, the genesis of the rule of law began with a formal understanding—originating from England—and developed into a substantive understanding in the course of the twentieth century, especially overshadowed by the Nazi terror. In the wake of this, a substantive conception took root first in the Council of Europe and later in the EU. The Council of Europe, with the Venice Commission, has contributed to forming the current understanding of the rule of law in the Union in a fundamental way. The case law, both of the ECtHR and the ECJ, has given the concept contours and has made it flourish. Even though the TEU does not contain a legal definition of the rule of law, the fundamental value has been given concrete shape by the above institutions and organs and others.

In the twenty-first century, politicians have become more aware of the importance to guarantee the rule of law in light of the massive backsliding in several member states. While the Union sought to safeguard democracy, human rights, and the rule of law by enforcing them as requirements for accession countries, it was surprised by member states taking a firm path outside the Union's fundamental values. When faced with increasing violations, the Union acted hesitantly and helplessly, in particular when it comes to the member state Hungary, which has repeatedly violated the fundamental values since 2010. In response to further threats by Hungary and other member states, both the Union and the Council of Europe developed safeguards for the rule of law. While the checklist by the Venice Commission helps to identify breaches of the rule of law, the 2014 Union Rule of Law Framework provides a sophisticated toolbox for responding to breaches of the rule within a (pre-)Article 7 TEU procedure, infringement proceedings and, since January 2021, the conditionality mechanism. When Poland moved in a similar direction in 2015, the Union was better prepared. Since then, the Commission has initiated several infringement proceedings at the ECJ and activated the preventive mechanism of Article 7 TEU against Poland. Only then was the action taken against Hungary intensified, but more slowly and not as harshly as against Poland, where the Polish government feels that it has been treated unfairly compared to Hungary.[285] Nevertheless, both member states have not been impressed by the different procedures against them, have continued undeterred with populist leaders "act[ing] like children testing the boundaries of their actions and keep pushing as far as they can."[286] The head of the last independent Hungarian radio station concluded that "the probability of fair, independent judgments is much lower than at that time [translated by the author]."[287]

Part of the Union toolbox for preventing and resolving breaches of the rule of law in the member states is the new annual Rule of Law Report. The first Report in 2020 monitors the decline of the rule of law in several member states. Hungary and Poland as the two member states with the most controversial record regarding the rule of law are addressed in using euphemistic language:[288] "The report presents the situation in Poland or Hungary as one where a largely intact system of constitutional checks and balances is being attacked. In fact, in both countries key ones were already removed a while ago and the authoritarian developments are already institutionally entrenched."[289] The comparative analysis, therefore, is misleading due to different starting points: on the one hand member states with rule of law deficiencies democratic and, on the other hand, member states like Hungary and Poland autocratic.[290] Furthermore, the report touches superficially on the consequences for the rule of law situation in the member states owing to the COVID-19 pandemic. Not only does the COVID-19 pandemic seem to be a pretext for expanding power in Hungary and Poland, but also for stagnation in the Union in dealing with both countries. During the third wave in mid-February 2021, the Hungarian government enacted a decree, which contains a complete ban on public assemblies with at least two persons. Judicial review at the Hungarian Constitutional Court, however, is a farce: judicial independence and impartiality are missing because the government-friendly judges decide in favor of the government.[291] At the Union level, the ongoing Article 7 (1) TEU procedures against both countries largely stood still in 2020.[292] In mid-January 2021, the European Parliament adopted a resolution on ongoing hearings under Article 7(1) of the TEU regarding Poland and Hungary and expressed its concern that "the hearings are not organized in a regular, structured, and open manner [and] that the failure by the Council to make effective use of Article 7 of the TEU continues to undermine the integrity of the common European values."[293] The resolution also refers to the conditional mechanism to protect the Union's budget.[294]

Against this background, it is to be feared that the pandemic might even accelerate the worsening of the rule of law in Hungary and Poland. Nevertheless, the commission's latest action against Hungary and Poland offer little hope for stronger and more consistent efforts to improve the rule of law situation. In particular, the newly introduced conditionality mechanism could prove to be an effective tool if the Union ventures to apply it. The ongoing resistance of both member states and the currently escalating dispute with the EU are comprehensible because of their financial dependence on the Union. This is especially true in Hungary, whose only stable financial resource is EU funds. However, Poland, as the biggest monetary benefactor from the EU, is also financially in need of EU payments. The statement of Poland's prime minister in which he affirmed Poland's remaining in the EU after the Polish constitutional court's verdict should be seen against this background. Nevertheless, the concern persists about a "legal *polexit*" and, associated with this, a political disruption in the EU. A severe withdrawal of EU funds would, therefore, hit the Hungarian and Polish governments hard and would threaten the financial system of favoring supporters and disadvantaging opponents as well as consolidating power. However, the extent to which the Union Rule of Law Framework is effective in practice remains to be seen.

NOTES

1. Joana Gill, "The Rule of Law: what is it and why is it important?" updated September 30, 2020, https://bit.ly/3uYjWGe.

Please note that this article considers events until October 7, 2021.

2. European Commission, "Reasoned Proposal in accordance with Article 7(1) of the Treaty of the European Union regarding the rule of law in Poland. Proposal for a

Council decision on the determination of a clear risk of a serious breach by the Republic of Poland of the rule of law," published December 20, 2017, https://bit.ly/3x1XCh2.

3. European Parliament, "The situation in Hungary European Parliament resolution of 12 September 2018 on a proposal calling on the Council to determine, pursuant to Article 7(1) of the Treaty on European Union, the existence of a clear risk of a serious breach by Hungary of the values on which the Union is founded (2017/2131(INL))," published September 12, 2018, https://bit.ly/3v00kSp.

4. Günter Wilms, *Protecting Fundamental Values in the European Union through the Rule of Law. Articles 2 and 7 TEU from a Legal, Historical and Comparative Angle* (Florence: European University Institute, 2017), 3.

5. World Justice Project, "Rule of Law Index 2020," 16, accessed January 14, 2021. https://bit.ly/3djKT1f.

6. Freedom House, "Nations in Transit 2020. Dropping the Democratic Façade," 2, accessed January 17, 2021, https://bit.ly/3wZGEQj.

7. Werner Schroeder, "The European Union and the Rule of Law–State of Affairs and Ways of Strengthening," in *Strengthening the Rule of Law in Europe: From a Common Concept to Mechanisms of Implementation*, ed. Werner Schroeder (Oxford / Portland: Hart Publishing, 2016), 4.

8. Schroeder, "The European Union and the Rule of Law," 4.

9. Jörg Polakiewicz and Jenny Sandvig, "The Council of Europe and the Rule of Law," in *Strengthening the Rule of Law in Europe: From a Common Concept to Mechanisms of Implementation*, ed. Werner Schroeder (Oxford / Portland: Hart Publishing, 2016), 117.

10. Schroeder, "The European Union and the Rule of Law," 25.

11. Martin Loughlin, *Foundations of Public Law* (New York: Oxford University Press, 2010), 314–24.

12. Polakiewicz and Sandvig, "The Council of Europe," 117.

13. Claus Dieter Classen, *Nationales Verfassungsrecht in der Europäischen Union: Eine integrierte Darstellung von 27 Verfassungsordnungen* (Baden-Baden: Nomos, 2013), 56–62.

14. Theodore Konstadinides, *The Rule of Law in the European Union: The Internal Dimension* (Oxford / Portland: Hart Publishing, 2017), 55.

15. Brian Tamanaha, *On the Rule of Law. History, Politics, Theory* (New York: Cambridge University Press, 2004), 91.

16. Tamanaha, *On the Rule of Law*, 92.

17. Tamanaha, *On the Rule of Law*, 92–93.

18. Tamanaha, *On the Rule of Law*, 93; Konstadinides, *The Rule of Law*, 55.

19. Joseph Raz "The Rule of Law and Its Virtue," in *The Authority of Law. Essays on Law and Morality*, ed. Joseph Raz (Oxford: Clarendon Press, 1979), 214.

20. Tamanaha, *On the Rule of Law*, 94.

21. Lary May, "Bystanders, the Rule of Law, and Criminal Trials," in *Getting to the Rule of Law*, ed. James E. Fleming (New York: New York University Press, 2011), 248–59

22. Friedrich von Hayek, *The Constitution of Liberty* (London: Routledge & Kegan, 1960), 86.

23. Lon Fuller, *The Morality of Law* (New Haven / London: Yale University Press, 1969), 200–24.

24. Herbert Hart, "Problems of the Philosophy of Law," in *Essays in Jurisprudence and Philosophy*, ed. Herbert L.A. Hart (Oxford: Clarendon Press, 1983), 111–18.

25. Raz "The Rule of Law," 226.

26. Tamanaha, *On the Rule of Law*, 95.

27. Jürgen Habermas, "Reconciliation through the Public Use of Reason: Remarks on John Rawls's Political Liberalism," *The Journal of Philosophy* 92, no. 3 (1995): 130.

28. Tamanaha, *On the Rule of Law*, 100.

29. Tamanaha, *On the Rule of Law*, 100.

30. Ronald Dworkin, *A Matter of Principle* (Oxford: Clarendon Press, 1985), 11.

31. Tamanaha, *On the Rule of Law*, 104.

32. John Ferejohn, "Judicializing Politics, Politicizing," *Law and Contemporary Problems* 65, no. 3 (2002): 43–44.

33. Ferejohn, "Judicializing Politics," 56–57.

34. Norman Marsh, "The Rule of Law as a Supra-National Concept," in Oxford Essays in Jurisprudence, ed. Anthony G. Guest (Oxford: Oxford University Press, 1961), 243–45.

35. Organization for Security and Co-operation in Europe, "Document of the Copenhagen Meeting of the Conference on the Human Dimension of the CSCE (de)," 3, published June 29, 1990, https://bit.ly/3agfjzB.

36. Tamanaha, *On the Rule of Law*, 112.

37. International Commission of Jurists, *The Rule of Law in A Free Society: A Report of the International Congress of Jurists* (Geneva, 1959), VI–II; Tamanaha, *On the Rule of Law*, 113.

38. Albert Venn Dicey, *An Introduction to the Study of the Law of the Constitution* (London: MacMillan, 1961), 182–205.

39. Laurent Pech, "The Rule of Law as a Constitutional Principle of the European Union." *Jean Monnet Working Paper* 4, no. 9 (2009), 36–41, accessed February 3, 2021, https://bit.ly/3agpiEY.

40. Rainer Grote, "Rule of Law, Rechtsstaat and Etat de droit," in *Constitutionalism, Universalism and Democracy–A comparative analysis*, ed. Christian Starck (Baden-Baden: Nomos Verlagsgesellschaft, 1999), 278–91.

41. Grote, "Rule of Law," 304.

42. Pech, "The Rule of Law as a Constitutional Principle," 42–43.

43. Pech, "The Rule of Law as a Constitutional Principle," 44.

44. Tamanaha, *On the Rule of Law*, 3.

45. See further on this, Tímea Drinóczi and Agnieszka Bień-Kacała, "Illiberal constitutionalism and the European Rule of Law in Rule of Law," in Common Values, and Illiberal Constitutionalism: Poland and Hungary within the European Union, ed. Tímea Drinóczi and Agnieszka Bień-Kacała (London/New York: Routledge, 2021), 10–20.

46. Pech, "The Rule of Law as a Constitutional Principle," 47.

47. Council of Europe, "Statute of the Council of Europe. ETS No. 001," Preamble, Article 1, published May 5, 1949, https://bit.ly/2Q81dJJ.

48. Council of Europe, "Statute of the Council," recital 3.

49. Council of Europe, "Statute of the Council," Article 3.

50. Council of Europe, "Statute of the Council," Article 4.

51. Council of Europe, "Statute of the Council," Article 5(a).

52. Council of Europe, "Statute of the Council," Article 8.

53. Werner Schroeder, "The Rule of Law As a Value in the Senses of Article 2 EU: What Does It Mean and Imply?" in *Defending Checks and Balances in EU Member States. Taking Stock of Europe's Actions*, ed. Arnim von Bogdandy, Piotr Bogdanowicz, Iris Canor, Christoph Grabenwarter, Maciej Taborowski and Matthias Schmidt (Berlin: Springer-Verlag, 2021), 108.

54. Council of Europe, "Warsaw Declaration," published March 16/17, 2005, https://bit.ly/3gdRrjZ.

55. Laurent Pech and Joelle Grogan, "Meaning and Scope of the EU Rule of Law," 35–38, published April 4, 2020, https://bit.ly/3ttHzX2.

56. European Commission for Democracy through Law (Venice Commission), "Report on the Rule of Law," 9–10, published April 4, 2011, https://bit.ly/32k3a8l.

57. European Commission for Democracy, "Report on the Rule of Law," 10.

58. European Commission for Democracy through Law (Venice Commission), "The Rule of Law Checklist," 10, published May 2016, https://bit.ly/3aiEkdz.

59. European Commission for Democracy, "The Rule of Law Checklist," 13.

60. European Commission for Democracy, "The Rule of Law Checklist," 13–14.

61. Elisabeth Steiner, "The Rule of law in the Jurisprudence of the European Court of Human Rights," in *Strengthening the Rule of Law in Europe: From a Common Concept to Mechanisms of Implementation*, ed. Werner Schroeder (Oxford / Portland: Hart Publishing, 2016), 139.

62. Golder v. the United Kingdom (App no 4451/70 (ECtHR. 1975)) para 34.

63. Engel and Others v the Netherlands (App no 5100/71; 5101/71; 5102/72; 5354/72; 5370/72 (ECtHR. 1976)) para 69.

64. Amuur v. France, App no 19776/92 (ECtHR. 1996) § 50.

65. Steiner, "The Rule of Law," 143, 154.

66. *E.g.,* Klass and Others v. Germany, App no 5029/71 (ECtHR. 1978) § 55.

67. Stafford v. the United Kingdom App no 46295/99 (ECtHR. 2002) § 78.

68. *E.g.,* Maktouf and Damjanović v. Bosnia and Herzegovina, App no 2312/08 and 34179/08 (ECtHR. 2013) § 49.

69. Baka v. Hungary, App no 20261/21 (ECtHR. 2016) §§ 73–79, 121–22.

70. *E.g.,* Bellet v France, App no 23805/94 (ECtHR.1995) § 36.

71. *E.g.,* The Sunday Times v the United Kingdom, App no 6538/74 (ECtHR. 1979) § 55.

72. *E.g.,* Čonka v. Belgium, App no 51564/99 (ECtHR.2002) § 90.

73. Assanidze v. Georgia, App no 71503/01 (ECtHR. 2004) § 129.

74. *E.g.,* Beian v. Romania, App no 30658/05 (ECtHR.2007) § 39.

75. The Sunday Times v. the United Kingdom, § 49.

76. Hans Petter Graver, "A New Nail in the Coffin for the 2017 Polish Judicial Reform," published December 2, 2020, https://bit.ly/3dlqGIw.

77. Guđmundur Andri Ástráđsson v. Iceland, App no 26374/18 (ECtHR. 2020) abstract p. 1, §§ 253–90.

78. Guđmundur Andri Ástráđsson v. Iceland, abstract p. 1, § 290.

79. Polakiewicz and Sandvig, "The Council of Europe," 116.

80. Reczkowicz v. Poland, App no 43447/19 (ECtHR 2021), Press Release.

81. Council of Europe, "Memorandum of Understanding between the Council of Europe and the European Union," § 23, published March 11, 2007, https://bit.ly/3ggpYOK.

82. Council of Europe, "Memorandum of Understanding," § 24.

83. Polakiewicz and Sandvig, "The Council of Europe," 120.

84. Sergo Carrera et al., *The Triangular Relationship between Fundamental Rights, Democracy and the Rule of Law in the EU: Towards an EU Copenhagen Mechanism* (Brussels: CEPS Paperbacks, 2013), 17.

85. Laurent Pech, "The Rule of Law in the EU: The Evolution of the Treaty Framework and Rule of Law Toolbox," 5–10, published March, 2020, https://bit.ly/3djKoU.

86. Walter Hallstein, "Die EWG als Schritt zur Europäischen Einheit," in *Walter Hallstein–Europäische Reden*, ed. Thomas Oppermann (Stuttgart: Deutsche Verlags-Anstalt, 1979), 109 and Walter Hallstein, "Die EWG–Eine Rechtsgemeinschaft," in *Walter Hallstein–Europäische Reden*, ed. Thomas Oppermann (Stuttgart: Deutsche Verlags-Anstalt, 1979), 341.

87. Schroeder, "The European Union and the Rule of Law," 6.

88. Secretariat of the Commission of the European Communities, "Declaration on European Identity," *Bulletin of the European Communities* 6, no. 12 (1973): 118.

89. Les Verts v. Parliament, C 294/ 83 (ECJ. 1986) § 23.

90. Pech, "The Rule of Law in the EU," 11–12.

91. Pech, "The Rule of Law as a Constitutional Principle," 12.

92. Ex Article 6(1) TEU.

93. Ex Article 7 TEU.

94. Ex Article 49 TEU.

95. Pech, "The Rule of Law in the EU," 13.

96. Article 21(1) TEU.

97. Articles 255, 263(1) (4), 269 TFEU.

98. Laurent Pech and Kim Lane Scheppele, "Illiberalism Within: Rule of Law Backsliding in the EU." *Cambridge Yearbook of European Legal Studies* 19, no. 3 (2017): 3–47.

99. Artur Nowak-Far, "The Rule of Law Framework in the European Union: Its Rationale, Origins, Role and International Ramifications," in *Defending Checks and Balances in EU Member States. Taking Stock of Europe's Actions*, ed. Arnim von Bogdandy, Piotr Bogdanowicz, Iris Canor, Christoph Grabenwarter, Maciej Taborowski and Matthias Schmidt (Berlin: Springer-Verlag, 2021), 306–7.

100. Viviane Reding, A new Rule of Law initiative," Speech, European Parliament, Strasbourg, March 11, 2014, https://bit.ly/2QGTCSz.

101. For a critical analysis, see Peter Oliver and Justine Stefanelli, "Strengthening the Rule of Law in the EU: The Council's Inaction," *Journal of Common Market Studies* 54, no. 5 (2016): 1078–79.

102. Pech, "The Rule of Law in the EU," 16–17.

103. European Commission, "The 2020 EU Justice Scoreboard," 2, published August, 2020, https://bit.ly/3ga0en0.

104. European Commission, "The 2020 EU Justice Scoreboard," 56.

105. European Commission, "Commission Recommendation (EU) 2016/1374 of 27 July 2016 regarding the rule of law in Poland," published July 27, 2016, https://bit.ly/3mU0Hv2.

106. Art 7(1) TEU.

107. European Commission, "Reasoned Proposal."

108. European Parliament, "The situation in Hungary."

109. Pech, "The Rule of Law in the EU," 26–28.

110. European Commission, "Strengthening the rule of law within the Union. A blueprint for action," published July 17, 2019, https://bit.ly/3ac6eaY.

111. European Commission, "Strengthening the rule of law within the Union."

112. European Commission, "2020 Rule of Law report. The rule of law situation in the European Union," published September 30, 2020, https://bit.ly/3slHFPe.

113. Ángeles Pérez Marín, "The European Public Prosecutor's Office. Protecting the Union's financial interests through Criminal Law," *Eucrim* 1 (2020): 36–41.

114. Pech, "The Rule of Law in the EU," 32; Stefan Voigt, *Taking the Rule of Law Seriously–How the EU Could Foster Its Own Values*, ILE Working Paper Series No 24 (Hamburg: University of Hamburg, Institute of Law and Economics (ILE), 2019), 1.

115. Schroeder, "The Rule of Law," 113.

116. Marcus Klamert and Dimitry Kochenov, "Article 2 TEU," in The Treaties and the Charter of Fundamental Rights–A Commentary, ed. Manuel Kellerbauer, Marcus Klamert and Jonathan Tomkin (Oxford: Oxford University Press, 2019), 24–25; Stelio Mangiameli, "Article 2 [The Homogeneity Clause]," in *The Treaty on European Union–A Commentary*, ed. Hermann-Josef Blanke and Stelio Mangiameli (Berlin / Heidelberg: Springer-Verlag, 2013), 112; Pech, "The Rule of Law in the EU: The Evolution"; disagreeing, see Schroeder, "The Rule of Law," 109–10.

117. Schroeder, "The European Union and the Rule of Law," 9; Laurent Pech and Joelle Grogan, "Unity and Diversity in National Understandings of the Rule of Law in the EU," published April 4, 2020, https://bit.ly/3aiERfz.

118. Monica Claes and Matteo Bonelli, "The Rule of Law and the Constitutionalisation of the European Union," in *Strengthening the Rule of Law in Europe: From a Common Concept to Mechanisms of Implementation*, ed. Werner Schroeder (Oxford / Portland: Hart Publishing, 2016), 267.

119. European Commission, "Communication from the Commission to the European Parliament and the Council. A new EU Framework to strengthen the Rule of Law," published March 11, 2014, https://bit.ly/3tBfL3f.

120. European Commission, "Strengthening the rule of law within the Union"; European Commission, "Further strengthening the Rule of Law within the Union. State of play and possible next steps," published April 3, 2019, https://bit.ly/3glxqYV.

121. European Commission, "A new EU Framework to strengthen the Rule of Law," 4.

122. European Commission, "A new EU Framework to strengthen the Rule of Law," 4.

123. European Commission, "A new EU Framework to strengthen the Rule of Law," 4.

124. Schroeder, "The Rule of Law," 119–20.

125. European Commission, "Strengthening the Rule of Law within the Union."

126. Laurent Pech and Joelle Grogan, "Meaning and Scope," 22–23.

127. European Commission, "A new EU Framework to strengthen the Rule of Law," 4.

128. Schroeder, "The Rule of Law," 122.

129. Pech and Grogan, "Meaning and Scope," 23.

130. Schroeder, "The Rule of Law," 114.

131. European Commission, "Further strengthening the Rule of Law within the Union," 1–2.

132. *E.g.*, Algera and others v Common Assembly,C-7/56 and C-4 to 7/57 (ECJ. 1957) p. 55.

133. *E.g.*, Alpha Steel Ltd. v Commission, C 14/81 (ECJ.1982) § 10.

134. *E.g.*, Klomp v Inspectie der Belastingen, C-23/68 (ECJ. 1969) § 13.

135. *E.g.*, Cargill BV v Commission, C-248/89 (ECJ. 1991) § 17–24.

136. E.g., E.ON Energie AG v Commission, C 89/11 P (ECJ. 2012) § 127–34.

137. E.g., Italian Constitutional Court in DB v Commissione Nazionale per le Società e la Borsa (Consob), C-481/19 (ECJ. 2021) § 38.

138. E.g., M. M. v Minister for Justice, Equality and Law Reform, C-277/11 (ECJ. 2012) § 86.

139. E.g., AM & S Europe Limited v Commission, C-155/79 (ECJ. 1982) § 18.

140. E.g., UBS Europe SE and Alain Hondequin and Others v DV and Others, C-358/16 (ECJ. 2018) §§ 60–70.

141. E.g., Technische Universität München v Hauptzollamt München-Mitte, C269/90 (ECJ. 1991) §14.

142. Thomas von Danwitz, "The Rule of Law in the Recent Jurisprudence of the ECJ," *Fordham International Law Journal* 37, no. 5 (2014): 1315–16.

143. Schroeder, "The Rule of Law," 120; Peter van Elsuwege and Femke Gremmelprez, "Protecting the Rule of Law in the EU Legal Order: A Constitutional Role for the Court of Justice," *European Constitutional Law Review* 16, no. 1 (2020): 12.

144. Thomason Danwitz, "The Rule of Law in the Recent Jurisprudence of the ECJ." In *Strengthening the Rule of Law in Europe: From a Common Concept to Mechanisms of Implementation*, ed. Werner Schroeder (Oxford / Portland: Hart Publishing, 2016), 157.

145. Yassin Abdullah Kadi & Al Barakaat International Foundation v Council & Commission, C-402/05 P and C-415/05 P (ECJ. 2008) § 316.

146. Yassin Abdullah Kadi & Al Barakaat International Foundation, § 334.

147. Yassin Abdullah Kadi & Al Barakaat International Foundation, § 285.

148. Von Danwitz "The Rule of Law," 159.

149. Von Danwitz "The Rule of Law," 159.

150. Von Danwitz, "The Rule of Law," *Fordham*, 1328–29.

151. Von Danwitz, "The Rule of Law," *Fordham*, 1329.

152. Digital Rights Ireland and Seitlinger and Others v Ireland, C-293/12 and C-594/12 (ECJ. 2014) § 48.

153. E.g. Algera and others v Common Assembly, 63–64.

154. Commission v Hungary, C-288/12 (ECJ. 2014) §§ 54, 75–80.

155. Commission v Hungary, C-288/12 (ECJ. 2014) § 51–55.

156. Associação Sindical dos Juizes Portugueses v Tribunal de Contas, C-64/16 (ECJ. 2018) the ruling concerned the issue of salary reduction of judges concerning the violation of judicial independence and developed further this concept which had been previously raised e.g. in the case Graham J. Wilson v Ordre des avocats du barreau de Luxembourg, C-506/04 (ECJ. 2006) as regards the rules applicable to the composition of judicial bodies that are in charge of hearing appeal proceedings.

157. Pech and Platon, "A Court of Justice," 1827; Scheppele et al., "EU Values Are Law, after All: Enforcing EU Values through Systemic Infringement Actions by the European Commission and the Member States of the European Union," *Yearbook of European Law* 39, no. 1 (2021): 4–5.

158. Associação Sindical dos Juizes Portugueses, §§ 32–34.

159. Commission v Hungary, C-78/18 (ECJ. 2020).

160. Commission v Hungary, C-78/18 (ECJ. 2020) §§ 110–43

161. Commission v Hungary, C-66/18 (ECJ. 2020) §§ 234, 243.

162. Commission v Hungary, C-66/18 (ECJ. 2020) §§ 68–93.

163. Commission v Hungary, C808/18 (ECJ. 2020) §§ 314–15.

164. Scheppele et al, "EU Values Are Law," 43.

165. Commission v Poland, Case C-441/17 (ECJ. 2017).

166. Commission v Poland, Case C-619/18 (ECJ. 2018).

167. Commission v Poland, Case C-791/19 (ECJ. 2020).

168. Scheppele et al, "EU Values Are Law," 43.

169. Commission v Poland, C-619/18 (ECJ. 2018).

170. A.K. and Others v Sąd Najwyższy, C-585/18, C-624/18, S-625/18 (ECJ. 2019) §§ 152–53.

171. A.K. and Others, § 166.

172. A.B. and Others v Krajowa Rada Sądownictwa and Others C-824/18 (ECJ. 2021).

173. A.B. and Others, §§ 96, 139, 165.

174. Naczelny Sąd Administracyjny. Komunikat w sprawie wyroków NSA dotyczących odwołań od uchwał KRS w przedmiocie przedstawienia (nieprzedstawienia) wniosków o powołanie do pełnienia urzędu na stanowisku sędziego Sądu Najwyższego. May 6, 2021. https://bit.ly/3hda202.

175. E.g., Alekszij Torubarov v Bevándorlási és Menekültügyi Hivatal, C-556/17 (ECJ. 2019).

176. Van Elsuwege and Gremmelprez, "Protecting the Rule of Law," 31.

177. Pech and Grogan, "Meaning and Scope," 19.

178. Lydia Gall, "Judgement In, Damage Done in Hungary. EU Action Needed to Reverse Rule of Law Breakdown," published October 13, 2020, https://bit.ly/3agvnRU; more precisely on university autonomy in Hungary, see Somody in this volume.

179. Nowak-Far, "The Rule of Law Framework," 315–16; Petra Bárd and Sergio Carrera, "The Commission's Decision on 'Less EU' in Safeguarding the Rule of Law: A play in four acts," 2, published March 8, 2017, https://bit.ly/3mQzolb.

180. Ahtisaari et al, "Report on the Austrian Government's Commitment to the Common European Values, in Particular Concerning the Rights of Minorities, Refugees and Immigrants, and the Evolution of the Political Nature of the FPÖ (The Wise Men Report)," *International legal materials: current documents* 40, no. 1 (2001).

181. Scheppele and Pech, "Didn't the EU Learn."

182. Pech and Scheppele, "Illiberalism Within," 10.

183. Ahtisaari et al, "Report on the Austrian Government's Commitment," 120.

184. European Commission, "A new EU Framework to strengthen the Rule of Law," 5.

185. Emmanuel Crabit and Nicolaas Bel, "The EU Rule of Law Framework," in *Strengthening the Rule of Law in Europe: From a Common Concept to Mechanisms of Implementation*, ed. Werner Schroeder (Oxford / Portland: Hart Publishing, 2016): 200–201.

186. José Manuel Durão Barroso, "State of the Union 2012 Address," Speech, European Parliament, Strasbourg, September 12, 2012, https://bit.ly/32h0UyG.

187. Bárd and Carrera, "The Commission's Decision," 4.

188. European Commission, "A new EU Framework to strengthen the Rule of Law," 3, 6.

189. Emmanuel Crabit and Nicolaas Bel, "The EU Rule of Law Framework," in *Strengthening the Rule of Law in Europe: From a Common Concept to Mechanisms of Implementation*, ed. Werner Schroeder (Oxford / Portland: Hart Publishing, 2016), 204.

190. European Commission, "A new EU Framework to strengthen the Rule of Law," 7–8.

191. Linda Senden, *Soft law in European Community law* (Oxford / Portland: Hart Publishing, 2004), 148–49.

192. Nowak-Far, "The Rule of Law Framework," 320.

193. Nowak-Far, "The Rule of Law Framework," 322.

194. European Commission, "Further strengthening the rule of law within the Union," 3.

195. European Commission, "Reasoned Proposal."

196. European Parliament, "The situation in Hungary."

197. Micha Šimečka, "The establishment of an EU Mechanism on Democracy, the Rule of Law and Fundamental Rights (debate)," Statement, European Parliament, Brussels, October 20, 2020; Daniel Kelemen, "Europe's Other Democratic Deficit: National Authoritarianism in Europe's Democratic Union," *Government and Opposition* 52, no. 2 (2017): 223–27; Dimitry Kochenov and Laurent Pech, "From bad to worse? On the Commission and the Council's rule of law initiatives," published January 20, 2015, https://bit.ly/3mQC1Dz.

198. Kim Lane Scheppele and Laurent Pech, "That These Rule-of-Law Interventions Don't Work?" published March 9, 2018, https://bit.ly/2OZoHQQ.

199. Freedom House, "Nations in Transit 2020," 2.

200. European Commission, "Further strengthening the rule of law within the Union," 10–14.

201. European Commission, "Further strengthening the rule of law within the Union," 11–13.

202. European Commission, "2020 Rule of Law report."

203. European Commission, "The EU's Rule of Law Toolbox," published April, 2019, https://bit.ly/3uRbE39.

204. European Commission, "2020 Rule of Law report," 4.

205. Regarding the aspect of judicial independence, see European Commission, "2020 Rule of Law report," 10–11; concerning Bulgaria, see Radosveta Vassileva, "Kolevi: Bulgaria's 10-Year Cat-and-Mouse Game with the Council of Europe and the Venice Commission," published February 12, 2020, https://bit.ly/3dno9gT.

206. For a more detailed analysis on the rule of law backsliding in Hungary, see Somody, in this volume. See for an informative visualization of the constitutional development Tímea Drinóczi and Agnieszka Bień-Kacała, "Preface," in Common Values, and Illiberal Constitutionalism: Poland and Hungary within the European Union, ed. Tímea Drinóczi and Agnieszka Bień-Kacała (London/New York: Routledge, 2021), xvi.

207. As addition after completion, the section will refer to the first Rule of Law Report. The second Rule of Law Report concerning Hungary see European Commission, "2021 Rule of Law Report. Country Chapter on the rule of law situation in Hungary," published July 20, 2021, https://bit.ly/37Cu3qI and concerning Poland see European Commission, "2021 Rule of Law Report. Country Chapter on the rule of law situation in Poland," published July 20, 2021, https://bit.ly/37BpmgX.

208. Kriszta Kovács and Gábor Attila Tóth, "Hungary's Constitutional Transformation," *European Constitutional Law Review* 16, no. 1 (2011): 187–98. See also Tímea Drinóczi and Agnieszka Bień-Kacała, "Illiberal constitutionalism," 20 ff. using the term "illiberal constitutionalism" to describe the transformation of Poland's and Hungary's constitutional system to a stage of incompatibility with EU values.

209. Peter Wilkin, "The Rise of 'Illiberal' Democracy: The Orbánization of Hungarian Political Culture," *Journal of World-Systems Research* 24, no. 1 (2018): 24.

210. Wilkin, "The Rise of 'Illiberal' Democracy," 23–25.

211. European Commission, "2020 Rule of Law Report. Country Chapter on the rule of law situation in Hungary," 1, published September 30, 2020, https://bit.ly/2QuplWK.

212. European Commission, "Country Chapter Hungary," 1, 2–7.

213. See more specifically on attacks on judicial independence and media pluralism in Hungary, Somody in this book.

214. European Commission, "Country Chapter Hungary," 1, 17–19.

215. Katarzyna Gajda-Roszczynialska and Krystian Markiewic, "Disciplinary Proceedings as an Instrument for Breaking the Rule of Law in Poland," *Hague Journal on the Rule of Law* 12, no. 3 (1969): 457.

216. Urszula Jaremba, "The rule of the majority vs. the rule of law: how Poland has become the new enfant terrible of the European Union," *Tijdschrift voor Constitutioneel Recht* 7, no. 3 (2016): 262.

217. Kriszta Kovács and Kim Lane Scheppele, "The fragility of an independent judiciary: Lessons from Hungary and Poland—and the European Union," *Communist and Post-Communist Studies* 51, no. 3 (2018): 6.

218. Gajda-Roszczynialska and Markiewic, "Disciplinary Proceedings," 458.

219. Dariusz Mazur, "Annual report for 2020: From bad to worse–the Polish judiciary in the shadow of the 'muzzle act'," 3, published December 31, 2020, https://bit.ly/2OSEkcC.

220. European Commission for Democracy, through Law (Venice Commission), "Poland. Joint Urgent Opinion," 14, published January 16, 2020, https://bit.ly/3mQBvp.

221. European Commission, "2020 Rule of Law Report. Country Chapter on the rule of law situation in Poland," 1, published September 30, 2020, https://bit.ly/3snsnJC.

222. European Commission, "2020 Rule of Law Report. Country Chapter on the rule of law situation in Poland," 1, 8, published September 30, 2020, https://bit.ly/3snsnJC.

223. European Commission, "Country Chapter Poland," 11.

224. As noted in the recent Greco reports: "Fourth Evaluation Round: Corruption prevention in respect of members of parliament, judges and prosecutors," published September 22, 2021, https://bit.ly/3ijzzV8 and "Fifth Evaluation Round: Compliance Report Poland," published September 27, 2021, https://bit.ly/3ijqgV3.

225. European Commission, "Country Chapter Poland," 13–14.

226. Pawel Florkiewicz and Alan Charlish, "Polish Lower House Passes Media Reform Bill, which U.S. Denounces," published August 12, 2021, https://reut.rs/3CQuah1.

227. Pawel Marcisz, "The Lex TVN and the End of Free Media in Poland," published August 15, 2021, https://bit.ly/2WtF5g5.

228. European Commission, "September infringements package: key decisions," published September 23, 2021, https://bit.ly/3mbhIk3.

229. European Commission, "Country Chapter Poland," 1.

230. European Commission, "Country Chapter Poland," 17.

231. Amnesty International, "Hungary: LexNGO finally repealed but a new threat is on the horizon," published May 18, 2021, http://bitly.ws/dHF6.

232. European Commission, "February infringements package."

233. European Commission, "October infringements package: key decisions," published October 30, 2020, https://bit.ly/3ggWIaf.

234. Jennifer Rankin, "EU urged to Suspend Funds to Hungary over 'grave breaches of the rule of law'," published July 7, 2021, https://bit.ly/3xHVA4G.

235. European Commission, "October infringements package"; European Commission, "December infringements package: key decisions," published December 3, 2020, https://bit.ly/3v8nmGT.

236. European Commission, "Rule of Law: European Commission launches infringement procedure to safeguard the independence of judges in Poland," published April 29, 2020, https://bit.ly/3x0ul6k.

237. European Commission, "Rule of Law: European Commission refers Poland to the European Court of Justice to protect independence of Polish judges and asks for interim measures," published March 31, 2021, https://bit.ly/3aeQDYn.

238. Court of Justice of European Union, "Press release no. 130/21, The disciplinary regime for judges in Poland is not compatible with EU law Court of Justice of European Union," published July 15, 2021, https://bit.ly/2UO3Dz8.

239. Alicja Ptak, "Poland to dissolve judges' Disciplinary Chamber to meet EU demands," published August, 7, 2021, https://reut.rs/3AwhucR.

240. European Commission, "Independence of Polish judges: Commission asks European Court of Justice for financial penalties against Poland on the activity of the Disciplinary Chamber," published September 7, 2021, https://bit.ly/3hfiOts.

241. European Commission, "Independence of Polish judges: Commission asks European Court of Justice for financial penalties against Poland on the activity of the Disciplinary Chamber," published September 7, 2021, https://bit.ly/3hfiOts.

242. Daniel Tilles, "Polish Ruling Party Approved Opposition Candidate for Human Rights Commissioner," published July 8, 2021, https://bit.ly/2VFnm4C.

243. EURACTIV, "Impasse deepens in Poland over new ombudsman," published May 14, 2021, https://bit.ly/3fF0D03.

244. Wlodarczak-semczuk and Morland, "Key Polish rulingon primacy of EU law delyed," published August 31, 2021, https://www.reuters.com/world/europe/polish-court-rule-primacy-eu-law-amid-deepening-row-with-brussels-2021-08-31/.

245. Rule of Law, "The PM filed a Petition with the Constitutional Tribunal about the Superiority of Polish Law over EU law," published March 30, 2021, https://bit.ly/2ULuVWM.

246. Reuters, "EU Commission Says Poland Cannot Question Primacy of EU law," published June 10, 2021, https://reut.rs/36yZPV1.

247. Court of Justice of European Union, "Communiqué de Presse no. 127/21, La Pologne doit suspendre immédiatementl'application des dispositions nationales relatives notamment aux compétences de la chambre disciplinaire de la Cour suprême," published July 14, 2021, https://bit.ly/2VOPiDj.

248. Maria Wilczek, "Polish court ruling against EU legal jurisdiction moves Polexit one step closer," published October 7, 2021, https://bit.ly/3uQzfSO.

249. Regarding the primacy of national law, the PiS government refers to the ruling of the German Federal Constitutional Court on the Public Sector Purchase Programme (judgment of 5 May 2020 2 BvR 859/15, 2 BvR 980/16, 2 BvR 2006/15, 2 BvR 1651/15). In doing so, the PiS government deliberately misunderstands the German Court and exploits its ruling for its own purposes to undermine the rule of law in Poland further. In contrast to the Polish Constitutional Tribunal, the German Court is independent, not a political puppet. The German Court's reasons to adopt an ultra vires act and the Polish government's dismantling of the independence of the judiciary are in all respects not comparable with each other (Thomas Guddat, "Ein Paukenschlag in Karlsruhe, der bis nach Warschau zu hören war," published July 12, 2020, https://forumdialog.eu/2020/07/12/ein-paukenschlag-in-karlsruhe-der-bis-nach-warschau-zu-hoeren-war/#_ftn11).

250. Court of Justice of European Union, "Press release no. 173/21, Transfers without consent of a judge from one court to another or between two divisions of the

same court are liable to undermine the principles of the irremovability of judges and judicial independence," published October 6, 2021, https://bit.ly/3DmR2nD.

251. European Commission, "EU founding Values: Commission Starts Legal Action against Hungary and Poland for Violations of Fundamental Rights of LGBTIQ People," published July 15, 2021, https://bit.ly/3r9PWI13; fearing the withholding of EU funds, first polish regions started to withdraw from the resolution against LGBTQ people, see e.g. Daniel Tilles, "Polish region withdraws anti-LGBT resolution amid EU funding threat," published September 22, 2021, https://bit.ly/3 F. 3RyIP.

252. Scheppele et al, "EU Values Are Law," 3.

253. European Commission for Democracy, through Law (Venice Commission), "Interim Report on the Measures taken in the EU Member States as a Result of the COVID-19 Crisis and their Impact on Democracy, the Rule of Law and Fundamental Rights," 10, 13, published October 8, 2020, https://bit.ly/3e9azNg.

254. European Commission for Democracy, "Interim Report," 15.

255. European Commission for Democracy, "Interim Report," 15.

256. Hungary Today, "Coronavirus: Parliament Votes to Extend State of Emergency," published October 11, 2020, https://bit.ly/3e6psj.

257. HYPERLINK "https://www.rferl.org/author/rfe-rls-hungarian-service/opvuq_" \o "RFE/RL's Hungarian Service" RFE/RL's Hungarian Service, "Hungary's Orbán Seeks Continued Emergency Powers For COVID-19 Response," published February 15, 2021, https://bit.ly/3gh5rtc.

258. Council of Europe, "Respecting democracy, rule of law and human rights in the framework of the COVID-19 sanitary crisis: A toolkit for member states," 2, published April 7, 2020, https://bit.ly/2Q5RfII.

259. Council of Europe, "Complete list of the Council of Europe's treaties," last updated April 7, 2021, https://bit.ly/3x0iDIV.

260. Ireland v United Kingdom, App no 5310/71 (ECtHR. 1978) § 207.

261. European Commission for Democracy through Law (Venice Commission), "Respect for Democracy, Human Rights and the Rule of Law during States of Emergency–Reflections," 3, published May 26, 2020, https://bit.ly/2PZjHMD.

262. European Commission for Democracy, "Poland. Joint Urgent Opinion," 3–4.

263. European Commission for Democracy, "Respect for Democracy," 14.

264. European Commission for Democracy, "Respect for Democracy," 18–19.

265. European Commission, "2020 Rule of Law report," 6.

266. European Commission, "2020 Rule of Law report," 6–7.

267. European Commission, "2020 Rule of Law report," 6.

268. European Commission, "Country Chapter Hungary," 8.

269. European Commission, "Country Chapter Hungary," 15.

270. European Commission, "Country Chapter Hungary," 16.

271. European Commission, "Country Chapter Poland," 16.

272. European Commission for Democracy, "Interim Report," 6–7.

273. Jaap de Zwaan, "The European Union and the Rule of Law: A new instrument," published December 22, 2020, https://bit.ly/3e4RJXH.

274. Jan, "Hungary, Poland block 2021-2027 EU budget, recovery package," published November 16, 2020, https://reut.rs/3dltDso.

275. European Parliament and Council, "Regulation of the European Parliament and of the Council on a General Regime of Conditionality for the Protection of the Union Budget," published December 16, 2020, https://bit.ly/3afJnex.

276. European Parliament and Council, "General Regime of Conditionality for the Protection of the Union Budget," Article 6 in conjunction with Article 4.

277. European Council, "European Council meeting (10 and 11 December2020)–Conclusions," published December 11, 2020, https://bit.ly/3afWa0I.

278. Aleksejs Alemanno and Hubertus Chamon, "Conditionality Mechanism: What's in it?" published December 30, 2020, https://bit.ly/3x2tcv9; Scheppele et al., "Compromising the Rule of Law while Compromising on the Rule of Law," published December 13, 2020, https://bit.ly/3ga28nE; optimistic, see Julinda Beqiraj, "The 'Regulation on a general regime of conditionality for the protection of the Union budget' and its contested implementation," published January 19, 2021, https://bit.ly/3agtwMW.

279. European Parliament, "European Parliament resolution of 16 December 2020 on the Multiannual Financial Framework 2021–2027, the Interinstitutional Agreement, the EU Recovery instrument and the Rule of Law Regulation," published December 14, 2020, https://bit.ly/3dm40aR, recitals 4–5.

280. European Parliament, "Application of Regulation (EU, Euratom) 2020/2092: the Rule of Law conditionality mechanism," published March 25, 2021, https://bit.ly/3uULLQ2, § 14.

281. European Parliament, "Application of Regulation," § 13.

282. European Parliament, "The creation of guidelines for the application of the general regime of conditionality for the protection of the Union budget," July 8, 2021, https://bit.ly/3seGFOv.

283. Tamanaha, *On the Rule of Law*, 141.

284. Simon Chesterman, "An International Rule of Law?" *The American Journal of Comparative Law* 56, no. 2 (2008): 332.

285. Vasiliki Poula and Eponine Howarth, "The European Commission's Rule of Law Report: a key tile in the mosaic of rule of law protection in the EU," published October 22, 2020, https://bit.ly/3doAz8s.

286. Tímea Drinóczi and Agnieszka Bień-Kacała, "Illiberal constitutionalism and the European Rule of Law in Rule of Law," in *Common Values, and Illiberal Constitutionalism: Poland and Hungary within the European Union*, ed. Tímea Drinóczi and Agnieszka Bień-Kacała (London/New York: Routledge, 2021), 20.

287. András Arató, "Der Feind zahlt mit," 5, *Süddeutsche Zeitung* 59, no. 5 (2021): 4.

288. Laurent Pech, "Doing more harm than good? A critical assessment of the European Commission's first Rule of Law Report," published December 9, 2020, https://bit.ly/3ggY5pp.

289. Daniel Hegedüs, "The European Commission's Missed Rule-of-Law Opportunity," published October 1, 2020, https://bit.ly/3mRJXEw.

290. Pech, "Doing more harm than good?".

291. Kriszta Kovács, "Hungary and the Pandemic: A Pretext for Expanding Power," published March 11, 2021, https://bit.ly/32kfXaW.

292. Pech et al., "1825 Days later: The End of the Rule of Law in Poland (Part I)," published January 13, 2021, https://bit.ly/2Qvm9dm; Kovács, "Hungary and the Pandemic."

293. European Parliament, "Application of Regulation," § 1, 3. European Parliament, "Ongoing hearings under article 7(1) of the TEU regarding Poland and Hungary," published January 16, 2020, https://bit.ly/304EEKS, §1,3

294. European Parliament, "Application of Regulation," § 6. European Parliament, "Ongoing hearings under article 7(1) of the TEU regarding Poland and Hungary, " published January 16, 2020, https://bit.ly/304EEKS, § 6

REFERENCES

Ahtisaari, Maritti, Frowein, Jochen, and Oreja Oreja. "Report on the Austrian Government's Commitment to the Common European Values, in Particular Concerning the Rights of Minorities, Refugees and Immigrants, and the Evolution of the Political Nature of the FPÖ (The Wise Men Report)." *International legal materials: current documents* 40, no. 1 (2001): 102–23.

Alemanno, Aleksejs and Hubertus Chamon. "Conditionality Mechanism: What's in it?" Published December 30, 2020. https://bit.ly/3x2tcv9.

Amnesty International. "Hungary: LexNGO finally repealed but a new threat is on the horizon." Published May 18, 2021. http://bitly.ws/dHF6.

Arató, András. "Der Feind zahlt mit." *Süddeutsche Zeitung* 59, no. 5 (2021): 4.

Bakó, Beáta. "Hungary's Latest Experiences with Article 2 TEU: The Need for 'Informed' EU Sanctions." In *Defending Checks and Balances in EU Member States. Taking Stock of Europe's Actions*, edited by Arnim von Bogdandy, Piotr Bogdanowicz, Iris Canor, Christoph Grabenwarter, Maciej Taborowski and Matthias Schmidt, 35–69. Berlin: Springer-Verlag, 2021.

Bárd, Petra and Sergio Carrera. "The Commission's Decision on 'Less EU' in Safeguarding the Rule of Law: A Play in Four Acts." Published March 8, 2017. https://bit.ly/3mQzolb.

Barroso, José Manuel Durão. "State of the Union 2012 Address." Speech, European Parliament, Strasbourg, September 12, 2012. https://bit.ly/32h0UyG.

Beqiraj, Julinda. "The 'Regulation on a general regime of conditionality for the protection of the Union budget' and its contested implementation." Published January 19, 2021. https://bit.ly/3agtwMW.

Carrera, Sergo, Elspeth Guil and Nicholas Hernanz. *The Triangular Relationship between Fundamental Rights, Democracy and the Rule of Law in the EU: Towards an EU Copenhagen Mechanism.* Brussels: CEPS Paperbacks, 2013.

Chesterman, Simon. "An International Rule of Law?" *The American Journal of Comparative Law* 56, no. 2 (2008): 331–61.

Claes, Monica and Matteo Bonelli. "The Rule of Law and the Constitutionalisation of the European Union." In *Strengthening the Rule of Law in Europe: From a Common Concept to Mechanisms of Implementation*, edited by Werner Schroeder, 265–89. Oxford / Portland: Hart Publishing, 2016.

Classen, Claus Dieter. *Nationales Verfassungsrecht in der Europäischen Union: Eine integrierte Darstellung von 27 Verfassungsordnungen*. Baden-Baden: Nomos, 2013.

Crabit, Emmanuel and Nicolaas Bel. "The EU Rule of Law Framework." In *Strengthening the Rule of Law in Europe: From a Common Concept to Mechanisms of Implementation*, edited by Werner Schroeder, 197–206. Oxford / Portland: Hart Publishing, 2016.

Council of Europe. "Complete list of the Council of Europe's treaties." Last updated April 7, 2021. https://bit.ly/3x0iDIV.

Council of Europe. "Respecting democracy, rule of law and human rights in the framework of the COVID-19 sanitary crisis: A toolkit for member states." Published April 7, 2020. https://bit.ly/2Q5RfII.

Council of Europe. "Memorandum of Understanding between the Council of Europe and the European Union." Published March 11, 2007. https://bit.ly/3ggpYOK.

Council of Europe. "Warsaw Declaration." Published March 16/17, 2005. https://bit.ly/3gdRrjZ

Council of Europe. "Statute of the Council of Europe. ETS No. 001." Published May 5, 1949. https://bit.ly/2Q81dJJ. §

Court of Justice of European Union. "Press release no. 173/21, Transfers without consent of a judge from one court to another or between two divisions of the same court are liable to undermine the principles of the irremovability of judges and judicial independence." Published October 6, 2021. https://bit.ly/3DmR2nD.

Court of Justice of European Union. "Communiqué de Presse no. 127/21, La Pologne doit suspendre immédiatementl'application des dispositions nationales relatives notamment aux compétences de la chambre disciplinaire de la Cour suprême." Published July 14, 2021. https://bit.ly/2VOPiDj.

Court of Justice of European Union. "Press release no. 130/21, The disciplinary regime for judges in Poland is not compatible with EU law Court of Justice of European Union." Published July 15, 2021. https://bit.ly/2UO3Dz8.

De Zwaan, Jaap. "The European Union and the Rule of Law: A New Instrument." Published December 22, 2020. https://bit.ly/3e4RJXH.

Dicey, Albert Venn. *An Introduction to the Study of the Law of the Constitution*. Tenth Edition. London: MacMillan, 1961.

Dworkin, Ronald. *A Matter of Principle*. Oxford: Clarendon Press, 1985.

Drinóczi, Tímea and Bień-Kacała, Agnieszka. "Illiberal Constitutionalism and the European Rule of Law in Rule of Law." In *Common Values, and Illiberal Constitutionalism: Poland and Hungary within the European Union*, edited by Tímea Drinóczi and Agnieszka Bień-Kacała, 3–40. London / New York: Routledge, 2021.

EURACTIV. "Impasse deepens in Poland over new ombudsman." Published May 14, 2021. https://bit.ly/3fF0D03.

Euronews. "EU wants daily fines for Poland over its controversial judiciary reforms." Published September 7, 2021. https://bit.ly/38QcwMs.

European Commission. "September infringements package: Key decisions." Published September 23, 2021. https://bit.ly/3mbhIk3.

European Commission. "Independence of Polish judges: Commission asks European Court of Justice for financial penalties against Poland on the activity of the Disciplinary Chamber." Published September 7, 2021. https://bit.ly/3hfiOts.

European Commission. "EU founding values: Commission starts legal action against Hungary and Poland for violations of fundamental rights of LGBTIQ people." Published July 15, 2021. https://bit.ly/3r9PWH3.

European Commission. "February infringements package: Key decisions" Published February 18, 2021. https://bit.ly/3agtV1U.

European Commission. "Rule of Law: European Commission refers Poland to the European Court of Justice to protect independence of Polish judges and asks for interim measures." Published March 31, 2021. https://bit.ly/3aeQDYn.

European Commission. "The 2020 EU Justice Scoreboard." Published August, 2020. https://bit.ly/3ga0en0.

European Commission. "2020 Rule of Law report. The rule of law situation in the European Union." Published September 30, 2020. https://bit.ly/3slHFPe.

European Commission. "The EU's Rule of Law Toolbox." Published April, 2019. https://bit.ly/3uRbE39.

European Commission. "2021 Rule of Law Report. Country Chapter on the rule of law situation in Hungary." Published July 20, 2021. https://bit.ly/37Cu3qI.

European Commission. "2021 Rule of Law Report. Country Chapter on the rule of law situation in Poland." Published July 20, 2021. https://bit.ly/37BpmgX.

European Commission. "2020 Rule of Law Report. Country Chapter on the rule of law situation in Hungary." Published September 30, 2020. https://bit.ly/2QuplWK.

European Commission. "2020 Rule of Law Report. Country Chapter on the rule of law situation in Poland." Published September 30, 2020. https://bit.ly/3snsnJC.

European Commission. "October infringements package: Key decisions." Published October 30, 2020. https://bit.ly/3ggWIaf.

European Commission. "December infringements package: Key decisions." Published December 3, 2020. https://bit.ly/3v8nmGT.

European Commission. "Rule of Law: European Commission launches infringement procedure to safeguard the independence of judges in Poland." Published April 29, 2020. https://bit.ly/3x0ul6k.

European Commission. "Strengthening the rule of law within the Union. A blueprint for action." Published July 17, 2019. https://bit.ly/3ac6eaY.

European Commission. "Further strengthening the Rule of Law within the Union. State of play and possible next steps." Published April 3, 2019. https://bit.ly/3glxqYV.

European Commission. "Reasoned Proposal in accordance with Article 7(1) of the Treaty of the European Union regarding the rule of law in Poland. Proposal for a Council decision on the determination of a clear risk of a serious breach by the Republic of Poland of the rule of law." Published December 20, 2017. https://bit.ly/3x1XCh2.

European Commission. "Commission Recommendation (EU) 2016/1374 of 27 July 2016 regarding the rule of law in Poland." Published July 27, 2016. https://bit.ly/3mU0Hv2.

European Commission. "Communication from the Commission to the European Parliament and the Council. A new EU Framework to strengthen the Rule of Law." Published March 11, 2014. https://bit.ly/3tBfL3f.

European Commission for Democracy through Law (Venice Commission). "Poland. Joint Urgent Opinion." Published January 16, 2020. https://bit.ly/3mQBvp7.

European Commission for Democracy through Law (Venice Commission). "Respect for Democracy, Human Rights and the Rule of Law during States of Emergency–Reflections." Published May 26, 2020. https://bit.ly/2PZjHMD.

European Commission for Democracy through Law (Venice Commission). "Interim Report on the Measures taken in the EU Member States as a Result of the COVID-19 Crisis and their Impact on Democracy, the Rule of Law and Fundamental Rights." Published October 8, 2020. https://bit.ly/3e9azNg.

European Commission for Democracy through Law (Venice Commission). "The Rule of Law Checklist." Published May 2016. https://bit.ly/3aiEkdz.

European Commission for Democracy through Law (Venice Commission). "Report on the Rule of Law." Published April 4, 2011. https://bit.ly/32k3a8l.

European Council. "European Council meeting (10 and 11 December 2020)–Conclusions." Published December 11, 2020. https://bit.ly/3afWa0I.

European Parliament. "The creation of guidelines for the application of the general regime of conditionality for the protection of the Union budget." Published July 8, 2021, https://bit.ly/3seGFOv.

European Parliament. "Application of Regulation (EU, Euratom) 2020/2092: the Rule of Law conditionality mechanism." Published March 25, 2021. https://bit.ly/3uULLQ2.

European Parliament and Council. "Regulation of the European Parliament and of the Council on a General Regime of Conditionality for the Protection of the Union Budget." Published December 16, 2020. https://bit.ly/3afJnex.

European Parliament. "European Parliament resolution of 16 December 2020 on the Multiannual Financial Framework 2021–2027, the Interinstitutional Agreement, the EU Recovery instrument and the Rule of Law Regulation." Published December 14, 2020. https://bit.ly/3dm40aR. European Parliament. "Ongoing hearings under article 7(1) of the TEU regarding Poland and Hungary." Published January 16,2020. https://bit.ly/304EEKS.

European Parliament. "The situation in Hungary. European Parliament resolution of 12 September 2018 on a proposal calling on the Council to determine, pursuant to Article 7(1) of the Treaty on European Union, the existence of a clear risk of a serious breach by Hungary of the values on which the Union is founded (2017/2131(INL))." Published September 12, 2018. https://bit.ly/3v00kSp.

Ferejohn, John. "Judicializing Politics, Politicizing." *Law and Contemporary Problems* 65, no. 3 (2002): 41–68.

Florkiewicz, Pawel and Charlish, Alan. "Polish lower house passes media reform bill, which U.S. denounces." Published August 12, 2021. https://reut.rs/3CQuah1.

Freedom House. "Nations in Transit 2020. Dropping the Democratic Façade." Accessed January 17, 2021. https://bit.ly/3wZGEQj.

Fuller, Lon L. *The Morality of Law*. New Haven / London: Yale University Press, 1969.

Gajda-Roszczynialska, Katarzyna and Krystian Markiewicz. "Disciplinary Proceedings as an Instrument for Breaking the Rule of Law in Poland." *Hague Journal on the Rule of Law* 12, no. 3 (1969): 451–83.

Gall, Lydia. "Judgement In, Damage Done in Hungary. EU Action Needed to Reverse Rule of Law Breakdown." Published October 13, 2020. https://bit.ly/3agvnRU.

Gill, Joana. "The Rule of Law: what is it and why is it important?" Published September 30, 2020, 2021. https://bit.ly/3uYjWGe.

Graver, Hans Petter. "A New Nail in the Coffin for the 2017 Polish Judicial Reform." Published December 2, 2020. https://bit.ly/3dlqGIw.

Greco. "Fourth Evaluation Round: Corruption prevention in respect of members of parliament, judges and prosecutors." Published September 22, 2021. https://bit.ly/3ijzzV8.

Greco. "Fifth Evaluation Round: Compliance Report Poland." Published September 27, 2021. https://bit.ly/3ijqgV3.

Grote, Rainer. "Rule of Law, Rechtsstaat and 'Etat de droit.'" In *Constitutionalism, Universalism and Democracy–A Comparative Analysis*, edited by Christian Starck, 277–306. Baden-Baden: Nomos Verlagsgesellschaft, 1999.

Guddat, Thomas. "Ein Paukenschlag in Karlsruhe, der bis nach Warschau zu hören war," published July 12, 2020, https://forumdialog.eu/2020/07/12/ein-paukenschlag-in-karlsruhe-der-bis-nach-warschau-zu-hoeren-war/#_ftn11.

Habermas, Jürgen. "Reconciliation Through the Public Use of Reason: Remarks on John Rawls's Political Liberalism." *The Journal of Philosophy* 92, no. 3 (1995): 109–31.

Hallstein, Walter. "Die EWG als Schritt zur Europäischen Einheit." In *Walter Hallstein–Europäische Reden*, edited by Thomas Oppermann, 103–12. Stuttgart: Deutsche Verlags-Anstalt, 1979.

Hallstein, Walter. "Die EWG–Eine Rechtsgemeinschaft." In *Walter Hallstein–Europäische Reden*, edited by Thomas Oppermann, 341–48. Stuttgart: Deutsche Verlags-Anstalt, 1979.

Hart, Herbert L.A. "Problems of the Philosophy of Law." In *Essays in Jurisprudence and Philosophy,* edited by Herbert L. A. Hart, 88–119. Oxford: Clarendon Press, 1983.

Hegedüs, Daniel. "The European Commission's Missed Rule-of-Law Opportunity." Published October 1, 2020. https://bit.ly/3mRJXEw.

Hungary Today. "Coronavirus: Parliament Votes to Extend State of Emergency." Published October 11, 2020. https://bit.ly/3e6psjl.

International Commission of Jurists. *The Rule of Law in a Free Society: A Report of the International Congress of Jurists*. Geneva, 1959.

Jaremba, Urszula. "The Rule of the Majority vs. the Rule of Law: How Poland has Become the New Enfant Terrible of the European Union." *Tijdschrift voor Constitutioneel Recht* 7, no. 3 (2016): 262–74.

Kelemen, Daniel. "Europe's Other Democratic Deficit: National Authoritarianism in Europe's Democratic Union." *Government and Opposition* 52, no. 2 (2017): 211–38.

Klamert, Marcus and Dimitry Kochenov. "Article 2 TEU." In *The Treaties and the Charter of Fundamental Rights–A Commentary*, edited by Manuel Kellerbauer, Marcus Klamert and Jonathan Tomkin, 22–30. Oxford: Oxford University Press, 2019.

Kochenov, Dimitry and Laurent Pech. "From bad to worse? On the Commission and the Council's rule of law initiatives." Published January 20, 2015. https://bit.ly/3mQC1Dz.

Konstadinides, Theodore. *The Rule of Law in the European Union: The Internal Dimension*. Oxford / Portland: Hart Publishing, 2017.

Kovács, Kriszta. "Hungary and the Pandemic: A Pretext for Expanding Power." Published March 11, 2021. https://bit.ly/32kfXaW.

Kovács, Kriszta and Kim Lane Scheppele. "The fragility of an independent judiciary: Lessons from Hungary and Poland–and the European Union." *Communist and Post-Communist Studies* 51, no. 3 (2018): 1–12.

Kovács, Kriszta and Gábor Attila Tóth. "Hungary's Constitutional Transformation." *European Constitutional Law Review* 16, no. 1 (2011): 183–203.

Loughlin, Martin. *Foundations of Public Law*. New York: Oxford University Press, 2010.

Mangiameli, Stelio. "Article 2 [The Homogeneity Clause]." In *The Treaty on European Union–A Commentary*, edited by Hermann-Josef Blanke and Stelio Mangiameli, 109–56. Berlin / Heidelberg: Springer-Verlag, 2013.

Marcisz, Pawel. "The Lex TVN and the End of Free Media in Poland." Published August 12, 2021. https://verfassungsblog.de/the-lex-tvn-and-the-end-of-free-media-in-poland/.

Marsh, Norman S. "The Rule of Law as a Supra-National Concept." In *Oxford Essays in Jurisprudence*, edited by Anthony G. Guest, 223–64. Oxford: Oxford University Press, 1961.

May, Lary. "Bystanders, the Rule of Law, and Criminal Trials." In *Getting to the Rule of Law*, edited by James E. Fleming, 241–64. New York: New York University Press, 2011.

Mazur, Dariusz. "Annual report for 2020: From bad to worse–the Polish judiciary in the shadow of the 'muzzle act'." Published December 31, 2020. https://bit.ly/2OSEkcC.

Nowak-Far, Artur. "The Rule of Law Framework in the European Union: Its Rationale, Origins, Role and International Ramifications." In *Defending Checks and Balances in EU Member States. Taking Stock of Europe's Actions*, edited by Arnim von Bogdandy, Piotr Bogdanowicz, Iris Canor, Christoph Grabenwarter, Maciej Taborowski and Matthias Schmidt, 306–31. Berlin: Springer-Verlag, 2021.

Oliver, Peter and Justine Stefanelli. "Strengthening the Rule of Law in the EU: The Council's Inaction." *Journal of Common Market Studies* 54, no. 5 (2016): 1075–84.

Organization for Security and Co-operation in Europe (OSCE). "Document of the Copenhagen Meeting of the Conference on the Human Dimension of the CSCE (de)." Published June 29, 1990. https://bit.ly/3agfjzB.

Pech, Laurent. "The Rule of Law in the EU: The Evolution of the Treaty Framework and Rule of Law Toolbox." Published March, 2020. https://bit.ly/3djKoUV.

Pech, Laurent. "Doing more harm than good? A critical assessment of the European Commission's first Rule of Law Report." Published December 9, 2020. https://bit.ly/3ggY5pp.

Pech, Laurent. "The Rule of Law as a Constitutional Principle of the European Union." *Jean Monnet Working Paper* 4, no. 9 (2009). Accessed February 3, 2021. https://bit.ly/3agpiEY.

Pech, Laurent and Joelle Grogan. "Unity and Diversity in National Understandings of the Rule of Law in the EU." Published April 4, 2020. https://bit.ly/3aiERfz.

Pech, Laurent and Joelle Grogan. "Meaning and Scope of the EU Rule of Law." Published April 4, 2020. https://bit.ly/3ttHzX2.

Pech, Laurent and Sébastien Platon. "A Court of Justice. Judicial independence under threat: The Court of Justice to the rescue in the *ASJP* case." *Common Market Law Review* 55, no. 6 (2018): 1827–54.

Pech, Laurent and Kim Lane Scheppele. "Illiberalism Within: Rule of Law Backsliding in the EU." *Cambridge Yearbook of European Legal Studies* 19, no. 3 (2017): 3–47.

Pech, Laurent, Wachowiec, Patryk and Dariusz Mazur. "1825 Days later: The End of the Rule of Law in Poland (Part I)." Published January 13, 2021. https://bit.ly/2Qvm9dm.

Pérez Marín, Ángeles. "The European Public Prosecutor's Office. Protecting the Union's financial interests through Criminal Law." *Eucrim* 1 (2020): 36–41.

Polakiewicz, Jörg and Jenny Sandvig. "The Council of Europe and the Rule of Law." In *Strengthening the Rule of Law in Europe: From a Common Concept to Mechanisms of Implementation*, edited by Werner Schroeder, 115–34. Oxford / Portland: Hart Publishing, 2016.

Poula, Vasiliki and Eponine Howarth. "The European Commission's Rule of Law Report: a key tile in the mosaic of rule of law protection in the EU." Published October 22, 2020. https://bit.ly/3doAz8s.

Ptak, Alicja. "Poland to dissolve judges' Disciplinary Chamber to meet EU demands." Published August, 7, 2021. https://reut.rs/3AwhucR.

Rankin, Jennifer. "EU urged to suspend funds to Hungary over 'grave breaches of the rule of law'." Published July 7, 2021. https://bit.ly/3xHVA4G.

Raz, Joseph. "The Rule of Law and Its Virtue." In *The Authority of Law. Essays on Law and Morality*, edited by Joseph Raz, 210–29. Oxford: Clarendon Press, 1979.

Reding, Viviane. "A New Rule of Law Initiative." *Speech, European Parliament*, Strasbourg, March 11, 2014. https://bit.ly/2QGTCSz.

Reuters. "Polish court delays ruling on primacy of EU law for the fourth time." Published September 30, 2021. https://reut.rs/3kZL9q.

Reuters. "EU Commission says Poland cannot question primacy of EU law." Published June 10, 2021. https://reut.rs/36yZPV1.

RFE/RL's Hungarian Service. "Hungary's Orban Seeks Continued Emergency Powers For COVID-19 Response." Published February 15, 2021. https://bit.ly/3gh5rtc.

Rule of Law. "The PM filed a petition with the Constitutional Tribunal about the superiority of Polish law over EU law." Published March 30, 2021. https://bit.ly/2ULuVWM.

Rutynowska, Eliza. "The ombudsman: a watchdog, not a lapdog." Published March 15, 2021. https://bit.ly/2QpDTqG.

Senden, Linda. *Soft law in European Community law*. Oxford / Portland: Hart Publishing, 2004.

Scheppele, Kim Lane, Kochenow, Dimitry Vladimirovich and Barbara Grabowska-Moroz. "EU Values Are Law, after All: Enforcing EU Values through Systemic Infringement Actions by the European Commission and the Member States of the European Union." *Yearbook of European Law* 39, no. 1 (2021): 1–21.

Scheppele, Kim Lane, Pech, Laurent and Sébastien Platon. "Compromising the Rule of Law while Compromising on the Rule of Law." Published December 13, 2020. https://bit.ly/3ga28nE.

Scheppele, Kim Lane and Laurent Pech. "Didn't the EU Learn That These Rule-of-Law Interventions Don't Work?" Published March 9, 2018. https://bit.ly/2OZoHQQ.

Schroeder, Werner. "The Rule of Law As a Value in the Senses of Article 2 EU: What Does It Mean and Imply?" In *Defending Checks and Balances in EU Member States. Taking Stock of Europe's Actions*, edited by Arnim von Bogdandy, Piotr Bogdanowicz, Iris Canor, Christoph Grabenwarter, Maciej Taborowski and Matthias Schmidt, 106–26. Berlin: Springer-Verlag, 2021.

Schroeder, Werner. "The European Union and the Rule of Law–State of Affairs and Ways of Strengthening." In *Strengthening the Rule of Law in Europe: From a Common Concept to Mechanisms of Implementation*, edited by Werner Schroeder, 3–34. Oxford / Portland: Hart Publishing, 2016.

Secretariat of the Commission of the European Communities. "Declaration on European Identity." *Bulletin of the European Communities* 6, no. 12 (1973): 118–22.

Šimečka, Micha. "The establishment of an EU Mechanism on Democracy, the Rule of Law and Fundamental Rights (debate)." Statement, European Parliament, Brussels, October 20, 2020.

Steiner, Elisabeth. "The Rule of law in the Jurisprudence of the European Court of Human Rights." In *Strengthening the Rule of Law in Europe: From a Common Concept to Mechanisms of Implementation*, edited by Werner Schroeder, 135–54. Oxford / Portland: Hart Publishing, 2016.

Strupczewski, Jan. "Hungary, Poland block 2021-2027 EU budget, recovery package." Published November 16, 2020. https://reut.rs/3dltDso.

Tamanaha, Brian Z. *On the Rule of Law. History, Politics, Theory*. New York: Cambridge University Press, 2004.

Tilles, Daniel. "Polish region withdraws anti-LGBT resolution amid EU funding threat." Published September 22, 2021. https://bit.ly/3 F. 3RyIP.

Tilles, Daniel. "Polish ruling party approved opposition candidate for human rights commissioner." Published July 8, 2021. https://bit.ly/2VFnm4C.

Van Elsuwege, Peter and Femke Gremmelprez. "Protecting the Rule of Law in the EU Legal Order: A Constitutional Role for the Court of Justice." *European Constitutional Law Review* 16, no. 1 (2020): 8–32.

Vassileva, Radosveta. "Kolevi: Bulgaria's 10-Year Cat-and-Mouse Game with the Council of Europe and the Venice Commission." Published February 12, 2020. https://bit.ly/3dno9gT.

Voigt, Stefan. *Taking the Rule of Law Seriously–How the EU Could Foster Its Own Values*. ILE Working Paper Series No 24. Hamburg: University of Hamburg, Institute of Law and Economics (ILE), 2019.

Von Danwitz, Thomas. "The Rule of Law in the Recent Jurisprudence of the ECJ." In *Strengthening the Rule of Law in Europe: From a Common Concept to Mechanisms of Implementation*, edited by Werner Schroeder, 155–69. Oxford / Portland: Hart Publishing, 2016.

Von Danwitz, Thomas. "The Rule of Law in the Recent Jurisprudence of the ECJ." *Fordham International Law Journal* 37 no. 5 (2014): 1311–47.

Von Hayek, Friedrich A. *The Constitution of Liberty*. London: Routledge & Kegan, 1960.

Wilczek, Maria. "Polish court ruling against EU legal jurisdiction moves Polexit one step closer." Published October 7, 2021. https://bit.ly/3uQzfSO.

Wilkin, Peter. "The Rise of 'Illiberal' Democracy: The Orbánization of Hungarian Political Culture." *Journal of World-Systems Research* 24, no. 1 (2018): 5–42.

Wilms, Günter. *Protecting Fundamental Values in the European Union through the Rule of Law. Articles 2 and 7 TEU from a legal, historical and comparative angle*. Florence: European University Institute, 2017.

World Justice Project. "Rule of Law Index 2020." Accessed January 14, 2021. https://bit.ly/3djKT1f.

Chapter 9

The Future of International Criminal Justice Cooperation

A Retreat from the Rule of Law?

Yvon Dandurand and Jessica Jahn

INTRODUCTION

In a globalized world, international cooperation has become essential in most aspects of social and economic life, as well as in critical sectors such as public health, security, environmental protection, development, or population flow. However, the focus in this chapter is on the specific need for international cooperation in criminal matters (or international criminal justice cooperation) based on the rule of law and respect for human rights, governed by an international legal framework, and supported by international institutions. Such cooperation has evolved over the years and now takes many forms, some of them more crucial than others.

The growing transnational nature of crime, partly the result of globalization, digitalization, and mobility trends, has made international cooperation an indispensable part of the international community's crime prevention and criminal justice agenda. In fact, the security and development challenges posed by organized crime, illicit economies, and corruption seem only to diversify and intensify.[1] However, the relative importance that policymakers attach to international criminal justice cooperation often depends on how they perceive the threats posed by transnational organized crime, corruption, and the exploitation of illicit markets, and on the strength of their resolve to counter such threats.

Whether one is investigating or prosecuting crimes across borders, transferring fugitives, protecting witnesses, exchanging evidence, or forfeiting assets, success usually hinges on interstate cooperation. Unfortunately, while organized crime and illicit markets proliferate globally, there is a global political tendency toward deglobalization and purely national solutions. Yet, to be fully effective in a globalized world, multilateral criminal justice cooperation must ultimately be supported by multilevel governance structures that address the complex political, legal, and logistical challenges that international cooperation in criminal matters inevitably faces. At this point, however, instead of greater cooperation to fight crime, multilateral responses remain disjointed, insufficient, and reactive.[2]

A hard-won achievement of the last decades was the establishment of international legal frameworks based on a commitment to the rule of law, the protection of human rights, and the reaffirmation of state sovereignty serving as a basis for legal harmonization and enabling international criminal justice cooperation. Yet, in spite of the progress achieved over the last twenty years at the bilateral, regional, and international levels, international cooperation in the investigation and prosecution of serious crimes remains deficient. The multilateral cooperation regime "has not yielded the expected dividends in terms of effective international cooperation."[3] The proliferation of cooperation arrangements, however necessary, did not prove to be an appropriate substitute for a more comprehensive, integrated international legal framework for cooperation in criminal matters, one in which the separate modalities of cooperation are used in a more effective and complementary manner.[4]

Year after year, the World Economic Forum's global risks reports sound the alarm about the intensification of global risks and the lack of collective will to tackle them.[5] Similarly, the 2020 World Drug Report concluded that drug trafficking has never been more international in nature, warning that "[d]espite the fact that international cooperation is the foundation of the international drug framework, its effectiveness is barely measured at the global level."[6] The growing threats of organized crime and corruption combined with the diminishing ability of states, working alone or together, to counter them are the result of state-centered politics and a diminishing support for multilateralism. While the Kyoto Declaration, adopted at the most recent UN Congress on Crime Prevention and Criminal Justice, notes the importance of multilateral cooperation,[7] the "impotence of political will" continues to prevent meaningful progress.[8]

One cannot trust the official discourse about the present international cooperation regime and its successes. False or misleading arguments about the rule of law or national sovereignty are used to defend the regime's failures and hide its growing desuetude. The discourse is plainly intended to justify the states' frequent noncompliance with their international obligations rather than to encourage a reconsideration of the existing cooperation regime. At a time when multilateralism itself is under siege, international cooperation is often discussed without reference to the global decline in all forms of international cooperation and political compromise.

Deep but still uncertain geopolitical changes and the decline of the rule-based liberal order have seemingly led to a gradual retreat from the rule of law and shrunk states' commitment to the implementation of a comprehensive rule-based international criminal justice cooperation regime. Many states increasingly prefer informal approaches to cooperation that reaffirm their sovereignty but are not necessarily tethered to the rule of law and human rights. The weakening of multilateral cooperation regimes is certainly not unique to the criminal justice sector and its fight against transnational crime. However, the precariousness of the present situation and the social, human, and economic costs resulting from the shortcomings of the current international cooperation regime are perhaps not yet fully appreciated.

With an eye toward the future, this chapter reflects on the state of international criminal justice cooperation, arguing that the legacy tools and mechanisms on which international cooperation still relies are unable to adapt to the pace of changing patterns in transnational organized crime. Various geopolitical and other uncertainties have all but paralyzed multilateral attempts to improve the current criminal justice cooperation regime. The chapter highlights some of the fault lines and fragility of that, reflects on apparent shifts in cooperation trends, and offers five scenarios or possible futures for international criminal justice cooperation in the foreseeable future. It concludes with a comment of possible complementarity or synergies between these scenarios.

LIMITATIONS OF THE GLOBAL COOPERATION REGIME

Even at the best of times, various practical, legal, and political factors can hamper international criminal justice cooperation. The most common ones include differences in cultural and legal traditions, languages, or political orientations. To these we must add a narrow interpretation of state sovereignty, the absence of enabling national legislation, the absence of channels of communication for the exchange of information and intelligence, divergences in approaches and priorities, and corruption of public officials. Laws, bilateral treaties, conventions, and formal coordination mechanisms may open some pathways to enhanced cooperation, but the success of these initiatives always depend on relationships of trust, reciprocity, and mutual respect between states, and ultimately on the extent to which states perceive cooperation as in their own best interests.[9]

It is easy to conclude that international cooperation did not grow fast enough to keep up with the pace of change in patterns of transnational crime, the movement of criminals and their growing technological sophistication.

By most accounts and in most parts of the world, this international cooperation regime remains weak, fragmented, and capricious.[10] It is becoming profusely clear that current international cooperation legacy mechanisms and processes are largely inefficient in light of the new technologies and the constant shifts in criminal patterns, not to mention the paralyzing politicization of international cooperation in criminal matters. For example, as we have argued elsewhere, some of the international legal frameworks have proven inadequate as a basis for international cooperation and the protection of migrants and victims of trafficking.[11]

This is the case, for instance, in the exchange of electronic data through the mutual legal assistance (MLA) process, which entails bilateral or multilateral agreements that usually include due process safeguards.[12] According to the European Commission, electronic evidence is required in about 85 percent of criminal investigations, of which about two-thirds (65 percent) involve evidence that is either stored or controlled by technology companies in another jurisdiction.[13] In view of the anticipated "data-sharing storm,"[14] prompted in part by the rising global uptake of the Internet of Things, blockchain applications, and cryptocurrencies, cross-border digital data has and will only continue to become a necessity for criminal justice actors, on which they must depend to investigate and prosecute a range of serious crimes.[15] Yet, the MLA process remains painfully slow compared to the speed at which criminal investigations develop and digital data can be moved, tampered, or deleted.[16] Rather than increasing international cooperation for the investigation and prosecution of serious crimes, MLA has added layers of cumbersome administrative processes and legal uncertainty, without any guarantee that the digital data in question can even be extracted.[17] These issues are further exacerbated by the time-sensitive nature of electronic evidence, differences between legal systems, the clash of bureaucracies, the protection of sovereignty and, in many instances, the incapacity of law enforcement and states to work together to overcome their differences.[18]

Evidence of the practical and technical limitations of the MLA regime is compelling, but the shortcomings are also part of the broader failure of states to adequately address the underlying and more politically inflammatory concerns around the jealous protection of data sovereignty,[19] the politicization of international cooperation,[20] and conflicting policy paradigms and priorities in the area of cyber governance.[21]

Because existing methods of cooperation remain utterly complex and generally inadequate, they are increasingly replaced by informal and much more controversial alternatives.[22] Some of these alternatives are outside existing legal frameworks and are not subject to independent oversight or effective scrutiny. Clear legal standards have yet to be formulated, despite the fact that "effective, as opposed to perfunctory and impotent, oversight and controls are as indispensable today as they were thirty years ago."[23] Some observers also expressed a concern over the emergence of national and international entities and processes, together with specialist liaison networks, functioning outside existing governance and accountability frameworks.[24] Others have observed that frustrations with the current systems of extradition and transfer of suspects,[25] law enforcement data and information sharing,[26] and most other modalities of cooperation have driven many states to find alternatives and to engage in a number of behaviors that threaten human rights and disrupt the free flow of information across borders.[27]

Some of the main fault lines in the current international criminal justice regime have not only been obvious for a long time, but they are quickly widening. Some of these fault lines are the result of unsettled international policy, including a gridlock in cyber policy, policy paralysis in migration policy, and competing interests in environment protection and climate policy. These unresolved policy ambiguities have a direct impact on international criminal justice cooperation. Obviously protracted international policy disagreements are not new but trying to prevent and resolve international problems within an effective international cooperation is doomed to fail.

Failure to Address New Challenges

With the growing prevalence of new and emerging forms of crime, such as cybercrime, environmental crime, and crime related to falsified medical products, policymakers, and practitioners increasingly find themselves in need of specialized and innovative policies, tools, and operations.[28] In most cases, the transnational nature of such crimes requires coordinated international responses, yet the development of such tools has yet to receive sufficient attention. Meanwhile, combating such crimes demands coordination at the national level among various stakeholders, many of whom do not typically cooperate in criminal matters, including agencies responsible for protecting the environment, health, or cultural heritage, as well as the private sector. Indeed, that coordination is necessary not only for domestic investigations and prosecutions but also in the execution of foreign requests.[29]

Cyber-insecurity, in particular, is especially revealing of states' unwillingness to sacrifice sovereignty in favor of effective criminal justice cooperation. The nature of cyber-enabled criminality poses significant challenges in terms of international cooperation, yet "there is no overarching consensus among UN member states on the best ways to tackle it."[30] In fact, Walker observed that there are two different competing approaches to cyber governance. On the one hand, Russia, China, and several developing countries advocate for "digital sovereignty," under which territorial jurisdiction and nonintervention would be at the forefront of a state-led process. On the other hand, Western states, including the United States, the EU, and Canada, generally champion a "multi-stakeholder model," involving private companies, academic experts, and practitioners in decision-making that might not necessarily respect sovereign interests.[31] Such incompatible policy paradigms may complicate cooperation efforts and make it unlikely that UN member states may agree on new cybercrime treaty. As Woods aptly put it, "if it is good, it will not be signed by all relevant parties, and if it is signed by all relevant parties, it will not be good."[32]

Even so, some progress in harmonizing legislation and enforcement approaches has been achieved at the regional level, most notably the implementation of the Budapest Convention on Cybercrime and its forthcoming Second Additional Protocol on Enhanced Cooperation and Disclosure of Electronic Evidence. The bar for international cooperation in fighting cybercrime has repeatedly being lowered, sometimes suggesting that states should pursue international cooperation without requiring full harmonization of national legislation, as long as national laws are sufficiently compatible to simplify and expedite the various forms of such cooperation.[33] At the same time, as cybercrime is mostly de-territorialized, states are encouraged to legislate on "extraterritorial jurisdiction over citizens and persons ordinarily resident on their territory, irrespective of where those acts were committed and whether they constitute offences in the foreign jurisdiction."[34]

Technology can be both a facilitator and an inhibitor of international cooperation. It unfortunately has not yet been placed fully at the service of international cooperation. Moreover, new asymmetries between countries in terms of their respective technological capacity have emerged, making it difficult for them to engage in fruitful cooperation in criminal matters. There are also disparities between states in terms of their case management systems and the capacity of their central authorities to deal with the increasing volume and complexity of work relating to new and sophisticated forms of crime.[35] The growing backlog of assistance requests is obviously a concern that needs to be addressed.

Limits of Existing Review and Amendment Mechanisms

There remains the hope that the review processes associated with conventions, such as the Budapest Convention, the United Nations Convention Against Transnational Organized Crime (UNTOC), or the United Nations Convention Against Corruption (UNCAC), will eventually lead to improvements in the current international criminal justice cooperation mechanisms.

The political priority accorded to the UNTOC and its protocols has waned quickly after its adoption in 2000 and there is no evidence that it has been widely used or that it has somehow significantly improved international cooperation or deterred organized criminals from continuing and expanding their activities globally.[36] There are "significant global gaps in its implementation" and little evidence that it has played much of a role as far as law enforcement cooperation is concerned.[37] The Conference of the Parties (COP) to the UNTOC finally adopted, after much delay, a mechanism for the review of the implementation of the convention and the protocols thereto.[38] However, the mechanism is slow, far from transparent and heavily politicized. The fact that states parties to that convention have taken eighteen years to agree on a review mechanism which can only take place over many years to come, combined with the many limitations they imposed on the process, betray the paltry importance that they attach to reviewing the actual implementation of the cooperation regime envisaged by the convention, holding each other accountable to deliver on their commitment, and strengthening that regime as required. Unified international pressure applied to states that do not live up to their commitments is a rarity.

By comparison, the first cycle of the review mechanism to the UNCAC began in 2010 and has since revealed many shortcomings of the regime, especially in relation to international cooperation. For instance, according to a report on the progress by states parties in implementing selected chapters of the UNCAC, most parties reported "no extradition cases in relation to which the Convention had been used as a legal basis or that no statistics were kept in that regard,"[39] observing that bilateral or regional agreements are generally preferred to facilitate cooperation. In relation to the implementation of chapter V on asset recovery, the Conference of the States Parties to the UNCAC found that states typically had little experience in MLA requests, resulting in an inability to assess the extent to which article 55, paragraphs 1–2, had been implemented by some parties.[40] Similarly, the majority of parties reported that no assets had been returned to another state, owing mainly to a lack of requests for such cooperation.[41] Among other things, such findings clearly point to the failure of the UNCAC to foster and support cooperation, as well as the continued asymmetries in states' ability to cooperate, despite the considerable investments made in capacity building and technical assistance.

From a broader perspective, one might question whether and to what extent we can expect these formal review mechanisms to form a consensus around necessary changes and deliver more powerful forms of cooperation. In fact, it is not clear what these international review processes or the international institutions which are the "custodians" of the relevant international treaties can actually do to reset these processes and enhance the existing regime. The current fundamental deficiencies of the present international criminal justice cooperation regime and associated mechanisms are not likely to be resolved by global or regional institutions. The latter, being primarily accountable to internal bureaucracies rather than external constituencies, "can play a useful role as conveners and centers of information sharing, but they lack the capacity to act at scale."[42] That being said, it is hard to disagree with Secretary General Antonió Guterres's message that, in the context of wide rejection of globalism and aggressive nationalism, "a multipolar world needs more multilateral governance, not less."[43]

The Pillars of International Cooperation in Criminal Matters

International cooperation is enabled by multilateral treaties, bilateral agreements, and national laws, but such instruments are not ends in themselves as partnerships invariably depend on sustained relationships of mutual recognition, trust, and reciprocity. The principle of good faith is a fundamental canon of general international law.[44] It underlies all forms of internal cooperation and, more generally, relationships between states in the execution of their treaty obligations.

The principle of reciprocity has always been a building block of international cooperation in criminal matters. Reciprocity is determined in part by a state's capacity to cooperate, but also by its capacity to compel others to cooperate and to respond firmly to noncompliance with existing agreements. However, reciprocity is being redefined in an ad-hoc and mostly transactional manner, without reference necessarily to a broader normative framework. To different extents, various asymmetries between participating states determine the kind of reciprocity that is possible or the cooperation that is deemed desirable by individual states.[45]

Trust building and the development of working relationships to advance future cooperation are also important and rely on the good faith principle. They serve to lower the cost of cooperation.[46] Yet, trust is difficult to develop and is easily eroded. A lack of trust between states and participating agencies often explains why requests for collaboration are ignored or denied. There may not even be transparency about the reasons why requests are denied, "which in some cases results from uncertainty about the recipient country's ability to maintain the confidentiality of a given request or protect the sources and methods of collection, which, in turn, limits the timely sharing of information."[47] For example, exchange of information and intelligence is unlikely when another country's key law enforcement or justice institutions are perceived as corrupt and untrustworthy. Without trust, the mutually reinforcing attribute of reciprocity withers or may be improperly leveraged as bargaining power for political gain, whereby states withhold or offer cooperation for concessions sometimes in other domains of strategic interest. In the zero-sum game played by certain states, the type of long-term relationships that are needed to address contemporary threats tend to be sacrificed for short-term advantages.

One must also remember that states' interests are multidimensional and that cooperation in criminal matters agreements and other transactions transcend negotiations around criminal matters issues. Everything is on the table for a deal, in particular the interests that appeal to the states involved in these negotiations/transactions and their respective policy goals. In many countries, even those that purport to abide by the rule of law, the decision whether to extradite for criminal matters is ultimately made by a political official, such as a minister of justice or a minister of foreign affairs and secretary of state, thus blurring the thin line between politically motivated and independent law enforcement decision-making. International cooperation efforts are thus inherently imbued with state power and global politics.

Sovereignty and the Pursuit of National Interests

Gordon Brown, a former UK prime minister, recently summarized the challenge as follows: "There is a huge disconnect between where we are physically—more interconnected, more independent, more integrated than ever before—and where we are geopolitically—tribal, protectionist and disconnected."[48]

International criminal justice cooperation is essentially the tributary of other forms of international cooperation. The former cannot be understood without reference to the latter and both are intimately linked to the states' own perceived broad interests. Indeed, extradition and other forms of criminal justice cooperation are related to other aspects of international cooperation between countries and can be used as a foreign policy tool in negotiating agreements concerning various cooperation issues.[49]

As Patrick rightly noted, "weak international cooperation is a choice, not an inevitability."[50] However, to the extent that international criminal justice cooperation is failing, it does so because of the states' ambivalence and diminishing commitment to a multilateral, rule of law-based cooperation regime. States are still torn between their desire for effective cooperation in fighting crime and mitigating other security threats, and their distrust of each other and obsessive commitment to preserving national sovereignty. The states' retreat from a cooperation system based on the rule of law is perhaps not that surprising and neither is the emergence of alternatives to that system. As Zakaria reminds us all, "nations have created mechanisms and institutions to cooperate and solve problems. But in the end, in extremis, they walk alone."[51]

The desuetude of the global international criminal justice cooperation regime does not affect every country equally. In fact, interstate competition prevails now more than ever over a willingness to face transnational threats together. There are also issues about the costs associated with participation in the current regime, the upkeep of the present regime and structures, and who should bear these costs. Many of the current discussions about existing cooperation mechanisms revert to "burden sharing."

Asymmetries of Means and Capacities

There are often fundamental asymmetries of political interests, cooperation preferences, means and capacity among states facing specific transnational organized crime threats. States obviously do not have the same crime control priorities or interests. This becomes obvious when considering the different interests of producing states, as compared to consuming states (drugs, firearms, forced labor, etc.) or states of origin versus transit or destination states (immigration, migrant smuggling, human trafficking, etc.). Furthermore, states do not have the same law enforcement and criminal justice capacity, nor do they have the same capacity to engage in effective international cooperation. At the same time, new asymmetries are emerging that further complicate international cooperation (e.g., control over the Internet, access to certain technologies, etc.). All of these asymmetries will continue to make international cooperation in criminal matters a very challenging task and should explicitly be taken into account in all efforts to enhance international criminal justice cooperation and to fight transnational organized crime.[52]

DISTURBING TRENDS

Because it is essentially political and dependent on so many other complex factors, international criminal justice cooperation is perpetually in an unstable state. There is no "steady state" because of constantly evolving international relations and the fact there are just too many ways in which progress in international cooperation can be derailed. However, what is particularly alarming is that no clear vision has emerged of what a desirable or acceptable end state might embody, especially in relation to effective international cooperation.

Even though changes in systems cannot be measured on a Richter scale, they can have a profound impact and transform the systems. In this section, several shifts and trends that affect international cooperation are identified, including challenging geopolitics, shifting alliances, and waning faith in international institutions, among others. While the general trends do not apply equally to all forms of cooperation or to all regions, they figure prominently in discussions around cooperation.

Geopolitical Tensions and Uncertainties

International criminal justice cooperation is on very shaky ground. In an increasingly fragmented world where most issues become a reason for contention among states, the stable interstate relationships that are needed for all forms of cooperation are lacking. In fact, the mounting geopolitical and geo-economics tensions among the world's most influential countries was identified as "the most urgent global risks at present" in the World Economic Forum's 2019 Global Risks Report.[53]

A new balance of power is being shaped by emerging economic, demographic, and technological forces and, with it, a turbulent and largely unsettled geopolitical landscape. As states increasingly question the value of long-standing frameworks, they turn inward and view challenges and opportunities through narrow nationalist and unilateral lenses, they tend to pursue their own agendas and alliances, multilateral cooperation regimes and mechanisms are regarded as less important.[54] At best, they are seen as instruments to promote their own best interests.

Global cooperation against transnational crime and related security threats can prevail over global dysfunction if states and their leaders are willing to change course. These leaders must clearly identify areas in which their national interests merge or are at least compatible. However, future progress will likely remain marred by a "trust recession" in multilateralism and global institutions.[55] This is significant because trust and reciprocity are the necessary engines of international cooperation in criminal matters. This lack of congruity in the international response to organized crime, and cybercrime especially, is connected to a growing breakdown in trust among governments, even at national and regional levels.[56]

In the present high-turbulence era, states seem to have lost faith in the value of working together. Multilateral institutions—ostensibly foundational to the rule-based international criminal justice cooperation regime—are not as effective as they were meant to be in preventing and responding to organized crime and other security threats. The turbulence accentuates interstate rivalries and threatens to undermine the international community's ability to mitigate critical global risks,[57] including transnational organized crime, cybercrime, crimes against the environment, and corruption. Clearly, there is a pressing and urgent need for stronger multilateralism and international cooperation, yet states continue to demonstrate a rather myopic view of the challenges that lie ahead and what is needed to overcome them.

The relative failure of international cooperation structures and mechanisms to deliver on the promise of a coordinated and effective response to the COVID-19 pandemic has exposed international cooperation as a mirage and exposed the "terrible consequences of faltering global cooperation."[58] In other areas, for example, in the context of international migration, international cooperation has often led to restrictions on migratory flows and created greater illicit markets for movement and opportunities for organized crime. These and other examples of institutionalized international cooperation are testing the faith of the most fervent defenders of internationalism. Faith in international institutions and their ability to coordinate action, foster cooperation, and manage transnational threats has been seriously affected. As some experts have observed, there has been a critical loss of faith in the value of international cooperation and the world has not been this bereft of most rudimentary forms of cooperation since the 1930s.[59] The institutionalization of international governance sought to impose the rule of law and provide a basis for cooperation other than raw power. In matters of international criminal justice cooperation, the results are largely unconvincing.

Weakened International Order and Faith in International Institutions

Much attention is given these days to the renewed perils to which democracies are exposed, including autocracy's global ascendance and the rising support for authoritarian and xenophobic populist movements that are openly contemptuous of the rule of law.[60] It may not be an exaggeration to refer to some current global trends as an impending crisis of legitimacy and a serious threat to our institutions, including multilateral institutions.[61] A deconsolidation of the rule of law and a gradual suffocation of international criminal justice cooperation are more than a theoretical possibility.

Underpinning this possibility is the unmet challenge of adapting the basic tenets of the international liberal order, which include liberal democracy, the rule of law, and shared sovereignty, to the contemporary landscape of an interdependent world increasingly unconstrained by borders. Instead, states have used international cooperation to support antiquated notions of sovereignty and undermine the liberal order. Many air their grievances with the liberal order under the veil of upholding national sovereignty while at the same time encroaching on the sovereignty of other states. Even if sovereignty may have demonstrated itself as somewhat versatile in the past, the potential success of such an adaptation will require systemic global change, including perhaps disruptions to the present distribution of power and transformations to institutions—a politically unappealing and formidable task to which many global leaders are either willfully blind or wholly resistant. To this, one may add the broader failure of international institutions to find common ground among states on key issues that challenge conventional notions of sovereignty and build a consensus around a vision for the future of international criminal justice cooperation.

Changes in Nature and Scope of Political Alliances

Historically, international criminal justice cooperation has had its strong moments, for example, during the days of the so-called war on drugs during which temporary alliances were created and transnational cooperation was bought, extorted, or otherwise compelled. However, support for that approach has eroded over the years and that basis of international cooperation in criminal matters has become more fragile. According to Tenant, "the process leading up to the 2016 UN General Assembly Special Session (UNGASS) exposed a fault line in the previous international consensus that had been in place since the 1998 UNGASS, and the 2009 Political Declaration and Plan of Action."[62] Latin-American governments, supported by civil society, advocated for a new agreement on international drug policy, a more human-rights-centered approach, including a move away from a law enforcement.

Public Debate and Public Support for International Cooperation

Over the last two decades, the public has become more aware of the challenges and political issues surrounding international criminal justice cooperation. After the 9/11 terrorist attacks in the United States, the renewed war against terrorism placed enormous pressure on existing international cooperation mechanisms and new international alliances emerged. The global instruments against terrorism, the UNTOC and the UNCAC were seen as strong bases for international law enforcement cooperation.[63] Public attention was drawn on terrorism prevention practices that raised serious concerns about exceptional and very problematic international cooperation practices that ran contrary to the Rule of Law, human rights principles and international standards (e.g., kidnapping, extraordinary renditions). These practices underscored the need to ensure that "states adhere to the rule of law, including the basic principles, standards and obligations of criminal and international law that define the boundaries of permissible and legitimate State action against terrorism."[64]

Generally speaking, however, international criminal justice cooperation in criminal matters rarely attracts a lot of public attention, except perhaps when specific cases of failure of existing mechanisms become breaking news. Nevertheless, it seems that international cooperation issues are increasingly debated in public and in the media, even if that tends to take place in a context where international cooperation is deeply politicized and powerful states use sophisticated strategy to influence the global information supply chain. Public support for renewed international cooperation is shaky and unlikely to improve unless governments can show the population the concrete benefits from international cooperation.

States' Disinvestment in Multilateral Cooperation Mechanisms

The obsoleteness and ineffectiveness of existing international criminal justice cooperation mechanisms are obvious. For most states, the current legacy mechanisms supporting that cooperation are impractical, unaffordable, and unsustainable: they can only lose at this game because it is fundamentally rigged. As a result of a growing trust deficit—not that the "trust capital" was ever that significant—states are progressively disinvesting themselves from the global international criminal justice cooperation regime and show a growing preference for bilateral, regional, and generally less formal and less binding forms of cooperation arrangements.

For instance, confiscation of proceeds of crime is a key tool for tackling organized crime, corruption and any crime motivated by financial profit. However, international cooperation agreements, which would otherwise be encouraged by the prospect of return and sharing of assets between the countries involved, often require that the assets in question are linked to an offense of which an individual was convicted and are sometimes inadequate to deprive criminals of their ill-gotten gains. More powerful instruments, such as extended confiscation or non-conviction-based confiscation, are required but are at present limited to some bilateral formal or informal arrangements for that purpose.[65]

The resulting states' disinvestment in multilateral criminal justice cooperation structures and mechanisms and their increased reliance on informal and mostly bilateral modes of cooperation is a worrying trend. These arrangements may be limited in scope, but tend to be useful in the short-term resolution of cooperation issues. The trend is far from ideal because it encourages criminal organizations to displace their activities toward the weakest links in a very loosely knitted web of cooperation. As a result, some states become even more vulnerable than before to the activities of organized crime, including cases where criminal organizations risk capturing the state or hijacking local institutions. Feedback loops are thus created as the disengagement of key countries lead others to do the same.

Case Studies of Flashpoints

There are numerous examples of international disputes flaring up over issues of cooperation in criminal matters, many of them related to extradition but also other crucial areas of cooperation. These flashes attract media attention, stir nationalistic feelings, and pressure political leaders to take action to resolve the incidents, if not to review the country's whole approach to criminal justice cooperation. Many countries still refuse to extradite their own nationals. Furthermore, one naturally expects international cooperation to be complicated by political considerations and obstacles when the alleged crime involves a political figure or when the crime is committed for political purposes. This is the case, for example, with the strained judicial cooperation relationship between Turkey and Russia following the assassination of Saudi journalist Jamai Khashoggi at the Saudi consulate in Istanbul in October 2018. This is why international cooperation in cases of highly politicized incidents of alleged corruption by elected officials is so sensitive and complicated. This is also why international criminal justice cooperation relating to incidents of alleged terrorism or violent extremism has been particularly difficult and has sometimes been responsible for major setbacks in international cooperation.

Consider also the example of the Huawei executive, Meng Wanzhou, who was arrested more than three years ago by Canadian authorities at the Vancouver airport, at the request of the United States, on fraud charges related to US sanctions against Iran. Soon after her arrest, Meng was released on bail by a British Columbian court and, more than three years later, she is still awaiting a resolution of the extradition request. At an early stage in the process, the then American president, Donald Trump, said that he would intervene in the case if it served his country's national interests, specifically that he might drop the charges against Ms. Meng if he secured a favorable trade deal with China. Ms. Meng alleges that she faced abuse of process during her arrest. Her lawyers have argued that she was unlawfully detained, searched, and interrogated as part of a plan between Canadian and American authorities to have border officers misuse their customs and immigration process to covertly collect evidence for the FBI.[66] On December 11, 2018, Meng was released on bail by a British Columbian court, while US president Donald Trump said he would intervene in the case if it would serve national interests.

Among other things, the arrest and the prolonged court process relating to the extradition request has created a diplomatic crisis between China and Canada. On December 10, 2018, former diplomat Michael Kovrig and businessman Michael Spavor, two Canadian citizens, were arrested and held in China and much later accused of espionage.[67] Their arrest is widely viewed in Canada as a retribution for the arrest of Ms. Meng, which occurred nine days prior to the arrests of the two Canadians. Nearly three years later, they are both still being detained in China. The situation reveals how international criminal law cooperation can be purposefully tied to trade negotiations and concessions. In fact, as the president of the United States was announcing that the signing of a "phase one trade agreement" between the United States and China was eminent, we learned that the prime minister of Canada, Justin Trudeau, called on the United States not to sign a trade deal with China unless Beijing agreed to release the two Canadians. China's response was to demand the immediate release of Meng Wanzhou and to warn Canada that it should "stop colluding with others" to pressure China. A spokesperson for the Chinese Foreign Ministry, Geng Shuang, is quoted as saying during a regular press briefing: "When you pull out chestnuts from the fire at the behest of others, you will only end up hurting yourself," a Chinese expression referring to doing someone else's dirty work. The Canadian prime minister has been under considerable internal political pressure, largely by civil society, to intervene, stop the extradition process, and obtain the release of the two Canadian "hostages." Mr. Trudeau's response was that Canada remains firmly committed to the rule of law and Ms. Meng's case will be handled by the justice system. His position has consistently been that unilaterally Ms. Meng's extradition process "would embolden China to detain other Canadians to further its political goals" and "endanger thousands of Canadians who travel to China and around the world by letting countries know that a government can have political influence over Canada by randomly arresting Canadians."[68]

Another example that attracted global attention is that of Hong Kong's Fugitive Offenders and Mutual Legal Assistance in Criminal Matters Legislation (Amendment) Bill, which was proposed by the Hong Kong government in 2019 to establish a mechanism for the transfer of fugitives not only for Mainland China but for Taiwan and Macau, areas that were excluded in the existing laws. Opposition to the Bill was virulent and widespread and hundreds of thousands of people took to the streets in protest for many weekends in a row. Other countries expressed their concern as well.[69] The Bill was never adopted, but in 2020, China adopted a new national security law for Hong Kong that immediately went into effect. The law, passed in China's Standing Committee of the National People's Congress, includes sixty-six articles and covers four areas of criminal activity: secession, subversion, terrorism, and collusion with foreign or external forces. Those convicted of such crimes face maximum sentences of life imprisonment. The law grants mainland China more powers to intervene in Hong Kong's affairs and establishes a national security agency in Hong Kong outside of the jurisdiction of the local government. The law also grants mainland authorities jurisdiction in "complex" cases such as those involving a foreign country or issues that are deemed to pose a major and imminent threat to national security.[70] Chinese officials defended the law as an important measure to curtail anti-government protests in Hong Kong like those that sprung up in June 2019. Other countries reacted negatively and several of them immediately suspended their extradition agreements with Hong Kong.[71] Some of them, like Canada, also removed special trade treatments for sensitive exports to Hong Kong.

THE FUTURE OF INTERNATIONAL COOPERATION

We must let go of comfortable assumptions of the past and abandon the illusion that strong international cooperation will emerge more or less spontaneously from the antiquated regime and the legacy international mechanisms with which we are now left. Given the menace of transnational crime and the perils linked to transnational crime and organized crime groups' control over licit and illicit markets, the stakes are too high to stick which might have worked in the past and hope for the best.

We are obviously going through a period of high turbulence, with complex and uncertain trends unfolding in an ambiguous and volatile environment. Our reflex, or perhaps the wisest choice in such a turbulent and uncertain environment, is probably to distrust all predictions.[72] However, rejecting "any foresights as meaningless flannel" can only lead to myopic planning and flawed strategies.[73]

Anticipating or predicting the future is truly a complicated task. Some trends were identified above, but a trend is not necessarily a prediction. One may not always anticipate new breakthroughs or major disruption in existing patterns, one can nevertheless extrapolate carefully from observed trends. Possible futures, or scenarios, can be identified that are at least capable of helping policymakers to approach emerging challenges more competently.

Trying to apply probabilistic forecasting (calculating realistic odds to arrive at plausible futures) may not help us understand the future of international cooperation in criminal matters, especially since matters of international criminal justice cooperation are always wrapped in some secrecy. There are often no records, no data, no numbers to estimate any probability. However, scenario planning (or some form of strategic forecasting) is not only possible but also very likely worthwhile. This kind of planning exercise involves identifying the main uncertainties that characterize a situation and how they might affect existing systems, and then trying to imagine how different combinations of events may yield outcomes that are significantly different from what mere extrapolation of the present would suggest.[74]

It is not futile to attempt to predict the kind of changes that may affect international criminal justice cooperation in the foreseeable future.[75] At this stage, it probably does not require a lot of foresight to predict the continuing deterioration and growing irrelevance of the existing international cooperation regime in criminal matters. International cooperation is at an all-time low. If further deterioration of the current international cooperation regime is what the future has in store, then there are good reasons to worry. There is possibly no other option than trying to imagine a different future for international cooperation in criminal matters. The question may be: what is stopping us from imagining a better path forward?

Tetlock and Gardner proposed a distinction between the "big questions" and the "small questions" about the future and argued that we are mostly interested in the big questions (i.e., what really matters), but unfortunately these questions cannot be quantified or scored.[76] Considering the future of international cooperation in criminal matters, a cluster of questions come to mind. First, one may wonder about the sustainability of the current cooperation regime, its architecture, and the mechanisms and institutions that support it. What precisely is worth saving from the current regime? What are the crucial missing elements? There are also questions about the role that the UN and other multilateral mechanisms could realistically play in reversing the states' growing disinvestment from the current regime and in promoting more effective international cooperation. What would it take for states to invest or reinvest in more effective multilateral mechanisms of international cooperation in criminal matters? What kind of event or action, political or other, could serve as a wake-up call for states and break the current lethargy? Can a discussion of the future on international criminal justice cooperation lead to concrete action unless it is grounded in a better understanding of emerging forms of crime, the accelerating impact of technology on both crime and crime control, and some insight into the future of transnational organized crime? Can states engage in perfecting the existing cooperation regime unless they recognize how badly they actually need it?

What we propose in the next section is a brief discussion of scenarios that can be anticipated based on present trends in international criminal justice cooperation. Five distinct but not necessarily incompatible scenarios are suggested: (1) "together" forecasts a situation where states forge the political will and willingness to compromise toward refashioning the existing cooperation mechanisms; (2) "unbound" reflects a world in which states increasingly rely on bilateral or regional cooperation frameworks, possibly leading to new cooperation zones; (3) "going alone" proposes greater use of unilateral actions by states to achieve their aim, bypassing existing cooperation mechanisms and agreements; (4) "retreat" sees the accelerated use of informal cooperation arrangements or alternatives to the potential detriment of the rule of law and human rights; and (5) "renewal" posits that states could be compelled to reimagine the international cooperation regime and undertake radical reform efforts, including establishing a binding arbitration mechanism to resolve unilateral-related disputes.[77]

In proposing such scenarios, our goal is not to try to map out the currents or tidal changes that may affect international cooperation. We do not make any attempt either to speculate on the potential for a major event (political or other) to disrupt current trends and create new possible scenarios. Although some of these scenarios can clearly appear more preferable or more likely than others, we leave it to readers to draw their own conclusions in that regard. Finally, we recognize that, in order to be useful as planning tools, any scenario or vision of the future must be connectable to decisions in the present.[78]

FIVE SCENARIOS FOR INTERNATIONAL CRIMINAL JUSTICE COOPERATION

Scenarios are narrative descriptions of possible futures based on an analysis of current trends. None of the optimistic or grim outcomes one can forecast are inevitable, but there should be no doubt that change has already been seeded. At this moment, imaginable scenarios are made even fuzzier and harder to define because of the various international relations and geopolitical trends currently at play, some converging and others diverging. Nevertheless, a snap back to the old order is very improbable.

As the next geopolitical era is being shaped, many uncertainties persist and it is hard to predict where the distribution of power will settle. To the extent that the world order is influenced by the global superpowers, there remains much ambiguity around which state, if any, will lead the adaptation of the order, including by extension the factors that influence cooperation patterns and mechanisms. To be effective, the adaptation may need to be as deep as the constellation of forces that led to the fragility of the order in the first instance. Those who bide their time, waiting for a return of past arrangements, will be ill-prepared for what lies ahead and their own vulnerability to transnational organized crime will most likely be exacerbated.[79] Cooperation, as mentioned previously, is facing many vexing challenges, rendering it perhaps a "wicked" problem.

Of the many possible approaches to these challenges, what is likely to be the prevalent one? Will most states build on the years of efforts and substantial progress in international cooperation and attempt to modernize and strengthen multilateral mechanisms (*Together*) or will they further explore new pathways to cooperation at the bilateral, regional, or subregional levels (*Unbound*)? Will more countries, particularly powerful ones, disengage from existing multilateral mechanisms and decide to go their own way, pursuing extraterritorial jurisdiction, relying on informal and often problematic alternatives to current mechanisms and using their power and influence to coerce others into bilateral informal or formal cooperation arrangements (*Go alone*)? Will the growing tendency of states to retrench from the rule of law and the global cooperation regime signal the end of these regimes (*Retreat*)? Another possibility is that as a result of disruptive technologies or other factors, the social and economic costs of organized crime and corruption may become so steep and so politically damaging (e.g., in relation to cybercrime, crime against the environment, state capture by organized crime groups, or financial crime) that the international community may be shaken out of its current lethargy and embark on an urgent project to fundamentally rethink and retool international cooperation within multilateral institutions (*Renewal*). What follows are further descriptions of the possible scenarios.

Together: Perfecting the Existing International Cooperation Regime

The present international criminal justice cooperation regime is under great stress, but most states understand that fully retreating from it is not really an option. Perfecting that regime, within the multilateral institutions that support them, therefore may appear as a reasonable response to current challenges. Can participating states, as has been suggested,[80] agree that it is time to update and reinvigorate the regime with measures that take into account lessons learned, as well as global changes that have occurred since the regime was first instituted? Could the current limitations of global criminal justice cooperation mechanisms or the factors that lead countries to bypass formal procedures and procedural protections be addressed? Would the perfecting of existing mechanisms prevent states from resorting to problematic, informal, and sometimes unilateral alternatives?[81]

An increasingly polarized world is one where the main axes of international cooperation will be redefined along different lines.[82] That polarization is further politicizing international criminal justice cooperation and will likely increase the growing tendency of some of the states to tear down anything that constrains national sovereignty with rules, and if necessary, retreat from the rule of law and the protection of human rights.

Reinventing and future-proofing the architecture of the existing international cooperation regime might be a monumental undertaking, although an indispensable one. It is not easy to navigate the complicated swirl of geopolitical changes, competing interests, limited multilateral capabilities, and external trends in an era of unrelenting change and complex challenges.

At present, the global international criminal justice cooperation regime is essentially rudderless. There is no one at the helm and in the absence of competent leadership; it is not clear where credible initiative to improve the current situation may come from at this juncture. The current lack of leadership within the global international cooperation regime will likely continue to make the *Together* scenario less likely to succeed, unless new leadership emerges. Will the necessary leadership emerge to make this reform process possible?

Unbound: Growing Preference for Bilateral and Regional Agreements

An accelerating shift toward bilateralism (or regionalism) is also a probable scenario. It would reflect a pragmatic and realistic adaptation to exigent circumstances, including new global polarization, the weakness of the global cooperation regime, and the growing retreat of key participants from that regime. Since there is no broad-scale program to simplify international criminal justice cooperation at the global level, to reconsider the legal basis of existing tools and mechanisms, or to transform the process into a more efficient and effective administrative one, turning to bilateral or regional solutions makes a lot of sense for countries eager to proceed with like-minded partners. In fact, among some like-minded countries with a past experience of successful cooperation, there is a discernible trend toward the simplification of the process of extradition to make it more effective against various forms of transnational crime.[83] Some experts have actually suggested that promoting the execution of bilateral treaties or equivalent functional agreements should be encouraged in order to prevent unilateral action or other problematic alternatives to conventional forms of cooperation.[84]

This scenario may not necessarily be an indication of weak cooperation. International asymmetries translate into what some have referred to as "state preferences." Identifying these preferences may help explain the motives and calculations behind states' policies and practices with respect to international criminal justice cooperation. Money and Lockhart observed that most states are strategic and that they pursue or refuse cooperation to the extent that it serves their interests.[85] They explain states' preferences or choices from an economic point of view in terms of the perceived costs of transactions, costs of inaction, and costs of negotiation, as well as the burden of multilateral agreements as compared to the lesser burden of bilateral or regional agreements. For example, a consideration of the costs and benefits of cooperation on readmission is clearly a factor that shaped and led to the proliferation of bilateral agreements relating to the process of readmission through which individuals who are not allowed to stay on the territory of a country (e.g., unauthorized migrants, rejected asylum-seekers or stateless persons) are expelled or removed, whether in a coercive manner or not.[86]

States' growing preferences for informal, nonbinding agreements, may be explained in terms of their interests in promoting renegotiation in the presence of uncertainty and shifting power.[87] Similarly, states often use unilateral noncompliance as a renegotiating strategy. Informal arrangements make such renegotiating easier and less costly in the short term. States may anticipate that acting in ways that others consider unlawful may bring about change to legal rules going forward. "Unilateral action of this kind can disrupt the status quo and prompt renegotiation that would not have occurred through purely collective decision-making processes."[88] However, as Meyer argues, these international dynamics prevent formal renegotiation and create long-term costs for states that can inhibit short-term cooperation. Incentives for engaging in long-term, multilateral, rule-based formal agreements progressively vanish.

Major international criminal justice cooperation agreements reflect to varying extents the power distribution of the past. As power is shifting across many important areas of international cooperation, making long-term international agreements less attractive to rising powers, states want the flexibility to obtain better cooperative terms in the future. They attempt to respond to this fluctuating power by relying increasingly on informal, more easily renegotiable bilateral agreements. Meyer explains that this turn of event does not necessarily represent a retreat from cooperation. Rather, "it reflects an effort to cooperate under conditions that make long-term agreements difficult to reach"; informal agreements are preferred because they are the best available option under the current and uncertain circumstances.[89]

Some states have little to offer others in terms of cooperation, yet have a dire need for cooperation from other states, especially neighboring states. One can imagine the proliferation of transnational cooperation "bubbles" based on particular criminal threats or localized strategies to control crime (or a particular type of transnational crime) within a bubble. New cooperation zones may emerge from the current context. These zones, depending on the type of transnational crime targeted, may not be defined geographically as much as in terms of a shared interest in facing a specific transnational crime threat.

Going Alone: Growing Unilateralism

In the short term, unilateralism may be an attractive option, mostly for powerful states that can make it work and are less concerned about long-term consequences of such an approach. It is quite clear that participation in and compliance with multilateral agreements, including their specific terms, are in many ways imposed by powerful states on others. However, these multilateral obligations quickly fall into desuetude when these same powerful states either lose interest, decide to proceed unilaterally or bilaterally, or signal their indifference to other states. In addition to formal and informal bilateral or regional agreements, powerful states also have the option of unilateral action to fight certain kinds of organized crime (asserting extraterritorial powers, etc.), many of them illegal and very problematic for the world order and the rule of law. That too is part of the strategic calculations in which states engage. In the future, powerful states will continue to leverage their material capabilities, relationships, and information in a more rapid, integrated, and adaptive mode than in the past.[90] In doing so, they will shape the future of international cooperation and this, in effect, may take place largely outside of multilateral institutions and mechanisms. In some instances, unilateral methods actually go directly against Article 4(2) of the UNTOC through which states parties agree that sovereignty forbids the unilateral use by one party of its law enforcement authority in another. However, some countries have circumvented the convention by creating extraterritorial jurisdictions to enable their law enforcement agencies to operate abroad.[91]

It is also interesting to note that, in a world where the United States has long exerted territorial jurisdiction over the main technology companies while the majority of Internet users permanently reside elsewhere, states have responded to the American hegemony over electronic evidence by enacting data localization laws, deploying government-sponsored hacking, and adopting other unilateral alternative measures for data access. Experts have started to sound the alarm on the grave unintended consequences of such unilateral measures for the functioning of the Internet, civil liberties, and cybersecurity, but the alarms appear to remain unheard.

Retreat: Increase Reliance on Informal Arrangements and Alternate Methods

Uncertainty affects international criminal justice cooperation in many of the same ways in which it affects the effectiveness and efficiency of national criminal justice system.[92] When uncertain about the response of other states, the outcomes of their own cooperation efforts, or the future of international cooperation agreements, states predictably look for alternatives. This fourth scenario assumes that the current trend that sees states increasingly rely on informal cooperation arrangements and often problematic methods will not only continue but accelerate out of the necessity to more effectively address the localized impact of transnational crime.

Frustrated with the cost, burden, and inefficiencies of the global cooperation regime, why would state not try to rely on simpler, more informal, and nonbinding arrangements at the bilateral or regional levels? According to Money and Lockhart,[93] more states are likely to prefer informal cooperation arrangements because it allows them most of the time to: (1) avoid any unnecessary loss of national sovereignty; (2) avoid limiting their policy choices due to binding agreements; (3) avoid publicity and transparency; (4) modify or nullify agreements fairly quickly and with few detrimental consequences; (5) avoid having to make formal, visible pledges to states with which they are otherwise not necessarily aligned or in a positive relationship; (6) avoid any enforcement mechanisms and any costs/punishment for noncompliance with formal agreements; (7) avoid the national scrutiny that formal cooperation agreements would attract since they tend to require specific parliamentary or legislative acceptance or ratification; and (8) allow the executive branch of government to act without legislative or judicial authorization. To these reasons, one can add the states' greater ability, when proceeding informally, to limit the scope of their cooperation to modes and forms that suit their interests or to turn a blind eye to potential human rights abuse and derogation to the rule of law and the states' obligations under international law.

Informal arrangements typically do not have any real enforcement mechanism, but rely on other factors (political, diplomatic, economic, practical, etc.) to support reciprocity, predictability, and coherent applications. There will continue to be instances where states will be coerced to cooperate with another more powerful one in order to avoid various detrimental consequences (including the prospect of unilateral action by the more powerful states to the detriment of sovereignty considerations). We can also expect these agreements to be limited in scope to the type of criminal activities that parties share an interest in controlling (at least within their respective territory). This is in part because different types of cooperation are better suited to deal with different kinds of crime, different threats, and different circumstances (including the asymmetries discussed above).

Unfortunately, some of these informal bilateral arrangements, like the unilateral approaches discussed earlier, rely on methods that amount to a circumvention of existing treaties or an affront to the sovereignty of another nation. Some of them are in direct violation of international treaties. This obviously has wider implications from the point of view of policy, human rights, and the rule of law.

Renewal: Radical Review and Renewal of the Multilateral Regimes

The kind of integrated system called for many years ago by the International Bar Association is as urgently required today as was then to ensure political neutrality, the protection of human rights, and the preservation of the rule of law and international standards of legality.[94] Under this fifth scenario, states would undertake to reaffirm the relevance of the rule of law and the primacy of human rights in international criminal justice cooperation. However, if states continue to concentrate on their individual crime control priorities and targets, or focus on immediate geostrategic goals and advantages, they will surely fail to reimagine or adapt international cooperation mechanisms to the demands of our time. Opportunities for action on key priorities may slip away.

Supra-state mechanisms could be considered to ensure accountability, resolve disputes among participants, and ensure compliance, including perhaps the power to impose sanctions. The threat of consequences is applied too erratically and sporadically to have any real impact except perhaps in the most blatant and defiant cases of noncompliance. Addressing the question of states' noncompliance with their obligation under the relevant treaties might emerge as a priority, but to date efforts to establish consequences for a state's noncompliance with treaty obligations have not been very successful.

States may be amenable to the establishment of binding arbitration mechanism to resolve disputes arising out of unilateral action by another state or a state's willful failure to comply with its international cooperation obligation. Sadoff suggests that such binding arbitration would be preferable to relying on domestic courts, human rights bodies, or the International Court of Justice, which all have their jurisdictional constraints.[95] Sadoff also suggests that, in cases of a dispute over an extradition request involving political offenses or extradition of a national, the matter could be submitted for prosecution to a permanent UN-based tribunal established for that purpose.

The *Renewal* scenario obviously raises several questions. What would it take for states to find the motivation to initiate such radical reforms? Can a radically different cooperation regime accommodate a much wider range of views and values than previous regimes were able to integrate in the past? Would states ever accept enforceable legal restrictions on their behavior at home and abroad? What role can multilateral organizations play in mobilizing state support for a transformation of the current regime? Alternatively, would it be wise for a small group of like-minded states to gradually initiate such reforms, pressuring other states to participate by leveraging trade, humanitarian aid, and diplomatic relations over time? Can civil society do anything to exert pressure toward such a scenario?

CONCLUSION

Informed by several observed trends and uncertainties, this chapter proposed five scenarios and possible futures related to international criminal justice cooperation. The scenarios are still insufficiently distinguished from each other and might to a certain extent coexist. They need further exploration. In the meantime, they will hopefully support a consideration of potential pathways toward the kind of international criminal justice cooperation that is now more needed than ever. There is a chance that states might find a way to end this area of impunity and oppose transnational organized crime more effectively.

NOTES

1. Ian Tennant, *Vienna Calling: A Briefing to the Incoming Head of the UNODC* (Geneva: Global Initiative Against Transnational Organized Crime, 2019). https://bit.ly/3vCVvzb.

2. Global Initiative against Transnational Organized Crime. *Draft strategy—2021–2023* (Geneva: Global Initiative, 2020).

3. Yvon Dandurand and Vivienne Chin, "Implementation of Transnational Criminal Law: Issues and Challenges," in *Routledge Handbook on Transnational Criminal Law*, edited by Neil Boister and Robert J. Currie (London: Routledge, 2015), 435–452.

4. Yvon Dandurand, Gerardo, Colombo, and Nikos Passas. "Measures and Mechanisms to Strengthen International Cooperation Among Prosecution Services." *Crime, Law and Social Change* 47 (2007): 261–289.

5. World Economic Forum, *The Global Risks Report* (Geneva: WEF, 2018); World Economic Forum, *The Global Risks Report* (Geneva: WEF, 2019); World Economic Forum, *The Global Risks Report* (Geneva: WEF, 2020).

6. United Nations Office on Drugs and Crime, *World Drug Report* (Vienna: United Nations, 2020), 34.

7. United Nations, *Kyoto Declaration* (Vienna: Congress on Crime Prevention and Criminal Justice, 2021).

8. Franco Berardi "Bifo," *Futurability: The Age of Impotence and the Horizon of Possibility* (London: Verso, 2017), 161.

9. Yvon Dandurand, "International Cooperation," in *Human Trafficking*, edited by John Winterdyk, Benjamin Perrin and Philip Reichel (Boca Raton: CRC Press, 2012), 233.

10. Dandurand and Chin, *Implementation*, 435–452.

11. Yvon Dandurand and Jessica Jahn, "The Failing International Legal Framework on Migrant Smuggling and Human Trafficking," in *The Palgrave International Handbook on Human Trafficking*, edited by John Winterdyk and Jackie Jones (London: Palgrave, 2020), 783–800.

12. Summer Walker, *Cyber-insecurities: A Guide to the UN Cybercrime Debate* (Geneva: GI-TOC, 2019).

13. European Commission. *Recommendation for a council decision authorising the opening of negotiations in view of an agreement between the European Union and the United States of America on cross-border access to electronic evidence for judicial cooperation in criminal matters* (Brussels: European Commission. 2019).

14. Nora Ni Loideain, "A Port in the Data-Sharing Storm: The GDPR and the Internet of Things." *Journal of Cyber Policy* 2 (2019): 1–19.

15. Ian Brown, and Douwe Korff, "Foreign Surveillance: Law and Practice in a Global Digital Environment." *European Human Rights Law Review* 3 (2014): 243–251.

16. Joe Barton, "Reforming the Mutual Legal Assistance Treaty Framework to Protect the Future of the Internet." *Ohio State Law Journal Furthermore* 79 (2018): 91–112.

17. Jonah Force Hill, "The Growth of Data Localization Post-Snowden: Analysis and Recommendations for U.S. Policymakers and Industry Leaders." *Lawfare Research Paper Series* 2 (2014): 1–41.

18. United Nations, *International cooperation and technical assistance to prevent and address all forms of crime: Terrorism in all its forms and manifestations, and new and emerging forms of crime—working paper* (Vienna: Fourteenth United Nations Congress on Crime Prevention and Criminal Justice, 2020).

19. Jonathan Mayer, "Government Hacking." *The Yale Law Journal* 127 (2018): 570–662.

20. Dandurand, *International Cooperation*, 233.

21. Summer Walker, *Cyber-insecurities: A Guide to the UN Cybercrime Debate* (Geneva: GI-TOC, 2019).

22. David A. Sadoff, *Bringing International Fugitives to Justice: Extradition and Its Alternatives* (New York: Cambridge University Press, 2018).

23. Christine Galvagna, "The Necessity of Human Rights Legal Protections in Mutual Legal Assistance Treaty Reforms." *Notre Dame Journal of International and Comparative Law* 9, no. 2 (2019): 84.

24. Clive Harfield, "The Organization of 'Organized Crime Policing' in its International Context." *Criminology and Criminal Justice* 8 (2008): 483–498.

25. Helen McDermott, "The Structure of International Cooperation in the Transfer of Suspects. Extradite or Abduct?." *International Criminal Law Review* 15, no 2 (2015): 254–297.

26. Walker, *Cyber-insecurities.*

27. Joe Barton, "Reforming the Mutual Legal Assistance Treaty Framework to Protect the Future of the Internet." *Ohio State Law Journal* 79 (2018): 91–112.

28. United Nations Office on Drugs and Crime, *World Drug Report* (Vienna: United Nations, 2020).

29. United Nations, *International Cooperation and Technical Assistance to Prevent and Address all Forms of Crime: Terrorism in all its forms and manifestations, and new and emerging forms of crime - working paper* (Vienna: Fourteenth United Nations Congress on Crime Prevention and Criminal Justice, 2020).

30. Tennant, *Vienna Calling.*

31. Walker, *Cyber-insecurities,* 3.

32. Andrew Keane Woods, "Mutual Legal Assistance in the Digital Age," in *Cambridge Handbook of Surveillance Law*, edited by David Gray and Stephen E. Henderson (Cambridge: Cambridge University Press, 2017), 659–676.

33. United Nations, *Report on the meeting of the Expert Group to conduct a comprehensive study on cybercrime, held in Vienna from 3 to 5 April 2018* (Vienna: United Nations, 2018), § 9. https://bit.ly/3c3nr7h.

34. United Nations, *Report on the meeting of the Expert Group to conduct a comprehensive study on cybercrime, held in Vienna from 3 to 5 April 2018* (Vienna: United Nations, 2018). https://bit.ly/34wk6to.

35. United Nations, *Activities of the United Nations Office on Drugs and Crime to promote the implementation of the provisions on international cooperation in the United Nations Convention against Transnational Organized Crime* (Vienna: Conference of the Parties to the United Nations Convention against Transnational Organized Crime, 2020a).

36. Ian Tenant, *The Promise of Palermo: A Political History of the UN Convention against Transnational Organized Crime* (Geneva: GI-TOC, 2020). https://bit.ly/3fUTQ1i.

37. Neil Boister, "The Cooperation Provisions of the UN Convention against Transnational Organized Crime: A 'Toolbox' Rarely Used?." *International Criminal Law Review* 16 (2016): 39–70.

38. Conference of the Parties to the United Nations Convention against Transnational Organized Crime. *Resolution 9/1. Establishment of the mechanism for the review of the implementation of the United Nations Convention against Transnational Organized Crime and the Protocols thereto* (Vienna: UNODC, 2018); Cecily Rose, "The Creation of a Review Mechanism for the UN Convention against Transnational Organized Crime and its Protocols." *American Journal of International Law* 114, no. 1 (2020): 51–67.

39. Conference of the States Parties to the United Nations Convention against Corruption. *Progress in implementing the mandates of the Open-Ended Intergovernmental Expert Group Meeting to Enhance International Cooperation under the United Nations Convention Against Corruption* (Vienna: UNODC, 2020), 7.

40. Conference of the States Parties to the United Nations Convention against Corruption. *Implementation of Chapter V (Asset Recovery) of the United Nations Convention against Corruption: Thematic Report by the Secretariat* (Vienna: UNODC, 2020), 14.

41. Conference of the States Parties to the United Nations Convention against Corruption. *Implementation of Chapter V (Asset Recovery) of the United Nations Convention against Corruption: Thematic Report by the Secretariat* (Vienna: UNODC, 2020), 15.

42. Nadioa Schadlow, "The End of American Illusion," *Foreign Affairs* 99, no. 5 (2020): 440.

43. Patrick Wintour, "UN Must Reform to Defend Enlightenment Values, Secretary General Says," *The Guardian*, May 10, 2017. https://bit.ly/3fHAHkB.

44. Helen McDermott, "The Structure of International Cooperation in the Transfer of Suspects. Extradite or Abduct?" *International Criminal Law Review* 15, no 2 (2015): 254–297.

45. Jean-Pierre Cassarino, *Dealing with Unbalanced Reciprocities: Cooperation on Readmission and Implications* (Washington, DC: Middle East Institute, 2012). https://bit.ly/3wRtCnf.

46. Jeanette Money and Sarah, P. Lockhart, *Migration Crisis and the Structure of International Cooperation* (Athens: University of Georgia Press, 2018), 272.

47. United Nations, *International cooperation and technical assistance to prevent and address all forms of crime: Terrorism in all its forms and manifestations, and new and emerging forms of crime—working paper* (Vienna: Fourteenth United Nations Congress on Crime Prevention and Criminal Justice, 2020), 8.

48. Gordon Brown, *Seven Ways to Change the World: How to Fix the Most Pressing Problems We Face* (London: Simon & Shuster, 2021), 19.

49. Jennifer Daskal, "Privacy and Security Across Borders," *The Yale Law Journal Forum* 128 (2019): 1029–1051.

50. Stewart Patrick, "When the System Fails: COVID-19 and the Costs of Global Dysfunction," *Foreign Affairs* 99, no. 4 (2020, July-August): 40–50.

51. Fareed Zakaria, *Ten Lessons for a Post-pandemic World* (New York: Norton, 2020), 1.

52. Dandurand and Chin, *Implementation*, 452.

53. World Economic Forum, *The Global Risks Report* (Geneva: WEF, 2019), 10.

54. World Economic Forum, *The Global Risks Report* (Geneva: WEF, 2019), 10.

55. David Lipton, "Trust and the Future of Multilateralism." Introductory Remarks for the Eurofi High Level Seminar, IMF First Deputy Managing Director David Lipton (30 April 2018). International Monetary Fund. https://bit.ly/2R6IC14.

56. Summer Walker, *Cyber-insecurities: A Guide to the UN Cybercrime Debate* (Geneva: GI-TOC, 2019).

57. World Economic Forum, *The Global Risks Report* (Geneva: WEF, 2020), 11.

58. Stewart Patrick, "When the System Fails: COVID-19 and the Costs of Global Dysfunction." *Foreign Affairs* 99, no. 4 (2020): 40.

59. John G. Ikenberry, "The Next Liberal Order: The Age of Contagion Demands More Internationalism, Not Less." *Foreign Affairs* 99, no. 4 (2020): 133–142.

60. Stevan Levitsky and Daniel Ziblatt, *How Democracies Die* (New York: Crown, 2018); Ronald Inglehart, "The Age of Insecurity: Can Democracy Save Itself?" *Foreign Affairs* 97, no. 3 (2018): 20–28; Yasha Mounk and Roberto Stefan Foa,"The End of the Democratic Century: Autocracy's Global Ascendance." *Foreign Affairs* 97, no. 3 (2018): 29–38; Yasha Mounk, "The Undemocratic Dilemma." *Journal of Democracy* 29, no. 2 (2018): 98–112.

61. Yvon Dandurand and Jessica Jahn, "The Fragility of a Culture of Lawfulness." *Bialostockie Studia Prawnicze* 23, no. 3 (2018): 13–26; Dennis J. Snower, *Toward Global Paradigm Change: Beyond the Crisis of the Liberal World Order* (Oxford: Blavatnik School of Government, University of Oxford, 2019); Liesbet Hooghe, Tobias Lenz, and Gary Marks, "Contested World Order: The Delegitimation of International Governance." *Review of International Organizations* 14, no. 4 (2018): 731–743.

62. Tennant, *Vienna Calling.*

63. United Nations Office on Drugs and Crime, *Handbook on Criminal Justice Responses to Terrorism* (New York: United Nations, 2009), 64.

64. United Nations Office on Drugs and Crime, *Handbook,* 69.

65. Tommaso Trinchera, "Confiscation and Asset Recovery: Better Tools to Fight Bribery and Corruption Crime." *Criminal Law Forum* 31 (2020): 49–79.

66. Liu Zhen, "Beijing hands over detained Canadians' case to prosecutors," *The Global Mail* (2019, December).

67. Tonda MacCharles and Grauer Perrin. "Justin Trudeau warns of China's growing threat as detained Canadians formally arrested," *Toronto Star*, May 16, 2019.

68. John Paul Tasker, "Trudeau rejects calls to release Meng Wanzhou," *CBC*, June 25, 2020. https://bit.ly/3wO3xp8.

69. Jeff Li, "Hong Kong-China extradition plans explained," *BBC News*. December 13, 2019.

70. Chris Buckley, "What China's New National Security Law Means for Hong Kong," *New York Times*, June 28, 2020. https://nyti.ms/2SDBLwB; Mark Gollom, "What you need to know about China's new national security law for Hong Kong," *CBC*. July 1, 2020. https://bit.ly/3g01QOw; Joanne Lee-Young, "New National Security Law Passed for Hong Kong Raises Concern in Vancouver," *Vancouver Sun*, June 3, 2020. https://bit.ly/3vG9XGt.

71. Stephen Castle, "U.K. Suspends Extradition Treaty with Hong Kong Over Security Law," *New York Times*, July 20, 2020. https://nyti.ms/2Tn8XJ2; Amanda Connoly, "Canada Suspending Hong Kong Extradition Treaty in Response to New Security Law," *Global News*, July 3, 2020. https://bit.ly/3p8yXUr.

72. Freija van Dujine and Peter Bishop, *Introduction to Strategic Foresight* (The Netherlands: Future Motions, Dutch Future Society, 2018), 10.

73. Richard Susskind, *Online Courts and the Future of Justice* (Oxford: Oxford University Press, 2019), 13.

74. Peter J. Scoblic and Philip E. Tetlock, "A Better Crystal Ball: The Right Way to Think About the Future." *Foreign Affairs* 99, no. 6 (2020): 10–18.

75. Giulio Calcara, "Rethinking Legal Research on Matters of International Police Cooperation: Issues, Methods and Raison d'Être." *Liverpool Law Review* 40 (2019): 95–111.

76. Philip Tetlock and Dan Gardner, *Superforecasting: The Art & Science of Prediction* (London: Random House, 2015).

77. See also: Yvon Dandurand and Jessica Jahn, *The Future of International Cooperation* (Geneva: GI-TOC, 2021).

78. Scoblic and Tetlock, *A Better Crystal Ball.*

79. World Economic Forum, *The Global Risks Report* (Geneva: WEF, 2020).

80. Peter Gastrow, *Adopted 18 Years ago, why has the UNTOC Still Not Achieved Its Aim?* (Geneva: GI-TOC, 2018). https://bit.ly/3uEzUVJ.

81. Helen McDermott, "The Structure of International Cooperation in the Transfer of Suspects. Extradite or Abduct?" *International Criminal Law Review* 15, no. 2 (2015): 254–297.

82. Fareed Zakaria, *Ten Lessons for a Post-pandemic World* (New York: Norton, 2020).

83. Neil Boister, "Global Simplification of Extradition: Interviews with Selected Extradition Experts in New Zealand, Canada, the US, and EU." *Criminal Law Forum* 29 (2017): 327–375.

84. Sadoff, *Bringing International Fugitives,* 597.

85. Jeanette Money and Sarah, P. Lockhart. *Migration Crisis and the Structure of International Cooperation* (Athens: University of Georgia Press, 2018).

86. Jean-Pierre Cassarino, *Dealing with Unbalanced Reciprocities: Cooperation on Readmission and Implications* (Washington, DC: Middle East Institute, 2012). https://bit.ly/34C4SD8.

87. Timothy Meyer, "Shifting Sands: Power, Uncertainty and the Form of International Legal Cooperation." *European Journal of International Law* 27, no. 1 (2016): 161–185.

88. Timothy Meyer, *Shifting Sands*, 164.

89. Timothy Meyer, *Shifting Sands*, 185.

90. National Intelligence Council. *Global Trends: The Paradox of Progress* (Washington: Office of the Director of National Intelligence, 2017). https://bit.ly/3c6tAQo.

91. Gastrow, *Adopted 18 Years Ago*. https://bit.ly/3yQIMuu.

92. Yvon Dandurand, "Criminal Justice Reform and the System's Efficiency." *Criminal Law Forum* 25 (2014): 383–440. https://bit.ly/3p9b4Mh.

93. Money and Lockhart, *Migration Crisis.*

94. International Bar Association Task Force on International Terrorism. *International Terrorism: Legal Challenges and Responses* (Ardsley: Transnational Publishers, 2004).

95. Sadoff, *Bringing International Fugitives.*

REFERENCES

Barton, Joe. "Reforming the Mutual Legal Assistance Treaty Framework to Protect the Future of the Internet," *Ohio State Law Journal Furthermore* 79 (2018): 91–112.

Berardi "Bifo," Franco. Futurability: The Age of Impotence and the Horizon of Possibility. (London: Verso, 2017).

Boister, Neil. "Global Simplification of Extradition: Interviews with Selected Extradition Experts in New Zealand, Canada, the US, and EU." *Criminal Law Forum* 29 (2017): 327–375.

Boister, Neil. "The Cooperation Provisions of the UN Convention against Transnational Organized Crime: A 'Toolbox' Rarely Used?," *International Criminal Law Review* 16 (2016): 39–70.

Boister, Neil. An Introduction to Transnational Criminal Law (Oxford: Oxford University Press. Castle, Stephen. "U.K. Suspends Extradition Treaty with Hong Kong Over Security Law." New York Times, July 20, 2020. https://nyti.ms/34BfrX32018).

Brown, Gordon, *Seven Ways to Change the World: How to Fix the Most Pressing Problems We Face* (London: Simon & Shuster, 2021).

Brown, Ian, and Korff, Douwe. "Foreign Surveillance: Law and Practice in a Global Digital Environment." *European Human Rights Law Review* 3 (2014): 243–251.

Buckley, Chris. "What China's New National Security Law Means for Hong Kong." New York Times, June 28, 2020. https://nyti.ms/3uM82z7.

Calcara, Gulio. "Rethinking Legal Research on Matters of International Police Cooperation: Issues, Methods and Raison d'Être." *Liverpool Law Review* 40 (2019): 95–111. https://bit.ly/3c7z79k.

Cassarino, Jean-Pierre. *Dealing with Unbalanced Reciprocities: Cooperation on Readmission and Implications* (Washington, DC: Middle East Institute, 2012). https://bit.ly/34vm7WS.

Conference of the States Parties to the United Nations Convention against Corruption. *Progress in Implementing the Mandates of the Open-Ended Intergovernmental Expert Group Meeting to Enhance International Cooperation under the United Nations Convention Against Corruption* (Vienna: UNODC, 2020a).

Conference of the States Parties to the United Nations Convention against Corruption. *Implementation of Chapter V (Asset Recovery) of the United Nations Convention against Corruption: Thematic Report by the Secretariat* (Vienna: UNODC, 2020b).

Connolly, Amanda. "Canada Suspending Hong Kong Extradition Treaty in Response to New Security Law," *Global News*, July 3, 2020. https://bit.ly/3z1BXqi.

Dandurand, Yvon and Jahn, Jessica. *The Future of International Cooperation* (Geneva: GI-TOC, 2021). https://bit.ly/33ydqOi.

Dandurand, Yvon and Jahn, Jessica. "The Failing International Legal Framework on Migrant Smuggling and Human Trafficking," In *The Palgrave International Handbook on Human Trafficking,* edited by John Winterdyk and Jackie Jones (London, Palgrave 2020): 783–800.

Dandurand, Yvon and Jahn, Jessica. "The Fragility of a Culture of Lawfulness." *Bialostockie Studia Prawnicze* 23, no. 3 (2018): 13–26.

Dandurand, Yvon and Chin, Vivienne. "Implementation of Transnational Criminal Law: Issues and Challenges." In *Routledge Handbook on Transnational Criminal Law*, edited by Neil Boister and Robert J. Currie (2015): 435–452. London: Routledge.

Dandurand, Yvon. "Criminal Justice Reform and the System's Efficiency." *Criminal Law Forum* 25 (2014): 383–440. https://bit.ly/2RaOTsM.

Dandurand, Yvon. "International Cooperation." In *Human Trafficking*, edited by in John Winterdyk, Benjamin Perrin and Philip Reichel (2012): 233. Boca Raton: CRC Press.

Dandurand, Yvon, Colombo, Gerardo and Passas, Nikos. "Measures and Mechanisms to Strengthen International Cooperation among Prosecution Services." *Crime, Law and Social Change* 47 (2007): 261–289.

Daskal, Jennifer. "Privacy and Security across Borders." *The Yale Law Journal Forum* 128 (2019): 1029–1051.

Conference of the Parties to the United Nations Convention against Transnational Organized Crime. *Resolution 9/1. Establishment of the mechanism for the review of the implementation of the United Nations Convention against Transnational Organized Crime and the Protocols Thereto* (Vienna: UNODC, 2018).

Edmonds-Poli, Emile and Shirk, David. "Extradition as a Tool for International Cooperation: Lessons from the U.S.-Mexico Relationship," *Maryland Journal of International Law, 33* (2018): 215–243. https://bit.ly/3c6TDXu.

European Commission. *Recommendation for a council decision authorising the opening of negotiations in view of an agreement between the European Union and the United States of America on cross-border access to electronic evidence for judicial cooperation in criminal matters* (Brussels: European Commission, 2019).

Force Hill, Jonah. "The Growth of Data Localization Post-Snowden: Analysis and Recommendations for U.S. Policymakers and Industry Leaders." *Lawfare Research Paper Series* 2 (2014): 1–41.

Galvagna, Christine. "The Necessity of Human Rights Legal Protections in Mutual Legal Assistance Treaty Reforms." *Notre Dame Journal of International and Comparative Law* 9, no. 2 (2019): 57–84.

Gastrow, Peter. *Adopted 18 Years ago, why has the UNTOC still not achieved its aim?* (Geneva: GI-TOC, 2018). https://bit.ly/3p7POGW.

Global Initiative against Transnational Organized Crime. *Draft strategy—2021–2023* (Geneva: GI-TOC, 2020).

Gollom, Mark. "What you need to know about China's new national security law for Hong Kong," *CBC*. July 1, 2020. https://bit.ly/3g418jo.

Granger, Serge. "Chine-Canada: à quand un traité d'extradition. Sans traité d'extradition, la Chine et le Canada gagneraient à signer des ententes bilatérales pour améliorer la mobilité entre les deux pays." *Policy Options*. August 29, 2016. https://bit.ly/34zZJvu.

Harfield, Clay. "The Organization of 'Organized Crime Policing' in its International Context," *Criminology and Criminal Justice* 8 (2008): 483–498. https://bit.ly/2SKNCJr.

Hooghe, Lesebet, Lenz, Tobias and Marks, Gary. "Contested World Order: The Delegitimation of International Governance." *Review of International Organizations* 14, no. 4 (2018): 731–743. https://bit.ly/3c8D4KR.

Ikenberry, John G. "The Next Liberal Order: The Age of Contagion Demands More Internationalism, Not Less." *Foreign Affairs* 99, no. 4 (2020): 133–142.

Inglehart, Ronald. "The Age of Insecurity: Can Democracy Save Itself?" *Foreign Affairs* 97, no. 3 (2018, May-June): 20–28.

International Bar Association Task Force on International Terrorism. *International Terrorism: Legal Challenges and Responses* (Ardsley: Transnational Publishers, 2004).

Li, Jeff. "Hong Kong-China extradition plans explained." *BBC News*. December 13, 2019.

Lipton, David. "Trust and the Future of Multilateralism." Introductory Remarks for the Eurofi High Level Seminar, IMF First Deputy Managing Director David Lipton (30 April 2018). International Monetary Fund. https://bit.ly/2R6CXIo.

Lee-Young, Joanne. "New National Security Law Passed for Hong Kong Raises Concern in Vancouver." *Vancouver Sun*, June 3, 2020. https://bit.ly/3uHB6r7.

Levitsky Stevan and Ziblatt, Daniel. *How Democracies Die* (New York: Crown, 2018).

Loideain, Nora Ni "A Port in the Data-Sharing Storm: the GDPR and the Internet of Things." *Journal of Cyber Policy* 2 (2019): 1–19.

MacCharles, Tonda and Perrin, Grauer. "Justin Trudeau warns of China's growing threat as detained Canadians formally arrested," *Toronto Star*, May 16, 2019.

Mayer, Jonathan. "Government Hacking," *The Yale Law Journal* 127 (2018): 570–662.

Meyer, Timothy. "Shifting Sands: Power, Uncertainty and the Form of International Legal Cooperation." *European Journal of International Law* 27, no. 1 (2016, February): 161–185.

McDermott, Helen. "The Structure of International Cooperation in the Transfer of Suspects. Extradite or Abduct?." *International Criminal Law Review* 15, no. 2 (2015): 254–297. https://bit.ly/3vEsVxi.

Money, Jeanette and Lockhart, Sarah, P. *Migration Crisis and the Structure of International Cooperation* (Athens: University of Georgia Press. 2018).

Mounk, Yasha and Foa, Roberto Stefan. "The End of the Democratic Century: Autocracy's Global Ascendance." *Foreign Affairs* 97, no. 3 (2018): 29–38.

Mounk,Yasha. "The Undemocratic Dilemma." *Journal of Democracy* 29, no. 2 (2018): 98–112.

National Intelligence Council. *Global Trends: The Paradox of Progress* (Washington: Office of the Director of National Intelligence, 2017). https://bit.ly/2SN20k7.

Patrick, Stewart. "When the System Fails: COVID-19 and the Costs of Global Dysfunction." *Foreign Affairs* 99, no. 4 (2020): 40–50.

Rose, Cecily. "The Creation of a Review Mechanism for the UN Convention against Transnational Organized Crime and its Protocols." *American Journal of International Law* 114 (2020): 51–67.

Sadoff, David. A. *Bringing International Fugitives to Justice: Extradition and Its Alternatives* (New York: Cambridge University Press, 2018).

Snower, Dennis. J. *Toward Global Paradigm Change: Beyond the Crisis of the Liberal World order* (Oxford: Blavatnik School of Government, University of Oxford, 2019).

Schadlow, Nadioa. "The End of American Illusion." *Foreign Affairs* 99, no. 5 (2020, September-October): 35–45.

Scoblic, Peter J. and Tetlock, Philip E. "A Better Crystal Ball: The Right Way to Think About the Future." *Foreign Affairs* 99, no. 6 (2020, November-December): 10–18.

Susskind, Richard. *Online Courts and the Future of Justice* (Oxford: Oxford University Press, 2019).

Tasker, John Paul. "Trudeau rejects calls to release Meng Wanzhou," *CBC*, June 25, 2020. https://bit.ly/3p8GEd2.

Tenant, Ian. *The Promise of Palermo: A Political History of the UN Convention against Transnational Organized Crime* (Geneva: GI-TOC, 2020). https://bit.ly/2TxC1xG.

Tennant, Ian. *Vienna Calling: A Briefing to the Incoming Head of the UNODC* (Geneva: GI-TOC, 2019). https://bit.ly/3fR6MF6.

Tetlock, Philip and Gardner, Dan. *Superforecasting: The Art & Science of Prediction* (London: Random House, 2015).

Trinchera, Tommaso. "Confiscation and Asset Recovery: Better Tools to Fight Bribery and Corruption Crime," *Criminal Law Forum* 31 (2020): 49–79.

United Nations Office on Drugs and Crime. *Handbook on Criminal Justice Responses to Terrorism* (New York: United Nations. 2009).

United Nations Office on Drugs and Crime. *World Drug Report* (Vienna: United Nations, 2020).

United Nations, *Activities of the United Nations Office on Drugs and Crime to promote the implementation of the provisions on international cooperation in the United Nations Convention against Transnational Organized Crime* (Vienna: Conference of the Parties to the United Nations Convention against Transnational Organized Crime, 2020a).

United Nations, *International cooperation and technical assistance to prevent and address all forms of crime: Terrorism in all its forms and manifestations, and new and emerging forms of crime - working paper* (Vienna: Fourteenth United Nations Congress on Crime Prevention and Criminal Justice, 2020).

United Nations, *Kyoto Declaration* (Vienna: Congress on Crime Prevention and Criminal Justice, 2021).

United Nations, *Report on the meeting of the Expert Group to conduct a comprehensive study on cybercrime, held in Vienna from 3 to 5 April 2018* (Vienna: United Nations, 2018). https://bit.ly/34xB62i.

van Dujine Freija and Bishop, Peter. *Introduction to Strategic Foresight* (The Netherlands: Future Motions, Dutch Future Society, 2018).

Walker, Summer. *Cyber-Insecurities: A Guide to the UN Cybercrime Debate* (Geneva: GI-TOC, 2019).

Wintour, Patrick. "UN Must Reform to defend Enlightenment Values, Secretary General Says," *The Guardian*, May 10, 2017. https://bit.ly/2RYa1Ts.

Woods, Andrew Kane. "Mutual Legal Assistance in the Digital Age." In *Cambridge Handbook of Surveillance Law,* edited by David Gray and Stephen E. Henderson (2017): 659–676. Cambridge: Cambridge University Press, 2017.

World Economic Forum, *The Global Risks Report* (Geneva: WEF, 2018).

World Economic Forum, *The Global Risks Report* (Geneva: WEF, 2019).

World Economic Forum, *The Global Risks Report* (Geneva: WEF, 2020).

Zakaria, Fareed. *Ten Lessons for a Post-Pandemic World* (New York: Norton, 2020).

Zhen, Liu. "Beijing hands over detained Canadians' case to prosecutors," *The Global Mail* (2019, December).

Chapter 10

Exordinum

William Schabas

In post–World War II Vienna, several years before Austria was admitted to membership in the United Nations and decades before its UN Office was established, journalist Holly Martens and his erstwhile friend Harry Lime, who had become a local gangster trafficking in counterfeit medicines, confronted each other on the *Riesenrad*, the city's iconic Ferris wheel.

> Holly, I'd like to cut you in, old man. There's nobody left in Vienna I can really trust, and we've always done everything together. When you make up your mind, send me a message—I'll meet you any place, any time, and when we do meet old man, it's you I want to see, not the police. Remember that, won't ya? Don't be so gloomy.
>
> After all it's not that awful. You know what the fellow said: in Italy, for thirty years under the Borgias, they had warfare, terror, murder and bloodshed, but they produced Michelangelo, Leonardo da Vinci and the Renaissance. In Switzerland, they had brotherly love, they had five hundred years of democracy and peace—and what did that produce? The cuckoo clock. So long Holly.[1]

The "fellow," of course, was Graham Greene, and the encounter was fictional. The scene comes toward the end of the Carol Reed film *The Third Man*, for which Greene wrote the screenplay based upon his novel. In the film, it is Orson Welles who makes the ominously Machiavellian remarks. Indeed, Machiavelli was a fan of the Borgias.

The climax of *The Third Man* is a chase through Vienna's sewers, with Lime metaphorically descending into the underworld, much like Don Giovanni in the final scene of Mozart's opera. He might well have been greeted there by the Florentine political philosopher Niccolò Machiavelli, who would surely have endorsed Lime's cynical assessment of the achievements of "five hundred years of democracy and peace" in Switzerland. Helvetia's five tranquil centuries certainly produced more than the cuckoo clock. It was in Geneva, in 1748, that the Baron de Montesquieu published his *Esprit des lois*, one of the pioneering treatises of the "rule of law."

In the vain hope that he might outwit the censor with a veiled attack on Napoleon III, Maurice Joly contrived an encounter in the underworld between Machiavelli and Montesquieu, first published in 1864 as *Dialogue aux enfers entre Machiavel et Montesquieu ou la politique de Machiavel au XIXe siècle*. Inspired by Joly's satire, Friedrich Forsthuber, Michael Platzer, Sławomir Redo, and Gerhard Reissner have produced this modern version of the debate, one that speaks to important contemporary themes of migration and climate change, as well as the efforts to undermine the rule of law underway in some European and other states.

The third recital of the preamble to the Universal Declaration of Human Rights states: "Whereas it is essential, if man is not to be compelled to have recourse, as a last resort, to rebellion against tyranny and oppression, that human rights should be protected by the Rule of Law."[2] During the drafting of the Declaration, the formulation of the "rule of law" had originally appeared in the article concerning equality before the law and it was only in the final weeks of the negotiations that it was moved to the preamble. Unfortunately, there is no explicit mention of the rule of law in the treaties derived from the Universal Declaration as part of the International Bill of Rights. The authoritative organ for the interpretation of the International Covenant on Civil and Political Rights, the Human Rights Committee, has nevertheless referred to "the principles of legality and rule of law inherent in the Covenant."[3]

In the early decades of the International Bill of Rights, the importance of accountability, including criminal prosecution, in the protection and promotion of human rights was not in the forefront. Human rights activists were more focused on the fundamental rights of the accused and of the prisoner, tending to view criminal justice as a threat to individual freedoms rather than a means for their enforcement. Nuremberg was understood as a curious experiment, unlikely to be repeated, rather than as unfinished business. This was despite the implied call in the first human rights treaty to be adopted by the General Assembly, Article VI of the Convention on the Prevention and Punishment of the Crime of Genocide,[4] that a permanent international criminal tribunal be established. That vision, of course, has changed radically in the last quarter century.

Since World War II, the European institutions—principally the Council of Europe and the European Union—have been among the most steadfast defenders of the rule of law. The European Union has served as the backbone for new formations like the International Criminal Court. The Council of

Europe as well as the Organization for Security and Cooperation in Europe have developed the principal legal framework for protection of minorities. But the rule of law is under a renewed attack, not only from outside Europe but from within its very heart.

The idea that history repeats itself has been attributed to Karl Marx. To Mark Twain is attributed a more nuanced version: "History doesn't repeat itself, but it rhymes." Today, there are some who reference the blank verse of the 1930s, the debacle of the rise of fascism and its disastrous aftermath for the entire planet. But there is an important difference that suggests this is not merely another stanza in a recurring saga. In contrast with the first part of the previous century, there are now robust international institutions. They are rooted in the protection of the principle of the rule of law, starting with the United Nations, but including the regional European institutions as well as those in other parts of the world, for example, the United States of America. They were built to withstand such onslaughts. Their survival is a matter of urgency. Their weakening and eventual destruction is at the top of the agenda of the dark forces, of the modern-day Machievellis.

Figure 10.1 Marian Turski, Holocaust Survivor (Head of the International Auschwitz Committee, 2021, Chair of the Council of the Museum of the History of Polish Jews in Warsaw, Deputy Chair of the Association of the Jewish Historical Institute of Poland, Journalist and Recipient of the French National Order of the Legion of Honour), Addressing the International Day of Commemoration in Memory of the Victims of the Holocaust (January 27, 2019) at the United Nations Headquarters (New York, NY, USA). *Photo credit: United Nations Photo/Evan Schneider.*

Only a year ago, the world commemorated the 75th anniversary of the liberation of Auschwitz. Moving ceremonies marked the somber date. One of the survivors, Marian Turski (Figure 10.1), spoke there where more than a million Jews and members of other vulnerable minorities were systematically murdered. In the audience were some of the despots who now threaten to dismantle the rule of law, within their own countries and beyond. "Auschwitz didn't come out of the blue" Turski warned. "The 11th commandment is: Thou shalt not be indifferent . . . Do not be indifferent when any minority is discriminated against. Democracy depends on the rights of minorities being protected."[5]

NOTES

1. Orson Welles, *Cucoo Clock Speech*, https://bit.ly/3gFBmmM.
2. United Nations General Assembly resolution 217 A (III), Universal Declaration of Human Rights, 10 December 1948, https://bit.ly/3h2DBzR.
3. General Comment 29, States of emergency (article 4): International Covenant on Civil and Political Rights, § 16, https://bit.ly/35E1JDs. For other references, see: Concluding Observations, Chile, CCPR/C/CHL/CO/5,§ 3; Concluding Observations, Russia, CCPR/CO/79/RUS, § 23, available through the United Nations Treaty Body Database, https://bit.ly/2TPwN0c.
4. Convention on the Prevention and Punishment of the Crime of Genocide, 78 U.N.T.S. 277.
5. Marian Turski. *Thou Shall Not Be Indifferent.* With a Foreword by Olga Tokarczuk, Wołowiec: Wydawnictwo Czarne/Warsaw: Association of the Jewish Historical Institute of Poland, 2021, 149, 153.

BIBLIOGRAPHY

Convention on the Prevention and Punishment of the Crime of Genocide, 78 U.N.T.S. 277.

Turski, Marian. *Thou Shall Not Be Indifferent.* With a foreword by Olga Tokarczuk, Wołowiec: Wydawnictwo Czarne/Association of the Jewish Historical Institute of Poland, 2021.

United Nations Digital Library, International Covenant on Civil and Political Rights, General Comment 29, States of emergency. International Covenant on Civil and Political Rights. https://bit.ly/35E1JDs.

United Nations General Assembly resolution 217 A (III), Universal Declaration of Human Rights, 10 December 1948. https://bit.ly/3h2DBzR.

Welles, Orson. *Cuckoo Clock Speech*, September 2, 1949. https://bit.ly/3gFBmmM.

Chapter 11

Dialogue in Hell between Montesquieu and Machiavelli on Climate Change, Migration, and the Rule of Law

Friedrich Forsthuber, Michael Platzer, Sławomir Redo, and Gerhard Reissner

PREFACE

Blue-sky. Photographs of Montesquieu's and Machiavelli's busts. Text below to be communicated by a male voice, in contemporary English.

Welcome, Ladies and Gentlemen! Today we will get to know Montesquieu's liberal thoughts from his preindustrial era and Machiavelli's conservative thoughts of Renaissance. Although neither one or the other could foresee how the current debate on climate change, migration, and the rule of law might have been related to their ever-relevant thinking, these days the validity of their arguments still holds water. The following dialogue between them conveys the urgent message to rehabilitate the rule of law not through populistic calls but through civic education.

This dialogue keeps with the original character and dynamics of the exchange of the two great masters of moral philosophy and political science. Montesquieu is a real scientist of culture. Machiavelli considers himself a neutral moral analyst. His sheer interest in human society is to retain the rule. Political actors, not philosophical spectators, are the exemplars of prudence.

Montesquieu is a virtuous person and philosopher. He is honest and unafraid to speak his mind. He gives up when an action is immoral. Machiavelli strongly held back by his historical reflections is less a modern thinker than Montesquieu seized by imminent future. Unlike him, Machiavelli knows that being "good" has its limits. With his own sense of virtue, Machiavelli is only "good" when this is useful for increasing his power. He is not good when this does not pay off.

On the other hand, our modern day "Montequieus" could learn something from the "political" Machiavelli, by making compromises to reach the "greater good" or to seek temporary allies to gain an important goal. In the end, lofty goals are only meaningful if they are implementable.

For their regimes, they both seek support from the underprivileged. Montesquieu encourages the people to appreciate and enlarge freedom. Hence reading Montesquieu's work *Persian Letters* with a romantic interpretation of the trip of two Muslims to France, one may come to sympathize with "the Other." Montesquieu is worried that real civic virtue is unsustainable in large republics—the contemporary prototype could be the European Union. The EU's survival is not only harmed by external demagoguery, trumpeting the fear of "the Other," but also by the dearth of internal rule of law effective controls. Machiavelli explicitly seeks it in exchange for the promise of security and a false freedom.

Montesquieu bets power not on personal skills of their seekers but on institutional arrangements which advance social justice and well-being. Machiavelli's works emphasize that a wise ruler should rely on what is under his own control. These rulers arouse enmity against immigrants, hence—using the United Nations terminology—they point to actual concerns for "safe, orderly and regular" migration. Machiavelli knows that skillfully exploiting such concerns makes sense, but this also has its limits. Even the most powerful people can be destroyed when they are conceited and challenged by someone with even greater skill.

This script focuses their dialogue on the contemporary issues of climate change, migration, and the rule of law. Both lived in the Little Ice Age (1300–1850) with its unstable climate. Both knew that nature was a force to be reckoned with, but they differed on how to react to the world of nature. Montesquieu, convinced of the perfect climate of France for sustainable life, felt that by understanding the world of nature people can develop amicable lifestyles in harmony with it and a moral agency to promote larger freedom where climate permits. While he was not seized by any public emergency, he always insisted that, in any case, fomenting fear does not help to make people wiser but only contaminates thinking. Machiavelli, aware of various floods that ravaged his republic, felt that it was fortune and managerial skill of a ruler that helps to counter natural disasters.

Times have changed, so some of their views may seem compatible neither for the drama of climate change nowadays nor with social justice developments. Starting with the most incongruent one, in the lifetime of these two *dramatis personae* there had not been anything like today's civil society, but only some simple elements, which were the "tumults" or rebellions.

In comparison with Machiavelli, Montesquieu's civic engagement in Paris was quite cultivated. He often frequented various literary salons, spoke there in public and discussed philosophical works of others. But in neither case this had anything to do with checks on the authority of a ruler. Regarding Machiavelli's Florentine civic life, he occasionally met the city's intellectuals with whom he discussed political and literary matters, but the rest of his social time he spent in his community in taverns "rotting," playing backgammon and drinking wine.

Likewise, in the lifetime of these two great men there was no phenomenon like "migration" that now causes a conflict of legal cultures. There was a conflict of values in settling, by war and violence, religious differences. But there was no mediation, restorative justice, or compensation for victims.

Next, Montesquieu and Machiavelli fundamentally differ whether someone who committed a crime should be punished. Montesquieu would be upset that someone may be pardoned for harming others. "I would be glad . . . to have a rule of justice that prevented them from harming me," he says in "My Thoughts."[1] For Machiavelli, killing someone for the common good and not for personal ambition is justified. Such a person should not enjoy impunity. We are familiar with both points of view in the debate over capital punishment, severity of punishment, and potential for rehabilitation.

Finally, Montesquieu criticized the Italian judicial administration of Machiavelli's time, because of the dependence of judges on the favors and whims of the prince. At his own time, Montesquieu criticized the administration for giving the legislative and judicial powers to the people, regarded as "the sovereign." By dispensing justice in this way, the sovereign's "general will" can destroy each private citizen's safety. In the landmark opinion on the independence of judiciary and political freedom, Montesquieu says, that there is no freedom "if the judiciary power be not separated from the legislative and executive. Were it joined with the legislative, the life and liberty of the subject would be exposed to arbitrary control; for the judge would then be the legislator. Were it joined to the executive power, the judge might behave with violence and oppression."[2]

Indeed, in Machiavelli's time, there was neither an independent judiciary nor the "rule of law." There was a nominal rule *by* law—a singularly pursued policy of a prince—whether just or unjust—for what he regarded as the "common good" (the Republic). Machiavelli was willing to sacrifice even himself in the republic's interest. Such commitment is criticized by Montesquieu.

However incongruent nowadays, these contrasting views on the rule of law and democracy appear, they have not in the least lost their competing currency. In some aspects, their worldviews are *not* mutually exclusive. After all, they both concentrated on the art of ruling and the mechanics of statecraft. Implicitly, both are federalists. However, European unification for Machiavelli is an anathema. Machiavelli believes that Europe's future is in small fatherlands, because where there are more states there are more able men. He only thinks about federating the Italian city-states, so they become independent of foreign power influence and eventually will govern themselves by their own judgment. "Own judgment" for Montesquieu, as the first modern confederalist, should be much more forthcoming and liberal, but successfully applicable only to single small countries (not their grouping). Federating any further would only be appreciated by others much later and will remain a contentious legal and political matter. For both, sky, sun, character of people never varies, as if they were the same cards, continually reshuffled and played at the table.

Both philosophies are a part of the United Nations thinking. The arguments of Montesquieu and Machiavelli continue to be relevant. But their original views obviously must be reinterpreted and adapted to interplay with current challenges and for those of the next decades.

As much as for them, so for us some of their statements have double ententes. We pursue them in the name of one or another thinker. But contrary to their own (if not dated now) intent we try to arrive at forming a majority view, as the case is with "leaving no one behind" declared by the 2030 United Nations Sustainable Development Goals Agenda. This is the concept bridging conservatism and liberalism faced with dramatic climate change—the driver for transformation.

PERSONAGES AND WORLDVIEWS

Black background. Two presenters walking into the middle stage with lights focused on them. A female presenter stops on the left. Off the cuff, she briefly presents the life of Montesquieu. A male presenter stops on her right; Presents the highlights of Montesquieu. At the time of their respective introductions, one actor after another walks onto the stage. They take respective seats in armchairs on the left and right and listen to the presentation, against background music.

Background music of their times or its contemporary interpretation: When Montesquieu is being introduced—"Versalles. Les Manches Vertes" by Giovanni Battista Lulli, when Machiavelli is being introduced—a Florentine song "Fortuna desperata."

Charles-Louis de Secondat, Baron de La Brède et de Montesquieu (1689–1755), was born in *Château La Brède* near Bordeaux (France), more than two centuries after Machiavelli. The man of science and letters, aware of the effects of the Thirty-years' war (1618–1648). *Conseiller à la Cour*

(Counsellor to the Court) then *Président à mortier* (principal magistrate) of the Parliament of Bordeaux. "Humanist" and "geographer" of law with a climatogical belief system and a "moral compass." Congenial, talkative, skeptically cheerful, trusting. Grew up in the same intellectual climate in which his ideas were produced. He is a modern idealist with some practical bent, but not an apostle of major progress. Aware what in the past absolutism did to Europeans and other people, he is looking for alternative way of governance in the world. He realizes that there are not many good people, so he proposes to start education with good laws. He believes in education and public engagement as agents of change. He is a gentle teacher of the virtue of moderation, advocate of humane, reasoned justice and punishment, in line with the intellectual climate, going slowly beyond the ancien regime. Rarely does he first look into specifics. More often he looks generally at developments and then makes specific recommendations for their in situ relevance. Like Aristotle, he recognizes the role of reason and passions in reacting to crime. Further, as an idealistic realist he argues that notwithstanding justice as an end in itself, the laws and their administration should pragmatically and effectively eliminate only some forms of evil by slowly adapting people's *mœurs* (mores/customs) and their need for larger freedom. Checks and balances allow for the promotion of goodness in and for people. He is a promotor of trust and moderator of people's conduct to interact with natural law. Being a Christian, he keeps himself at distance to the Catholic Church about which he occasionally expresses critical opinions. He also criticizes despotism as a concentration of arbitrary power—an evil artifact of life. Separation of powers within a state and the detachment of *l'état politique* from *l'état civil* (civil society) is the antidote. At his time, civility implied virtues—cultivating good manners and customs rather than organization of citizens, save, perhaps, the events in literary salons. Scientifically proven for him is that the "empire of climate" predetermines the mores of people: they are freer in the North than in the South. Yet addressing poverty is important everywhere. Successful families bring up their children in recognition of the hardships of life, and in modesty. Living in harmony with nature implies various forms of adaptation to it. He was skeptical about the mutability of character and climate. Changing the customs should be in line with the best laws people can bear. Regarding civic education, in contrast to Montesquieu's time and with due United Nations' respect for countries' cultural uniqueness, the contemporary global civic education message to which he could subscribe is that some original customs should not be left intact, hence United Nations crime prevention and criminal justice standards and norms and the role of women. He is a progenitor of the idea of looking at the development of people so no one is left behind, providing for their welfare. He is a precursor of "inclusive identity" for social change toward equality, however complex and distant this still is. He "loves the republic" as long as it provides for equality and moderation over public and private life. Montesquieu was a proponent of commerce, which advances progress and mores and is completely against corruption. He believes in incorporating the precepts of economy into the universality of other values into the "society of societies." He was a "Citizen of the world" who also intellectually invests in the paradigm of welfare and peaceful coexistence. Awarded with *L'ordre de la Mouche à miel* (the Order of the Honey Fly)—a parody of the great orders of chivalry—for loyalty and obedience to the perpetual dictate of the order the duchess Louise-Bénédicte de Bourbon. She honored "little men" who made big intellectual impact (*Piccola si, ma fa puri gravi le ferite*); "a stranger to his own country, better to understand it at last" (D'Alambert). Montesquieu's burial site in *Église Saint-Sulpice*, Paris, was destroyed during the French Revolution. His remnants were thrown into the Paris catacombs.

Niccolò di Bernardo dei Machiavelli (1469–1527) was born in Florence (Italy). He was an ambitious republican official, secretary of the Florentine government, middle-rank diplomat who assumed important legations to the city-states in the Italian peninsula, to France, and in the Germanic countries. After fourteen years of public life, he was suspected of conspiracy, arrested, imprisoned, and subjected to torture. Eventually, with no evidence, he was banished from Florence. For almost fifteen years, he was under house arrest in his nearby country estate in San Casciano. He regards himself as a good man. Cool and calculating thinker; he appears as "pure logic incarnate." He is a realist, energetic even impetuous in acting; distrustful, manipulative, and deceptive. He is neither really concerned with any international norms of his time nor with popular sentiments but only with the necessity of local survival and geographical expansion in the first place. He was a "Technician of law" dismissing natural law; keen on perfecting the "empire of laws"; a "spin doctor" to outwit those who are sincere, a "noble liar" egoistical to the bone. "Speaks like an angel"—subtly, but is sharp, critical; he borders on meanness. In fact, he is like arsenic—sweet and poisonous. While he pokes fun, with a smile on his lips he advises that people should follow their own ways of living without concern for the opinion of others as long as this does not offend Machiavelli. He positions himself with a *credo*: The more a ruler is perceived as a benign figure looking out for the welfare of his people, the more trusting his subjects will be. Appearing charming and humble, in fact, he is a bold usurper. Machiavelli is neither Christian nor pagan, but convinced of his "fast track to Heaven." He pursues religion and justice as instrumental means of the ruler's governance. He does so by advancing and normalizing in public life immoral standards of conduct that are socially inimical, expedient and should yield "the best deal" for him. Machiavelli looks for evil cases and moralizes on their strength.

On the other hand, Machiavelli's talents, political instincts, can be used to bring about positive developments. He is not a procrastinator, he is a doer, a self-appointed agent of change. Change should be not the effect of educated choice and engagement, but of a passive process of acceptance intended to inculcate fear of God and obedience to the law of the prince. He is a "merchant of fear" and manipulator of people's sentiments. Perversely, this is the source of moral enhancement which dignifies his subjects. Nominally, they are applauded for their devotion to the fatherland; they are also encouraged to enjoy "pedestrian pursuits—festivals, fashion, games," happy situations, just to make them stand by the ruler. With this simple approach, Machiavelli recommends cultivating support of his subjects, a sort of populism—participation without power. He is occasionally applauded for his acumen when he makes catchy historical analogies. His analogies are biased interpretations of selected past historical events in the interest of highlighting his power without consideration whether this is indeed true, moral, or legitimate. With his inherently evil human nature, Machiavelli passionately, hence without strict logical argument or impartiality, teaches from the past "truth" from "what men do" to live for own glory. Parents of children who want them to be educated as privileged youth may appreciate his teachings on how, at the cost of others, to become successful in life in a hostile world by taking his teachings to meet their children's own selfish goals. He is a cunning but still a reasonable ruler. While shrewdly pursuing his power, he knows that some forms of evil may bring him disapproval and deprive him of his glory, even depose him and make him criminally responsible. Therefore, he sees brutality as abominable and hardly useful. He uses a hammer and chisel instead. He likes pious cruelty. His interests are limited to the security of his own republic. He is not interested in commerce and its role in human relationships. Acquisition from someone else has only one sense—of enlarging power by force. He is an extreme example of "exclusive identity"—a model patriot in his own deepest sense, whereby only nominally the welfare of his like-minded compatriots is a priority over other people's welfare. He "loves the republic more than his soul." He himself is an example of a moderately living citizen. Austerity is his private preference. But he neither cares about other people getting rich nor those living in poverty, as long as both are complacent. An ardent nationalist, Machiavelli was buried in Florence in the Church of Santa Croce. His tomb bears the following epitaph: "Nicolas Machiavelli: No praise can equal this name alone" (*Tanto nomini nullum par elogium*).

Stage lights go on. Stage—option I: A shabby salon with carmine walls. Two old armchairs with one small table in-between. Carafe with water, two glasses. Behind a gated window with a view at a holy volcano Chachani (Peru)[3] *with a tower of the Church of the Nazarene in the foreground and a blue-sky in the background, respectively symbolizing the ambiguous beliefs of Machiavelli ("nether Christian nor pagan"), Montesquieu's distance to the Church; and the United Nations (blue-sky). "Hell" is represented by the volcano on the picture. On left and right walls two bookshelves with respective white-and-black book spines, symbolizing good and bad. Montesquieu and Machiavelli take their seats in the armchairs.*

Stage—option II: Additional semi-circular staircases on the far left and right with a Renaissance fireplace. On its top it holds a row of books with white, black-and-blue spines; in the middle a golden statue of Themis, Greek Roman Goddess. On the wall behind a picture with ecclesiastical keys (crossed) to Heaven. The window with the mentioned volcano view is on the entresol joining the staircases. At the end of the piece, Machiavelli and Montesquieu rise from the armchairs and walk toward their respective staircases.

Montesquieu speaks with a French accent. Machiavelli speaks with an Italian accent.

I.

Montesquieu: When I found myself in this place, I learned that you are one of those permanent (Oops!, *pardon*!) prominent residents in Hell, *Segretario* Machiavelli. I do not know how long I may stay here with you, but as long as we are together I take this opportunity of your prominence, and, hmm, would like to learn how did you earn your hellish reputation.

Machiavelli: Permanent resident? I have been here only since 1527! Hellish reputation? Let's see, if I really deserve it. Anyway, welcome, Baron de Montesquieu! As we are still awaiting in Hell our destined place in Eternity, indeed we can spend some time to discuss what comes as a total surprise to me, namely that not "The Prince" but climate is our ruler.

Montesquieu: D'accord! Let me start with my *credo*. I will "speak of the different peoples of Europe as I speak of the different peoples of Madagascar."[4] We are now in the twenty-first century. From what I see now it is clear, that climate makes itself the first of all "empires" in any place under the sun! I have said so when I lived on Mother Earth, and I confirm this now to you in this unenviable for us location. I am not sure whether my argument about climate is clear to everybody. I wonder if *you* experienced how climate had affected your way of thinking and living in Florence. I first saw your beautiful Florence that you left centuries ago. What a livable climate you have in Florence! Perhaps therefore you have not been privy to the weather extremities.

Machiavelli: [*Interrupts*] You are not right, Baron. I remember some weather extremities in Florence. I know what you are talking about.

Montesquieu: Bon, but even if you experienced yourself such extremities in your inland Florence, they cannot be compared to Rome which lies at the seashore. There I was struck by them. They had a debilitating effect on Rome. Various diseases were rampant. They must have originated from the unhealthfulness of Rome's coastal regions and from the harshness of the entire seashore area. When in the Vatican I was received by Cardinal de Polignac, the French Minister to the Holy See, I discussed with him why Romans are known for their bellicose spirit. I wondered with him whether their character comes from the stagnant water from old drains that turned into smelly soil cavities in the city. After all, it is full of ancient ruins left untouched for centuries. The Cardinal agreed with my suspicion. He said that in summer, vapors and insects arise from dried up places on the shore of the sea and from alum mines, so the air pollution in Rome becomes much more intense and agitating.

Machiavelli: You seem to say that the character of Romans is conditioned by the air they breathe! Aha, you think like me! Right, all Romans seem to me somewhat noxious. [*Triumphantly*] True! True! "To the Church, therefore, and to the priests, we Italians owe this first debt, that through them we have become wicked and irreligious."[5] But all people "are ungrateful, fickle, liars, and deceivers, they shun danger and are greedy for profit."[6]

Montesquieu: Hold on with your pathetic statement! You are mixing everything and making great analogies! I did not mean the Roman Church, but only the Romans! This may be only the way you think, because, for you evil makes the world go around.

Machiavelli: [*Caught in flagranti delicto*] *Bene*, let's take this up later. Please continue.

Montesquieu: I have studied this Roman problem carefully. Unlike you, *Sire*, I cannot draw such a negative conclusion about Italians, even if we reason the same way. Not only your conclusions are discouraging, but also your thinking is deceitful and unscientific.

Machiavelli: You are pressing heavy charges against me.

Montesquieu: Be that as it may, but before you may come to other conclusions, without further ado let me share some science with you. In my view, air reacts with nerve endings. If cold, it contracts them; if warm, it relaxes them. Contraction means added strength and vigor but decreases sensitivity. Relaxation means less physical strength but more active emotions. Northern peoples are morally virtuous because their senses are dull. Southern peoples are indolent and immoral because their senses are agitated and passions violent. The institutions in both regions will be in accordance with their respective characters. In moderate climates they tend to liberty and equality, in warm climates to tyranny and slavery. A good legislator must favor the advantages. He must respond the vices intrinsic to the climate.

Machiavelli: Do you think, there is something in the soil or climate that makes a country particularly adapted to the preservation of freedom?

Montesquieu: Excusez moi, you again have misunderstood me. As for the soil, I will make my point later. And I am not at all surprised by your question. It took me almost twenty years of studies to research it. Our general spirit anywhere in the world comes out of climate but morality is the combination of laws, religion, customs, and manners. It is up to the legislator to promote the spirit of the nation. In any place under the sun, it is the government that should always strive to encourage the virtues and discourage the vices prompted by the climate.

II.

Machiavelli: Virtues, vices? Sounds nice but it is very general. What may happen when people from the South come to the North? In short, how to deal effectively with the newcomers?

Montesquieu: Let's both take a look from the skies down to Mother Earth [*video of burning areas in North Africa, Australia, British Columbia, California, Corsica, Peloponnese and Siberia with people and animals seeking refuge*]. Do you see it ravaged by fires? How many people, wolves, foxes, bears and camels and other animals die there? Do you see that people and animals escape in search of safety and water? Do you see them climbing the walls and fences to escape misery? Aren't people sinning against nature? Do you think that they will stay put where they are now and not come to Italy or France for that matter? [*returns to his armchair*] And what about other calamities? Do you remember what happened to your people flooded in Florence? And what about your family fleeing Florence to escape the Black Death? You and your father survived, but you lost three other family members! Do you remember a good Samaritan story? I tell you, "[j]ustice to others is like charity to ourselves"[7]!

Machiavelli: [*Annoyed*] You are impressing me with your knowledge of life of Jesus, and the way when before Him the Troglodytes behaved—these primitive savages, hah? What a configuration!

Montesquieu: "If we can believe the historians, they were more like beasts than men"[8] but, but! they were "united by their uprightness as much as by the corruption of their fellows"[9]!

Machiavelli: [*Annoyed by the allusion that he is a beast and a corruptor*] Look, no question, of course, everybody wants to survive and live in safety. Wherever anybody comes from they have this right, especially when such calamities occur. If during such calamities I would have been in power, and regardless how successful I would be, I would do everything to make them and my folks safe and happy, so they all will carry me to Heaven in their arms if God gave them wings. [*Quaintly*] And as for the story about the robbed stranger helped by a passer-by? Do you want now to make me a robber? Hold on! That story from Jesus suggests that helping such people in dire need without expecting anything in return makes us truly go-od. [*Saying slowly*]. How would I know that my giving a stranger a hand will eventually ruin my well-being? In my view, "none will ever offer thanks to him who merely refrains from injury."[10] Why then should I be charitable and humane toward strangers when the reason that made strangers come does not make them grateful to me? Do you realize that they only want to take a ride with you without saying even *merci*? And how may I be sure that as a Samaritan I was not ambushed?

Montesquieu: [*Evidently provoked, emotionally and sarcastically retorts* ad hominem] I see, it is not "too easy to perform acts of evangelic charity when one's life is spent on sumptuous couches, with beautiful women, when upon going to bed and arising, great personages are eager to help you into or out of your shirt. Be a father of a family and not a despot, a patriarch and not a prince"![11] [*then upon a reflection asks*:] Hmm, does a father become poorer when he shares his knowledge with his family?

Machiavelli: Poorer? No, but "yes" when frustrated, if the teaching goes in vain or even worse–when my good will was exploited by someone who is not gratuitous.

Montesquieu: OK, but keeping only to your own words from "The Prince" that by nature all people are evil, should they do evil unto others as they would do unto you? [*wondering*]. I wonder since you consider them bad, what will you do next with these bad newcomers. Wouldn't you like rather to make them "good"?

Machiavelli: Good, but with the malignity of their spirit whenever they have a free occasion to commit crime? Impossible! Send them back home? Make them happy there? Who cares? [*Hesitating*] Look, wouldn't you agree that one should keep promises only as long as the conditions under which they have been left outlives them?

Montesquieu: Do you ask me how people should conduct themselves when they are in a guest house?

Machiavelli: Yes, in "The Prince" I said: "A wise ruler . . . cannot and should not keep his word when such an observance would be to his disadvantage, and when the reasons that caused him to make a promise are removed. If men were all good, this precept would not be correct. But since men are a wicked lot and will not keep their promises to you, you likewise need not keep yours to them."[12] I mean, when someone is mischievous, then I need not keep my promise.

Montesquieu: Hmm, yes, when *everybody* has a free occasion, *some* may be prompted by the malignity of their spirit to be ungrateful or even criminal. But for me this is an opportunity to be taken care of, but not for you, *Segretario* Machiavelli. And I am rather surprised that in this unenviable place we both are in now, you still disregard what the apostles Matthew and Luke said, that we should do unto others as we would like them do unto us. For you is better to stop strangers from coming and let them deal with their unlucky lot on their own in distant seas and lands. No mercy, no reciprocity, no commonality.

Machiavelli: Apostles? I don't care. As I said, I would not oppose strangers who genuinely and duly accept my house rules. But, first of all, with my harsh law I would deter strangers from coming. Second, when they come I would make my sumptuous laws clear not by my lavishness but prudence and parsimony. I would only carefully deal with strangers to obviate any fear of revenge from them. It will be sufficient therefore to be firm, parsimonious, and rigorous. That would be the limits of my assistance.

Montesquieu: Hmm, indeed "[p]rinces who lavish honors gain nothing by it . . . The more one rewards people, the more others deserve rewards."[13] But rigorous? Be that as it may but that's *not* a priority in my constitution. Yes, we both know that harsh laws do not deter, let alone do the justice which everybody seeks, yourself including. So I well understand you, and even William Shakespeare does when Hamlet says that "conscience does make cowards of us all."[14] But look at Florence right now: strangers are coming—unwelcomed. Should fear overcome us?

Machiavelli: Yes, I see who is arriving at Florence. Our social welfare is world known. We have a good reputation.

Montesquieu: I know that when you were in Florence as its Secretary, you dealt with foreign affairs either with force or fraud. In local affairs you either opted for your own benefit or for eliminating dangers. Whether you like it or not, now you would have to deal with both affairs at one time, and as if they were one. You have strangers with whom you can deal either way. So, since you so often speak of "people" you should tell me, the Florentine Secretary, how would you command your own people concerned with strangers? Can you imagine them all with minds burning of hatred or cooled by tolerance? Are the refugees or are we responsible for one another? If not us, who then is responsible for them? Do you have any advice?

Machiavelli: Advice? [*Guessing, nervously looking around*] . . . , well . . . *mi scusi*, let me think more about this. [*Then slowly says*] A flood of people is not like a natural flood. No precautions, dykes or fortresses will help. And I must warn you, Baron, that in "all cities and in all nations there do not prevail the same desires and passions"[15] so, surely, strangers will make a difference, because different people share different passions and desires. I see here a big problem.

Montesquieu: Bon. [*Next, stands up with the book, walks behind Machiavelli's armchair and keeping the book above his head, says:*] So let us look for advice we may both agree on. In "*De l'esprit des lois*" I wrote: "Nature is just to

all mankind; she rewards them for their industry, whilst an arbitrary power deprives people of its benefits, and then indolence and inaction seem to be their only happiness."[16] Neither in your or my time on Earth I could foretell that my advice to keep people industrious will be so minutely executed!

Machiavelli: Ah! So you think we agree? I am also of the opinion that "poverty and hunger are needed to make men industrious, but laws are also needed to make them good. When we do well without laws, when laws are not needed; but when good customs are absent, laws are at once required."[17]

Montesquieu: Well, even if we agree, making laws work is not so simple . . . [*Exclaiming*] *Segretario* Machiavelli! Since we agree that these newcomers should not upset our house rules and our sense of justice they must appreciate that our laws, religion, mores and manners are respected. Since you so carefully studied the monumental history of Rome by Livy, wouldn't you agree that "*fortiter sed suaviter*"—to act strongly, but gently—is the way to go with the strangers?

Machiavelli: Didn't I just say so before?

Montesquieu: You mean to be rigorous? I can imagine that there will be many strangers who will hesitate to share our sentiments, even if you approach them in the right manner. So, yes, I would be concerned with too many reacting to our rules with emotions, but even more with those people's ignorance of my own language! I have always stood for abolishing and unchaining slavery. But I am not for the unfettered flow of people and not for respecting my country's language and its humanistic culture. Nourishing the strangers with the virtues of living together in peace and justice is for me the most important! I worked to make ourselves be of the same spirit and to share the way of life that gives a chance to anyone to live in harmony with others and with nature.

Machiavelli: [*Puzzled*] Well, well, well . . . So?

Montesquieu: [*Boldly*] So, let's talk straight. You undertook important diplomatic missions in Europe. You spoke with Cesare Borgia, Catherine Sforza and Pope Julius II. You also talked with King Louis XII, from my native country and with the Holy Roman Emperor Maximilian II. You enjoyed that international *milieu*. But you also suffered from great hardships, the malignity of fortune as you said. Weren't you ostracized, imprisoned for one year, and tortured for three weeks hanged from your bound wrists, because of your alleged plot against the Medici? Do you remember that after the general amnesty you fell forever into disgrace in the Florentine political and diplomatic world, and you lost their trust?

Machiavelli: Yes, this all happened to me! But what this all has to do with strangers?

Montesquieu: [*Exclaiming*] You have enough to tell me what you felt when you experienced your malignity of fortune! How then I who never had been imprisoned and tortured can reply how to treat others? Certainly, you would not recommend the way you were treated by your own authorities to others. Wouldn't you?

Machiavelli: [*Agitated*] Yes, I felt mistreated, abandoned, and mistrusted. Indeed, those unfortunate strangers are abandoned, mishandled and mistrusted. But should they have a say in our matters? *Oh, la, la*! These strangers' lifestyles may sabotage our own security and *fortuna*. They do not share with us more than the drive for safety. That's very understandable, but not good enough! Strangers are changing our Fortune. She may be like "one of those destructive rivers that, when they become enraged, flood the plains, ruins the trees and buildings, raising the earth from one spot and dropping it onto another. Everyone flees before it; everyone yields to its impetus, unable to oppose it in any way. But although rivers are like this, it does not mean that we cannot take precautions with dikes and dams."[18] Do you want strangers if we fail to integrate them? I am afraid that if their way of life opposes ours we will be in for a very turbulent time. Our *fortuna* will be at stake.

Montesquieu: [*Surprised*] Turbulent time? Not necessarily so turbulent as you may imagine it. As you know, fear has a quick ear. It is so easy to instigate fear and ruin our human relations balance. My ear and mind encourage us to be clear on which side we are on: Be it prejudiced or judicious? Be just or moderate? I would not have asked you these questions, had it has not occurred to me that my own study *Observations sur l'Histoire Naturelle* [*he raises the treatise and assumes the posture of a lector*] on the pigmentations of insects, the parasitic life.

Machiavelli: [*Interrupts*] You speak about insects, parasitic life? What does this have to do with strangers? Are they parasites?

Montesquieu: Sounds this grotesque? Not for me, *Signor Segretario*. Just listen to me, please!

Machiavelli: I am all ears!

Montesquieu: I studied parasitic life of the mistletoe, the abdominal circulation of the frog, the foramen ovule and *ductus Botalli*. Last but not least, my experimental research on the nutritional value of vegetables have taught me to be very incisive but cautious in drawing conclusions about the nature of "things," including about us and others.

Machiavelli: [*Bewildered by this far fetching academic statement; dismissively and mockingly*] I know that in your early academic career you have been awarded. You forgot to add that you received *L'ordre de la Mouche à miel*—the Order of the Honey Fly for your intellectual pursuits, *oh, la, la*! [*Paternalistically*] *Chevalier* Montesquieu!

Montesquieu: [*Seriously, aware of his paltry but fiery posture, and the parody of the Order*]. Yes, I got that order as a token of my friends' appreciation for my fervid searches to learn the secrets of Mother Earth. So let me now be clear, and listen carefully to my *exposé*. *Écoute moi, Secrétaire*.

Machiavelli: Your scientific expositions are very elaborate, and I am really losing track of your volatile train of thought! I am not used to hear such expositions!

Montesquieu: Just listen! When I delivered to the Academy in Bordeaux that treatise on insects, parasites and frogs I realized how some of my own initial ideas through deduction may become clear and rational. *Cogito ergo sum*! No longer I let my passions prevail over my Reason. [*Stiffening*] So, let me now also be as clear and bold as you yourself always had been. I have come to the conclusion that those strangers traveling across the world to livable places want democracy as much as others who enjoy it. Everybody as a physical being is like other bodies governed by invariable laws from which democracy originated. And this is the law which I found and promote.

Machiavelli: Bene! What a parallel! But what this has to do with democracy? How come then those strangers do not contribute to democracy at home and, when they leave it, are such a burden to European democracies? The masses anywhere, whether in democracy or not, are tranquil, as long as someone does not encroach on their property or women. If you want to rule, keep this in mind. And that's the reason for the inaction of anybody of the plebeian sort, whether native or stranger. Both will eat from your hand, but they will bite it when you do not feed them. That's the misery of your democratic ideal. What really unifies people is just a simple ideology, laws and religion, not anything else!

Montesquieu: You seem to have forgotten about your own words: "They who would have their city become a great empire, must endeavor by every means to fill it with inhabitants; for without a numerous population no city can ever succeed in growing powerful. This may be achieved in two ways, by gentleness or by force. By gentleness, when you offer a safe and open path to all strangers who may wish to come and dwell in your city, so as to encourage them to come there of their own accord; or by force, when after destroying neighboring towns, you transplant their remaining inhabitants to live in yours."[19] So, why do you only talk about biting and feeding? What about encouraging educated strangers to live with us and utilizing their skills?

Machiavelli: Indeed so I have said, and I admit that "an act of benevolence will at all times have more influence over the minds of men than violence and ferocity."[20]

Montesquieu: Well, well, well, what an admission! So listen now to this: I cannot condemn newcomers who look for better life elsewhere, if they readily and truly offer their service and capacities in our shared welfare. I may paraphrase myself by saying that the richer a country is, the more foreigners are drawn by its wealth. I should add that also peace and justice are two golden assets which attract newcomers to a country which cherishes them.

Machiavelli: Yes, I remember you saying that justice to others is like charity to ourselves.

Montesquieu: The newcomers to Europe should not be treated as a burden to our democracy. Even those who are unskillful may serve it as long as they want to learn. They are not different from anybody else as much as we are from them. They may revive our democracy in new forms and ways, if also we want them to learn. We must be ready to show them what "property" for the security of democracy means. These strangers should be encouraged to respond in kind.

Machiavelli: A tit-for-tat?

Montesquieu: Yes. Those who appreciate this principle should be as free as we are, and we all should be respectful to one another. Those who don't appreciate it should leave us, unless they learn our house rules. That house rules' learning will be for them as well as for us. I want such laws that are reciprocal, decisive, forceful but humane and transformative for their welfare through schooling and other education that emancipates them.

Machiavelli: Transformative? Hah!, I will soon tell you what I think about it, but go on now, please.

Montesquieu: I will hold you to your word. Here are my words: "We can gauge ourselves and the newcomers by what we demand of ourselves and others with whom we live. We do not only want them to be just, enemies of fraud and deception, at least toward us—for as luck would have it, we are much less concerned that they be this way toward others. We also want them to be assiduous, obliging, tender, affectionate, sensitive. We would regard a friend as a dishonorable man, if he were to rest content with observing the rules of an exact justice toward us. Thus, there are certain duties that are different from those that come directly from justice. These duties are founded on propriety, and derive from justice only in the sense that it is just in general for men to have consideration for each other—not only in the things that can make society more useful to them, but also in the things that can make society more agreeable to all."[21]

Machiavelli: You speak again about reciprocity.

Montesquieu: Yes, because this is what makes the civic spirit and what serves order in the State. "It lets you feel joy in public tranquility, in the fair administration of justice, in the security of the magistrates, in the prosperity of those who govern, in the respect paid to the laws, in the stability of a country. Civic spirit is obeying the laws, even in cases where they are harmful to us, considering the general good they always bring us rather than the particular harm they sometimes bring us. Civic spirit is exercising with zeal, with pleasure, with satisfaction, that type of citizenry entrusted to everyone in the body politic."[22] These are my thoughts.

Machiavelli: [*Lightly; smiling*] "What an overwhelming flood of eloquence. Governments are overturned by such talk."[23]

Montesquieu: Veuillez m'excuser pour un si longue exposé!

III.

Machiavelli: I admit, this discussion shows how much we differ about the folks with whom a good ruler must deal with. I would never give so much credit to anybody, and especially to strangers. I am very candid in "The Prince." I stand for deceit and scheming to outmaneuver competitors and through false compliments subdue a victim and take control of anybody. If I was in that book not clear enough, I said so again in my comedy "The Mandrake Root."

Montesquieu: "The Mandrake Root," "*La Mandragola*"?, "*La Mandragore*"?—that famous comedy shown in Florence and Venice! Even Pope Leo X liked it!

Machiavelli: Pope's delight, and your generous reference make me happy to enjoy the authorship of my greatest artistic bestseller!

Montesquieu: Applause aside, I understand that a potion made of that root may stupefy a person who drinks it. That's quite an insidious way to control someone's mind! Isn't it?

Machiavelli: Hmm, be that as it may. That's exceptional. By and large I am for such control by more subtle means. Am I right, that you also know them? In your *répertoire* you recognize deception, even more monstrous then mine, Baron de Montesquieu! Didn't you write: "to indicate a great deception the English say: 'That is Jesuitically false'"[24]? Everybody knows what you mean by deception!

Montesquieu: Are you taking me for a ride? Yes, I recognize deception. Surely, the Jesuits are the masters in the art of intrigue! You may rather accuse me of self-deception, but you are guilty of intriguing!

Machiavelli: [*Hesitating*] . . . as long as people do not hate me, they let themselves be ruled. Only a few, those most ambitious think critically. I can easily deal with all of them in my own manner—through corruption! This is the simplest form of the rule by law to govern orderly over people and property. Deception or intrigue serve this purpose well. We must only be careful not to trespass on others' sanctified values. Keep, therefore, in mind that "men forget the death of their father more quickly than the loss of their patrimony."[25]

Montesquieu: [*Admitting*] True, continue, please.

Machiavelli: Within these limits, frankly, people really should take care of themselves. I only decide whether or not somebody or something is just and serves my ends. But this is a secondary matter. My first priority is to keep peace and security, and to make my people happy. "For in all republics, whatever the form of their government," a very few people desire power, "but all the rest, whose number is countless, only desire that they may live securely . . . [They] are well contented where The Prince enacts such laws and ordinances as provide for the general security, while at the same time the laws establish his own authority; and when he does this, and the people see that nothing will really induce them to violate these laws, they soon begin to live happily and without anxiety."[26]

Montesquieu: So this is your way to govern?

Machiavelli: Yes. Governance is nothing "else than . . . controlling your subjects so that it shall neither be in their power nor in their interest to harm you. And this is effected either by making such sure your dealing with them puts it out of their power to do you injury, or else by granting them benefits so that it would be folly in them to seek to change their condition."[27] Let them be occupied with festivals and shows!

Montesquieu: [*Sardonically*] Governance through popular hedonism, hah? Indeed, how simple and joyful this sounds! Does this mean that you take liberty from the people, but not material and personal possessions? What about holding a party ticket? Didn't you say in your comedy "The Mandrake Root," "if you are not in with the ruling party and don't have good connections, you can't even get a dog to bark at you."[28]?

Machiavelli: Certo, that's the way to rule! You seem to believe that good governance comes from what people feel and want to say. I see that their spirit must be kept in check. It should be molded, even expropriated, hence my quip about the dog. I do not accept criticism. When it comes, I tell you—you must be expedient. "Any harm done to a man must be of the kind that removes any fear of revenge."[29] I want to build and strengthen the rule of law only for my own sake, in the best interests of the glory of my republic and my successors. Simply put, *Monsieur* Montesquieu, "it is much safer to be feared than loved,"[30] and be "never either hated or despised."[31]

Montesquieu: [Showing disagreement]

Machiavelli: I see, you reject my idea for successful governance that leaves people to their own devices to think, judge and act within their own *small* worlds. You see them in a bigger world and you want to empower them, don't you?

Montesquieu: Wait, I have not even started to speak about the rule of law, while you already have concluded what is good for you, but that is *not* the Rule of Law. I see that here we differ drastically. Therefore, let me first tell you that, when it comes to educating people I see justice everywhere—from A to Z, from Arithmetic to Zoology. In my alphabet I want to teach people to be able to contribute to a just social order which is not only enjoyable because of festivities. Justice is not a thing, but a relation among things. I see justice that may make you and all of us everywhere to be fair, progressive. Justice is something eternal, universal and independent of human law. Justice should provide benefits for all. I am only saying that justice should respond to and help to shape up our morals and mores. In every place under the sun, we should deliver justice *toutes proportions gardées* and bring it up to higher standards. Neither I am a dreamer nor a hypocrite. In contrast with you, I do not think that masses should be falsely empowered, as indeed they were constituent people. This is unrealistic, I am sorry. I believe that over them and at the core of the ruling there should be the rule of law, not a despotic ruler who, in fact, strips these people

of their right to individual liberty. For me, this is what the independent judges should protect.

Machiavelli: Judges should rule the way I want them. Free people and states are those which are far from any external servitude and are able to govern themselves by their own judgments. For a ruler there is no court of appeal.

Montesquieu: [*Agitated*] What? No court of appeal? Independent judiciary is important for the ruler *and* the masses. It is so simple as that! Even if we differ in other things involved in the independence judges through their verdicts should balance out the claims people make. This may more readily happen when the independence of judges is well protected by the constitution—by law, that is, and not by your personal caprice, whims or fears, Machiavelli. That's what I call "*pouvoirs distributes*"[32]—distribution of powers. I do not care how one organizes the courts. . . . They can hand down verdicts from the *Palais de Justice* or render them even under a tree. It may be oak, pine or birch or any other tree or place, as long as a judge is only sworn to do justice, but not for its administrator or any other claimant, and adjudicates only in accordance with that law.

Machiavelli: You speak of something incomprehensible to me. In my courtyard, the judge is my guest, and follows my house rules. According to them, "there are two ways of contesting, the one by the law, the other by force; the first method is proper to men, the second to beasts; but because the first is frequently not sufficient, it is necessary to have recourse to the second. Therefore it is necessary for a prince to understand how to avail himself of the beast and the man."[33] Of course, there are different judges with whom we have to deal with. "Whilst it is easy to persuade them, it is difficult to fix them in that persuasion. And thus it is necessary to take such measures that, when they believe no longer, it may be possible to make them believe by force."[34] So I treat judges who do not play by my rules. I line them up! [*Pauses, then continues paternalistically*] My friend, do you still think of "[a] saintly judicial detachment from worldly pressures"[35]? About divine justice? Isn't this naive?

Montesquieu: [*Shocked*; *quickly but calmly*] And where are you now? Aren't you expecting divine justice in this place?

Machiavelli: [*Admits*] Fair enough, but you must know what Saint Augustine thought of justice! Don't you remember his story about Alexander the Great? The king asked the pirate: "What is your idea, in infesting the sea?" And the pirate answered with uninhibited insolence, "The same as yours, in infesting the earth! But because I do it with a tiny craft, I'm called a pirate; because you have a mighty navy, you're called an emperor."[36] Baron: People are concerned about their safety and welfare. Let's be frank: Prayers won't help, don't be so naive!

Montesquieu: You made a point, indeed! Justice must come fast. But why you have forgotten to add what Saint Augustine also said: "Remove justice, and what are kingdoms but gangs of criminals on a large scale? What are criminal gangs but petty kingdoms? A gang is a group of men under the command of a leader, bound by a compact of association, in which the plunder is divided according to an agreed convention. If this villainy wins so many recruits from the ranks of the discouraged and the demoralized that it requires additional territory, establishes a strong base, captures cities and subdues peoples, it then openly arrogates to itself the title of kingdom, which is usurped in the eyes of the world, not by the renouncing of aggression but by seizing territory with impunity."[37] This is corruption by laws. Corruption is "an incurable evil, because it is in the very remedy itself."[38] Regrettably, here I must agree with my distinguished predecessor, Ibn Khaldun of Tunis—may peace be upon him—who said about corruption in government. Government is "an institution which prevents injustice other than such as it commits itself."[39] That's why constraint of men by other men, my "*pouvoirs distributes*"—distribution of powers, should keep the government in check.

Machiavelli: Hmm, first you wanted to make me a robber, now I am a villain and evil corruptor who doesn't want to be kept in check, right? No! I regard myself a true master of *l'arte della stato* not a villain, robber, or corruptor. First of all, I am a good rhetor! Believe me, public opinion "can be made to express whatever one wants if the hidden springs of power are truly understood. But before thinking about controlling opinion, you have to disorient it, to unsettle its convictions by acting in astonishingly contradictory ways, constantly diverting it, mesmerizing it, little by little leading it astray. One of the great secrets of the day is to know how to manipulate popular prejudices and passions so as to create such a confused way of thinking that any common ground of understanding is impossible among people who speak the same language and have the same interests."[40]

Montesquieu: [*Sarcastically condescending*] So one citizen should fear another? No wonder then, that "one always marvels to see so much wit and so little enlightenment."[41] I opt for an opinion based on facts!

Machiavelli: Baron: Opinion is a mistress of success, as Shakespeare said. So yes, you can turn facts upside down. Anyway, anyone who thinks like me is my brother and sister. I welcome such "*me-toos*" in my home.

Montesquieu: [*Mockingly*] I am just visiting your home place, oops, *pardon*, this transition hot spot, *Segretario!*

Machiavelli: Look: from where we are now I still stand for a new order and new principles. It is me who keeps others in check. My turning black into white is the path of great men! Isn't it so that "evil lies so near the good, and both are so mixed up together, that you may readily seize the one when you think to grasp the other"?[42] Haven't you heard about great Ibn Zafar al-Siqilli of Sicily, then ruled by William the Bad. Like me this Sicilian Arab tells his Prince how to secure and exercise power. Another one was Han Fei of China who like me recommended a strict justice administration. I share their sense of transforming our world.

Montesquieu: Your distinguished predecessors?

Machiavelli: Yes. There are many great thinkers like me. Therefore, I tell you what they told me: One "should do as those prudent archers do who, aware of the strength of their bow when the target at which they are aiming seems too distant, set their sights much higher than the designated target, not in order to reach such a height with their arrow, but instead to be able, by aiming so high, to strike their target."[43] Baron de Montesquieu!, let's be frank: I am one of those prudent archers. My target is to achieve glorious ends with the wisdom of the ancients.

Montesquieu: Well, well, well. The end justifies the means? A catchy saying!

Machiavelli: Not mine, Baron. It came from our distinguished colleague Immanuel Kant, whom I do not see in our place.

Montesquieu: Immanuel Kant? The one whom people regard the forefather of the League of Nations and of the United Nations? The one who imagined a perpetual peace?

Machiavelli: Yes, that's him. I do not believe in any of his recommendations. These Machiavellians of peace are not of my kind! My own is that "it matters little what method a general follows, provided that he is skillful and that his ability makes him highly regarded by his men."[44] I also think that "inasmuch as men judge generally more by the eye than by the hand, there is nothing more important than by deceiving them."[45] One way or another they should be on one page with me. Method and image is everything! I enjoy deceiving! "Men are so simple and so much creatures of circumstance, that the deceiver will always find someone ready to be deceived."[46]

Montesquieu: Bon, indeed, deceit may be in the order of the day of everybody, and your illustrious predecessors are just cases in point. But I must warn you and your accolades who are so keen on it: "The reputation they have of excelling in their art discourages almost everyone from dealing with them, and [. . .] they find themselves for that reason deprived of all the advantages of collaboration."[47] [*Approaches Machiavelli*] Deceit is a successful tool for authority, but not for good governance. Bad faith never serves well.

Machiavelli: I must correct you [*mockingly*]: I only advise a "good faith of little account."[48]

Montesquieu: Indeed, and with that little of good faith, as you say, you serve all your commoners and take them for a ride. First, you pretentiously present yourself as an archer whom others should emulate, and command them to follow your deeds. Next, so they do not repent their misdeeds, you tell them to do more of the same for some illusive share of glory, and of impunity, too. And you move on at full gallop to build your own glory. In fact, through your "bad laws having made lazy men, they have been reduced to slavery because of their laziness."[49] You really start with making a man bad citizen, so you can eventually make him a good slave! [*Speaks boldly*] That's the way how with your *l'arte della stato* you really leave your people—men and women—behind: manipulated, morally crippled, mentally incapacitated as a bunch of blind followers teaching their children to follow suit. "Slavery is always preceded by sleep."[50]! By your *l'arte della stato* you really did not master any new order or new principle.

Machiavelli: I am reorganizing the foundations!

Montesquieu: Really? What you really do and admit is that you "propose to people anything that upon its face seems profitable and courageous, though there be really a loss concealed under it which may involve the ruin of the republic."[51] Moreover, as you also say, "the multitude will ever be most easily persuaded to it."[52] In fact, you merely usurped and ill-used your prerogatives for your personal pursuits. Yes, indeed, you turned black into white. You are an alchemist but not a physician. You impersonated yourself as the master of their universe, a God given judicial astrologist. Could there be anything more absurd than this role, and worse for the rule of law than your conduct misleading your own people?

Machiavelli: I find this not only normal but also desirable. I am convinced that you cannot do otherwise for if you do, you will not be supported by your people.

Montesquieu: Ecco! Chapeau bas! True! You said one has to be careful and know how to approach them. You warned "*Chi fonda in sul populo fonda in sul fango*"—"He who builds on the people, builds on mud."[53] True, you must be careful walking through the mud. Therefore, you should not abuse your people but get their support. This is exactly what you do in your own way: You buy their graces, but only for your own future. You exploit their naivety in governance and thrive on their indolence. I remember that you said, "[m]en are so thoughtless they'll opt for a diet that tastes good without realizing there's a hidden poison in it."[54] I studied people's thoughtlessness, their complacency or indecisiveness. You are right. These are the facts of life.

Machiavelli: Yes, "men are so simple, and so much creatures of circumstance, that the deceiver will always find someone ready to be deceived."[55] But continue, please.

Montesquieu: "Smart people follow their own route; they have new and hidden paths. They march where no one has been before. The word is new."[56] All the rest can be molded, if one wants to treat them like children. But I detest indolence and credulousness. I believe that as much as you can mold people in one way, you can also mold them in another way: to be proactive, critical and forthcoming. Even children can be critical! You may know that when I was a child, my parents who lived in the castle put me for three years in their servants' smallholding to appreciate other people's hardships. Then I felt the indolence of my caretakers. Since then I had wondered how "to predispose all men by our consideration, all men with whom we live."[57] And don't you remember what you said about industriousness and good laws? Do you agree?

Machiavelli: [*Trapped*] Certainly. And I repeat, people should be made industrious, but also kept occupied by festivals and spectacles!

Montesquieu: Hah! Then we both agree that mental indolence does not pay off for most people.

Machiavelli: Yes.

Montesquieu: And this is because "[w]e have no more right to demand complaisance of others than they have of us. [N]either of the two parties would have an expectation for the other if they were to wait for each other."[58] Surely, this would render our society harsh and barbarous. Am I right?

Machiavelli: Yes.

Montesquieu: Like it or not, may be you heard that even wolves reciprocate? So, if reciprocity is also so evident to you, wouldn't it then be a good custom to re-learn to reciprocate by animating and activating people's mutual regard, and by inculcating their industriousness and open-mindedness? One must create conditions in which people's indolence and indoctrinated mutual disregard do not lock them in poverty, whether material or of thought. We must practice this natural asset to respect and provide for one another. If not, then we "would render society harsh and make people barbarous."[59] Then indeed, you have people as you said, left behind. Children should be brought up in fairness and trust, adults led to live in peace and justice. They all should learn and live in mutual regard of one another. We need more integrity, more selflessness and more thoughtful minds to live in harmony with ourselves. There are ways in the natural order of things we must succumb to, but there are also other things we can improve ourselves. I am not for a single-man rule. That's my response to your new order and new principles.—*ordini nuovi* and *principi nuovi*! [*Clearly elated*] Let's with your *modi e ordini nuovi* seek indeed unknown waters and lands! That's a path as yet untrodden by anyone!

Machiavelli: [*Ironic*] Hmph! *ora vedo*, so then nobody will be left behind? That's very radical. *Huh*! What a dream! [*Resolved*] I am not for this "imaginary" world, I am not flying in reality beyond my ability to imagine.

Montesquieu: [*Agitated*] Really? Don't you remember your own words that "it is the nature of men to be bound by the benefits they confer as much as by those they receive"[60]? If you were a newcomer, how would you have felt after receiving them? So what about exercising this rule with newcomers? What about each part benefiting from the activity of the other? We explore our needs and look for advantages through our culture and our language, so the newcomers can follow the rules, share their sentiments but also the responsibilities and rights that make everybody understand our modern objectives and values, and our drive for ourselves and for them to be good citizens.

Machiavelli: Bon. I agree, but only as long as we play by our house rules.

Montesquieu: Bene. What about making this not in a happenstance but systemic way to make steadily, clearly and conditionally room for more freedom for us and them? Shouldn't we tell them that legitimate welfare and security comes with the host's price to be paid by hard work and commitment to humanistic values? What about treating strangers' new households in which they will be happy by themselves as places with their own growing assets, and not as new residents frustrated from whose misery we profit? If there is one single model that guarantees good legislation, then basing it on reciprocity would be it. If there is one single devious act which unifies everybody against, it is corruption. Don't you agree?

Machiavelli: Verità, sono d'accordo! When I deal with corrupt people, I am a beast. When I deal with honest people, I am a man.

Montesquieu: You yourself said that "good customs stand in need of good laws for their support, so laws, that they should be respected, stand in need of good customs."[61] So I only want us to withdraw from this deadlock in which we got ourselves into by cliché thinking that we should be one against another. I want everybody to learn the language of moderation and modern justice. It expands the limits of our thoughts and gets us out of this cul-de-sac. [*Exclaims*:] Niccolò, give me a hand!

IV.

Machiavelli: [*Makes the last attempt to turn table*] What a turn! You indeed are a man of science and a man of letters! But I fear that we both are now in a blind alley! You are a hypocrite, Baron, who on preaches democracy at home but endorses subjugation abroad! This is morally incomprehensible. Aren't these double standards?

Montesquieu: [*Puzzled*] *Che svolta*? *Veramente*? Nope! Imagine, you take a test in mathematics. The test has ten questions. You answered well to seven questions, but your colleague did better because he so answered to nine questions. By whose standard you should now be graded—his or the test's?

Machiavelli: Of course, by the test.

Montesquieu: So the standard is not 90 but 100 percent, right?

Machiavelli: Si.

Montesquieu: And so is with judging democracy, my friend. The difference with mathematics is that democracy is always on the horizon where higher standards are in sight. So there are no double but higher and lower standards. And now I may answer your first question about democracy and "The Persian Letters." In "The Persian Letters" I show two faces of one individual: of a young and old traveler—a visitor to Europe who quips about its customs and morals. In fact, I was the two-in-one who amused and not who thought. Where in my harem story did you find an independent judge? I only spoke about the ruler—a gatekeeper of despotism. My story about his Rule of Law is a *farce*. In fact, I wrote about his rule by law. Let me be clear: When the mores and character of a nation are fixed at a certain point, what is necessary to change them is not laws but a quiet revolution![62] If for you "fortune" is a woman, then for me "democracy" is female. *Vive la democratie*! *Vive la revolution*!

Machiavelli: Maybe my moral standards are poor. But I must remind you what Caesar said about the French "at the beginning the French were more than men, but in the end less than women."[63] Is this what you expect of democracy?

Montesquieu: Oh, you want to say that "people are less concerned with offending a man who makes himself loved than one who makes himself feared"[64]? So democracy with its soft power is not a match to your despotic rule? True, democracy is very vulnerable to abuse and some people are offending democratic rules. How not to ill-use democracy is my mission. That's why people must be vigilant and watch the rulers. And certainly you as the advocate of despotic rule will agree with our distinguished predecessor I mentioned before who said that your type of government is "an institution which prevents injustice other than such as it commits itself."

Machiavelli: Maybe then I am personally morally bankrupt, but not my "Prince," *Sire*! He is alive and kicking!

Montesquieu: Since you invoked the Sicilian Ibn Zafar in your favor, I should like to tell you that he endured a hard life accompanied by constant poverty. He was in such dire need that he was forced to agree that his daughter marries a man of a lower social station than his daughter's. Her husband sold his daughter as a slave. Despite his malignant fortune, Ibn Zafar has left behind one message of a penetrating wisdom. His message may be a tribute to understand your own malignity of fortune. He said: "A man's misfortunes correspond to his merits; and, by his patience under affliction, his share of merit may be known. He who has but little firmness in facing what he apprehends, will have but little chance of gaining what he hopes for."[65]

Machiavelli: Thank you for this recognition.

Montesquieu: I will also use here your own argument, that "[n]othing is harder to do, more dubious to succeed at, or more dangerous to manage, than making oneself a ruler and introducing a new order."[66] Your "Prince" played his card. Look around yourself and down at the misery of Mother Earth. [*the video footage shown again*]. We must universally recognize, resurrect and refit our minds with the Rule-of-Law idea that makes us grow in the interest of welfare of Mother Earth. This is my *ordini nuovi* and *principi nouvi*: Be loyal to Mother Earth! Support her!

Machiavelli: Ordini nuovi? Oh!, yes, I said so. While I see now Mother Earth burning and in despair, regrettably this has nothing to do with my order of things, but your insistence, Baron de Montesquieu, on the empire of climate. So, let's make a deal, Baron: your barrel of *Bordeaux* 2050 wine against my barrel of *Chianti* 2050 who is right! Our discussion has nothing to do with Mother Earth.

Montesquieu: Hmm, that's news to me! You earlier asked me about the quality of soil and liberties of people. Well, as a winemaker I know that *terroir,* that is climate, venue and wine culture make wine's essence. That may be quite a sour surprise to you, if I toast my "victory" drinking your *Chianti*! So, so much for the "taste" of liberties in 2050!

Machiavelli: Let's see. To make things even more sour, I must tell you that on my death bed I had a dream. A band of ragged, poorly dressed and miserable men were on their way to *Paradiso*. Next, I saw a crowd of solemnly attired, noble men of grave appearance. I recognized among them Plato, Plutarch, and Tacitus. They told me "'We are the damned of Hell.' I was happy to hear this, because in Hell I could discuss with them politics, whereas in Heaven I would languish in boredom among the saintly and blessed."[67] I still believe "that the true way of getting to Paradise is to learn the way to Hell in order to avoid it."[68] In short, I like *Paradiso* for the climate, but *Inferno* for the company! Right or wrong, we are now both in Hell, and I am happy to be with you, Baron de Montesquieu!

Montesquieu: [*Exclaiming*] *Caro Niccolò*! Let me tell you this: indeed, "I have seen descriptions of paradise that would make any man of sense avoid going there"[69]! so, perhaps, that's why we are both in Hell, although I realize God's greatness and my own littleness.

Machiavelli: Yes, I heard you saying this on your death bed.

Montesquieu: But didn't you say "I desire to go to Hell and not to Heaven. In the former I shall enjoy the company of popes, kings and princes, while in the latter are only beggars, monks and apostles"[70]? Don't you see in this *Inferno* all its nobles in fumes and toxic air? Do you see your friends intoxicated by power? Do you see others infused with your hidden poison? Aren't they your accolades and folks? What a crowd, and how hard is to breath! They all gave their hearts to the state of darkness. And yet in your last breath on the death bed I heard you saying "*Amo la patria mia più dell'anima*!"[71] You love Italy more than your soul! *Eh bien . . .* but since I consider myself a Frenchman only by chance, please tell me which of our two spirits can make Mother Earth fortunate again? Italian or French?

Machiavelli: [*Exclaiming; adrift, realizing the binary nonsense*] *Mi hai beccato, mascherina!!, mon ami Charles-Louis*! I trust only God may answer this.

Montesquieu: [*Exclaiming, assertively*] *Oh vraiment?! Oh veramente?!* [*puzzled, but agitated*] Not you, such a distinguished Italian mind?, not Mother Earth? God may answer this? Do you see around any stranded souls? Do you see these newcomers? Strangers like us? Aren't they as we are?

Machiavelli: [*Bewildered; looks up at the ceiling, with hands in prayer*] Eternal God, would you give our followers your own *laissez-passer* to avert the misfortune of Mother Earth?

DISCLAIMER

The story, all names, characters, and incidents portrayed in this dialogue are fictitious. No identification with actual persons (living or deceased) is intended or should be inferred.

ACKNOWLEDGMENTS

The script was originally inspired by the work of Maurice Joly *The Dialogue in Hell between Machiavelli and Montesquieu: Humanitarian Despotism and the Conditions of Modern Tyranny*, trans., ed. and with commentary by John S. Waggoner (Lanham-Boulder-New York-Toronto-Oxford: Lexington Books, 2003). It is based on (un)referenced texts from that work, as well as on a few ideas inspired by Peter Kreeft, *Socrates Meets Machiavelli*. Ignatius Press. Kindle Edition. In order to make the views of Montesquieu and Machiavelli up to present time, the authors of this script drew the most contemporarily sounding passages from the various translations of their works. In case of quoting Montesquieu's views, this practice was relatively rare in comparison with Machiavelli's works. In his case, the script draws on six English-language translations of "The Prince" (Machiavelli (a)-(f)) and three translations of "Discourses," among the translations of his other works. In this way the script accounts for the present-time philosophical, legal and social justice arguments between these two *dramatis personae*. The script also draws on the interpretative works of other authors named in the Bibliography. Both types of works from Humanities have been perused here in line with the credo, that "A work of art, be it a novel, a poem or a Scripture, must be read according to the laws of its genre" (Karen Armstrong, *The Lost Art of Scripture. Rescuing the Sacred Texts*. New York: Alfred A. Knopf, 2019, 9–10). To the named authors of those works belongs the credit for their academic originality and import. The authors thank Anna Alvazzi del Frate, Daniel Leisser, Kathryn Platzer, and Elżbieta Cieśla-Redo for their critique.

NOTES

1. Charles Montesquieu, *My Thoughts* [*Mes Pensées*], trans., ed., and with an introduction by Henry C. Clark (Indianapolis: Liberty Fund 2012), 1266 at 343.
2. Charles L. Montesquieu de Secondat. *The Spirit of Laws*, trans. T. Nugent (Kitchener, ON: Batoche Books, 2001), bk. VI.
3. https://bit.ly/3bQoupC (Accessed September 15, 2021).
4. Montesquieu, *My Thoughts*, 609 at 196.

5. Machiavelli. *Discourses on the First Decade of Titus Livius. The Collected Works of Niccolò Machiavelli: The Complete Works*. PergamonMedia, 2015, ch. XII, 5.

6. Machiavelli (a), *The Prince*, trans. George Bull (Penguin Books: Harmondsworth, Middlesex, England, 1983), bk. XVII, 96. [Other English language translations of the same title are alphabetically referenced below and in the Bibliography].

7. Translation after Mark Huliung, *Montesquieu and the Old Regime* (Berkeley-Los Angeles-London: University of California Press, 1976), 118. Charles L. Montesquieu. *Persian Letters: With Related Texts*, ed. Raymond N. Mackenzie (Indianapolis/Cambridge: Hackett Publishing Company, Inc., 2014. Kindle), Letter 12.

8. Charles Montesquieu. *Persian Letters* (Hackett Classics). Hackett Publishing Company, Inc. Kindle Edition, Letter 12.

9. Charles Montesquieu, *The Persian Letters*. Издательство Aegitas. Kindle Edition, Letter 12.

10. Niccolò Machiavelli, Discourses on Livy, in *Delphi Collected Works of Niccolò Machiavelli (Illustrated)* (Hastings, Essex, United Kingdom: Delphi Publishing Ltd, 2017), bk. I, ch. XVI, 3405.

11. Maurice Joly, *The Dialogue in Hell between Machiavelli and Montesquieu: Humanitarian Despotism and the Conditions of Modern Tyranny*, trans., ed. and with commentary by John S. Waggoner (Lanham-Boulder-New York-Toronto-Oxford: Lexington Books, 2003), 130.

12. Niccolò Machiavelli (b), *The Prince*, transl. and ed. Peter Bondanella, with introduction of Mauricio Virolli (Oxford: Oxford University Press, 2008), bk. XVIII, 114.

13. Montesquieu, *My Thoughts*, 1999 at 615.

14. William Shakespeare, *The Tragedy of Hamlet, Prince of Denmark*, Act III, Scene I,1776, https://bit.ly/3AUxdDj.

15. Machiavelli, *Discourses on the First,* bk. I, ch. XXXIX.

16. Montesquieu, *The Spirit*, bk. XIII, 3, 233.

17. Machiavelli, *Discourses on the First,* bk. I, ch. III, in *The Collected Works.*

18. Machiavelli (b), *The Prince,* bk. XXV, 138.

19. Machiavelli, *Discourses on the First,* bk. III, ch. II, in *The Collected Works.*

20. Discourses on the First Ten Books of Titus Livius, bk III, transl. Christian E. Detmold, in *The Prince Niccolò Machiavelli* (New York: Race Point Publishing, 2017), 163.

21. Montesquieu, *My Thoughts*, 1269, 347–348.

22. Montesquieu, *My Thoughts*, 1269 at 347–348.

23. Joly, *The Dialogue*, 130.

24. Montesquieu, *My Thoughts*, 581 at 191.

25. Niccolò Machiavelli (b) *The Prince*, bk. XVII, 111.

26. Machiavelli, *Discourses*, bk. XVI, ch. 5, in *The Collected Works.*

27. Machiavelli, *Discourses*, bk. II, ch. XXIII, in *The Collected Works.*

28. Niccolò Machiavelli, The Mandrake, in *The Essential Writings of Machiavelli,* ed. and trans. Peter Constantine. Introduction by Albert Russell Ascoli (New York: The Modern Library, 2007), scene 3 at 446.

29. Machiavelli (b), *The Prince*, bk. III, 65.
30. Machiavelli (b), *The Prince,* bk. XVII, 111.
31. Machiavelli (b), *The Prince,* bk. XIX, 120.
32. Montesquieu, *The Spirit*, bk XI.7, 184.
33. Machiavelli (e), *The Prince,* in *Delphi Collected Works,* bk. XVIII, 386.
34. Machiavelli (d), The Prince, transl. W. K. Marriot, in *The Collected Works*, ch. VI.
35. Frank I. Michelman, Machiavelli in Robes? The Court in the Election, in Arthur J. Jacobson and Michel Rosenfeld, The Longest Night, eds. *Polemics and Perspectives on Election 2000* (Berkeley Los Angeles London: The University of California Press, 2002), 256.
36. St. Augustine, *Concerning the City of God against the Pagans*, transl. H. Bettenson. Penguin, 1972, bk. IV, 4.
37. St. Augustine, *Concerning*, bk. IV, 4.
38. Montesquieu, *The Spirit*, bk. VI, 12, at 102.
39. In translation by Ernest Gellner. *Plough, Sword, and Book.* Chicago: University of Chicago Press 1992, 239.
40. Joly, *The Dialogue*, 39.
41. Montesquieu, *My Thoughts*, 1735 at 516.
42. Machiavelli, *Discourses,* in *Delphi,* bk. I, ch. XXXVII, 3767.
43. Machiavelli (b), *The Prince,* bk. VI, 74.
44. Niccolò Machiavelli, *The Discourses*, trans. Leslie J. Walker (London: Routledge, 2006), bk III, ch. 21, 526.
45. Cf. Machiavelli, *The Prince*. *The Collected Works,* bk. XVIII.
46. Machiavelli (b), *The Prince,* bk. XVIII, 100.
47. Montesquieu in his *Traité des devoirs* (1725, 439), quoted after Norbert Campagna, *Raison d'État*, in Montesquieu Dictionary, https://bit.ly/3gqOYBQ.
48. Machiavelli (d), *The Prince*, bk. XVIII, in the *Completed Works.*
49. Montesquieu, *The Spirit*, bk. XV.8 at 266.
50. Montesquieu, *The Spirit of the Laws*, bk. XIV.13 in translation of Melvyn Richter, *The Political Theory of Montesquieu* (Cambridge: Cambridge University Press, 1977), 263.
51. Machiavelli, *Discourses,* bk. I, ch. LIII, after Mauricio Viroli, *The Quotable Machiavelli.* (Princeton and Oxford: Princeton University Press, 2016), 190.
52. Machiavelli, Discourses, bk. I, ch. LIII, in *The Quotable*, 190.
53. Machiavelli (b), *The Prince*, bk. XVII, 96.
54. Niccolò Machiavelli (c), *The Prince*, transl. Tim Parks (UK: Penguin Random House, 2014), bk. 13, 55.
55. *Machiavelli* (a), *The Prince,* trans. George Bull, bk. XVIII, 100.
56. Montesquieu, *My Thoughts*, 807 at 236.
57. Montesquieu, *My Thoughts*, 1270 at 348.
58. Montesquieu, *My Thoughts*, 1270 at 348.
59. Montesquieu, *My Thoughts*, 1270 at 348.
60. Machiavelli, *The Prince,* bk. X, in *The Collected Works.*
61. Machiavelli, *Discourses,* ch. XVIII, in *The Collected Works.*

62. Cf. Montesquieu, *My Thoughts*, 499 at 174.

63. Niccolò Machiavelli, An Account of the Affairs of France, in *Delphi Collected Works*, 2538.

64. Machiavelli (e), *The Prince*, bk. XVII, in *Delphi Collected Works*, 194.

65. *Ibn Khallikan's Biographical Dictionary*, transl. Bn Mac Guckin de Slane, London: Oriental Translation Fund of Great Britain and Ireland and Bernard Quauitch, MDCCCLXVM, vol. III, 105.

66. Machiavelli (f), The Prince, in *The Essential Writings*, bk. VI, 564.

67. Marizio Viroli, *Niccolo's Smile. A Biography of Machiavelli*, transl. Antony Shugaar (New York: Hill and Wang, 2000), 3.

68. Letter of Machiavelli to Francesco Guicciardini, *The Letters of Machiavelli: A Selection Reprint Edition*, ed. and transl. Allan Gilbert (Chicago: The University of Chicago Press 1988), 198.

69. Montesquieu, *Persian Letters*, Letter 125.

70. Paul Thigpen, *From Last Words: Final Thoughts of Catholic Saints & Sinners*. Franciscan Media, 2006, 172.

71. Carta a Vettori del 16 de abril de 1527, in Mario Bonfantini, *N. Machiavelli, Opere*, (Milán-Nápoles: Ricardo Ricciardi Editore, 1963), 1136.

BIBLIOGRAPHY

Bonfantini, Mario. *N. Machiavelli, Opere*, Ricardo Ricciardi Editore: Milán-Nápoles, 1963.

Gellner, Ernest. *Plough, Sword, and Book*. Chicago: University of Chicago Press, 1992.

Joly, Maurice. *The Dialogue in Hell between Machiavelli and Montesquieu: Humanitarian Despotism and the Conditions of Modern Tyranny*, trans., ed. and with commentary by John S. Waggoner. Lanham-Boulder-New York-Toronto-Oxford: Lexington Books, 2003.

Ibn Khallikan's Biographical Dictionary transl. B^{n} Mac Guckin de Slane. London: Oriental Translation Fund of Great Britain and Ireland and Bernard Quauitch, MDCCCLXVM. vol. III.

Machiavelli, Niccolò. *Discourses on the First Ten Books of Titus Livius*, bk III, transl. Christian E. Detmold, in *The Prince* Niccolò Machiavelli, 163–234. New York: Race Point Publishing, 2017.

Machiavelli, Niccolò. *Delphi Collected Works of Niccolò Machiavelli* (Illustrated). Hastings, Essex, United Kingdom: Delphi Publishing Ltd, 2017.

Machiavelli, Niccolò. *The Collected Works of Niccolò Machiavelli: The Complete Works*. PergamonMedia, 2015.

Machiavelli, Niccolò. *The Essential Writings of Machiavelli* ed. and transl. Peter Constantine. Introduction by Albert Russell Ascoli Random House Publishing Group. Kindle Edition.

Machiavelli, Niccolò. *The Florentine Histories* transl. Laura F. Banfield, Harvey C. Mansfield. Princeton, NJ: Princeton University Press, 1988.

Machiavelli, Niccolò. *Discourses on Livy,* trans., Harvey C. Mansfield and Nathan Tarcov. Chicago: University of Chicago Press, 1996.

Machiavelli, Niccolò. *The Discourses,* trans. Leslie J. Walker. London: Routledge, 2006.

Machiavelli, Niccolò (a). *The Prince*, transl. George Bull. Harmondsworth: Middlesex, England, 1983.

Machiavelli, Niccolò (b). *The Prince*, transl. and ed. Peter Bondanella, with introduction of Mauricio Virolli. Oxford: Oxford University Press, 2008.

Machiavelli, Niccolò (c). *The Prince*, transl. Tim Parks. UK: Penguin Random House, 2014.

Machiavelli, Niccolò (d). *The Prince*, transl. W. K. Marriot, in *The Collected Works, The Collected Works of Niccolò Machiavelli: The Complete Works.* PergamonMedia, 2015.

Machiavelli, Niccolò (e). *The Prince,* in *Delphi Collected Works of Niccolò Machiavelli* (Illustrated). Hastings, Essex, United Kingdom: Delphi Publishing Ltd, 2017.

Machiavelli, Niccolò (f). *The Prince,* in *The Essential Writings of Machiavelli* ed. and transl. Peter Constantine. Introduction by Albert Russell Ascoli Random House Publishing Group. Kindle Edition.

Montesquieu, Charles L. de Secondat. *My Thoughts,* trans., ed. and with an introduction by Henry C. Clark. Indianapolis, IN: Liberty Fund, 1796/2012.

Montesquieu, Charles L. de Secondat. *The Persian Letters*, trans. Margaret Mauldon. Oxford: Oxford University Press, 2008.

Montesquieu, Charles-Louis de Secondat. *Persian Letters*, trans. C. J. Betts. Harmondsworth-Baltimore: Penguin Books, 1973.

Montesquieu, Charles. *The Persian Letters.* Издательство Aegitas. Kindle Edition.

Montesquieu, Charles L. de Secondat. *Persian Letters: With Related Texts*, ed. Raymond N. Mackenzie. Indianapolis/Cambridge: Hackett Publishing Company, Inc., 2014. Kindle.

Montesquieu, Charles L. de Secondat, *The Spirit of Laws*, trans. T. Nugent, Kitchener, ON: Batoche Books, 2001.

Shakespeare, William. *The Tragedy of Hamlet, Prince of Denmark.* https://bit.ly/3AUxdDj.

Thigpen, Paul. *From Last Words: Final Thoughts of Catholic Saints & Sinners.* Franciscan Media, 2006.

Viroli, Maurizio. *Niccolo's Smile: A Biography of Machiavelli.* New York: Farrar, Strauss & Giroux, 2000.

Viroli, Maurizio. *The Quotable Machiavelli.* Princeton and Oxford: Princeton University Press, 2016.

Chapter 12

On the Dialogues in Hell between Machiavelli and Montesquieu from the Perspective of Climate Change, Migration, and the Rule of Law

Sławomir Redo

INTRODUCTION

This chapter comments on the two dialogues between Machiavelli and Montesquieu: the dialogue preceding it and the imaginary dialogue scripted by a Parisian barrister Maurice Joly (1833–1878), who in 1864 anonymously published in Brussels (Belgium) a moral treatise entitled *The Dialogue in Hell between Machiavelli and Montesquieu*. These two dialogues are more than 150 years apart. However, the works of Machiavelli and Montesquieu from which we drew our intellectual inspiration to address climate change, migration, and the rule of law have been evergreen. Their respective republican and democratic views empower policy holders and advocates of one or another position to implement in practice what their masters wrote centuries ago.

What particularly inspired us as scripters is the seeming incompatibility of views of those two masters. Amid the imminent climate change catastrophe, in their works, then in Joly's and our dialogue, we sought to expose what is common in all of them. This we did for the readers—followers of one or another school of thought and action—to take our ideas into their own hands and work in concert with others to mitigate the imminent conundrum undermining the principles of justice and larger freedom, declared in the United Nations Charter. Clearly, however, had this not been the original Joly's idea to script his own dialogue, our dialogue would have not surfaced. Hence below my short account of his intellectual journey which resulted in the 1864 book, followed by a more incisive analysis of Montesquieu's and Machiavelli's intellectual positions and worldviews.

MAURICE JOLY AND HIS WORK

In an autobiographical account Joly recalled that "while walking on the terrace along the river near Pont Royal in bad weather," he had the idea of a fictional conversation between Montesquieu and Machiavelli in Hell. "It is Machiavelli who represents the policy of force as opposed to Montesquieu who represents the policy of justice; while Machiavelli will represent Napoleon III, who would describe his own abominable policies."[1]

The "Dialogue" was written as a defense of republicanism and a critique of the authoritarianism of Napoleon III. The book was seized by the French police at a border crossing, and Joly was easily identified. His trial took place in 1865 and he received a prison sentence of fifteen months for inciting hatred and contempt against the government.[2]

In 1868, the second edition of *The Dialogue* was issued in France under Joly's name. At that time, Joly joined the radical *French resistance* against the emperor. In 1870, at the time of Franco-Prussian war, the emperor surrendered. He was eventually deposed and exiled to England.

Soon after the collapse of the empire, Joly sought to obtain a civil service position from a successful friend who in 1871 became the president of the National Assembly. Joly failed. Disgruntled, he sued him, and started to publish articles on political subjects, attacking him and several other political figures, who were his old friends. "He was a lonely man, devoted to moral principles and apparently never forgave anyone who did not live up to his standards. Perhaps his keen insight into politics and society was sharpened by a passionate desire to remain pure and morally inviolate. If so, he paid with his life for his rigor. On July 16, 1878, he shot himself."[3]

MACHIAVELLI IN THE LIGHT OF CONTEMPORARY CRITIQUE

Progressive educators, thinkers, and philosophers, some of whom may be regarded as the progenitors of the United Nations views on justice, did not hesitate to criticize Machiavelli's original views. Antonio Gramsci in his "Prison Notebooks" contemplates the invertibility of his reasoning:

> It is commonly asserted that Machiavelli's standards of political behavior are practiced, but not admitted. Great politicians—it is said—start off by

denouncing Machiavelli, by declaring themselves to be anti-Machiavellian, precisely in order to be able to put his standards "piously" into practice. Was not Machiavelli himself a poor Machiavellian, one of those who "are in the know" and foolishly give the game away, whereas vulgar Machiavellianism teaches one to do just the opposite?[4]

Isaiah Berlin spares no word to brand Machiavelli's reasoning:

> The commonest view of him, at least as a political thinker, is still that . . . he is a man inspired by the Devil to lead good men to their doom, the great subverter, the teacher of evil, *le docteur de la scélératesse*, the inspirer of St. Bartholomew's Eve, the original of Iago. Ibis is the "murderous Machiavel" of the famous four hundred-odd references in Elizabethan literature . . . His name adds a new ingredient to the more ancient figure of Old Nick. For the Jesuits he is "the devil's partner in crime," "a dishonorable writer and an unbeliever," and *The Prince* is, in Bertrand Russell's words, "a handbook for gangsters" . . . a "vademecum for statesmen," a view tacitly shared, perhaps, by other heads of State . . . This is the view common to Protestants and Catholics . . . Cardinal Pole, Bodin and Frederick the Great, followed by the authors of all the many anti-Machiavels, among the latest of whom are Jacques Maritain and Leo Strauss.[5]

Leo Strauss quotes Eric Voeglin, an early post–World War II political historian, who congratulates Machiavelli on his groundbreaking contribution to post-constitutionalism which was the death knell of democracy: "It was Machiavelli . . . who achieved the theoretical creation of a concept of rulership in the post-constitutional situation."[6]

A political philosopher Waldemar Hanasz gives the review of opposite opinions: Machiavelli was called an "experimental scientist" [by Charles S. Singleton—added], "a thoroughgoing empiricist" [Leslie J. Walker, Leonid M. Batkin, Markus Fischer, Joseph Femia—added], a "Galileo of politics" [Giuseppe Prezzolini—added], and even "the inventor of the inductive method"[7] [Leslie J. Walker—added].[8]

In the *Stanford Encyclopedia of Philosophy*, his writings were found "maddeningly and notoriously unsystematic, inconsistent and sometimes self-contradictory."[9] Regarding contradictoriness, Maurice Merleau-Ponty, a French phenomenological philosopher, argues that Machiavelli is misunderstood because:

> He combines the most acute feeling for the contingency or irrationality in the world with a taste for the consciousness or freedom in man. . . . There is a way of repudiating Machiavelli which is Machiavellian; it is the pious ruse of those

> who turn their eyes and ours toward the heaven of principles in order to turn them away from what they are doing. And there is a way of praising Machiavelli which is just the opposite of Machiavellianism, since it honors in his works a contribution to political clarity.[10]

Machiavelli's political clarity is demonstrated by Terence Ball, who explains: "To seize the day, to act boldly and even ruthlessly, is the only way in which fickle fortune (*fortuna*) can be tamed, and genuine glory (*gloria*) and lasting fame (*fama*) secured." Machiavelli's metaphor is instructive. "Fortune," says Machiavelli, in a now-notorious aside, "is a woman, and it is necessary, if you wish to master her, to conquer her by force; [for] . . . she lets herself be overcome by the bold rather than by those who proceed coldly." *Virtù* is to politics what virility is to sex: It is the congeries of qualities that make for success in the activities in which the manly man, the virile *vir*, and the virtuoso prince are respectively engaged.[11]

In a similarly incisive opinion, Machiavelli's reasoning was found by Leo Strauss to be bold ("powerful rhetoric"), but unsystematic, a kind of "decayed" Aristotelian logic.[12] Strauss points out: "In order to realize the magnitude of Machiavelli's success it is necessary [to] . . . grasp his principle . . . : one must lower the standards in order to make probable, if not certain, the actualization of the right or desirable social order or in order to conquer chance; one must effect a shift of emphasis from moral character to institutions."[13]

In line with the above principle of "leveling down,"[14] Yves Winter concludes, regarding Machiavelli's views on crime and punishment: "He narrows what counts as irrationality and excess."[15]

The following assessment sums up all the above diversified reception of Machiavelli's "Prince":

> [It] was mixed from the start: some readers found in it a frank, sometimes ironic, description for the benefit of the people of the evil means used by bad rulers; others read in it evil recommendations to tyrants to help them maintain their power. The history of the reception of the Prince . . . discloses a book with many facets: the impious and amoral Machiavelli of the Jesuits; the republican champion of the people, who unveiled the evil practices of tyrants, of the Enlightenment and Romantic readers; the citizen and patriot who fought for the liberation of Italy of the "*Risorgimento*"; the nationalist author who realized the limits of popular sovereignty and the necessity of force during the Fascist era.[16]

The present public policy text on Joly's book places itself at the juncture of moral and political philosophy. Joly's book is the most accurate and authoritative iteration of Machiavelli's thoughts, as if it were original.

Montesquieu's final exclamation: "Eternal God, what have you permitted!" is the final evidence of Machiavelli's forceful reasoning in Joly's interpretation.

Through it, Joly points to the victory of regressive historicist Machiavellian thought over progressive modernist Montesquieuan moral thought. For Joly, and to a lesser extent for the original Montesquieu, moral progress is stoppable and its effects are reversible. Be that as it may, the original Montesquieu believed in the force of education and public engagement in the name of moral progress. But: "he refused . . . to believe that moral progress, happiness, security, freedom and all the valuable things in life necessarily increased. And felt no great confidence in the future. His was an interesting and exactly balanced mixture of a cyclical and linear view."[17]

Since Montesquieu's, and even more, Machiavelli's time, the current domestic and international jurisprudence document that common moral values have been considerably "leveled up." However, nobody knows how moral progress advances. Notwithstanding this dearth of knowledge with respect to the variables that may globally represent progress, for example, maternal and child mortality, life expectancy, and literacy rates, one may approximate and document its upward course. Moreover, such forms of progress are occasionally well administered and exercised. If only the sky had a limit and the horizon would not recede, such facts and figures would be more visible, appreciated, and regarded as proven.

The principle of "leveling down" commanded more by boldness than reasonableness unmistakably suggests why Montesquieu's argumentation for "leveling up" failed. He has not been enough of a *lex animator*. He acts by reversing by force, not by reason. However, wherever Machiavelli claims that the idea of the separation of powers may be more illusory than real, this requires a critical (more reasonable?) reflection after more than 500 years since the publishing of *The Prince* (1513), and more than 150 years after the publishing of *The Dialogue* (1864).

To this day it remains puzzling why *The Dialogue*, so intellectually powerful, essentially innocuous regarding Semitism, and so vital to democracy has stayed in the closet for so long. And when taken out of the closet, it has been abused for its content and for its intent.[18] In the interests of settling *The Dialogue* where it really belongs, that is as an illustration how major aspects of social justice may be challenged, this chapter focuses on authoritarian rule that inherently compromises the rule of law. Authoritarian rule with its abusive "power positivism"[19] and judges obligation to be only *lex loquent* debilitates the rule of law process and the "larger freedom" sought by the United Nations, since its proclamation in the Charter. Some ideologies, laws, and policies addressing the rule of law may thwart or facilitate its progressive agenda. The UN as a "benevolent conqueror"[20] or a supporter of positive social progress in any case envisions and animates socioeconomic development for 2030 and beyond. This involves the imminent reprioritization of the rule of law challenges from the domestic arena to a global arena, prompted by climate change and migration.

With the above in mind, and to return to the original essence of *The Dialogue* which should be a basis for the "leveling up" of democracy through legal positivism and strengthening of the separation of powers, I will first address the logic of both thinkers, and next focus on the relevance to the 2030 United Nations Sustainable Development Agenda.[21] This UN new legal order is within the reach of civic education and civil society—and it means the reversal of popular sovereignty.

In the absence of substantive discussion of this form of civic-mindedness in Joly's text and in contrast with his sparse drawing on the original statements of both interlocutors, this script provides genuine quotations from the original works of Machiavelli and Montesquieu, accompanied by Joly's own arguments. Of course, throughout the entire text, Machiavelli- and Montesquieu-type arguments are interlaced with our own. Our text ventures into the issue of who can make our societies into a world with strong institutions inspired by peace and justice, which themselves are being put at jeopardy by climate change.

The entire script seeks to mirror the ways in which these two great minds reasoned, as originally charted by Joly. Joly is an intellectual giant, indeed "a genius"[22] who delivered a book that is so rich and provocative for the rule of law that it should be more generally addressed by other commentators.

ON THE KINDS OF LOGIC

Both reason somewhat differently. Machiavelli bottom-up, Montesquieu top-down.

Machiavelli

In *The Prince*, Machiavelli draws extensively on inductive logic: "Most *B* are *A*; *C* is *B*; therefore, it is highly likely that *C* is *A*."[23] Stretching this canon, Machiavelli's "right opinion" allows him to then say: "If all men were good, this advice would be bad; but since men are wicked and will not keep faith with you, you need not keep faith with them."[24] He also does so in our dialogue trying to extend Montesquieu's observations on the "noxious air" prompting Romans to be bellicose to the Roman Church. He participates in the dialogue with one fixed idea. Hence, he "lacks most noble of scientific pretentions, the open mind" . . . as if "[s]omething was obscuring his view and predetermining his decisions."[25]

Encouraging others to follow his idea, his "right opinion," he continues with a *specific* premise that he wants to make *general*. For this he employs an exceptional example of evil conduct—in fact a criminal case.

His idea of *pathos* and *ethos* comes from the original teaching of Aristotle, but not from his logic. Aristotle's deductive logic starts with a universal premise. Next, it goes into a generic premise (probative example). It ends up with a specific conclusion (proof): "all *B* are *A*; *C* is *B*; therefore, *C* is *A*."[26] Aristotle argues that when it comes to rendering justice, rulers should apply a golden mean in moral virtues.

In difference with him, Machiavelli stepwise highlights a single case, as if it was general for moral virtues. He elevates that case by emphasizing its pathetic value—a model to follow; in fact, a mere probative instance, a sheer smokescreen. Next, under the guise of authoritative discovery, he deceptively and purely instrumentally invokes *ethos*, as if that example documented a laudable standard or norm. This implies that "bad" and "good" are one generalizable "quality" (i.e., they are not fixed parts of "bad" or "good" character). This salami-slicing tactic treats "good" as a detachable "quality." This detachment enables a "true common good"/a "good end."

The reasoning ends as a "conclusion" equivalent to a tenacious moral authority on the part of the reasoner. In so doing, Machiavelli eventually transforms that bad example into a good *exemplum*.[27] What is morally right to do to others, whatever they do to you, gives you the moral right to do the same moral wrongs to them as they do to you. Consequently, it is morally right to do what is morally wrong. The wrong in question is right, making evil good.[28] On an individual level, the most pronounced case of this transformative tactic is Machiavelli's ceremonial reinterpretation of the conduct of Agathocles of Syracuse (317–289 BC), a mass murderer and tyrant on behalf of whom Machiavelli eventually "speaks well of evil."[29]

For any unscrupulous decision-maker, let alone follower, this is the reasoner's "gateway to Hell" which eventually is entered by the follower because of the offer that cannot be refused. This way Machiavelli disconnects politics from ethics. As a "noble liar" he appeals to higher ends to relinquish a moral constraint. Gradually and subtly, the decision-maker introduces new conventional ethics and readiness "to reform Hell," that is, society/milieu on the ground with servile people excluded from sharing other benefits of his/her politics. Wherever the reasoner succeeds to introduce it institutionally, its proponents claim that "it is the law." Others were lured off guard. The "white-to-black" inversion is then announced as the eventually proper law the one and only *lex loquens*. This is like a prisoner accused of a crime who judges his/her judge and jury.[30]

Merleau-Ponty in his "Note on Machiavelli" concludes: "When the victim admits defeat, the cruel man perceives another life beating through those words;

he finds himself before another himself. We are far from the relationships of sheer force that hold between objects. To use Machiavelli's words, we have gone from "beasts" to "man"" [original text].[31] Moreover, he himself recommends to use native language in such a way that it "converts words that it has borrowed from others into its own use, and it is so powerful, that the borrowed words do not disorder it, but rather, it disorders theirs; because that which it bears from the others it pulls to itself in such a manner, that it seems to be its own."[32]

And to pursue this rhetoric further, Machiavelli recommends the use of native language in such a way that it "converts words that it has borrowed from others into its own use, and it is so powerful, that the borrowed words do not disorder it, but rather, it disorders theirs; because that which it bears from the others it pulls to itself in such a manner, that it seems to be its own."[33]

Aided by this language inversion, the "travel through Hell" for the rule by law continues. Because it risks reversal of "black into white" (hence the threat of punishment) to escape it Machiavelli provides canonical recommendation:

> We must . . . in order to be pardoned for our faults, commit new ones; redoubling the mischief, and multiplying fires and robberies; and in doing this, endeavor to have as many companions as we can; for when many are in fault, few are punished; small crimes are chastized, but great and serious ones rewarded. When many suffer, few seek vengeance; for general evils are endured more patiently than private ones. To increase the number of misdeeds will, therefore, make forgiveness more easily attainable, and will open the way to secure what we require for our own liberty. And it appears evident that the gain is certain; for our opponents are disunited and rich; their disunion will give us the victory, and their riches, when they have become ours, will support us. Be not deceived about that antiquity of blood by which they exalt themselves above us; for all men having had one common origin, are all equally ancient, and nature has made us all after one fashion. Strip us naked, and we shall all be found alike. Dress us in their clothing, and they in ours, we shall appear noble, they ignoble—for poverty and riches make all the difference. It grieves me much to think that some of you are sorry inwardly for what is done, and resolve to abstain from anything more of the kind. Certainly, if it be so, you are not the men I took you for; because neither shame nor conscience ought to have any influence with you. Conquerors, by what means soever, are never considered aught but glorious. We have no business to think about conscience; for when, like us, men have to fear hunger, and imprisonment, or death, the fear of hell neither can nor ought to have any influence upon them.[34]

Machiavelli legitimizes evil, in life course criminology known as a "stepping stone theory." Whether meant structurally or individually, "the way to

Hell" starts as an innocuous incremental process with no criminal stigma. The evilness of an entry act is being reduced to a palatable "small lie" when compared to great and serious rewardable acts. The subsequent successful small lies bolster the implementer's conscience. Because the increasingly greater acts pursued in the name of a glorious finale eventually exonerate and delegitimize the whole criminal conduct, they alleviate the fear of sanction ("Hell," hunger, prison). They eventually convert the rule of law to rule by law: thesis to anti-thesis. They encourage and legitimize impunity that may also be substantiated on religious grounds. They institutionalize new crime and sin, if you will.[35] And, indeed, this process of leveling down finds empirical support in contemporary experimental studies: Tested people were less likely to criticize the actions of others when their behavior eroded gradually, over time, rather than in one abrupt shift.[36]

This multilayer "words-to-deeds" process is slow. Its symbolic if not also conundrumical language expression is best captured by the oxymoron "ideological blackmail by the Rule of Law" voiced in the European Union by the RoL's opponents.[37] More innocuous expressions or words pass unheeded. As this inversion process continues, they are repeated—chiastic, often in reverse order (e.g., "*Pleasure's a sin, and sometimes sin's a pleasure*"—Lord Byron, in *Don Juan*). Occasionally, this involves anadiplosis—repeating the same word in the next sentence. This order gradually subverts the importance of liberal "middle way" values by eliminating or, at least, diminishing any gray area between "white" and "black."[38]

Chiastic inversion is more clearly identifiable in fictional writings (e.g., in Byron's *Don Juan* or Machiavelli's *Discourses*) than in present politics where anadiplosis (repetition) is more readily pursued. However, in any case, words build a chain of unfolding inferences, eventually with a dead-end relationship.

It is exactly this premonitive context which helps us to see Hegel's moral repugnance for the "Inverted World" (*Verkeherte Welt*). There "sweet becomes sour, white becomes black and North becomes South. The inversions cover moral laws as well as natural ones: Honor becomes contempt and punishment becomes pardon."[39]

Machiavelli amorally promotes criminal conduct to ascertain absolute "heavenly" rule as his despotic vision to be virtuous in appearance only—not moral but "excellent" anyhow.

"Whatever politics demands [becomes] virtuous."[40] This is his "effectual truth."[41] Revealed and promulgated as the sum of the practical conditions, it should justify if not also guarantee his impunity and eternal glory through manipulatively legitimizing his understanding of "common good" as a republican virtue.[42] "[I]in the world there are only ordinary people; and the few [honest] have no place, while the many have a spot on which to lean."[43]

In this perspective, certainly Hitler comes to mind when he says to Goebbels: "Whether right or wrong, we must win. That is the only way. And it is morally right and necessary. And when we have won, who will ask us about the method? In any case, we have chalked up so much that we have to win, otherwise our entire people—and in first place we ourselves, with all that is dear to us—will be wiped out."[44]

This sounds perverse and insidious. And as if Nazi rhetoric did not make it perverse enough, it is underpinned by the Machiavellian idea of revitalizing past glories and projecting them into the future while using Christianity for political purposes, with which it has no connection. Machiavelli thus pulled Christian from its original "right versus wrong" canon and made it into a "civic religion." He misappropriated its objectives. Using the cloak of religion, he inverted Christian values in the name of his own posthumous secular glory.

Perhaps Machiavelli's views are most dramatically expressed in a passage from *La Mandragora* ("The Mandrake Root") where Callimaco says,

> [T]he worst you can get from it is that you'll die and go to Hell. But how many others have died! And in Hell how many worthy men there are! Are you ashamed to go there? This implies that good and evil are absolutes. Evil is objectively, God-proclaimed, evil. There is no utilitarian or consequentialist escape here—evil cannot be transformed into good. Evil lands you in hell. Nevertheless, it is politically necessary to do evil. So you must accept that. You perform the evil, and then you must courageously endure the punishment. After all, as Machiavelli tells us, there are some very worthy people in hell. . . There is a lot of bravado involved here. It is even rather impressive. Nevertheless, it is clear that it does not get you out of hell. Evil is evil. And you pay the penalty in hell.[45]

Disguising the sinister side of this false inversion of values ultimately relies on being able to manipulate the people into continuing to blindly accept it by concealing it under the cloak of the church's transcendental moral authority. Both the real and the imagined Machiavelli clearly assume that people are suggestible, credulous, manipulable, and lazy. No logic is needed to ponder whether the ruler's skilful governance is right or wrong for their country; mere folk wisdom will suffice. Thus adults, manipulated like children, behave as if they cannot differ right from wrong.

Montesquieu

Montesquieu's logic starts with a Cartesian-type disclaimer that he is free from prejudices and superstitions: "I speak of the different peoples of Europe as I speak of the different peoples of Madagascar."[46] Next, he acts as a citizen to determine the order of things. For this he follows Thomistic logic: formulating and postulating, for instance, that "the government be so constituted as one man need not be afraid of another."[47] Further, he poses questions—probative examples: "Does this art of politics make our histories more splendid than those of the Greeks and Romans?" Finally, he offers answers: "Those who raise men dishonoured by their morals to the highest positions offer quite a bad opinion of themselves."[48] Occasionally, however, he mixes deduction with induction.[49] Then, like Machiavelli, he generalizes a particular historical case to draw conclusions about the desired ideal legal order. Unlike Machiavelli who for this sake would conquer *fortuna* (or challenge, Fortune), he contends that Fortune, that is climate, wins.

For Montesquieu, people are dependent on their government being amenable to modernization and investment in the common good (and less on laws, customs, and mores in descending order). In several different contexts, he persuades people to abandon their cherished beliefs, not by directly challenging them, but by making the alternatives more attractive.[50] Unlike Machiavelli with his mentality of exclusion, Montesquieu is in favor of inclusion through words, deeds, and institutions.

This is why in *The Spirit of Laws*,[51] Montesquieu pays homage to the idea of trade, which fosters international ethics of reciprocity and propriety to moderate people's conduct. Consequently, wherever Machiavelli "levels down" through negative associations, Montesquieu "levels up" through positive associations. Wherever Machiavelli analyses, alludes to, and recasts historical cases to highlight the autocrat's future glory, Montesquieu analyses, provides evidence of, and advocates institutional conduct for the better future of humankind. Whereas Montesquieu applies the Golden Rule, Machiavelli straight from Hell "propels the Un-Golden rule to the heights of constitution making, and asks the legislator to strike with the law"[52] [original language].

Robert von Mohr wrote: "Machiavelli has sinned, but he has been even more sinned against."[53] In our dialogue we keep this claim in mind. However, we do follow neither the "sinning" or the "sinned against" approach exclusively. What drives our dialogue is "United Nations logic,"[54] which overrides the interlocutors' arguments to arrive at an implementation of the UN vision of the rule of law in the age of climate change.

ON THE TRUTH, MORALITIES, AND MIGRATION

Private and Public Morality

In *The Dialogue* by Joly, Machiavelli boldly explains to Montesquieu:

> My only crime was to speak the truth to peoples and to kings—not the moral truth, but *the political truth* [emphasis added], not the truth as it ought to be, but as it is and always will be . . . only of moral and political facts deduced from one eternal truth: the evil instinct in man is more powerful than the good. Man is more attracted by evil than by good and fear and force have more sway over him than reason. . . . Have you ever seen a single state conduct itself according to the principles that govern private morality?[55]

In contrast, Montesquieu in *The Dialogue* by Joly is moderate. He sees private and public morality as *de lege ferenda* parts of universal morality. He plainly equates morally universal conduct with what is "written in all religions and . . . imprinted in luminous characters in the conscience of man."[56]

Machiavelli in his statement in *The Dialogue* intentionally blurs the line between what is de facto true ("moral truth") and what is only "true" politically ("political truth")—one morality for ordinary human beings and another for princes. Hannah Arendt, German-US philosopher (1906–1975), and survivor of the Holocaust, called this bluff, explaining:

> It is clearly an attempt to change the record, and as such, it is a form of action. The same is true when the liar, lacking the power to make his falsehood stick, does not insist on the gospel truth of his statement but pretends that this is his "opinion," to which he claims his constitutional right. This is frequently done by subversive groups, and in a politically immature public the resulting confusion can be considerable. The blurring of the dividing line between factual truth and opinion belongs among the many forms that lying can assume, all of which are forms of action.[57]

At the time of writing, she believed that "organized lying" was a marginal phenomenon, given the absence of at the time of the post-truth politics of today. However, hypothesizing that this form of lying may be popular in politics she finds, that:

> Only where a community has embarked upon organized lying in principle, and not only with respect to particulars, can truthfulness as such, unsupported by the distorting forces of power and interest, become a political factor of the first order. Where everybody lies about everything of importance, the truthteller, whether he knows it or not, has begun to act; he, too, has engaged himself in political business, for, in the unlikely event that he survives, he has made a start toward changing the world . . . Since the liar is free to fashion his "facts" to fit the profit and pleasure, or even the mere expectations, of his audience, the chances are that he will be more persuasive than the truthteller. Indeed, he will usually have plausibility on his side; his exposition will sound more

> logical, as it were, since the element of unexpectedness—one of the outstanding characteristics of all events—has mercifully disappeared. It is not only rational truth that . . . stands common sense on its head; reality quite frequently offends the soundness of common sense reasoning no less than it offends profit and pleasure.[58]

As a moral philosopher, Arendt tried to understand the moral plasticity of respectable bourgeois Germans who succumbed to Nazi moral standards in the 1930s and reverted to universal standards after the war. She was preoccupied by the question of how some individuals managed to remain decent in spite of these black/white standards. She believed that to remain decent defies universal morality. Decency ultimately rests with a self that rejects intimacy with criminal conduct. She credited such people's decency to an inner standard of judgment, a self-evidently clean conscience.[59] Finally, as if entirely dismissing the relevance to her argument of the "conscience of mankind" as set out in the preamble to the Universal Declaration of Human Rights' (UDHR), Arendt asked: "'The Rights of Man': What Are They*?*" She criticized the Declaration for its "lack of reality," that is, its lack of capacity for action in the world of national and territorial sovereignty,[60] for, in fact, its lack of normative constitutionalism.[61]

She soon softened her criticism of UDHR. While in the English-language publication referenced above, she originally wondered if there were any human rights at all, Arendt did find one right in the German translation of the same text entitled, "There Is Only One Human Right."[62] This is "the right to have rights" of migrant peoples who are not citizens of any political community.[63]

Unlike in *The Dialogue* by Joly, the dialogue scripted in this book follows the Montesquieuan understanding of morality, as per its UN interpretation. In line with it, António Guterres as the United Nations High Commissioner for Refugees (2011), in the "Remarks at the opening of the judicial year of the European Court of Human Rights" (ECtHR) stated that by working over the past fifty years to define and defend the rights of refugees, internally displaced and stateless people, the Court has helped to make Arendt's notion a reality.[64]

The migration crisis which started in 2015 showed that this is a misconception. In 2020, the ECtHR in the case *N.D. and N.T v. Spain*[65] considered United Nations and European human rights instruments regarding refugee rights. The case was prompted by the Spanish authorities' rush to carry out collective expulsions (pushbacks or "hot returns") to Morocco of illegal entrants to the Spanish territory of Melilla in North Africa. The Court, adjudicating the claim of two young asylum applicants, concluded that the practice of the Spanish authorities indiscriminately applying expulsion to every individual, irrespective of whether they sought asylum or not, did not amount to a violation of the prohibition of collective expulsions under Article 4 Protocol 4 of the European Convention of Human Rights (ECHR). The Court emphasized that an applicant seeking ECHR protection must first document concrete factual or legal grounds which, under international or national law, would have precluded the applicants' removal had they been registered individually. Finally, the Court requested that states provide genuine and effective access to legal entry mechanisms for the purposes of asylum and employment.

In a concurring individual—very sublime—opinion Judge Aleš Pejchal offered a more systematic insight into the ECtHCR verdict. He noted that the quest for justice starts first with the applicants' effective and genuine protection of fundamental rights, freedoms, and duties in their home countries which ratified the African Charter of Human and People's Rights. Among the duties the Charter obliges

> [t]o preserve the harmonious development of the family and to work for the cohesion and respect of the family; to respect his parents at all times, to maintain them in case of need; 2. To serve his national community by placing his physical and intellectual abilities at its service . . . 6. To work to the best of his abilities and competence, and to pay taxes imposed by law in the interest of the society.[66]

The applicants could not prove before the Court how their duties had been unfairly contested by their home countries' governments. In his opinion, the judge indicated that the lack of concrete evidence of the applicants' unfair treatment cannot be compensated by their general claim that they sought fairness as justice in another legal community over the border fence they climbed. While the applicants' claim stands up to scrutiny as an idealistic academic argument advanced by John Rawls, in their court case this must be evidenced by concrete "serious problems," something of "exceptional nature" as a result of which they felt incapable of pursuing their particular rights and exercise particular duties vis-à-vis their home countries and continent.[67]

The judge concluded:

> In my view, practically speaking and allowing for a touch of overstatement, the Spanish security forces committed one small mistake. When returning all the persons involved in the climbing of the fence back to Moroccan territory, they could have informed them that if they were not satisfied with the situation of human rights protection in their home countries, they could bring an action before the African Court on Human and Peoples' Rights, which was competent in the matter.[68]

In this chapter, the ensuing reflections on migration (a disappointing reality for Arendt), climate, and the rule of law are addressed in the sequence of the previous chapter. Some of these reflections go behind and beyond what is said in our script. These are my own reflections on the Machiavellian and Montesquieuan approaches, both brilliantly and very nuancedly pursued by Maurice Joly, and—of course—reflections on original works of both great thinkers.

ON CLIMATE

In our dialogue climate change features as the driver of migration. In this context—but bearing in mind, of course, that the Sustainable Development Goals were centuries ahead of Machiavelli and Montesquieu—the two discuss the importance of the natural environment in creating and sustaining political communities. Machiavelli does not connect climate with the different manners and mores people may display, nor with their mentality. As a matter of fact, as if the response to natural disasters and other calamities would be one and the same across the world, he argued that human conduct in times of such emergencies is a 50–50 struggle between luck and human ingenuity.

Yet it would be hard to disagree with him that, literally, is a commonplace reaction to take precautions "with dikes and dams" so "flood would not have produced the enormous upheavals that it has, or it would not have struck here at all."[69] In fact, in the same literal sense of a well-regulated power to resist adversity he may be considered the progenitor of the concept of promoting resilient lives and livelihoods for achieving progress toward the UN Sustainable Development Goals—so far the most serious and versatile plan to counter climate change. This idea has been reinforced by the regular reports of the Intergovernmental Panel on Climate Change.

Regarding Montesquieu in *The Spirit of Laws*," he seconds such an attitude to disaster mitigation: "When a state is depopulated by particular accidents, by wars, pestilence, or famine, there are still resources left. The men who remain may preserve the spirit of industry; they may seek to repair their misfortunes, and calamity itself may make them become more industrious."[70]

However, he sees corruption as a hindrance to disaster mitigation: "This evil is almost incurable when the depopulation is prepared beforehand by interior vice and a bad government."[71] Machiavelli, as the chief political corruptor, is silent on this problem.

ON MIGRATION

While migration increases due to natural disasters, in less critical times migration remains a normal process. If we regard Machiavelli's original view about the helpful role of strangers in his princedom as an indication of his general attitude to that form of migration, then he seemingly would qualify as a proponent of sound migration governance. "Safe, orderly and regular migration" are the key objectives of the 2018 UN global compact for migration.[72] However he was an ardent nationalist exclaiming on his death bed "*Amo la patria mia più dell'anima*!"[73] His cynical acceptance of strangers through a skills-based immigration policy is only utilitarian ("the greatest good for the greatest number"). It is evidently instrumental, self-interested, and selfish. Yet, he knows that "fortresses do much more harm than good."[74] Therefore, he would rather oppose the incursions of outsiders, and if this happens, he would count on the ruler's strong institutions to limit their impact, rather than on infrastructure: "[W]ho can bring together a strong army can do without building fortresses, while he who has not a strong army ought not to build them, but should carefully strengthen the city . . . All other expedients are costly in time of peace, and in war useless."[75]

It looks as if building fortresses, walls, dikes, dams, will not help in the flow of undocumented migrants. But this does not mean that for him fortresses were obsolete. Confronted by Francesco Guicciardini's (one of the greatest Renaissance historians and his patrons) penetrating query: "Ought we then to blame medicine because faith in it might render us less cautious in preserving our health?" Machiavelli was again silent.[76]

Machiavelli's reserve regarding strangers is to some extent supported by Montesquieu who contemplated the effects of Rome's conquest of the Italian Peninsula, resulting in extending its rule to new inhabitants. They were simply absorbed, but not assimilated, let alone integrated. Consequently, Montesquieu concedes:

> Forced to fight against those who were, so to speak, the hands with which it enslaved the world, Rome was lost. It was going to be reduced to its walls; it therefore accorded the coveted right of citizenship to the allies who had not yet ceased being loyal . . . and gradually to all. After this, Rome was no longer a city whose people had but a single spirit, a single love of liberty, a single hatred of tyranny–a city where the jealousy of the senate's power and the prerogatives of the great, always mixed with respect, was only a love of equality. Once the peoples of Italy became its citizens, each city brought to Rome its genius, its particular interests, and its dependence on some great protector. The distracted city no longer formed a complete whole. And since citizens were such only by a kind of fiction, since they no longer had the same magistrates, the same walls, the same gods, the same temples, and the same graves, they no longer saw Rome with the same eyes, no longer had the same love of country, and Roman sentiments were no more.[77]

On its face, the above argument appears to be evergreen. However, the difference is that not current "Romans" (e.g., the European Union, the USA) but undocumented migrants are in the conquest through "waters and lands." In the present time of interstate and interregional controversies and conflicts involving migration are very volatile, just to mention the influx of migrants from Central America to the USA, and from Western Asia and Africa to the European Union. Occasionally instigated by governments from those regions, undocumented migration has prompted a new "Machiavellian moment" (J. G. A. Pocock's argument about destabilization of state institutions). How to go about excessively diversified "feeling rules" and "emotion norms" while retaining stability of host countries' ideals and institutions is a very pertinent question.[78] With the growing proportion of aging people worldwide less open to newcomers, the empathy of native residents dwindles. Building up loyalty necessary to caring for the common good is a must.

Regrettably, contemporary multiculturalism—Liav Orgad reminds us—does not emphasize what people have in common, but on what they differ.[79] If the differences are too broad, multiculturalism jeopardizes citizen's self-confidence, fuels ethnic crime, hatred and fear. Paraphrasing Orgad's question,[80] if strangers could not be more integrated, can they be more educated? If the present call for acceptance of multiculturalism does not work, can assimilation through industriousness, that is, through work ethics and honesty be a way to move forward?

Coming back to Montesquieu's liberal question "Does this art of [immigration-added] politics make our histories more splendid than those of the Greeks and Romans?," the answer is that absorbed but not integrated migrants have in fact been the European Union's parallel societies-aliens in the European polity, if not lose canons.

EU's integrity is at stake. Thus comes again the question "Ought we then to blame medicine because faith in it might render us less cautious in preserving our health?," as if asking whether fencing alone would indeed be *the* medicine to defend Europe's welfare.

Therefore, in our dialogue, the fictional Montesquieu goes beyond his original canonical considerations in *The Spirit of Laws* and echoed in *The Dialogue* by Joly, for example, "that all people's different spirit, their moral characteristics and the way of thinking and acting result from a unique combination of climate, religion, laws, maxims of government, history, mores and manners,"[81] as if those are not amenable to change and Global North's welfare would be at stake. Notwithstanding the evident uniqueness of mores, in our dialogue Montesquieu reemphasizes what he originally said in "My Thoughts" about the natural Golden Rule, and what he means by advancing justice locally. He not only corners Machiavelli regarding the Golden Rule, but also insists on rights and responsibilities of newcomers, including educating them in democratic house rules as their potential stakeholders. Machiavelli does not oppose this idea, but he would still be cautious to welcome them.

Machiavelli was probably the first to weigh lavish expenditures on governance which may bring rulers' downfall. In our dialogue he speaks there about being prudent and parsimonious in expenditures, and about avoiding hatred and contempt by keeping his people happy, while also reinforcing their work ethic ("industriousness").

Montesquieu would also have reservations regarding excessive welfarism: "Princes who lavish honors gain nothing by it. . . . The more one rewards people, the more others deserve rewards."[82] This is our allusion to the reform of immigrants' social welfare benefits by their conditioning on the guest country's house rules.

Any welfare state whose residents enjoy governmental unconditional handouts are at the risk of welfare dependency. Nowadays, this is a hotly debated issue regarding the universal basic income (UBI). Article 25 of the UDHR states that "everyone has the right to a standard of living adequate for the health and well-being of himself and of his family."[83] The intention of UBI is to ensure that no one will be left behind.[84] From this perspective—writes Andrew Rigby—"we can see that welfare strategies have been a key means of defending the state and the established order from social unrest as well as an expression of humanitarian concern for the plight of the dispossessed and marginalised."[85]

Both thinkers to various extents seem to share the fear that strangers bring into their worlds the novelty they may not easily take on board, as if the cowardly conscience of Hamlet (after all a Machiavellian character) would completely thwart them. In difference with Machiavelli, Montesquieu sees light at the end of the tunnel. He wants to temper cowardice by shifting our attention from human interactions to people's interactions with nature. Therefore, he is inclined to develop for newcomers and natives a supra loyalty—of lifestyles in harmony with Mother Earth (to use the expression of the 2030 Agenda). This could be his own premonition of "triple win" which is the UN's orientation (SDG 12.8). For Machiavelli, any harmony, whether with nature and/or newcomers, is beyond his imagination.

We contextualize these contrasting reactions and seek to reconceptualize the "Machiavellian moment." We point to global civic education as not widely recognized, rationalized, and rationed medicine to contribute to welfare and preserve moral health. In other words, and more specifically, in countries experiencing (ir)regular (im)migration, that is, whether those wherefrom "strangers" come or where natives confront them, there should be "fortresses, walls, dykes, embankments" built, but mainly through the rule of law education.

In technical assistance terms, preserving welfare and moral health may start with locally focused partakers' mutual benefits.[86] Mutual benefits have been cynically acknowledged by Machiavelli. In *The Prince*, he said: "[T] he nature of men is such that they find themselves obligated as much for the benefits they confer as for those they receive."[87] In our dialogue Montesquieu recalls that statement. But his own genuine appreciation of the Golden Rule must have come from Hugo Grotius's deeper understanding of that obligation.[88] It originates not from the benefits but from mutual needs which go beyond self-interest.[89] Within these extant needs, Grotius presupposed peoples' social appetite (*appetitus societatis*). It drives them to contribute to justice for peaceful coexistence with others, even if not completely attainable. This appetite dictates to live up to promises, give back what is illegitimately acquired, compensate for what is wrongfully damaged, and to be punished for a crime.[90] Hence, technical assistance for preserving welfare and moral health should start with the account of locally focused partakers' needs and mutual benefits.

These have been some very elementary standards of domestic and international intercourse. It is thus self-explanatory why in our dialogue Montesquieu and Machiavelli concur that "if there is one single model that guarantees good legislation, then basing it on reciprocity would be it. If there is one single devious act which unifies everybody against, it is corruption."

When people are on the move, other values change their order. In short, "[p]eople give meaning to rights by exercising them."[91] The United Nations special rapporteur on extreme poverty and human rights notes:

> According to the World Bank, at 2°C degrees of warming, 100–400 million more people could be at risk of hunger and 1–2 billion more people may no longer have adequate water . . . Climate change could result in global crop yield losses of 30 percent by 2080, even with adaptation measures . . . Between 2030 and 2050, it is expected to cause approximately 250,000 additional deaths per year from malnutrition, malaria, diarrhoea, and heat stress . . . With people in poverty largely uninsured, climate change will exacerbate health shocks that already push 100 million into poverty every year . . . Even under the best-case scenario, hundreds of millions will face food insecurity, forced migration, disease, and death. Climate change threatens the future of human rights and risks undoing the last fifty years of progress in development, global health, and poverty reduction . . . [D]democracy and the rule of law, as well as a wide range of civil and political rights are every bit at risk.[92]

Indeed, they are. Two factors evidently contribute to this risk. First, according to the results of the sixth World Value Survey (2010–2014), among the citizens of emerging powers prevail material "survival values," that is, priority of security over liberty, nonacceptance of homosexuality (i.e., of post-modernistic drive for tolerance of lesbians, gays, transexuals, and bisexuals (LGTB)), abstinence from political action, distrust of outsiders and a weak sense of happiness.[93] People migrate because they are generally tired of living in the unfair state system.[94]

Among the citizens of northern countries (where the system is fairer) the "post-material" self-expression emancipative values prevail (freedom of thought, social equality, increasing tolerance of LGTB), especially in those countries where to today most of the refugees and migrants flock. In short, what emerges is the prioritization of basic existential values over post-material liberal "higher-order" values.[95]

Second, the fact that the Western Hemisphere's economy may by 2050 account for less than half of the world's economy suggests that a new value consensus should emerge, if the institutional framework of the emerging powers will keep pace with the growth of their gross domestic product. Emancipative education should assist in breaking the dominant cycle of material and intellectual poverty in the Global South to broaden the avenues for meeting the ethical living standards of the Global North host countries. There is neither moral reason nor moral politics without successful anti-corruption in any place.

Consequently, in both groups of countries there should be "zero tolerance" of corruption and to violating the three above rights: to security, life, and dignity. Their reciprocal and emancipative essence is elementary to both types of values, if corruption, exclusion, and violence are not to be in the order of the day.[96] The way to bridge the global division in understanding the value of these priorities is not just arguing about seemingly fateful differences in their meaning but in getting over them and acting together. Notwithstanding them, a worldwide and sustainable value consensus should be strengthened.

In the Global North, there are encouraging examples of urban stewardship immigrant-integration projects that may contribute to just that. They show how through a commensurate implementation of these three rights, security and freedom of natives and migrants can be satisfied.[97] Whatever is their bigger *chapeau*, for example, whether they de facto respond to the shift of values, contribute to living in harmony with nature (SDG 12.8) or/and to inculcate critical thinking (SDG 4.7) such stewardship projects appear to be the most approximate, viable and readily deliverable form of civic education at its best. With due account of target groups, they may be multiplied at the grassroots level: in the city streets and residential areas, in kindergartens, schools, and at universities.

The global shift of values is very drastic. Denmark may be the leading example. Whether or not driven by the doctrine of "cultural defense" (Liav Orgard), or "cultural self-preservation," that country has been drastically modifying its own immigration policy. This Scandinavian par excellence cradle of universal social justice idealized in the UN Charter, the country which first in the world ratified the 1951 UN Refugee Convention, the country which in 1995 hosted the first ever World Summit for Social Development, and in 1999 advocated Hugo Grotius's self-preservation doctrine for twenty-first century's humanitarian intervention,[98] has since 2021 dramatically tightened its own acceptance criteria for asylum seekers. Applicants will be flown to an asylum processing facility to a faraway third country. Those already in Denmark face heightened naturalization and permanent residence requirements (e.g., language exam, regressed welfare entitlements, no criminal record). The non-Western immigrants already living in Danish cities where the immigrant-attributed crime rates have been found critical are being dispersed across the capital and other municipalities.[99]

The effect of resettlement of male refugees who move is that they have an estimated 5.8 percent higher employment rate than refugees who stay put in their Danish original residence. For female refugees, the effect of resettlement on employment is not significant. This may be the effect of moving on subsequent employment or the reverse, that is, the effect on moving from having found a job farther away. Both male and female refugees who move from the initial municipality have an estimated 2–5 percentage point higher probability of being enrolled in education.[100]

Globally, as of this writing there are about 260 million people living outside of their original country of birth, out of which 22 percent in the European Union. Most of them found themselves there because of their rights-based reasons (family reunion, asylum and other admissions for humanitarian reasons).

Some 70 percent of native Europeans say that integrating immigrants is a necessary investment in the long run for their country, but the evidence shows that educationally immigrants fall behind the natives. They emphasize that successful integration is the responsibility of both immigrants and of the host society. Some 40 percent of surveyed natives say integration has not been successful in their local area or country. It takes one generation (i.e., 20–25 years) for differences in labor force participation rates between natives, labor migrants, former refugees, and dependent family members to disappear. Without intensive integration measures and efforts, the situation is most difficult for certain groups of migrant and refugee women.[101]

If inclusion is problematic just in one region with reasonably operating welfare and educational systems (though fragmented), how will the world by 2050 cope with increasing numbers of environmental migrants? While 2050 forecasts vary from 25 million to 1 billion, with 200 million being the most widely cited estimate, quite a portion of migrants will look for their sustainable livelihood opportunities abroad.[102] For one or another rights-based reason, there altogether may be ca. 500 million people living outside of their original country of birth.

If to relate the above verdict of the ECtH'R in the context of our dialogue, then Montesquieu's and the like-minders' insistence on emancipating the Southerners really highlights where Global North and South find themselves nowadays. Without developing legitimate opportunities for self-determination and self-realization of people in their countries of birth, without genuinely democratic rule, the world faces an unenviable conundrum. The sublime message of Judge Pejchal may be a prolegomena to broaden the avenues for orderly, safe, and regular migration in the future rather than reaching out for it "over the border fence." As of this writing, "hot returns" only spark heated reactions and convulsive counteractions. Hopefully, they will prompt "cooled off" transformative solutions.

ON GOVERNANCE AND THE RULE OF LAW

In other words, however counterintuitively this may sound, upfront there should be a genuine rule-of-law reform in the Global South countries wherefrom migrants leave to look for better life chances. Regrettably, the post–World War II history of Global North technical assistance (except for Scandinavian countries) hardly shows that the rule of law governance mattered. For quite a long time, technical assistance to Global South was motivated by malevolent exploitative goals.[103]

Where migration is a livelihood strategy for centuries, technical assistance must be very radically different from places in which it has been a relatively new development. A "benevolent conqueror's" *toutes proportions gardées* reform may help to reorchestrate and instrumentalize technical assistance—measured by the Rule-of-Law commensurate *needs* and *benefits*. "*Each party benefits from the activity of the other* [emphasis added]."[104] Underscored in our dialogue, Montesquieu's *pouvoirs distributes*[105] should be at the root of technical assistance. This should be a Montesquieuan antidote for the stupefying potion served by Machiavelli-type of governance-powered mandrake root idea to control people's minds for the absolutist rule.

In our dialogue, Montesquieu and Machiavelli argue that in the rule-of-law governance there are no double standards, as if that dialogue was only limited to *intra vires* v. *ultra vires* (within or beyond ruler's legal power). In fact, those two thinkers argue about the superiority of national constitutions and other parliamentary laws over the EU's founding treaty. Machiavelli says: "Judges should rule the way I want them. Free people and states are those which are far from any external servitude and are able to govern themselves by their own judgments. From a ruler there is no court of appeal." Montesquieu says:

> I do not care how one organizes the courts. . . . They can hand down verdicts from the Palais de Justice or render them even under a tree. It may be oak, pine or birch or any other tree or place. It does not matter whether you as a judge stand under a tree, sit or climb to the top—but only as long as you get there in a fair way. So only by yourself—with no claimants' support. You must only adjudicate in accordance with that law. It may be oak, pine or birch or any other tree or place. It does not matter whether you as a judge stand under a tree, sit or climb to the top—but only as long as you get there in a fair way. So only by yourself—with no claimants' support. You must only adjudicate in accordance with that law.

Machiavelli is adamantly clear: in his courtyard, a judge plays only by his rules. They are sufficiently harsh to counter disloyalty.

This debate on the scope of independence of judiciary has continued since the establishment of the EU. It has never been so volatile as it is nowadays. At present it takes place between the EU's "old" and "new" members. For the new members alleging double standards is a smoke screen to wield political power over justice, which by its nature is always *ultra vires*. New laws, and rules of disciplinary responsibility should guarantee it *intra vires*.

Montesquieu understands this political limitation well. Therefore, in our dialogue justice in his view is always on the horizon as it recedes, while countries and people move forward. Justice evolves in effect of an intangible relation within and beyond human mind. Independent judiciary means that its reorganization must not erode the separation of powers. As per *The Spirit of Laws,* he explains in our dialogue: "Justice is not a thing, but a relation among things. I see justice that may make you and all of us everywhere fair, progressive. Justice is something eternal, universal and independent of human conventions."

Montesquieu interprets justice in the pursuit of larger freedom, as if he would have precipitated its UN understanding. He levels justice up. In *The Dialogue* by Joly, Machiavelli levels justice down. He bluntly states that the university curricula must contain the interpretation of constitutional law the way he wants. No superior law, no discussion of pros and cons, no *de lege lata* vs *de lege ferenda*. Justice is cast in stone.

Machiavelli's counsels exploit feeble, wicked human nature and masses' passivity which mindlessly accept what the ruler says. He disregards the viability of any right actions by the "masses," because they are incapable of following the intentions and logic of authorities. The "masses," says Machiavelli, only and "constantly want to be distracted by novelties, surprises, and dramatic moves."[106] The almost defeated Montesquieu utters: "Truly, you are to be admired. What strength of mind! What deeds!"[107]

In our dialogue, Montesquieu does not give up and provocatively asks Machiavelli: "Pedestrian hedonism, hah?" Could indeed Montesquieu's moral pessimism be "reversed"? I believe so. In the best interest of prosperous and democratic future, there is only one way to make this happen: proving in practice that in time of climate change, migration security, and freedom are compatible concepts. A judicious implementation of three rights constitutive for liberal democracy: the right to security, the right to life and the right to dignity is vital to meet that interest.[108]

There is also clear evidence regarding other local cultural norms whose commonplace persistence is likewise detrimental to equality, namely the assertion about the indolence of people. Machiavelli is very critical about the listlessness of his compatriots. They "live a lazy indolent life free from trouble and inconvenience" which is "the cause of our degeneracy and the present neglect of military discipline."[109]

In our dialogue, Montesquieu and Machiavelli agree that because of that indolence *regardless of people's place of living* "[h]e who builds on the people, builds upon mud."[110] And so Joly in his own text thinks about people's indolence, hence about the chances for democratization. Via him Montesquieu, who compares Europe to India, says that there through "a system of castes . . . the people are turned into a herd of slaves, led . . . by the hand of priests and trembling under the rod of the master."[111] Answering in Joly's dialogue to Montesquieu's argument that "huge numbers of people whose poverty chains them to their work"[112] must react to the absolute rule, Machiavelli cynically responds that "popular sovereignty" meets these people's condition because of their "infinite baseness."[113] It demonstrates itself soon after expressing their vital concerns. Then they become indifferent to politics and religion. No measure of equality will cure this. They are "incapable of tolerating the frustrations of a free society and patient to the point of martyrdom with all the outrages of audacious despotism."[114]

In *The Spirit of Laws*, Montesquieu is especially pessimistic about Southerners: their energies are sapped by excessive heat which reduces their governance ability.[115] In *The Dialogue* by Joly, these are "people [who] doze peacefully in the degradation of slavery."[116] In our dialogue, Montesquieu is quoted saying: "Slavery is always preceded by sleep."[117]

For long the interpretation of intellectual inferiority and physical imbalance, if not enslavement, has dominated the Northerners' thinking about the Global South. If to confront this offensive argument with the UDHR terms, then Southerners' inaction would involve their tolerance of fear and acceptance of want, their resignation from the freedom of speech, and dismissal of the rule of law. In the SDGs terms (see the preamble), this would fly in the face of people's dignity, their prosperity, and of peaceful, just and inclusive societies.

But such a confrontation would be misleading. It looks dated in the sense of Montesquieu's original view about the superior moderate climate of France that enables its people exemplary personal disposition to pursue and enjoy good, even under absolutist government. Not just France but any country with the average temperature of 72 degrees Fahrenheit (22 degrees Celsius) allows for psychophysiological comfort. This disposition was proven by contemporary comparative US-China study on the dependent on climate human personality traits. It documented that as the climate change continues, such traits are evidenced irrespective of a country. The studied residents explored the outside environment, looked for new experiences, encountered others, engaged in a wider range of activities. Thus, they positively influenced their personalities, albeit—surprisingly—to a lesser degree among the surveyed US Americans than Chinese.[118] In sum, these findings only suggest that the extent of personality changes vary across cultures. No other conclusion could be reached about Montesquieu's thesis.

We dismissed it in our dialogue, based on the findings from two experimental investigations of personality changes in Indian school populations (teachers and students). The first experiment involved 321 junior school boys recruited from the lowest caste and 321 boys from the three highest castes. Grade 6 and 7 boys were requested to solve as many mazes as they could out of a given packet, with monetary incentives. When caste was not publicly announced, there were no caste differences in performance. However, when caste was publicly announced, the number of mazes solved by low caste boys dropped by a dramatic 25 percent. When caste was announced but a random draw of a name determined who in a session of six would be paid for the mazes he solved, the caste gap in performance disappeared. To the extent that the findings can be generalized to economic performance in north India, where caste distinctions remain marked, the authors say that their findings suggest that the aggregate economic effect on society of expectations associated with caste are unambiguously negative.

The experiment proved that:

- The negative learner's self-perception works like a self-fulfilling prophecy. It locks in the economic disadvantage because of the pre-defined content of own expectations.
- These expectations are not a consequence of a "culture of poverty" per se, but of its enduring legacy that hampers positive personal attitudinal changes.
- Since the aggregate effect of economic deprivation (injustice) on the expectations associated with the in-group is clearly negative, motivating a learner

to perform better may alleviate the enduring feeling of personal inferiority. In the long run it may alleviate prejudice of others and the impoverished future in general culture.[119]

Another study on the education system involved the relationship between teachers' incentives and primary students' performance (grades 1–5) in Andhra Pradesh—a rural province in southeast India. The study involved 500 tested and "control group" schools. The researchers found that from the two types of such incentives (a bonus based on the improvement in performance on assessment tests by their students ["individual incentive"] versus a bonus based on the improvement in performance of all students in the tested schools ["group incentive"]):

- Students in schools where teachers received either individual-based or school-based incentive pay did better than students in control group schools in all five grades, all districts, and at all levels of test question difficulty.
- Cash incentives to teachers not only boosted student performance more than providing inputs, they were also more cost-effective. Students in these schools performed better than those in schools that received cash grants for supplies or an extra teacher. At the same time, paying teachers based on the performance of their students was more cost-effective.
- There was very limited evidence that the program had different effects based on school characteristics such as the size of the school or the quality of its infrastructure. There was difference in results based on student demographics, including gender, household literacy, household caste, and baseline score. Affluence, however, did play a role: students from more affluent families showed a better response to the teacher incentive program.
- Students also did better in subjects for which teachers did not receive incentive pay.[120]

These two findings are very important for improving educational performance generally. They suggest that statistical findings on climate and durable inequalities in no way define social justice reforms anywhere in the world. Breaking out of the cycle of self-imposed cycle of poverty of thought may be instrumental to breaking out of the self-sustaining cycle of material poverty. This may happen by incentivizing students and teachers, thus eventually motivating structural reforms for social justice. The incentivized education aiming at "leveling up" counters indolence.

However, this does not imply automatic mastering of civil competence: acceptance, integrity, respect, and fairness. In a large field experiment on civic education (almost 1,300 upper secondary students from 59 classes in Sweden) its more advanced level was tested. The students' performance was tested by comparing two methods of imparting civic education: teacher-cantered education with deliberative student-role education.

For this purpose, the experimenters distributed two teaching materials. One was inspired by the UDHR, and another one explaining "What is democracy?" The latter teaching material outlined the basic idea of democratic decision-making. It included issues like the concept of, and criteria for, democracy, what nondemocratic governance is and examples of totalitarian regimes throughout history. Using one or the other method, students were expected to become familiar with human rights and democratic decision-making in an orderly manner. In the latter way, the general instruction to students was to focus on discussing and listening, helping each other to develop arguments, respecting each other's opinions, and not offending one another. The core part of the teaching consisted of the group exercises termed "deliberation scenario dilemmas." Each lesson included two or three deliberation scenario dilemmas. The experimenters concluded that there was little evidence that deliberative education significantly increases civic competence.[121]

The results of these three experiments are unequivocal insofar as concerns the incentivizing *versus* participatory role of teachers and students. In my limited teaching experience of the deliberative Socratic case study method,[122] its success depended largely on inspiratory interaction between a teacher and students, on internal students' cooperation reinforced by very forward-looking, inquisitive, and principled teacher's performance aiming at a joint pragmatic and paradigmatic outcome for those who may become social justice reformers. For a teacher, this is a much more tedious but insightful thought experiment that yields through such a deliberative method of scenario dilemmas quite hopeful and viable conclusions.

Summing up these three experiments, educational results depend on the ways and methods of interaction.[123] This is a two-way street with traffic outages.

CONCLUSION

On a bigger street map, the moral reason and moral politics are at a cross-roads. This is exactly the place where Machiavelli's and Montesquieu's views could be in a creative tension—between the reflex of own self-preservation and the humanitarian reflex. Sustainable livelihood with its rights and duties is a green traffic light that should regulate the right-way movement. The United Nations' and like-minded countries' technical assistance based on common needs and mutual benefits ("triple win") is the way to go.[124] Both types of moral entrepreneurship are meant for a laudable aim of orderly, safe, and regular migration—as long as they serve Mother Earth well.

The United Nations will hear Machiavellian and Montesquieuan calls. It will have to respond humanely and effectively to the shift in universal values.

More than a century and a half ago, a French liberal economist Frederic Bastiat said "that only those who endorse extreme views are likely to succeed in politics, while moderates will always be abandoned and vanquished in the middle."[125] In the same fateful way, a contemporary French political educator Raymond Aron said: "[h]aving political opinions is not a matter of having an ideology once and for all; it is a question of taking the right decisions in changing circumstances."[126] It is this context in which I find more pragmatic the recent advice of a German political scientist Uwe Backes:

> Political extremisms that act within the framework of legality may, in such a way—like poisons that, in small doses, develop healing effects—give an impetus to course corrections, point to neglected problem areas and, last—aside from their disintegrating effects—bring about integrative effects. The friends of the constitutional state should therefore refrain from a Manichaean crusade mentality, which, due to the resolution of mercilessly combating extremism has led to the behavioral patterns of the antipodes. For a middle which wishes to push its aims to their final conclusion, itself becomes extreme.[127]

Yet *paradigmatic* rule-of-law advice relevant to the emancipative essence of the rights to security, life, and dignity should really focus on ascertaining their viability amid climate change and migration. In this sense, no doubt, Montesquieu belongs to the precursors of modern constitutionalism. Oddly enough, so does the real and fictional Machiavelli. Both historical personages believed in man's jurisdiction on Earth, not solely determined by Heavens or the stars. In Joly's interpretation, both are teachers of legislators and thinkers: Machiavelli as the amoral teacher of autocracy and evil, Montesquieu as the moral teacher of larger freedom and progress. Machiavelli with his deceitful "Un-Golden rule" teaches: "Do unto others as you can expect they will do unto you." Montesquieu with his ethic of trust and moderation teaches justice, peace, tolerance according to the Golden Rule "Do unto others as you would have them to do unto you." This progressive rule is emblematic to and ecumenical for the United Nations' larger moral purpose, that is, "larger freedom."

As shown above, the legal orders pursued by both philosophers are often incompatible. Machiavelli's *ordini nuovi* and *principi nouvi* incapacitate people, Montesquieu's laws with his *pouvoirs distributes* emancipate them. Yet in any group of people—whether guided by conservative or liberal values—there are individuals less or more malleable to indoctrination or cooperation as well as those who are rationalists with less or more reasonable arguments. Machiavellism is "greening."[128] There are Montesquieuan moments in Machiavellian republicanism.[129]

Building the bridge into the dialogue between Machiavelli and Montesquieu through their exchanges on "fortresses and dykes" (as if against the flood of migrants) and on sour wine may seem to be anecdotic if not also ambiguous conjunctures. However, the message flowing from their dialogue is systemic and simple.

Regarding sour wine, the Conference of the Parties to the United Nations Framework Convention on Climate Change heard that climate adaptation and policies and actions are as slow as wine making and wine transitions.[130] These two factors together may lead to the demise if not death of Bordeaux wine. Consequently, metaphorically or not, the demise of *vin Château de la Brède* (the home place of Montesquieu) may be symbolic to the tarnished sense of freedom. If Montesquieu's moral optimism will not win, will Machiavelli *vin Santo del Chianti* remain the offer one cannot refuse? Regarding environmental migration, the UN global compact for orderly, safe, and responsible migration offers an opportunity to review and incorporate both developments in the international migration governance agenda.

Two world wars may suggest that Machiavelli was more realistic than Montesquieu. After 500 years since *The Prince* and almost 200 years since *The Spirit of Laws* the UN was brought to life.

The world visions of Machiavelli and Montesquieu no longer are as viable for the post-2030 world as they had been until 1945. If Montesquieu indeed meant "the psychic transformations that would transpire as the Western language of freedom the Eastern language of despotism by writing challenging messages upon the tabula of the mind,"[131] then the United Nations language of transformative justice is truly the medium in which larger freedom should be inscribed into it. But—Machiavelli says—"the visionary who has armed force on his side has always won through, while unarmed even your visionary is always a loser."[132] In his own opinion, Florence of his time had been both in a "disarmed mode" and a "servile mode."[133]

Save some religions, until the establishment of the UN such a passive-aggressive mode had never been viable. The UN is an unarmed ecumenical visionary that occasionally succeeds. The organization "calls upon" "urges," "condemns," "notes," "requests." The secretary general also "alerts," "warns," "regrets," and so on. Whether the UN's success is in the benevolent conquest or conquest by surrender, is Machiavelli's forceful reasoning really applicable to all times? Or is his own direct and urgent political call to seek a path to reach unknown "waters and lands" dated?

Hence a few more questions:

Why did *The Dialogue* by Joly place both *dramatis personae* in Hell? How soon will the Machiavellis of the present become the Montesquieus of the future? How many more conflagrations are in the offing before humankind reasserts the inherent sense of freedom from tyranny and oppression promoted in the UDHR which emerged straight from the conflagrations of Auschwitz and other concentration camps? How soon will member states inculcate globally the 2030 Agenda's recommended lifestyle in harmony with nature to create people's inclusive identity for the world's sustainable development with the rule of law? How soon will the rule of law paradigm in favor of Mother Earth's welfare receive its definitive momentum, so we all will not become losers? How soon we will appreciate this greening sense of "Justice to others is like charity to ourselves"[134]? If Machiavelli's subterranean influence matters in the United Nations, can it be now channeled for common good?

Consequently, and finally, if to approach Machiavelli's *ordini nuovi* and *principi nouvi* not in his but United Nations terms (so conscious of them), then this would mean that any people and peoples who may be left behind on the way to genuine social progress deserve encouragement and support for dignified and emancipatory treatment—larger freedom, however difficult this is in the time of shifting global values. This emancipatory treatment is needed for breaking away from the inculcated cycle of material and intellectual poverty—to various extents all over the world, and everywhere because of climate change. Hopefully, this will become new *vera cognizione* (using Machiavelli's term)—the impulse to great actions as well as the knowledge of how to perform them.[135] Otherwise, as Marie von Ebner-Eschenbach (1830–1916) said, "[w]ho doesn't know anything, has to believe everything."

Attention and response of like-minded UN member states and civil societies matter, numbers count, the clock ticks.

NOTES

1. Herman Bernstein, *The Truth About "The Protocols of Zion"* (New York: Covici Friede, 1935), 16–17.
2. Hans Speier, "The Truth in Hell: Maurice Joly on Modern Despotism," *Polity* 10, no. 1 (1977): 19–20.
3. Speier, *The Truth*, 21.
4. Antonio Gramsci, *Prison Notebooks,* ed. and transl. Quentin Hoare and Geoffrey Nowell Smith (ElecBook: London, 1999), 332–333.
5. Isaiah Berlin, *Against the Current: Essays in the History of Ideas*, 2nd ed., ed. Henry Hardy (Princeton-Oxford: Princeton University Press, 2013), 44.
6. Leo Strauss, *What is Political Philosophy? and Other Studies* (Chicago & London: The University of Chicago Press), 101.
7. In fact, this method was first popularized by Francis Bacon (1561–1626), posthumously recognized as the Third Plato. However, Bacon credited Machiavelli for the development of his own kind of inductive reasoning.

8. Wojciech Hanasz, "Machiavelli's Method Revisited: The Art and Science of Modelling," *The Review Journal of Political Philosophy* 8 (2010): 1.

9. Cary Nederman, "Niccolò Machiavelli," *The Stanford Encyclopedia of Philosophy* (Summer 2019 Edition), https://stanford.io/3aF24Zp.

10. Ted Toadvine and Leonard Lawlor, eds., *The Merleau-Ponty Reader* (Evanston, IL: Northwestern University Press 2007), 128–129, 134.

11. Terence Ball, "The Picaresque Prince: Reflections on Machiavelli and Moral Change," *Political Theory* 12, no. 44 (1984): 528.

12. Strauss, *What Is*, 47. See further Redo in this volume, ch. 2. For a critique of Strauss' arguments, see: Adrian Blau, "Anti-Strauss," *The Journal of Politics* 74, no. 1 (2012): 142–155.

13. Strauss, *What Is*, 46–47.

14. A prototype of "backward induction." Game theorists regard it as a compelling scientific process of reasoning from the end of a problem or situation to determine a sequence of optimal actions. It is occasionally pursued by historians who speculate alternative course of actions.

15. Yves Winter, *Machiavelli and the Orders of Violence* (Cambridge University Press: Cambridge, 2018), 97.

16. Giovanni Giorgini, "Five hundred years of Italian scholarship on Machiavelli's Prince," *The Review of Politics* 75 (2013): 625.

17. Alan Macfarlane, *Montesquieu and the Making of the Modern World* (Cambridge: CAM Rivers Publishing, 2018), 13.

18. Cf. Frankel, *Review*.

19. Vittorio Hösle, "Morality and Politics: Reflections on Machiavelli's 'Prince,'" *International Journal of Politics, Culture, and Society* 3, no. 1 (1989): 52–54.

20. Christian Volk, "The Law of the Nations and The Civil Law of The World. On Montesquieu's Political Cosmopolitanism," in *Order, and International Law System. The Early History of International Legal Thought from Machiavelli to Hegel*, ed. Stefan Kadelbach, Thomas Kleinlein and David Roth-Isigkeit (Oxford: Oxford University Press, 2017), 242.

21. A/RES/70/1, Transforming our world: the 2030 Agenda for sustainable development. 25 September 2015.

22. Steven Frankel, "Review: The Dialogue in Hell between Montesquieu and Machiavelli: Humanitarian Despotism and the Conditions of Modern Tyranny," *Interpretation–a Journal of Political Philosophy* 12 (2004): 97.

23. Blagden, *Induction*, 196, ftn.4.

24. Peter Kreeft. *Socrates Meets Machiavelli*. Ignatius Press. Kindle Edition.

25. Cf. Joseph Kraft, "Truth and Poetry in Machiavelli," *The Journal of Modern History* XXIII, no. 2 (June 1951), 116.

26. cf. Blagden, *Induction*, 196, ftn.4.

27. John P. McCormick, "Machiavelli's Agathocles: From Criminal Example to Princely Exemplum," in Michèle Lowrie and Susanne Lüdemann eds. *Exemplarity and Singularity Thinking through Particulars in Philosophy, Literature, and Law* (London-New York: Routledge, 2016), 123–129.

28. Peter Kreeft, *Socrates Meets Machiavelli*. Ignatius Press. Kindle Edition.

29. McCormick, *Machiavelli's*, 124.

30. Kreeft, Peter. *Socrates Meets Machiavelli*. Ignatius Press. Kindle Edition.

31. Merlau-Ponty, *Reader*, 124.

32. Niccolò Machiavelli, "Discorso o dialogo intorno alla nostra lingua," transl. William J. Landon, in *Politics, Patriotism, and Language: Niccolò Machiavelli's "Secular Patria" and the Creation of an Italian National Identity*, New York: Peter Lang Publishing, 2005, 258.

33. Niccolò Machiavelli, "Discorso o dialogo intorno alla nostra lingua," transl. William J. Landon, in *Politics, Patriotism, and Language: Niccolò Machiavelli's "Secular Patria" and the Creation of an Italian National Identity*. New York: Peter Lang Publishing, 2005, 258.

34. Niccolò Machiavelli, *History of Florence and of the Affairs of Italy. From The Earliest Times To The Death of Lorenzo the Magnificent* (USA: Start Publishing LLC, 2013), bk. III, ch. III, 138–139.

35. Sebastian de Grazia. *Machiavelli in Hell* (New York: Vintage Books, 2003), 54, 56, 314–317, 337–338.

36. Francesco Gino, and Max H. Bazerman, "When Misconduct Goes Unnoticed: The Acceptability of Gradual Erosion in Others' Unethical Behavior," *Journal of Experimental Social Psychology* 45, no. 4 (2009): 708–719.

37. Felicitas Benziger, "The New Rule of Law Mechanism: 'Ideological Blackmail Tool' or Legitimate Means to Protect the EU's Values?," *International Law Blog*. Fresh perspectives on international law, December 15, 2020, https://bit.ly/3nKUK5X.

38. cf. Chabod after Barbara Spackman, "Machiavelli and Maxims," *Yale French Studies* 77 (1990): 143, ftn 9-10 and 190.

39. GWF Hegel. *Phenomenology of Spirit*, trans. AV Miller (Oxford University Press, 1977), 158.

40. Clifford Orwin, "Machiavelli's Unchristian Charity," *American Political Science Review* 72, no. 4 (Dec. 1978): 1218.

41. Niccolò Machiavelli (a). *The Prince*, transl. and ed. Peter Bondanella, with introduction of Mauricio Virolli. Oxford: Oxford University Press, 2008, bk XV, 107.

42. Charles N. R. McCoy, "The Place of Machiavelli in the History of Political Thought," *The American Political Science Review* 37, no. 4 (1943): 640, ft. 25; Julian Korab-Karpowicz, *On the History of Political Philosophy: Great Thinkers from Thucydides to Locke* (Boston: Pearson Education/Routledge: 2012/2016), 120.

43. Machiavelli (a), *The Prince*, bk. XVIII, 116.

44. Ian Kershaw, *Hitler 1936–45: Nemesis* (Penguin Books: London, 2001), 372.

45. Philip Kain, J. *Hegel and Right: A Study of the Philosophy of* Right (Albany, NJ: State University of New York Press, 2018), 153.

46. Charles Montesquieu, My Thoughts [*Mes Pensées*], trans., ed., and with an introduction by Henry C. Clark (Indianapolis: Liberty Fund 2012), 196.

47. Charles L. de Secondat Montesquieu. *The Spirit of Laws*, trans. T. Nugent (Kitchener, ON: Batoche Books, 2001), XI.6, 173.

48. Montesquieu, *My Thoughts*, 395; Cf. Corey Robin, "Reflections on Fear: Montesquieu in Retrieval," *American Political Science Review* 94 (2004): 352.

49. Robert Shackleton. *Montesquieu: A Critical Biography* (New York: Oxford University Press, 1961), 309–310.

50. Andrea Radasanu, "Montesquieu on Ancient Greek Foreign Relations: Toward National Self-interest and International Peace," *Political Research Quarterly* 66, no.1 (2013): 4.

51. Montesquieu, *The Spirit*, bk. X.3; XX, 1–2.

52. de Grazia, *Machiavelli*, 302. Wherever Montesquieu in good faith may expect genuine reciprocity, Machiavelli in bad faith calls for it only to continue the "Un-Golden rule."

53. Robert von Mohr, *Die Gesichichte und Literatur der Staatwissenschaften*, 3 vols (Erlangen: Verlag von Ferdinand Enke, 1858), III, 54.

54. Sławomir Redo, "The Relevance of Philosophical and Religious Ideas to the United Nations Quest for Universalizing Criminal Justice," in Helmut Kury and Sławomir Redo, eds. *Crime Prevention and Justice in 2030. The UN and the Universal Declaration of Human Rights* (Cham: Springer, 2021), 575–602.

55. Maurice Joly, *The Dialogue in Hell between Machiavelli and Montesquieu: Humanitarian Despotism and the Conditions of Modern Tyranny*, trans., ed. and with commentary by John S. Waggoner (Lanham-Boulder-New York-Toronto-Oxford: Lexington Books, 2003), 10, 160.

56. Joly, *The Dialogue*, 165.

57. Hannah Arendt, Truth and Politics, in *Truth: Engagements Across Philosophical Traditions* David Wood and José Medina, eds. (Oxford: Blackwell Publishing 1967/2005), 306.

58. Arendt, *Truth*, 306.

59. Hannah Arendt, *The Origins of Totalitarianism* (New York: Penguin Modern Classic 2017), 593–607.

60. Hannah Arendt, "Human Rights. What are They?," *Modern Review* 3 (1949) no. 1: 476–483.

61. Christine E. J. Schwöbel, *Global Constitutionalism in International Legal Perspective,* (Leiden: Martinus Nijhoff Publishers 2011), 115.

62. Hannah Arendt, "Es gibt nur ein einziges Menschenrecht," *Die Wandlung* IV (1949): 754–770.

63. Christoph Menke, Birgit Kaiser and Kathrin Thiele, "The 'Aporias of Human Rights' and the 'One Human Right': Regarding the Coherence of Hannah Arendt's argument," *Social Research* 74 no. 3/I (2007): 739–762.

64. António Guterres, United Nations High Commissioner for Refugees; Remarks at the Opening of the Judicial Year of the European Court of Human Rights, 28 January 2011.

65. European Court of Human Rights, Case of N.D. and N.T. v. Spain, https://bit.ly/3ldbhwG.

66. Case of N.D. and N.T. v. Spain.

67. Case of N.D. and N.T. v. Spain.

68. Case of N.D. and N.T. v. Spain.

69. Machiavelli (a), *The Prince*, bk. XXV, 137–138.

70. Montesquieu, *The Spirit*, bk. XXIII. 28, 458.

71. Montesquieu, *The Spirit*, bk. XXIII. 28, 458.

72. A/RES/73/195, Global Compact for Safe, Orderly and Regular Migration (19 December 2018).

73. Lettere (Machiavelli)/Lettera XXVIII a Francesco Vettori, https://bit.ly/3y5GDtx.

74. Niccolò Machiavelli, Discourses On The First Decade Of Titus Livius, in *The Collected Works of Niccolò Machiavelli: The Complete Works*. PergamonMedia, 2015, bk. XXIV.

75. Machiavelli, *Discourses*, bk. XXIV.

76. Pasquale Villari, *The Life and Times of Niccolò Machiavelli* (2 vols: London: T.F. Unwin, 1992), II, 702.

77. Montesquieu, *Considerations on the Causes of the Greatness of the Romans and their Decline*, trans. with notes and an introduction by David Lowenthal (New York/London: The Free Press/Collier-Macmillan 1794/1965), 59.

78. Helmut Kury and Sławomir Redo, eds., *Refugees and Migrants in Law and Policy. Challenges and Opportunities for Global Civic Education* (Cham: Springer 2018), xxx; 880–881.

79. Liav Orgad, *The Cultural Defence of Nations. A Liberal Theory of Majority Rights* (Oxford: Oxford University Press, 2015), 4.

80. Orgad, *The Cultural*, 161.

81. Joly, *The Dialogue*, 13 and 164.

82. Montesquieu, *My Thoughts*, 1999 at 615.

83. UN doc. A/217 III Universal Declaration of Human Rights, 10 December 1948.

84. Inez Wijgaarde, Jebamalai Vinanchiarachi and Jeff Readman, Universal Basic Income (UBI) for Reducing Inequalities and Increasing Socio-Economic Inclusion: A Proposal for a New Sustained Policy Perspective, in Helmut Kury and Sławomir Redo, *Crime Prevention and Justice in 2030. The UN and the Universal Declaration of Human Rights* (Cham: Springer, 2021), 107–124.

85. Andrew Rigby, War, Revolution and Coronavirus: The Human Security case for universal income, https://bit.ly/3iDwpeS (accessed October 1, 2021).

86. Sławomir Redo, "For More United Nations Rule-of-Law 'Win-Win' Technical Assistance Outcomes amid Migration," *Studia Iuridica Toruniensia* XXIX (2021):315-349.

87. Machiavelli (a), *The Prince,* bk. X, 93.

88. Montesquieu, *My Thoughts*, 1537 at 441.

89. Hugo Grotius, *The Rights of War and Peace*, edited and with an Introduction by Richard Tuck, from the Edition by Jean Barbeyrac (Indianapolis: Liberty Fund, 2005). Vol. 1, Prolegomena, XVIII.

90. Redo, *For More United Nations.*

91. Raymond C. Offenheiser, Susan H. Holcombe, "Challenges and Opportunities in Implementing a Rights-Based Approach to Development: An Oxfam America Perspective," *Nonprofit and Voluntary Sector Quarterly* 32, no. 2 (June 2003): 286. doi: 10.1177/0899764003251739.

92. UN doc. A/HRC/41/39, §§ 26–28, 65.

93. Yilmaz Esmer and Thorleif Pettersson, eds., *Measuring and Mapping Cultures: 25 Years of Comparative Values Surveys* (Leiden: Brill, 2007).

94. Ortrun Merkle, Julia Reinold, and Melissa Siege, *A Study on the Link between Corruption and the Causes of Migration and Forced Displacement* (Deutsche Gesellschaft für Internationale Zusammenarbeit, 2017), 33, 78, and 112.

95. Esmer and Pettersson, *Measuring.*

96. Joao Nunes, "Reclaiming the Political: Emancipation and Critique in Security Studies," *Security Dialogue* 43, no. 4 (2012): 345–361.

97. Sławomir Redo, "Criminological Reflections on the Golden Rule and Urban Stewardship for Safety," *Eastern European Journal of Transnational Relations* 2, no. 1 (2018): 57–70.

98. Danish Institute of International Affairs, Hmanitarian Intervention: Legal and Political Aspects. Copenhagen 1999.

99. Michel Pace, Denmark's immigrants forced out by government policies, *Chatham House*, 28 June 2021, https://bit.ly/3l6SKDl.

100. Vilde Hernes, https://bit.ly/3l6SKDlJacob Nielsen Arendt, Pernilla Andersson Joona and Kristian Rose Tronstad, *Nordic Integration and Settlement Policies for Refugees. A Comparative Analysis of Labour Market Integration Outcomes* (Nordic Council of Ministers: TemaNord 2019:5290), 106.

101. European Strategy and Policy Analysis System, Global Trends to 2030: The Future of Migration and Integration, n.d., https://bit.ly/3yJsDpp.

102. International Organization for Migration, *A Complex Nexus*, n.d. https://bit.ly/2YkbLsU.

103. Sławomir Redo, From Good Samaritan Parable to Golden Rule in Technical Assistance: The United Nations 2030 Sustainable Development Goals Agenda and Culture of Lawfulness, in Alexander Balthasar and Marcin Lech, eds., *Europäische Perspektiven des internationalen Rechts zu Beginn des 21. Jahrhunderts. Schriftenreihe der Landesvertedigunsakademie* (Wien: Jan Sramek Verlag, 2022), 73–94.

104. Adam C. Day, and Charles T. Hunt, "Stabilisation Operations and the Problem of Non-Linear Change: A Relational Approach to Intervening in Governance Ecosystems." *Stability: International Journal of Security & Development* 9, no. 1 (2020): 7, doi: https://doi.org/10.5334/sta.727.

105. Montesquieu, *The Spirit*, bk XI.7, 184.

106. Joly, *The Dialogue*, 74.

107. Joly, *The Dialogue*, 74.

108. Helmut Kury and Sławomir Redo, *Refugees*, 870–871.

109. Niccolò Machiavelli, *The Art of War.* A Revised edition of the Ellis Farneworth, transl. with an Introduction by Neal Wood (Cambridge MA: Da Capo Press, 2001), 80–81.

110. Machiavelli (a), *The Prince*, bk. IX, 90.

111. Joly, *The Dialogue*, 32.

112. Joly, *The Dialogue*, 176.

113. Joly, *The Dialogue*, 26.

114. Joly, *The Dialogue*, 26.

115. Montesquieu, *The Spirit*, bk. XIV. 2, 249 and XIV.10, 252.

116. Joly, *The Dialogue*, 167.

117. Montesquieu, *The Spirit of the Laws*, bk. XIV.13, transl. Melvyn Richter, *The Political Theory of Montesquieu* (Cambridge: Cambridge University Press, 1977), 263.

118. Wenqui Wei, Jackson G. Lu, Adam D., Galinsky *et al.* "Regional ambient temperature is associated with human personality," *Nature Human Behavior* 1 (2017): 890–895, doi:10.1038/s41562-017-0240-0.

119. Karla Hoff and Piryanka Pandey, "An experimental investigation of an Indian caste." *World Bank Policy Research Working Paper* 3351. World Bank: Washington DC, June 2004. https://bit.ly/3tM9xNM.

120. Karthik Muralidharan and Venkatesh Sundararaman, Teacher Performance Pay: Experimental Evidence from India?, *NBER Working Paper* 15323 https://bit.ly/3yF0q2Y.

121. Mikael Persson, Klas Andersson, Pär Zetterberg, Joakim Ekman and Simon Lundin, Does Deliberative Education Increase Civic Competence? Results from a Field Experiment, *Journal of Experimental Political Science* 7 (2020): 199–208, doi:10.1017/XPS.2019.29.

122. Sławomir Redo, "Is Socrates Mortal? On the Impact of Socratic Logic on Teaching and Learning the United Nations Crime Prevention Law," in Helmut Kury and Sławomir Redo, eds. *Crime Prevention and Justice in 2030. The UN and the Universal Declaration of Human Rights* (Cham: Springer, 2021), 623–636.

123. Cf. Timothy Young, "Classroom Discipline à la Niccolo Machiavelli," *Phi Delta Kappan* 60, no. 10 (June 1979): 746.

124. Redo, *For More United Nations.*

125. Quoted after Aurelian Craiutu, *A Virtue for Courageous Minds: Moderation in French Political Thought* (Princeton and Oxford: Princeton University Press, 2012), 249.

126. Quoted after Aurelian Craiutu, *Faces of Moderation: The Art of Balance in an Age of Extremes* (Haney Foundation Series/University of Pennsylvania Press. Kindle Edition), 286.

127. Uwe Backes, Meaning and Forms of Political Extremism in Past and Present, *Central European Political Studies Review* IX, no. 4 (2007): 262.

128. Tony Brenton, *The Greening of Machiavelli: The Evolution of International Environmental Politics* (London: Routledge, 2019).

129. Johnson Wright, "Montesquieuan Moments: The Spirit of the Laws and Republicanism," *Journal of the Western Society for French History* 35 (2007): 149–169.

130. *Day 8 from COP 24 in Katowice: Accelerating Climate Action and The Future of Wine* by Michele Ghering, https://bit.ly/3yHopPb.

131. Mark Hulliung, *Montesquieu and the Old Regime* (Berkeley-Los Angeles-London: University of California Press, 1976), 117.

132. Niccolò Machiavelli (b), *The Prince*, transl. Tim Parks (UK: Penguin Random House, 2014), bk. VI, 23.

133. Niccolò Machiavelli, *Discourses on Livy*, trans. Harvey C. Mansfield and Nathan Tarcov (Chicago and London: The University of Chicago Press, 1966), bk. 1, ch. 49 at 101; Thomas Karako, Understanding the Things of State: On Machiavelli's Use of Modo, Ordine, and Via, in Hugh Liebert, Gary L. McDowell, and Terry L. Price, eds. *Executive Power in Theory and Practice* (New York: Palgrave MacMillan, 2012), 73.

134. In "*The Persian Letters*" (Letter 12), in translation of Mark Huliung, *Montesquieu and the Old Regime* (Berkeley-Los Angeles-London: University of California Press, 1976), 118; Charles L. Montesquieu, *Persian Letters: With Related Texts*, ed. Raymond N. Mackenzie (Indianapolis/Cambridge: Hackett Publishing Company, Inc., 2014. Kindle Edition), Letter 12.

135. Cf. Martin Fleisher, "The Ways of Machiavelli and the Ways of Politics," *History of Political Thought* 16, no. 3 (Autumn 1995): 353.

BIBLIOGRAPHY

Arendt, Hannah. "Human Rights. What are They?" *Modern Review* 3, no. 1 (1949): 476–483.

Arendt, Hannah. "Es gibt nur ein einziges Menschenrecht." *Die Wandlung* IV (1949): 754–770.

Arendt, Hannah. Truth and Politics, in *Truth: Engagements Across Philosophical Traditions* David Wood, José Medina eds. 295–314. Oxford: Blackwell Publishing, 1967/2005.

Backes, Uwe. "Meaning and Forms of Political Extremism in Past and Present." *Central European Political Studies Review* IX, no. 4 (2007): 242–262.

Ball, Terance. "The Picaresque Prince: Reflections on Machiavelli and Moral Change." *Political Theory* 12, no. 44 (1984): 521–536.

Benziger, Felicitas. "The New Rule of Law Mechanism: 'Ideological Blackmail Tool' or Legitimate Means to Protect the EU's Values?." International Law Blog. Fresh perspectives on international law, December 15, 2020. https://bit.ly/3nKUK5X.

Berlin, Isaiah. Against the Current: Essays in the History of Ideas, 2nd ed., ed. Henry Hardy Princeton-Oxford: Princeton University Press, 2003.

Bernstein, Herman. *The Truth about "The Protocols of Zion."* New York: Covici Friede, 1935.

Blagden, David. "Induction and Deduction in International Relations: Squaring the Circle Between. Theory and Evidence." *International Studies Review* 18 (2016): 193–213.

Blau, Adrian. "Anti-Strauss." *The Journal of Politics* 74, no. 1 (2012): 142–155.

Bonfantini, Mario. *N. Machiavelli, Opere*, Ricardo Ricciardi Editore: Milán-Nápoles, 1963.

Brenton, Tony. *The Greening of Machiavelli: The Evolution of International Environmental Politics*. London: Routledge, 2019.

Cohn, Norman. *Warrant for Genocide. The Myth of the Jewish World-conspiracy and the Protocols of the Elders of Zion*. New York: Harper & Row, 1966.

Craiutu, Aurelian. *A Virtue for Courageous Minds: Moderation in French Political Thought*. Princeton and Oxford: Princeton University Press, 2012.

Craiutu, Aurelian. *Faces of Moderation: The Art of Balance in an Age of Extremes*. Haney Foundation Series/University of Pennsylvania Press. Kindle Edition.

Day, Adam C. and Charles T. Hunt. "UN Stabilisation Operations and the Problem of Non-Linear Change: A Relational Approach to Intervening in Governance."

de Michelis, Cesare. *Protocolli dei savi di Sion*. Lincoln, NE: The University of Nebraska Press, 2004.

Eco, Umberto. Introduction, in Will Eisner, *The Plot. The Secret Story of the Protocols of the Elders of Zion,* v–vii. New York-London: W. W. Norton Company, 2005.

"Ecosystems." *Stability: International Journal of Security & Development* 9, no. 1 (2020): 1–23. doi: https://doi.org/10.5334/sta.727.

Esmer, Yilmaz and Thorleif Pettersson, eds., *Measuring and Mapping Cultures: 25 Years of Comparative Values Surveys*. Leiden: Brill, 2007.

European Court of Human Rights. Case of N.D. and N.T. v. Spain. https://bit.ly /3ldbhwG.

European Strategy and Policy Analysis System. Global Trends to 2030: The Future of Migration and Integration, n.d. https://bit.ly/3yJsDpp.

Fleisher, Martin. "The Ways of Machiavelli and the Ways of Politics." *History of Political Thought* 16 (Autumn 1995), no. 3: 330–355.

Frankel, Steven. "Review: The Dialogue in Hell between Montesquieu and Machiavelli: Humanitarian Despotism and the Conditions of Modern Tyranny." *Interpretation–A Journal of Political Philosophy* 12, no. 1 (2004): 95–103.

Gehring. Michele. *Day 8 from COP 24 in Katowice: Accelerating Climate Action and The Future of Wine*. https://bit.ly/3yHopPb.

Giorgini, Giovanni. "Five Hundred Years of Italian Scholarship on Machiavelli's Prince." *The Review of Politics* 75 (2013): 625–640.

Gramsci, Antonio. *Prison notebooks*, ed. and transl. Quentin Hoare and Geoffrey Nowell Smith. ElecBook: London, 1999.

Grotius, Hugo. *The Rights of War and Peace*, edited and with an Introduction by Richard Tuck, from the Edition by Jean Barbeyrac. Indianapolis: Liberty Fund, 2005, Vol. 1.

Guterres, António. United Nations High Commissioner for Refugees; Remarks at the opening of the judicial year of the European Court of Human Rights, 28 January 2011. https://bit.ly/3Bpw6LB.

Hanasz, Wojciech. Machiavelli's Method Revisited: The Art and Science of Modelling. *The Review Journal of Political Philosophy* 8 (2010): 1–31.

Hegel, G. W. F. *Phenomenology of Spirit*, trans. AV Miller. Oxford: Oxford University Press, 1977.

Hernes, Vilde, Jacob Nielsen Arendt, Pernilla Andersson Joona and Kristian Rose Tronstad, *Nordic Integration and Settlement Policies for Refugees. A Comparative Analysis of Labour Market Integration Outcomes*. Nordic Council of Ministers: TemaNord 2019:5290.

Hoff, Karla, and Piryanka Pandey. "An experimental investigation of an Indian caste." World Bank Policy Research Working Paper 3351. World Bank: Washington DC, June 2004. https://bit.ly/3tM9xNM.

Hösle, Vittorio. "Morality and Politics: Reflections on Machiavelli's 'Prince.'" *International Journal of Politics, Culture, and Society* 3, no. 1(1989): 51–69.

Hulliung, Mark. *Montesquieu and the Old Regime*. Berkeley-Los Angeles-London: University of California Press, 1976.

International Organization for Migration. *A Complex Nexus*, n.d. https://bit.ly /2YkbLsU.

Joly, Maurice. *The Dialogue in Hell between Machiavelli and Montesquieu: Humanitarian Despotism and the Conditions of Modern Tyranny*, trans., ed. and with commentary by John S. Waggoner. Lanham-Boulder-New York-Toronto-Oxford: Lexington Books, 2003.

Karako, Thomas. Understanding the Things of State: On Machiavelli's Use of Modo, Ordine, and Via, in Hugh Liebert, Gary L. McDowell, and Terry L. Price, eds. *Executive Power in Theory and Practice,* 55–82. New York: Palgrave MacMillan, 2012.

Korab-Karpowicz, Julian. *On the History of Political Philosophy: Great Thinkers from Thucydides to Locke*. Boston: Pearson Education/Routledge: 2012/2016.

Kraft, Joseph. "Truth and Poetry in Machiavelli." *The Journal of Modern History* XXIII, no. 2 (June 1951): 109–121.

Kreeft, Peter. *Socrates Meets Machiavelli.* Ignatius Press. Kindle Edition.

Kury, Helmut and Sławomir Redo (Eds.), *Refugees and Migrants in Law and Policy. Challenges and Opportunities for Global Civic Education*, 863–913. Cham: Springer, 2018.

Macfarlane, Alan. *Montesquieu and the Making of the Modern World.* Cambridge: CAM Rivers Publishing, 2018.

Machiavelli, Niccolò (a). *The Prince*, transl. and ed. Peter Bondanella, with introduction of Mauricio Virolli. Oxford: Oxford University Press, 2008.

Machiavelli, Niccolò (b). *The Prince*, transl. Tim Parks. UK: Penguin Random House, 2014.

Machiavelli, Niccolò. *Discourses on Livy*, trans. Harvey C. Mansfield and Nathan Tarcov. Chicago and London: The University of Chicago Press, 1966.

Machiavelli, Niccolò. *History of Florence and of the Affairs of Italy. From The Earliest Times To The Death of Lorenzo the Magnificent* (USA: Start Publishing LLC, 2013).

Machiavelli, Niccolò. *The Art of War.* A Revised edition of the Ellis Farneworth, transl. with an Introduction by Neal Wood. Cambridge MA: Da Capo Press, 2001.

Machiavelli, Niccolò. *The Collected Works of Niccolò Machiavelli: The Complete Works.* PergamonMedia 2015. Kindle Edition.

McCormick, John. "Machiavelli's Agathocles: From Criminal Example to Princely Exemplum." in Michèle Lowrie and Susanne Lüdemann eds. *Exemplarity and Singularity Thinking through Particulars in Philosophy, Literature, and Law*, 123–129 London-New York: Routledge, 2016.

Menke, Christoph, Birgit Kaiser and Kathrin Thiele. "The 'Aporias of Human Rights' and the 'One Human Right': Regarding the Coherence of Hannah Arendt's Argument." *Social Research* 74, no. 3/I (2007): 739–762.

Merkle, Ortrun, Julia Reinold, and Melissa Siege, *A Study on the Link between Corruption and the Causes of Migration and Forced Displacement.* Deutsche Gesellschaft für Internationale Zusammenarbeit, 2017.

Merleau-Ponty, Maurice. A Note on Machiavelli, in Ted Toadvine, Leonard Lawlor. *The Merleau-Ponty Reader*, 123–134 (Evanston, IL: Northwestern University Press, 2007).

Montesquieu, Charles L. de Secondat, *The Spirit of Laws*, trans. T. Nugent, Kitchener, ON: Batoche Books, 2001.

Montesquieu, Charles. "Essai sur les causes qui peuvent affecter les esprits et les caracteres," in *Oeuvres completes de Montesquieu*, R. Callois, ed. 2 vols. Paris: Gallimard, 1748/1949.

Montesquieu, Charles. *My Thoughts* (*Mes Pensées*), trans., ed., and with an introduction by Henry C. Clark. Indianapolis: Liberty Fund, 2012. https://bit.ly/389a7cL.

Montesquieu. *Considerations on the Causes of the Greatness of the Romans and Their Decline*, trans. with notes and an introduction by David Lowenthal. New York/London: The Free Press/Collier-Macmillan 1794/1965.

Muralidharan, Karthik and Venkatesh Sundararaman. Teacher Performance Pay: Experimental Evidence from India?, *NBER Working Paper* 15323. https://bit.ly/3yF0q2Y.

Nederman, Cary. "Niccolò Machiavelli." In *Stanford Encyclopedia of Philosophy*. Stanford University, 1997- (Summer 2019 Edition). https://stanford.io/2QLJaci.

Niccolò Machiavelli, "Discorso o dialogo intorno alla nostra lingua," transl. William J. Landon, in *Politics, Patriotism, and Language: Niccolò Machiavelli's "Secular Patria" and the Creation of an Italian National Identity*. New York: Peter Lang Publishing, 2005.

Nunes, Joao. "Reclaiming the Political: Emancipation and Critique in Security Studies." *Security Dialogue* 43, no. 4 (2012): 345–361.

Offenheiser, Raymond C., Susan H. Holcombe. "Challenges and Opportunities in Implementing a Rights-Based Approach to Development: An Oxfam America Perspective." *Nonprofit and Voluntary Sector Quarterly* 32, no. 2 (June 2003): 268–306.

Orgad, Liav. *The Cultural Defence of Nations. A Liberal Theory of Majority Rights*. Oxford: Oxford University Press, 2015.

Orwin, Clifford. "Machiavelli's Unchristian Charity." *American Political Science Review* 72, no. 4 (Dec. 1978): 1217–1228.

Pace, Michel. Denmark's immigrants forced out by government policies, *Chatham House*, June 2021, 28. https://bit.ly/3l6SKDl.

Pate, Gayatri. "How 'Universal' Is the United Nations' Universal Periodic Review Process? An Examination of the Discussions Held on Polygamy." *Human Rights Review* 18 (2017): 459–483.

Persson, Mikael, Klas Andersson, Pär Zetterberg, Joakim Ekman and Simon Lundin. Does Deliberative Education Increase Civic Competence? Results from a Field Experiment, *Journal of Experimental Political Science* 7 (2020): 199–208. 10.1017/XPS.2019.29.

Radasanu, Andrea. "Montesquieu on Ancient Greek Foreign Relations: Toward National Self-Interest and International Peace." *Political Research Quarterly* 66, no. 1 (2013): 3–17.

Redo, Sławomir. "Criminological Reflections on the Golden Rule and Urban Stewardship for Safety." *Eastern European Journal of Transnational Relations* 2, no. 1 (2018): 57–70.

Redo, Sławomir. "For More United Nations Rule-of-Law 'Win-Win' Technical Assistance Outcomes amid Migration." *Studia Iuridica Toruniensia* XXIX (2021): 315-349.

Redo, Sławomir. "The Relevance of Philosophical and Religious Ideas to the United Nations Quest for Universalizing Criminal Justice," in Helmut Kury and Sławomir Redo, eds. *Crime Prevention and Justice in 2030. The UN and the Universal Declaration of Human Rights,* 575–602. Cham: Springer, 2021.

Redo, Sławomir. "The Transformative Power of the United Nations Post-2015 Sustainable Development Goals and Crime Prevention Education for a New Culture of Lawfulness," in John Winterdyk, ed. *Crime Prevention. International Perspectives, Issues, and Trends*, 1–32. Boca Raton-London-New York: CRC Press. Taylor & Francis Group, 2017.

Redo, Sławomir. "Is Socrates Mortal? On the Impact of Socratic Logic on Teaching and Learning the United Nations Crime Prevention Law," in Helmut Kury and Sławomir Redo, eds., *Crime Prevention and Justice in 2030. The UN and the Universal Declaration of Human Rights*, 623–636. Cham: Springer, 2021.

Redo, Sławomir. *Blue Criminology. The Power of United Nations Ideas to Counter Crime Globally,* Report Series 53 (Helsinki: European Institute for Crime Prevention and Control, affiliated with the United Nations (HEUNI)), 2012.

Redo, Sławomir. From Good Samaritan Parable to Golden Rule in Technical Assistance: The United Nations 2030 Sustainable Development Goals Agenda and Culture of Lawfulness, in Alexander Balthasar and Marcin Lech, eds., *Europäische Perspektiven des internationalen Rechts zu Beginn des 21. Jahrhunderts. Schriftenreihe der Landesvertedigunsakademie*, 74–94. Wien: Jan Sramek Verlag, 2022.

Rigby, Andrew. War, Revolution and Coronavirus: The Human Security Case for Universal Income. https://bit.ly/3iDwpeS. Accessed October 1, 2021.

Robin, Corey. "Reflections on Fear: Montesquieu in Retrieval." *American Political Science Review* 94, no. 2 (2000): 347–360.

Schwöbel, Christine E. J. *Global Constitutionalism in International Legal Perspective.* Leiden: Martinus Nijhoff Publishers, 2011.

Shackelton, Robert. *Montesquieu: A Critical Biography.* New York: Oxford University Press, 1961.

Spackman, Barbara. "Machiavelli and Maxims." *Yale French Studies* 77 (1990): 137–155.

Speier, Hans. "The Truth in Hell: Maurice Joly on Modern Despotism." *Polity* 10, no. 1 (1977): 18–32.

UN doc. A/217 III Universal Declaration of Human Rights, 10 December 1948.

UN doc. A/RES/73/195, Global Compact for Safe, Orderly and Regular Migration, 19 December 2018.

Villari, Pasquale *The Life and Times of Niccolò Machiavelli.* 2 vols. London: T.F. Unwin, 1892.

Volk, Christian. The Law of the Nations and the Civil Law of the World. On Montesquieu's Political Cosmopolitanism, in Stefan Kadelbach, Thomas Kleinlein, David Roth-Isigkeit eds., *Order, and International Law System. The Early History of International Legal Thought from Machiavelli to Hegel*, 240–262 (Oxford: Oxford University Press, 2017).

von Mohr, Robert. *Die Gesichichte und Literatur der Staatwissenschaften.* 3 vols. Erlangen: Verlag von Ferdinand Enke, 1858.

Wei, Wenqui, Jackson G. Lu, Adam D. Galinsky et al. "Regional ambient temperature is associated with human personality." *Nature Human Behavior* 1 (2017): 890–895, doi:10.1038/s41562-017-0240-0.

Wijgaarde, Inez, Jebamalai Vinanchiarachi and Jeff Readman. Universal Basic Income (UBI) for Reducing Inequalities and Increasing Socio-Economic Inclusion: A Proposal for a New Sustained Policy Perspective, in Helmut Kury and Sławomir Redo, ed., *Crime Prevention and Justice in 2030. The UN and the Universal Declaration of Human Rights,* 107–124. Cham: Springer, 2021.

Winter, Yves. *Machiavelli and the Orders of Violence.* Cambridge University Press: Cambridge, 2018.

Wright, Johnson. "Montesquieuan Moments: The Spirit of the Laws and Republicanism." *Journal of the Western Society for French History* 35 (2007): 149–169.

Young, Timothy. "Classroom Discipline à la Niccolo Machiavelli." *Phi Delta Kappan* 60, no. 10 (June 1979): 746.

Chapter 13

Faith in the United Nations and Arts Approaches to Conflict Prevention and Resolution

Marian Liebmann

INTRODUCTION

The UN naturally places great emphasis on "evidence-based crime prevention."[1] However, crime prevention through the arts is a clinical approach to conflict resolution, hence does not render itself to comparable methodological assessments with other types of crime prevention interventions. Different methods are needed to capture the effects and results of such interventions.

This may be exemplified by considering Picasso's painting *Guernica*, a mural he painted in 1937 as a protest against the bombing of the town of Guernica (a stronghold of Republican and Basque activity) by Nazi war planes. The whole town was devastated, with women and children targeted as most of the men were away fighting elsewhere. Although there are no tables of statistics citing the effect of this picture, the horrors it portrays have been seen by many around the globe, and its message about the futility of war and the evils of totalitarianism is plain to see. Spectators remember the visual impact much longer than a page of numbers. And because human beings often act from their emotions, this picture may have changed many people's attitudes toward war.

ARTISTS INSPIRED BY THE UNITED NATIONS

In the 75th year of the United Nations, it is good to reflect on the contribution of artists to the aims of the UN. In particular, Norman Rockwell, Jan Henryk de Rosen, and Sagenji Yoshida stand out as contributing to this.

NORMAN ROCKWELL (1894–1978)

Norman Rockwell's first drawing about the UN, entitled *United Nations*, was conceived in 1952 and executed in 1953, at the height of the Cold War and two years into the Korean War. His idea was to picture the United Nations as the world's hope for the future—he portrayed the founding fifty-one nations through fifty-one figures reflecting diverse cultures, religions, races, and ethnicities, to represent the aspirations of the new UN organization. It is thought he intended to use the drawing as a guide to a large painting, but it never made it to canvas.[2]

In 1961, Norman Rockwell completed his iconic painting *Golden Rule*, including the words, "Do unto other as you would have them do unto you" (common to all major religions and ecumenical philosophies) surrounded by sixty-five people representing the world's nations, using sketches from his travels and local people from different backgrounds. This painting and the drawing *United Nations* are both in the Norman Rockwell Museum, Stockbridge, Massachusetts, United States.

A mosaic version of *Golden Rule* was presented to the UN in 1985 as a gift on behalf of the United States by then-First Lady Nancy Reagan. It was the centerpiece of an exhibition in 2015, at which the then-secretary general Ban Ki-moon said, "I often walk by and see people as diverse as the painting itself–standing in awe at its moving image of humanity and its transcendent message of compassion and community that is at the heart of all world religions."[3,4]

JAN HENRYK DE ROSEN (1891–1982)

Jan Henryk de Rosen was a Polish painter and patriot, who became well known for his murals and mosaic works in cathedrals, both in Poland and in the United States, as well as several other countries. Some of his most famous works are to be found in Grace Cathedral, San Francisco, an Episcopal Cathedral founded in 1849 during the California Gold Rush.

Among these are a faux-tile mural behind the Chapel of Grace reredos from 1932, and the mural in the Chapel of the Nativity's Adoration from 1946 showing the Holy Family with the magi and shepherds. De Rosen also included a little image of his boyhood home in Warsaw in the mural. On a smaller scale, he painted exquisite panels for the original old High Altar which is now in the Chapel of St. Francis columbarium. The most visible works of De Rosen in Grace Cathedral are the historical aisle murals painted between 1949 and 1950, composed in a style blending elements of the early Italian masters Giotto and Mantegna. The cathedral is an international pilgrimage center.[5]

The original charter for the UN was signed in San Francisco, and its 50th anniversary celebration was held at Grace Cathedral in 1995. At that occasion, the idea was born to use this as the impetus to create a "United Religions" organization. After five years of planning, the Charter of the United Religions Initiative (URI) was signed, in June 2000. In 2015, the URI was invited to join the 70th anniversary of the creation of the United Nations at a day-long celebration at Grace Cathedral. The shared anniversary was no coincidence, as the URI takes its inspiration from the United Nations. It is seen by many as a positive, nonmilitary approach that may help deal with the rising violence of religious extremism.[6]

SAGENJI YOSHIDA (1925–1999)

Sagenji Yoshida was a designer and academic from Japan, professor at Tokyo University of the Arts.[7] One of his pictures, donated by the Asia Crime Prevention Foundation, hangs in a central position in the Rotunda of the Vienna International Centre, Ho-o Raigi (The Sacred Birds). "The sacred birds will descend to earth only when peace and justice rule the world," said the artist.[8] The two gold-dipped peace phoenixes invite every viewer to participate in the goal that is the center of all the efforts of the United Nations: peace. The paintings are based on one of the five scriptures of ancient Chinese Reiki philosophy.

BEETHOVEN'S NINTH SYMPHONY: ODE TO JOY

It is a firm tradition that the UN marks United Nations Day on October 24 each year with a concert including the final movement of Beethoven's Ninth Symphony in D Minor (1824), based on Schiller's poem "Ode to Joy" (1785).[9] In October 1960, Dag Hammarskjöld, the secretary general, announced that the concert that year would include the symphony in its entirety. He and colleagues died in an airplane crash at Ndola, Zambia, on September 18, 1961, and the symphony was played again as a tribute to him.

In his talk, Dag Hammarskjöld described the music as moving from harsh conflict and dark threats to the theme of reconciliation and joy in the last movement. He added:

> The road of Beethoven in his Ninth Symphony is also the road followed by the authors of the Preamble of the Charter. It begins with the recognition of the threat under which we all live, speaking as it does of the need to save succeeding generations from the scourge of war which has brought untold sorrow

> to mankind. It moves on to a reaffirmation of faith in the dignity and worth of the human person. And it ends with the promise to practice tolerance and live together in peace with one another as good neighbors and to unite our strength to maintain peace.[10]

Beethoven's Ninth Symphony has also been used to inaugurate or signify other important political events. In 1972, the Council of Europe adopted the prelude to the "Ode to Joy" as the Anthem of Europe to celebrate the shared values of the member states. In 1985, European Union leaders chose it as the official anthem of the EU. It was also used as a protest anthem by demonstrators in Chile during the Pinochet dictatorship. In 1989, Leonard Bernstein conducted a version of the symphony at the Brandenburg Gate to celebrate the fall of the Berlin Wall.[11] Last but not least, in 2021, the Ode was played as a part of an online video concert at the closure of the Fourteenth United Nations Congress on Crime Prevention and Criminal Justice.

QUAKER WORK IN CRIMINAL JUSTICE AT THE UNITED NATIONS

For over 350 years, Quakers have been deeply concerned about prison conditions, based on their own experience of suffering for their beliefs in British jails. Their belief of "that of God in everyone" has led them to emphasize the treatment and reinstatement of those who have offended against the law, rather than their punishment. There is a tradition of Quaker work in penal reform including work in prisons and community support. Quaker activity in criminal justice relates particularly to the testimonies to peace, community, and equality. Quakers also helped to start the two oldest human rights and penal reform organizations, Anti-Slavery International and the Howard League for Penal Reform.

The following quotation sums up the Quaker approach:

> We believe in overcoming evil with good. We must speak and act from our own inner light to the inner light in all others as Jesus did. He showed and taught love, respect and concern for all, particularly those rejected by others, reaching out to the good in them.

Nor in general does this loving approach have lesser expectations or demand less responsibility than does the infliction and acceptance of punishment. In personal relationships and in the broader context of community and international affairs, a positive response to aberrant or destructive behavior through reconciliation, restitution, and reparation may take longer but it will be more likely to encourage the good in all parties, restore those who are damaged, reduce resentment and bitterness, and enable all those involved to move toward fuller integration.[12]

Quakers believe that people have the potential to change. They value rehabilitation and education because these present people with opportunities to find and develop the best in themselves. They have campaigned for educational opportunities so that prisoners can find work when they are released. They advocate for improvements in prison conditions both because of the belief in treating people as equally as possible, and because they see better conditions as more conducive to rehabilitation. They have campaigned against the death penalty from their beginning in England in the 1650s and continue to do so.

Besides campaigning for change in the criminal justice system, Quakers have worked as judges, lawyers, police chiefs, prison directors, psychologists, psychiatrists, and prison chaplains, seeking to make changes from within. A particular example is the *Alternatives to Violence Project (AVP)*, begun in a New York jail in 1975 by Quakers responding to a request from prisoners for help in managing and reducing violent emotions and actions. Quakers presented this project as an example of violence prevention at a workshop at the 1995 UN Congress on Crime Prevention and the Treatment of Offenders in Cairo, Egypt. AVP[13] has now spread worldwide. In local communities Quakers are probation officers, hostel wardens, social workers, and victim support workers.[14]

Since 1985, a team of Quakers representing Friends World Committee for Consultation (Quakers) has participated in the UN Crime Prevention Congresses and Commissions. The Quaker delegations have been active participants, initiating ancillary meetings and workshops, and contributing relevant statements to plenary sessions. Their interests focus on the humanitarian aspects of criminal justice, such as rehabilitation of offenders, prison standards, use of firearms by law enforcement officials, life imprisonment, women in prison (now covered by the Bangkok Rules),[15] rights of children of prisoners and restorative justice. Workshops have included human trafficking, race in prisons, life sentences, the death penalty, minimum standards in prisons, and several aspects of restorative justice.

Many of the issues raised by Quakers at the United Nations come from studies carried out by the Quaker United Nations Office (QUNO) in Geneva and the Quaker Council for European Affairs in Brussels (QCEA),[16] for example, the Council of Europe's 1989 report, *Violence and Conflict Resolution in Schools.*[17]

Quakers have collaborated with other NGOs, such as the Howard League for Penal Reform,[18,19] Penal Reform International,[20] the International Commission of Catholic Prison Pastoral Care,[21] the Academic Council on the United Nations Systems,[22] and the World Society of Victimology.[23] They have contributed to expert group meetings on the *Handbook on Restorative Justice Programmes*,[24] resettlement and reintegration, and both the Bangkok Rules[25] and the Nelson Mandela Rules.[26]

These activities are in line with wider Quaker work on peace. In 1947, the Nobel Peace Prize was awarded jointly to Friends Service Council (Quakers) and American Friends Service Committee (Quakers) "for their pioneering work in the international peace movement and compassionate effort to relieve human suffering, thereby promoting the fraternity between nations." Friends World Committee for Consultation has held special consultative status as a nongovernmental organization since 1948 and general consultative status since 2002, allowing Quakers an active role in the UN.

In September 2015, the UN General Assembly adopted the 2030 Agenda for Sustainable Development that includes seventeen Sustainable Development Goals (SDGs). SDG 16 is the one most applicable to work in the criminal justice field: "Promote peaceful and inclusive societies for sustainable development, provide access to justice for all and build effective, accountable and inclusive institutions at all levels."

The Quaker work at the UN seeks to contribute toward achieving this end.[27]

RESTORATIVE JUSTICE: A SPECIAL INTEREST

In 1990, Quakers presented a statement to the Eighth UN Congress, emphasizing a justice system based on healing rather than revenge, and addressing the needs of victims, offenders and the community, rather than demanding punitive sanctions. This statement was the first on restorative justice to be made at the United Nations.[28] An outcome was the UN basic principles on the use of restorative justice in criminal matters in 2002.

Quakers continue to be very active in the development of restorative justice. This goes beyond concern for the prisoner to concern for the individuals and communities they have offended against, and harmed in some way. Restorative approaches involve ways of repairing the psychological and financial harm caused to victims, for example, by answering questions from the victim, making recompense, or some form of community service.

Restorative approaches involve the following elements:

- victim support and healing is a priority;
- offenders take responsibility for what they have done;
- there is dialogue to achieve understanding;
- offenders try to put right the harm done;
- offenders are supported in ways to avoid future offending;
- the community helps to reintegrate both victim and offender.

I have been part of the Quaker team for nearly twenty years, attending the sessions of the UN Commission on Crime Prevention and Criminal Justice in Vienna most years, and the Congresses in 2005, 2010, and 2015, in Bangkok, Salvador (Brazil), and Qatar respectively. My inputs have focused on restorative justice, as that is my field of experience and expertise, having been involved in the field since 1984.

MY WORK HISTORY

It may seem strange to include this, but without it the subsequent sections will make less sense.

At school I was an "all-rounder," equally good at most subjects. I had always loved art, but parental guidance meant that this was not regarded as a career choice. So when the time came to specialize, I chose science subjects as more useful. After university (Oxford), where I studied physics and mathematics, I trained as a teacher, and taught mathematics for three years in a junior high school. This was followed by a period of writing (and drawing) visual aids for mathematics in schools, a creative job but with little outside contact.

I was missing the human interaction, so went into adult education, in a day center for ex-offenders. There I ran literacy classes, role-play sessions, art classes and small group therapy sessions, and learned much about the world of offenders. I then trained as an art therapist but there were no jobs. I was lucky to find a job coordinating the first Victim Support Service, which gave me a useful perspective when I then trained as a probation officer. I could no longer just ignore what my clients had done, and was probably one of the first probation officers to talk to them about their victims and the harm they had caused (most probation work till then had focused on helping offenders with such things as accommodation and jobs).

Just before training as a probation officer, I discovered mediation. I attended a course in London run by two trainers from Philadelphia (USA), and "the lights went on" in my head. So when I was working in probation, I used this training and undertook several victim-offender mediations—the label "restorative justice" came later. I also ran courses for other staff promoting the idea. Fortunately, my chief probation officer gave me approval and backing, as the layers of management in between had little understanding of restorative justice.

I had joined Mediation UK (in its former guise as the Forum for Initiatives in Reparation and Mediation) as a member, and the post of director came up. I applied and was appointed. My job was to promote the concepts and practice of mediation in the fields of community, schools and criminal justice, as well as to fundraise to keep the organization afloat. The work in community mediation expanded rapidly to about 120 services, but there was continuing government reticence to support restorative justice.

After four years, I left the post of director, for family reasons—I was away from home too much. But I continued part-time as projects adviser, concentrating on the new (Labour) government interest in restorative justice. But with a downturn in funding, I and other staff were made redundant in 1998, and Mediation UK lost its funding completely and closed in 2006. So from 1998, I became an independent trainer and consultant in restorative justice, and have been fortunate in having opportunities to work in many different countries, especially in Africa and Eastern Europe.

Alongside the part-time work for Mediation UK, I also obtained a post as art therapist in an inner-city mental health team, where I developed work on art therapy and anger, using my previous experience in probation. I retired from this post in 2014, but still run art therapy workshops on conflict and anger themes, and undertake supervision of art therapists.

These varied experiences have focused on my two main passions, mediation/restorative justice and art therapy. And I have been very interested in exploring the boundaries and overlaps between these. Out of these have come my writings—I have written/edited twelve books on these subjects (and many chapters in other books), all of them in response to particular needs in the field.

WRITINGS—A SELECTION

Below I describe the books I have written/edited which are relevant to the theme of this chapter (there are others not included here).

Art Therapy for Groups (1st edition London: Croom Helm 1986, 2nd edition London: Routledge 2004).

- This book describes the practice of theme-based art therapy group work: how to run such groups, with examples and case studies, followed by over 300 themes to use with groups.

Art Therapy in Practice (London: Jessica Kingsley Publishers 1990, edited).

- This book describes art therapy practice in a variety of contexts in one geographical area, Bristol. It is designed to be accessible to other professionals, such as nurses, doctors, psychologists, social workers—people who might refer clients to art therapy.

Art Therapy with Offenders (London: Jessica Kingsley Publishers 1994, edited).

- Art therapy work with prisoners helps them to cope with their sentences and life in prison; and work with offenders in the community and in mental health secure units helps them to understand their offending, and avoid offending in the future.

Arts Approaches to Conflict (London: Jessica Kingsley Publishers 1996, edited).

- This book explores how the arts can be used to work with conflict. It includes drama, visual arts, music, movement, and storytelling; and a section on combined arts. It is still the only book on this topic, as far as I know.

Community and Neighbour Mediation (London: Cavendish Publishing Ltd 1998, edited).

- Community mediation includes mediation between disputing neighbors and other community issues. This book includes definitions, history, the mediation process, different models for delivering mediation, training and support of mediators, case studies, standards and accreditation, evaluation, and research.

Art Therapy, Race and Culture, jointly edited with Jean Campbell, Frederica Brooks, Jenny Jones and Cathy Ward (London: Jessica Kingsley Publishers 1999).

- This encourages art therapists to look constructively at race and culture, to acknowledge and celebrate them, rather than regard them as "problems" to be avoided. The book challenges traditional Eurocentric therapy practice and explores other more culturally appropriate models.

Mediation in Context (London: Jessica Kingsley Publishers 2000, edited).

- This book shows how mediation works in different contexts—family, schools, community (urban and rural), victim-offender, labor relations, workplace, commercial, medical, elders, environment and international.

Restorative Justice: How It Works (London: Jessica Kingsley Publishers 2007a).

- This book explains restorative justice to a wide audience, with over 200 case studies in a variety of contexts. It is the only restorative justice book to contain a chapter on arts approaches.

Art Therapy and Anger (London: Jessica Kingsley Publishers 2008, edited).

- This book shows the special contribution of art therapy to help people who have problems managing their anger. It includes work with children, offenders, mental health problems, new mothers, brain damage, cancer care, and a war veteran.

ARTS IN CRIMINAL JUSTICE

It is important to make a distinction between arts and arts therapy, although there are many overlaps. Arts work in criminal justice usually focuses on an activity—visual art, drama, music, dance movement, writing—with an end-point in mind, such as an exhibition, concert or play. These activities can be undertaken by others about criminal justice issues or involve offenders (and sometimes victims) as participants. Along the way, participants usually gain great benefit, sometimes life-changing in personal terms, or an entry into a new career they had never considered, such as artist or actor.

Arts therapy focuses on the personal needs of the participants, and here arts can make a big contribution to people who often have limited ability or experience of explaining themselves verbally. Arts can form a bridge to dealing with long-standing issues for offenders (and for victims). Along the way, participants may produce some good art or music, but that is not the main purpose. And sometimes art therapy leads clients to discover art, and they then enroll in art classes to pursue art for its own sake.

Most of my work has been with art therapy but I will include some examples of arts work in criminal justice here.

- *Koestler Arts* is the UK's best-known prison arts charity. It encourages people in the criminal justice system to change their lives by participating in the arts. They share their artworks with the public, so people can witness this diverse range of voices, stories, and talent. Every year, they have a large annual exhibition in a well-known concert hall, displaying the best from thousands of entries from prisons and secure units all over the UK. The exhibition is curated by different people each year, including actors in the criminal justice system, and the exhibition is staffed by trained ex-offenders. There are many awards for participants, paid for by members of the public.[29]

- *Shakespeare Comes to Broadmoor* is the title of a book recounting the performance of several of Shakespeare's tragedies in Broadmoor Hospital (a high secure mental health institution), to an audience of patients and staff. The performances were given by actors from the Royal Shakespeare Company, the Royal National Theatre, and a local amateur drama group. Workshops took place after the performances. Many of the issues raised by the plays had a ready resonance with the world of forensic psychotherapy.[30]

- *Playing for Time Theatre Company*, based in Winchester, was a collaboration between the University of Winchester and two prisons (one female, one male) over eleven years. Between 2003 and 2014, the project produced eleven plays attended by members of the public, including prisoners' families and friends. Four of the plays were specially commissioned for the project. Working with education staff, the project fostered the learning of many transferable skills, both cognitive and interpersonal. In an interview afterwards, one prisoner said, "Doing something like a play builds your character, it builds your self-esteem, builds your confidence. When you get out for a job interview, you get the confidence to sit in front of somebody." Sadly, the work finished in 2014, due to lack of funds.[31]

- *Geese Theatre* and *Clean Break Theatre* Companies are two other leading theater companies working in the criminal justice system in the UK. *Geese Theatre* specializes in the use of masks. *Clean Break Theatre* works with women in prison and in the community. And there are many more.[32,33]

Changing Tunes is a charity that uses music and mentoring to help people lead meaningful lives, free from crime. It was started by one man taking his guitar into Bristol prison in 1987 and being amazed at the difference learning and playing music together made to people's life chances. The project slowly grew to include new prisons and now works in several prisons in southwest England and the Midlands. The organization employs a diverse group of musicians who hold regular workshops in prisons and occasionally organize concerts in prisons and the community. "Our tutor is patient, doesn't judge us, and has helped me calm down through learning music," said one participant. Another said, after his release, "Working with *Changing Tunes* made me feel life is worth living."[34]

The National Criminal Justice Arts Alliance (UK) promotes arts organizations working in criminal justice, supports, and informs policy in this area and has an online Evidence Library which contains research and evaluation reports on the impact of the arts in criminal justice.[35]

ARTS AND CONFLICT

The arts have long been used to portray and describe conflict, whether in pictures of battle scenes, epic poems of heroism, clashing music, or plays depicting family and societal conflict. I have already mentioned Picasso's *Guernica* as a famous example. So it would seem a natural step to use the arts to resolve or transform conflict.

Arts approaches can provide special opportunities to develop and practice skills of conflict resolution:

- they involve participants actively, so that they actually experience—in role play for example—someone else's point of view;
- the engagement in an external activity can provide a new perspective, which may help resolve a situation;
- people can try out different options and ways of being, using arts media in a frame of reference parallel to everyday life;
- involvement in the arts engages the whole person, using their creativity and emotions, giving rise to new insights which may help change a situation;
- cooperative arts projects can teach methods of working together and resolving conflicts as they arise;
- Arts approaches can help those with limited verbal skills.[36]

My book *Arts Approaches to Conflict* contains examples of projects—drama, music, art, dance movement—which use the media to understand and resolve conflicts in a variety of ways. They cover different contexts, including schools, probation services, and prisons. I will choose just one example to illustrate the possibilities.

In a group of adults attending a set of sessions on "Art and Conflict," one exercise was to share a piece of paper without talking. One pair drew a line down the middle and determinedly kept to their own sides. In another pair (see figure 13.1: Two ways of sharing), one person kept gently to her side of the paper (on the left), with watery pinks and blues, while her partner (on the right) tried ever harder to engage her, which was interpreted as encroachment. In discussion, it became apparent that they had very different concepts of sharing: The person on the left thinking both would keep to their own sides of the paper, the person on the right thinking both would share the whole space. This difference can lie at the base of many conflicts, whether family or workplace or even international.[37]

Michelle LeBaron has done much recent work in this area, showing how artists can lead the way in resolving conflicts on a societal level. She calls such practices Transformative Arts Practices, which she describes as

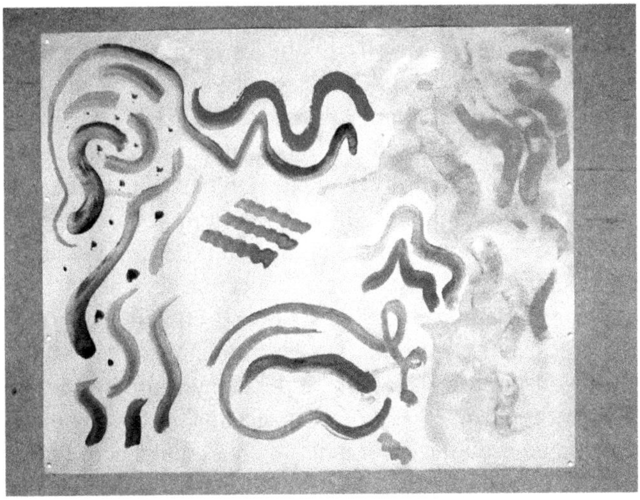

Figure 13.1 Two Ways of Sharing. *Photo credit: Marian Liebmann & Jessica Kingsley Publishers.*

"inclusive, welcoming diverse participants in the interests of resonant values such as strengthening belonging, building local capacity, leveraging community connections, increasing participation, and enhancing justice." She draws many of her examples from South and East Africa, providing a cross-cultural understanding of such arts work.[38]

MUSIC AND RECONCILIATION

Music Education and SDGs

In September 2015, the UN adopted the document *Transforming Our World: The 2030 Agenda for Sustainable Development*, a global agenda on sustainable development until 2030. There are seventeen Sustainable Development Goals, starting with SDG 1 "End poverty in all its forms everywhere" and including SDG 16 "Promote peaceful and inclusive societies for sustainable development, provide access to justice for all and build effective, accountable and inclusive institutions at all levels," probably the most relevant one to criminal justice concerns. The document *Culture in the Sustainable Development Goals: A Guide for Local Action* shows what cities can do to place culture at the center of local policies;[39] and the report *Culture in the Implementation of the 2030 Agenda: A Report by the Culture 2030 Goal Campaign* charts the progress of the campaign to include culture over the first four years of the SDGs.[40]

Several documents identify strands of music education as being particularly helpful in working toward sustainable development. It can bring about harmony, as shown by the World Orchestra of Peace founded by Georg Solti and the West-Eastern Divan Orchestra founded by Daniel Barenboim. It can help youth toward a positive future instead of gang violence, as shown by El Sistema and the Simon Bolivar Youth Orchestra in Venezuela.[41] More recently, the Isolation Choir has shown how remote voices can be pulled together during Covid times, alleviating mental health problems.

Ogunrinade points out how music education in the African context involves learning skills useful for life (cooperation and self-expression) and also for making a living, resulting in economic sustainability.[42] UNITAR (United Nations Institute for Training and Research) organized a seminar in November 2018 on music education and sustainable development, showing how music could be used internationally to create links between cultures.[43]

MUSIC IN CONFLICT RESOLUTION

In writing this section, I am indebted to two very experienced practitioners and theoreticians, who have practiced in this area for many years: Mark Smulian and June Boyce-Tillman. Both of them emphasize the role that music can have for everyone, as a source of enjoyment and also as a non-threatening nonverbal process which can help to bridge social and political divides.

Mark Smulian's work has included work with Israeli and Palestinian groups:

> The very act of "making" music with people who are our "enemies" transported us all to a space where the individual came into focus and ceased to be part of a larger, more threatening group.

He calls this the "Zone," a term also used by other people.[44] Out of these encounters, he formed the band WhiteFlag, which has toured internationally for many years. He calls it the Music of Compromise, based on listening, respect, and responsibility. Through music-making, people can begin to adopt some of the skills and attitudes and transfer them to everyday life. The building of trust is one of the most important elements of this. He sums up his work in one sentence: "Music does not assist the dialogue, music is the dialogue."

June Boyce-Tillman's work has spanned many spheres, mostly centered on music education in its widest sense, and moving on to music, healing, and spirituality. For many years, she worked in schools, where she helped groups of children to appreciate music through listening, performing, and composing. In all these aspects, she emphasized unity in diversity, using different methods of including individuals in cooperative activities, also using them to build social cohesion after conflicts.[45]

In her more recent work, June Boyce-Tillman has developed large-scale events on themes of peace, "Space for Peace," which also model the process of peaceful interaction.[46] She works with many groups from different parts of the community—schoolchildren, professional singers, people with learning disabilities, religious congregations and leaders (e.g., Muslim imams and Jewish rabbis and cantors), community choirs—who rehearse their own contributions as well as some simple peace chants. This involves a huge organizational cooperation. These often-disparate groups then perform in a cathedral where chairs have been removed to provide more space. She describes the concept of "liminality":

- a feeling of difference in relationship leading to a deep sense of peace;
- a paradoxical knowing so that diversity can exist within it easily;
- a sense of empowerment, bliss, realization;
- a feeling of an opening-up in the experience as boundaries start to dissolve;
- a sense of transformation, change.

June Boyce-Tillman also points out the work of Vegar Jordanger, who took Guided Imagery and Music to a critical phase of a dialogue with Chechen, North Ossetian, and Russian participants. This did not erase the differences, but resulted in transformation of group emotional tensions into a flowing "moment" of "collective vulnerability," resulting in a reconfiguration of human relations.[47]

ART THERAPY AND CRIMINAL JUSTICE

Narrative Approach: Use of Comic Strips

While I was working as a probation officer, I had the freedom to use art therapy approaches with several clients (I had qualified as an art therapist before working in probation). I found that comic strips or graphic stories were a very suitable medium for working with crime events. I asked probation clients (if they were willing to use simple art materials) if they could draw the events that led up to their crime. Many probation clients are not very articulate verbally, so this method was able to get beyond words, and also involved clients in telling their story from their own point of view. It could help them see what had led up to their offense, and then maybe see how they could avoid the offense next time. It could show patterns of offending and factors which were not obvious from verbal accounts, and also suggest areas for future work.

One of my first clients to do this had committed a sexual offense against a young woman on a bus, putting his hand up her skirt. When Ray described what led up to his offense, he said his car would not start and he was late for work. It was raining as he set out for the bus. He just missed one and caught the next, very worried about being late. I imagined a crowded bus and my client squeezing into a seat next to the young woman, and then maybe a conversation that went too far. However, his comic strip showed an empty bus apart from one person—the young woman. He went and sat next to her, then committed the offense. When I asked him when he knew he was going to commit the offense, he pointed to the picture where he was getting on the bus. So the offense was much more deliberate than his verbal account suggested.

The other interesting thing about the drawing was that he had drawn himself and the young woman side by side, both facing forward, not toward each other. This suggested to me that the offense was not about a relationship at all. Not wanting to leap to conclusions, I asked if he would draw a comic strip for his previous—and similar—offense. He had offered a lift to a local woman he only knew slightly "with a bit of a reputation" waiting at a bus stop. As they drove off, he put his arm across on to her leg. Again, he drew both of them looking straight ahead and talked of her as "forbidden fruit" rather than as a person.

This gave rise to much constructive work. It seemed that Ray committed sexual offenses when he was stressed, so one way to prevent them was for him to talk about his worries and try to get help with them. He also admitted to sexual fantasies, and was willing to attend a sex-offenders group which proved very helpful.[48]

Another client was a sixteen-year-old boy with a mild learning disability. He could write his name but little more. He had just left a special school where he had a reputation for violence. With violent offenses especially, offenders often say, "It just happened, I lost control and I can't remember anything." Asking them to draw a comic strip of the offense and how they came to commit it often helps them remember what happened. This then helps offenders acknowledge their responsibility and begin to look at the impact of their offense on their victim.[49],[50],[51]

The example in figure 13.2 (Comic strip of offense) shows one of Don's comic strips after he assaulted a girl at a bus stop.

1. Don and a friend at a bus stop (Don on the left).
2. Don going to the shop to buy a drink and a bar of chocolate.
3. Don back in the bus queue with two girls behind him.

Figure 13.2 Comic Strip of Offense. *Photo credit: Marian Liebmann & Jessica Kingsley Publishers.*

4. Don's friend making suggestive comments about the two girls.
5. The bus comes, with a crowd of people waiting to get on.
6. Don throws his drinks can on the ground but it goes on the girl's dress behind him. She is very angry. Don apologizes, but she is still angry.
7. Don punches her and she falls backward.
8. Everyone rushes over to her and Don runs off, now a little stick figure.
9. The bus stops, Don gets on and hides behind a seat in panic, as he hears sirens of ambulances rushing toward the scene.

Don had no prior relationship with the girl, and realized he was wrong to hit her, and felt ashamed. We were able to discuss how he could avoid such situations. This then led on to other work, in which Don did many pictures over a year.

He had a confused view of his violent father, so I suggested he drew a good and bad memory of him. His bad memory (see figure 13.3: Bad memory of father) shows his father drinking and beating Don up, with blood pouring out of Don's nose, mouth, and chest. His family and school assumed he would grow up to be like his father, so we discussed how he could include the "good bits" without the "bad bits." Three months later, he proudly told me he had achieved an incident-free week and had walked away from a potentially

Figure 13.3 Bad Memory of Father. *Photo credit: Marian Liebmann & Jessica Kingsley Publishers.*

Figure 13.4 Walking Away from Violence. *Photo credit: Marian Liebmann & Jessica Kingsley Publishers.*

violent situation (see figure 13.4: Walking away from violence). Doing the picture seemed to consolidate his new belief that he could change.[52,53]

VICTIM IMPACT WORK

Leicestershire Mediation Services developed the use of drawings as part of their Victim Impact Work with young offenders through the local Youth

Offending Team. They also used this approach with adult offenders. The program consisted of a five-session package of individual work, of which the first three sessions analyzed offenses from a victim perspective and the last two concentrated on developing strategies to avoid reoffending. The three "victim perspective" sessions took the client through an offense as experienced by:

1. The actual victim;
2. A "significant other" (of the client, e.g., mother, grandmother);
3. The client as a victim.

Each session looked at the victim's experience before, during, and after the offense. At each stage the physical, emotional, and cognitive/mental effects were examined.

Many clients have low emotional literacy and find these exercises really difficult. Visual methods can help to overcome this. Some of the techniques used were:

- Selecting images from a set of photographs to show how they thought victims might be feeling.
- Asking clients to make an image of their own victim if they could—if not, then an image of a "significant other" as victim.
- Asking clients to imagine a "pile of worries" a victim might have.
- Asking clients to draw the physical effects of their crime on a victim, e.g., churning stomach, feeling sick, headache.

Drawing pictures helped to make the effects more real than just talking, so that an emotional connection was made. Although this work was a self-contained package, it could also be part of preparation for restorative meetings with victims, if they wished to be involved.

An example of this kind of work took place with a young offender who had burgled the house of an elderly widow. He drew two pictures of his victim, Mary, before and after the burglary (see figures 13.5: Mary—before, and 13.6: Mary—after). The "before" picture shows an elderly but fit woman with gardening tools, smiling, labeled "Active, happy, lively and content." The "after" picture shows her downcast and immobile in a large armchair, labeled "Miserable, slumped, depressed, aged, broken, defeated, exhausted and losing the plot." This was then used to increase motivation to look at strategies for staying out of crime and making changes in lifestyle to achieve this.[54,55]

Figure 13.5 Mary–Before. *Photo credit: Marian Liebmann & Jessica Kingsley Publishers.*

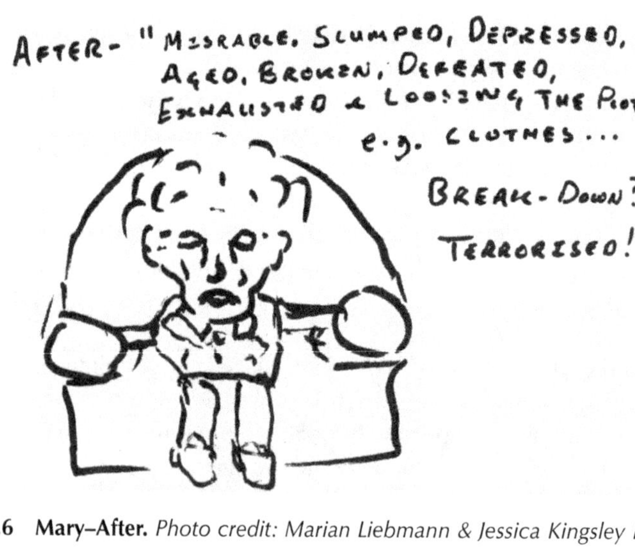

Figure 13.6 Mary–After. *Photo credit: Marian Liebmann & Jessica Kingsley Publishers.*

WORKING WITH ANGER: INDIVIDUAL WORK

This developed out of my work with offenders and comic strips. Anger is not the same as violence, but is often confused with it or is a precursor of violence. There seems to be a rising tide of unmanageable anger in children and adults in many societies—often with good reason. Anger often leads up to or is part of criminal events.

Anger involves the mind, the body and behavior—for "violent people," there may be habits built up over years to cope with emotional stress. So to be successful, anger management programs need to include three elements:

- The mind: Helping people to identify the perceptions and interpretations that generate anger;
- The body: Teaching relaxation and cooling-down techniques to help people to calm down so that they can think about things (when people are at the height of their anger, they are so aroused that they cannot think at all);
- Behavior: Teaching new skills, for example, assertiveness.

So anger management manuals tend to include:

- Exploration of what anger means to people;
- Anger diaries;
- Challenging perceptions;
- Awareness of physical symptoms;
- Relaxation techniques;
- Assertiveness;
- Positive self-talk.

My work on anger started with cofacilitating groups for violent offenders on probation (run along cognitive behavioral lines). I also worked with individuals to explore their violent behavior, what led up to it and how to develop alternative strategies of dealing with the situation. Several of them found such strategies quite alien to them at first, but came to value them in helping to keep them out of trouble.

Then I spent nineteen years as an art therapist working with individuals and groups in a Community Mental Health Team, and in response to a consultant psychiatrist asking, "Who can help me with all these angry clients?," developed a themed art therapy group on anger management. I ran this several times, with good results. More recently, I have run similar groups in African countries (Rwanda, South Africa, Tanzania, Uganda) mostly in the aftermath of war and violence.

Anger is a complex emotion, and, therefore, needs a complex response. Art therapy involves doing, thinking and feeling, as well as talking, so may have something particular to offer.

- It provides another way to communicate for people who find it hard to articulate verbally why they get angry;

- The process of doing the artwork slows clients down and helps them to reflect more on what is going on;
- Using art can be a less threatening way to approach issues;
- Using art provides the possibility of including many thoughts and feelings, often contradictory, on one page;
- There is no "right" or "wrong" way of doing art, so it provides a relief from the pressures of goal-oriented work;
- In group work, sharing the artwork helps people realize that they have things in common with each other, thereby overcoming isolation.[56]

WORKING WITH ANGER: THEMED GROUP

The themes I developed are based on a mixture of those used with probation clients, together with other exercises I have found helpful. They form a ten-session group.

1. *Introductions and ground rules*—essential for a group often frightened of their own and others' anger and possible violence. This session also includes a short time for participants to introduce themselves using dry art materials, such as pencils, oil pastels and felt-tip pens, before providing a wider range of art materials such as paints and clay.
2. *Relaxation and guided imagery*—relaxation is an important skill to learn, and guided imagery introduces the idea of a mental "safe place" to imagine in times of stress. This is followed up with a ten-minute relaxation at the end of each subsequent session, to embed the skill and provide a way of debriefing from any upsetting material in the session.
3. *What is anger?* What does it look like? Participants are often amazed at the different forms that anger can take, when they look at others' pictures—it can be portrayed as an explosion, an outburst, a "shut door," a spider's web, silence, and more.

4a. *Physical symptoms of anger*—this can include everyone's symptoms in the group on one "body outline" on a large piece of paper, turning a placid-looking person into a gruesome monster. The importance of this exercise is that physical symptoms often "kick in" before people realize "I am angry," so awareness of one's own physical symptoms can give time to take oneself out of a situation that can lead to destructive anger.

4b. *Anger—good or bad?* This exercise is often a surprise to participants, who may have been "sent" (though it is important to emphasize voluntary participation) or be preoccupied with the trouble they have experienced through their anger. Anger is important in protecting oneself or as a motivation to put injustices right.

5. *What's underneath the anger?* This is a key exercise focusing on identifying the hurt, unmet needs, and fears underlying anger, and can provide a way forward in working out how to meet the unmet needs and deal with the fears.
6. *Early family patterns*—this exercise often uncovers abuse in the family, and should be handled with care. It is placed two-thirds of the way through the group to allow for trust to build up, and also leaves enough time to debrief if it is upsetting. In short-term workshops, I usually omit this exercise.
7. *Anger and conflict*—this helps participants to look at the interaction between conflict and anger—conflict may lead to anger, or vice versa.
8. *Feelings and assertiveness, I-messages*—assertiveness (often using "I-messages") is a skill that helps people to stand up for themselves and speak about how they are affected by a situation, without attacking other people. In terms of art, I have translated the concept of assertiveness into art work about "the real you."
9. *Picture review*—this gives participants a chance to review their work and make a visual response to it.
10. *Group picture and ending*—there are many ways of doing this, for example, a joint picture, or people drawing/making gifts for each other, to round off the group and reflect on their learning.[57,58]

Steve was in his early thirties and suffered from depression, but also had long-standing problems with alcohol and anger. He had served several prison sentences for violence, and was rather skeptical about art therapy, but saw that he needed to do something about his anger. He explained, "I totally overreact and flip most of the time. I'm on my guard all the time. I'd like to be able to put my point across without being aggressive and violent, and handle wrong looks and bad-mouthing with different strategies." Two of his pictures illustrate this. Figure 13.7 (Anger = Violence) shows various implements of violence and figure 13.8 (Anger = Crime) shows Steve in prison, cut off from his partner and son. Clearly, he needed to "uncouple" anger from violence and crime, if he was going to have a chance of a nonviolent and crime-free life. He completed the group, acknowledging that it had (surprisingly, he said) kept him out of trouble. His picture of "the real you" (see figure 13.9: Peace, harmony, happiness) shows him playing with his son, with the anger, stress, and hurt lifting off. He arranged to continue the work with his probation officer.[59],[60]

Two books have been published in the UK to highlight arts therapies with offenders—*Art Therapy with Offenders*,[61] already mentioned above, and *Forensic Arts Therapies: Anthology of Practice and Research*.[62] The latter book extends the former by including all the arts therapies: visual art, music, drama, and dance movement.

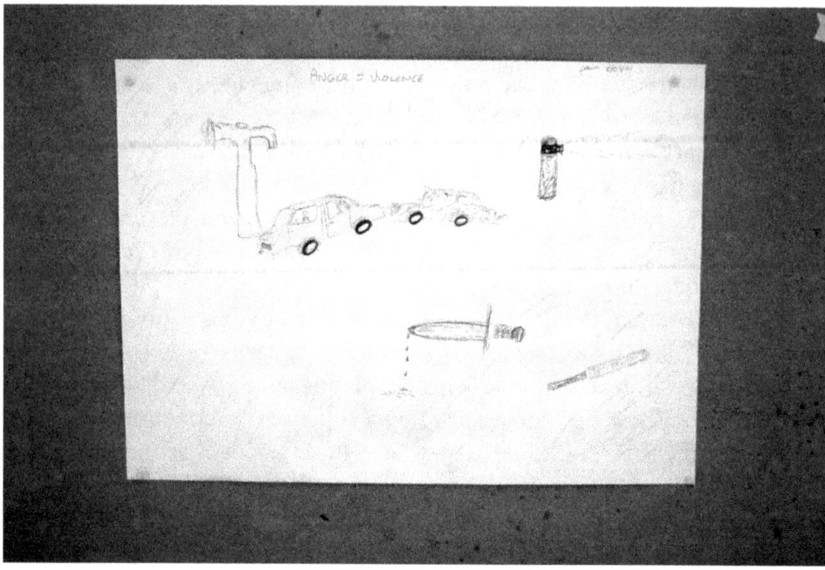

Figure 13.7 Anger = Violence. *Photo credit: Marian Liebmann & Jessica Kingsley Publishers.*

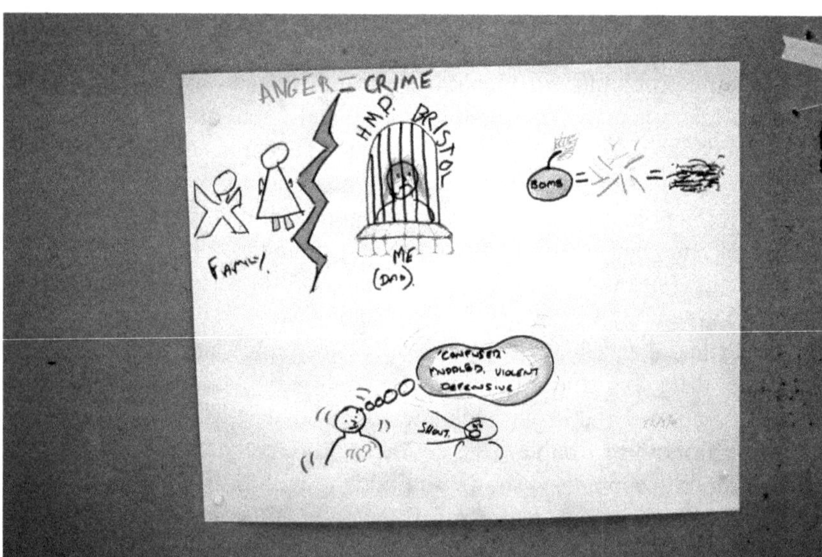

Figure 13.8 Anger = Crime. *Photo credit: Marian Liebmann & Jessica Kingsley Publishers.*

Figure 13.9 Peace, Harmony, Happiness. *Photo credit: Marian Liebmann & Jessica Kingsley Publishers.*

In the United States, the main person to contribute work and publications on art therapy in criminal justice settings is David Gussak. He cites the advantages of art therapy in prisons as it:

- has the advantage of bypassing rigid defenses, including pervasive dishonesty;
- promotes inadvertent unconscious disclosure, even while the client is not compelled to discuss therapeutic issues verbally, which might leave him vulnerable;
- takes advantage of the greater creativity inherent in the prison society, due to the intense need for diversion and escape;
- does not require that the inmate/patient knows, admits, or discusses what he has disclosed. Since the environment is already so dangerous, any unintended disclosure of insight can be more threatening;
- permits the inmate/patient to express himself in a manner acceptable to both the inside and outside culture;
- can produce mitigation of symptoms without verbal interpretation;
- is especially helpful in this environment, given the severe disabilities of this population, such as low levels of education, learning problems and other obstacles to verbal communication.[63,64,65,66]

ARTS APPROACHES TO RESTORATIVE JUSTICE

In my book *Restorative Justice: How It Works*, I included a chapter on arts approaches to restorative justice because the arts have a powerful effect, especially in working with the emotions involved in restorative justice. Examples include drama, such as theater groups going into prisons to present a play, then involving inmates in thinking about the impact of their crimes on victims; role-play; poems, songs, and pictures by offenders to donate to their victims; producing videos to use in crime prevention; community reparation projects such as murals for playgrounds (Liebmann).[67]

A more recent compilation of projects working at the intersection between art and restorative justice is *Restorative Imagination: Artistic Pathways*, published by the European Forum for Restorative Justice. It has three sections:

1. Restorative imagination;
2. Art as restoration and dialogue;
3. Making visible and giving voice through art.

The book contains many examples of arts work (art, music, drama, photography, video, writing) from all over Europe, and demonstrates the creativity of artists and restorative practitioners working together.

ARTWORK IN RESTORATIVE JUSTICE

In some Youth Offending Teams in the UK, artwork by young offenders is one way of making amends. Young people make pictures, posters, mosaics, silk paintings, and other items as gifts, either to their actual victims or to a charity. Sometimes they are encouraged to do pictures of their own feelings after committing their offense, to show victims they have thought about things. Sometimes they make things requested by victims, or pictures they think they will like, after meeting them at a Youth Offender Panel, mediation or restorative conference. Sometimes they make posters warning other young people of the consequences of their particular kind of crime. Photomontages of reparation work on large projects also have visual appeal.

One Youth Offending Team which made a special feature of this kind of work for some years was Oxfordshire Youth Offending Service, where Clair Aldington worked for six years as an artist and reparation supervisor, as well as being a trained facilitator of restorative conferences. She found that co-creating an art object with young people facilitated meaningful conversations about their offense, often when they could not articulate their feelings verbally. She described her first case:

CASE STUDY: THEFT FROM STORE

My first case was working with a young person who had stolen from a large national store. It was her first offense; she was embarrassed and remorseful about what she had done and wanted to make amends. She had stolen the item as a birthday gift for her brother. The young person was interested in beauty, and so we looked at the proportions of the face and the body, and designed two masks which expressed how she felt about what she had done. Once they were complete, I was not sure what to do with them. Co-creating the artwork with her enabled conversations about the offense, but at the end of the process I felt strongly that she should not keep the masks; our work together had been carried out as part of a court order which was aimed at enabling her to make reparation for the harm caused. I discussed it with a colleague and the most obvious course of action seemed to be to present it to the store (the people harmed—the victims) as a "reparative" gift. At this stage, it never occurred to me that we were proposing anything unusual.

On contacting the company, I learned that the store security officer had been disturbed by the experience of arresting the young person as she had been so distressed. He and the store manager expressed a desire to meet with us as a way of working through the incident.

The young person felt unable to attend a joint meeting with the store, but was happy for me and my manager to present her gift to them on her behalf. The store manager and security officer were delighted with the gift in terms of its "professional" looking presentation and the sentiments it expressed. The framed masks were hung in the store's staff room. As a result of the gifting, the young person's nationwide ban from the store was lifted and they said they would be happy to meet with her any time. I relayed this message to the young person and her mother who were relieved at the restorative outcome. This was the first time I witnessed the power of a piece of artwork to act as a conduit for communication between two parties in a conflict even when one of them is not present.[68]

Many other co-creations and gifts followed. Then, in 2007, Clair moved to the Shetland Islands in Scotland and cofounded an independent organization *Space2face* arts and restorative justice project, in which she continues the work. The following case studies are from her work there.

CASE STUDY: TREE

A son (in his early twenties) had committed assaults on family members (and others). The son had spent most of his late teens and early twenties in and out of prison. We spent two years working with the son and his parents in separate parallel processes. The parents were separated but chose to work together. The process took longer than anticipated due to the son's custodial stays. Each party created a tree to represent the three stages of their restorative process: Roots—facts (what happened?); Trunk—consequences (who was affected?); Leaves—future (what does everyone need in order to move on in a safer way?). The trees were exchanged in a face-to-face conference. Both sides used their trees as visual aids in the meeting to articulate their thoughts and feelings. Through the making process, they had co-created not only their tree, but their own restorative processes. Through describing their trees during the meeting, they were immediately having a restorative conversation.

"We've never been able to have this type of conversation before" (Mum).

CASE STUDY: BENCH

A son (in his early twenties) stole money fraudulently from his foster parents. As part of the son's restorative process, we spent a year with him co-creating a bench as a gift for his foster parents. We additionally employed a craftsperson to assist with the making. Concurrently, we were working with both foster parents. The father was, at first, unwilling to engage in a restorative process as he was too angry. As time progressed, this changed and he decided he would like to take part in a joint meeting. The bench had design features, such as a ship's wheels, that the son knew would resonate with his foster Dad. The son also wanted to replace an old bench in his foster parents' garden. As part of the formal joint meeting, the bench was gifted by the son to his foster Mum and Dad. They were overwhelmed, particularly by the album of photos that detailed the making process. Five years later, their relationship with their foster son remains strong and Mum is now a trustee of *Space2face*.

"The bench replaced the pain and harmed caused" (Mum).
"Doing this [restorative justice] is far harder than going to prison" (Son).[69],[70],[71]

Clair also references Kintsugi, a Japanese art in which the cracks of broken pottery are filled with a lacquer mixed with powdered silver, gold, or platinum, so that the cracks show up really visibly.

> The Japanese look at repair in a different way from how we see it in the West. In the West, we throw it away if it's cracked. I sometimes use Kintsugi as a representation of the restorative process. You can't take away damage done but can make something beautiful out of it. It will never be the same. The harm can still be seen. Harm can be physical or psychological and will never really go away, but restorative practice can help people to move on.[72]

Sometimes the results of Kintsugi can be even more beautiful than before.[73]

PLAYS ABOUT RESTORATIVE JUSTICE

There has been increasing interest in restorative justice as a topic for plays.

The Jack Manning Trilogy by David Williamson (2002)

- This trilogy explores community conferencing, bringing together the victims and perpetrators of a crime to attempt some kind of reconciliation.[74]

Face to Face

- When Glen comes face-to-face with the employee who rammed his Mercedes, he must acknowledge some responsibility for a series of incidents which helped provoke the crime.

A Conversation

- This revolves around the confrontation between the family of a rapist and murderer and the family of his victim. Between January and November 2017, the European Forum for Restorative Justice coordinated a film-making of this play, adapted to a European context and directed by Peter Harris, performed by the amateur theater group No Theatre and filmed by Oddbjørn Austevik and colleagues.[75]

Charitable Intent

- This focuses on the pressures and contradictions that erupt as workplace values change.

The Long Road by Shelagh Stephenson (2008)

- *The Long Road* deals with the devastating effects of knife crime, and how humanity and forgiveness can help restore hope and dignity. When 18-year-old Danny was killed in a random stabbing, his family struggled to cope with the senseless loss. His mother, wanting answers, decided to contact her son's killer, bringing them face-to-face, with remarkable consequences. Danny was stabbed by a girl over his brusque refusal to give her money for her bus fare, and the play shows the repercussions of his murder, from the perspective of a grieving middle-class family and the teenage killer in her prison cell. The attack arises in part from a lack of self-worth so crippling that a perceived insult is violently avenged.

It was written in collaboration with Synergy Theatre Project, using research conducted in prisons, and explores how restorative justice can help with rehabilitation. It was developed through meetings with perpetrators and victims of violent crime and has also been staged in several London prisons.[76,77]

After the Accident by Julian Armitstead (2008)

- This play uses the restorative justice system to explore the concept of dignity and the duties that everyone has to their community. Leon steals a car which results in the death of six-year-old Charley. Four years later, as his parole is coming up, Leon meets with Petra and Jimmy, Charley's parents. The action takes place around the restorative conference. In the event there are mistakes made by both sides. The play has been performed world-wide in many contexts, including one performance with an all-black cast.[78, 79]

La Mirada del Otro (The other's look) (2013)

- This play, about restorative justice and political violence, is the product of ten years research and artistic work conducted by the collective Project 43-2. The play focuses on restorative encounters between dissidents from the "Basque Homeland and Liberty" (*Basque Euskadi Ta Askatasuna*/ETA) in Spain and the families of their victims, presenting elements for transforming the conflict and promoting a culture of peace. It was performed more than 100 times in 70 different places (in Spanish with English subtitles), including Colombia, where a parallel was made to the peace process of the country. It was also performed at the European Forum for Restorative Justice Conference in 2019.[80]

The Listening Room by Harriet Madeley (2017)

- This play takes the true stories of five people whose lives were changed by a single violent crime, and explores what happens when the five victims of crime meet their aggressors via restorative justice. The play captures the tumult of emotions that many victims and offenders encounter when taking part in restorative justice. Motivations, retribution, rehabilitation, and forgiveness all feature in some way.[81]

CONCLUSION

This chapter has taken a journey through different applications of the arts in criminal justice, from professional artists honoring the UN to arts work in criminal justice settings, arts and conflict work, art therapy with offenders and the contribution of art and drama to work in restorative justice. It is clear that arts work offers a route for many people who find it difficult to express themselves verbally. It also offers an approach which can deliver unexpected results that verbal approaches simply cannot achieve.

Alongside this, we have seen that restorative justice has gained recognition and acceptance in the work of the UN. Quakers have been deeply involved in this, alongside people of other faiths. The Kyoto Declaration of the Fourteenth UN Congress, in its section on "reducing reoffending through rehabilitation and reintegration" includes a paragraph (42) on facilitating restorative justice processes.[82]

The journey of this chapter is also reflected in the art works mentioned, from the horrors of war depicted in Picasso's *Guernica* (1937) to the founding of the United Nations in 1945 and the completion of Rockwell's painting *Golden Rule* in 1961. De Rosen's murals and Yoshida's *Sacred Birds* are also part of this. And the journey continues with the SDGs, initiated in 2015, which mention "promotion of a culture of peace and non-violence, global citizenship and appreciation of cultural diversity and of culture's contribution to sustainable development" (SDG 4.7) and "promote peaceful and inclusive societies."[83]

I hope that this chapter has opened doors to a collaboration of art and faith in the prevention of crime and conflict. It is to be hoped that further opportunities to do such work will be made available to a wider group of people in the criminal justice system, as well as those outside it.

ACKNOWLEDGMENTS

I would like to acknowledge Jessica Kingsley Publishers for the use of material previously published in the following books written/edited by me:

Art Therapy in Practice (1990); *Arts Approaches to Conflict* (1996); *Restorative Justice: How It Works* (2007); *Art Therapy and Social Action (my chapter)* (2007); *Art Therapy and Anger* (2008).

I would like to acknowledge the contribution of Clair Aldington, whose practice has shown the potential of co-created art work in restorative justice.

Finally, I would like to acknowledge the contribution of the clients who contributed their work for us to learn from them.

NOTES

1. United Nations Office on Drugs and Crime (UNODC), "Kyoto declaration on advancing crime prevention, criminal justice and the rule of law: toward the achievement of the 2030 Agenda for Sustainable Development" (2021).

2. Norman Rockwell Museum (2014).

3. UN News, "'Golden Rule,' iconic Norman Rockwell mosaic, rededicated at UN Headquarters" (2014).

4. Association of Art Museum Directors, "Norman Rockwell at the United Nations" (2015).

5. Michael Lampen, "John De Rosen: Mural Master," in *Tales From the Crypt: Archival Pieces from Michael Lampen, Grace Cathedral's Archivist.*

6. United Religions Initiative, "The UN and URI Celebrate Their Anniversaries Together at Grace Cathedral" (2015).

7. Japan Traffic Culture Association (2019).

8. United Nations Information Service, 2019. "Art in Vienna UNO City" (2019).

9. Schiller, Friedrich, *Ode to Joy ('An die Freude')* (1786).

10. Andrew W. Cordier and Wilder Foote, eds, *Public Papers of the Secretaries-General of the United Nations, Vol. 5 Dag Hammarskjöld 1960-6* (New York and London: Columbia University Press, 1972), 224–25.

11. Simon Scott, "The Music and Morality of Beethoven's Mighty Ninth" (2019).

12. Six Quakers, 1979, Section 23.102 in *Quaker Faith & Practice.*

13. AVP International. https://avp.international.

14. Quakers in the World, "Crime and Justice" (2019).

15. United Nations Office on Drugs and Crime (UNODC), "The Bangkok Rules" (2010).

16. QUNO: www.quno.org; QCEA: www.qcea.org.

17. Jamie Walker, *Violence and Conflict Resolution in Schools: A Study of the Teaching of Interpersonal Problem-solving Skills in Primary and Secondary Schools in Europe* (1989).

18. Howard League: www.howardleague.org.

19. Howard League, "History of the Howard League for Penal Reform" (2017).

20. Penal Reform International. www.penalreform.org

21. International Commission of Catholic Prison Pastoral Care. https://iccppc.org.

22. Academic Council on the United Nations Systems (ACUNS). https://acuns.org.

23. World Society of Victimology. www.worldsocietyofvictimology.org.

24. United Nations Office on Drugs and Crime (UNODC), *Handbook on Restorative Justice Programmes* (2020).

25. United Nations Office on Drugs and Crime (UNODC), "The Bangkok Rules" (2010).

26. United Nations Office on Drugs and Crime (UNODC), "The United Nations Standard Minimum Rules for the Treatment of Prisoners (the Nelson Mandela Rules)" (2015).

27. UN Department of Economic and Social Affairs, Disability, "#Envision2030: 17 goals to transform the world for persons with disabilities" (2019).

28. Friends World Committee for Consultation, "A Statement on Restorative Justice" (1990).

29. Koestler Arts. https://www.koestlerarts.org.uk.

30. Murray Cox ed., *Shakespeare Comes to Broadmoor "The Actors are Come Hither": The Performance of Tragedy in a Secure Psychiatric Hospital* (London and Philadelphia: Jessica Kingsley Publishers, 1992).

31. Annie McKean, & Kate Massey-Chase eds., *Playing for Time Theatre Company: Perspectives from the Prison* (Bristol: Intellect Books, 2019).

32. Geese Theatre. http://www.geese.co.uk.

33. Clean Break Theatre. https://www.cleanbreak.org.uk.

34. Changing Tunes. https://www.changingtunes.org.uk.

35. National Criminal Justice Arts Alliance. https://www.artsincriminaljustice.org.uk/our-work/.

36. Marian Liebmann, ed., *Arts Approaches to Conflict* (London: Jessica Kingsley Publishers, 1996), 2–3.

37. Marian Liebmann, *Arts,* 166–67.

38. Michelle LeBaron, *Changing Our Worlds: Arts as Transformative Practice* (2018).

39. United Cities and Local Governments/UCLG & Culture 21, "Culture in the Sustainable Development Goals: A Guide for Local Action" (2018).

40. Culture2030Goal campaign. 2019. "Culture in the Implementation of the 2030 Agenda: A Report by the Culture 2030 Goal Campaign" (2019).

41. Katalin Bogyay, "Music and Sustainable Development in the framework of UNESCO's International Year of Cultural Rapprochement" (2010).

42. David Olusegun and Ade Ogunrinade, "Music Education as a Pillar to Sustainable Development in Nigeria," *Journal of Economics and Sustainable Development* 6, no. 3 (2015): 83–86.

43. United Nations Institute for Training and Research, "UNITAR Hosts Seminar on Music Education and Sustainable Development" (2018).

44. Mark Smulian, "Let Music Lead" (2020).

45. June Boyce-Tillman, "Getting Our Acts Together: Conflict Resolution Through Music," in *Arts Approaches to Conflict* (1996): 209–236.

46. June Boyce-Tillman, "Making Musical Space for Peace," in *Peace and Policy. Dialogue of Civilization for Global Citizenship* Vol. 15, *Music and Solidarity: Questions of Universality, Consciousness and Connection* (Toda Peace Institute 2011).

47. Vegar Jordanger, "Healing Cultural Violence: Collective Vulnerability through Guided Imagery with Music," in Olivier Urbain ed. *Music and Conflict Transformation: Harmonies and Dissonances in Geopolitics* (London: I. B. Tauris, 2008), 136–154.

48. Marian Liebmann, "'It Just Happened': Looking at Crime Events," in Marian Liebmann ed. *Art Therapy in Practice* (1990): 140–43.

49. Marian Liebmann, *It Just Happened*, 135–139.

50. Marian Liebmann, "Letting Go and Getting Framed." *Probation Journal* March issue, (1991): 25–31.

51. Marian Liebmann, ed., *Art Therapy with Offenders* (London: Jessica Kingsley Publshers, 1994), 258–263.

52. Marian Liebmann, *Letting Go*, 25–31.

53. Marian Liebmann, "Working with Anger Using Art," in Phil Bowen and Stephen Whithead, eds. *Curing Violence: How we Can Become a Less Violent Society* (The Centre for Justice Innovation, 2018), 173–75.

54. Marian Liebmann, "Arts Approaches to Restorative Justice" in *Restorative Justice: How It Works* (2007): 383 394.

55. Marian Liebmann, "Using Visual Arts Approaches to Enhance Victim Awareness," In *Restorative Imagination: Artistic Pathways* (2017): 78–79.

56. Marian Liebmann, ed., *Art Therapy and Anger* (2008): 14–15.

57. Marian Liebmann, *Art Therapy for Groups* (2004): 112–113.

58. Marian Liebmann, "Art Therapy for Anger Management." In *Forensic Arts Therapies: Anthology of Practice and Research* (2016): 71–72.

59. Marian Liebmann, "Art Therapy for Anger Management." 74–76.

60. Marian Liebmann, "Working with Anger Using Art." In *Curing Violence: How We Can Become a Less Violent Society* (2018): 175–177.

61. Marian Liebmann, ed., *Art Therapy with Offenders* (1994).

62. Kate Rothwell, ed., *Forensic Arts Therapies: Anthology of Practice and Research* (London: Free Association Books, 2016), 69–85.

63. David Gussak, "Art Therapy with Prison Inmates: A Pilot Study." *The Arts in Psychotherapy* 31, no. 4 (2004): 245–249.

64. David Gussak, "Art Behind Bars" (2013).

65. David Gussak, *Art and Art Therapy with the Imprisoned: Re-Creating Identity* (2020).

66. David Gussak and Marcia Sue Cohen-Liebman, "Investigation vs. Intervention: Forensic Art Therapy and Art Therapy in Forensic Settings." *The American Journal of Art Therapy* 40, no. 2 (2001): 123–135.

67. Marian Liebmann, "Arts Approaches to Restorative Justice," in *Restorative Justice: How It Works* (London; Jessica Kingsley Publishers, 2007), 383–418.

68. Clair Aldington, "The Role of the Arts and Gifting in the Restorative Process," in *Restorative Imagination: Artistic Pathways,* Emanuela Biffi. and Brunilda Pali eds. (Leuven, Belgium: European Forum for Restorative Justice, 2017), 55–56.

69. Clair Aldington, *The Role*, 57–62.

70. Clair Aldington, Leaflet/poster for European Forum for Restorative Justice Conference, Tirana (2018).

71. Clair Aldington, "Empowering Individuals Through Merging the Arts with Restorative Approaches." *Resolution 64,* summer issue (2019): 14–15.

72. Clair Aldington, *Empowering*, 14.

73. Audrey Harris, "Kintsugi: The Art of Broken," in *Restorative Imagination: Artistic Pathways* (2017): 36.

74. David Williamson, *The Jack Manning Trilogy* (Sydney: Currency Press, 2002).

75. European Forum for Restorative Justice (2017).

76. Shelagh Stephenson, *The Long Road* (London: Methuen Drama, 2008).

77. Restorative Justice Council, "Could you forgive your son's killer?" (2019).

78. Julian Armistead, *After the Accident* (London: Methuen Drama, 2011).

79. Amnesty International UK (2008).

80. European Forum for Restorative Justice, "Theatre Play *La Miranda del Otro*" (2019).

81. Harriet Madeley, *The Listening Room* London: John Tow Foundation (2017).

82. United Nations Office on Drugs and Crime (UNODC), Kyoto Declaration, section 42 (2021).

83. UN doc. A/RES/70/1.

BIBLIOGRAPHY

Aldington, Clair. "The role of the arts and gifting in the restorative process," in *Restorative Imagination: Artistic Pathways,* eds., Emanuela Biffi and Brunilda Pali, 54–63. Leuven, Belgium: European Forum for Restorative Justice, 2017.

Aldington, Clair. Leaflet/poster for European Forum for Restorative Justice Conference, Tirana, 2018.

Aldington, Clair. "Empowering individuals through merging the arts with restorative approaches." *Resolution 64,* summer issue. London: Restorative Justice Council, 2019, 14–20.

Armitstead, Julian. *After the Accident.* London: Methuen Drama, 2011.

Amnesty International UK, Julian Armitstead wins Amnesty International UK and ice and fire Protect The Human Playwriting Competition. 2008. Press release accessed September 1, 2019. https://bit.ly/2Yu2Gfi.

Association of Art Museum Directors. 2015. "Norman Rockwell at the United Nations." Accessed August 30, 2019. https://bit.ly/3d7g6BK.

Bogyay, Katlin. "Music and Sustainable Development in the framework of UNESCO's International Year of Cultural Rapprochement." Presented on the XVth International Summer University at ISES. July 1, 2010, Kőszeg, Hungary.

Boyce-Tillman, June. "Making Musical Space for Peace," in *Peace and Policy Dialogue of Civilization for Global Citizenship,* vol. 15, *Music and Solidarity: Questions of Universality, Consciousness and Connection,* ed. Laurence, Felicity and Urbain, Olivier, 85–201. New Brunswick and London: Transaction Publishers, 2011.

Boyce-Tillman, June. "Getting Our Acts Together: Conflict Resolution Through Music," in *Arts Approaches to Conflict,* ed. Marian. Liebmann, 209–236. London: Jessica Kingsley Publishers, 1996.

Campbell, Jean and Marian Liebmann. Frederica Brooks, Jenny Jones, and Cathy Ward. eds. *Art Therapy, Race and Culture*. London: Jessica Kingsley Publishers, 1999.

Changing Tunes. 2019. Accessed August 15, 2021. https://www.changingtunes.org.uk.

Clean Break Theatre, 2019. Accessed August 15, 2021. https://www.cleanbreak.org.uk.

Cordier, Andrew. W. and Wilder Foote. eds., *Public Papers of the Secretaries-General of the United Nations Vol 5 Dag Hammarskjöld 1960-6*. New York:

Columbia University Press, 1975, 224–25. Audio version, accessed June 15, 2021. https://bit.ly/3k1vMe9.

Cox, Murray. ed. *Shakespeare Comes to Broadmoor 'The Actors are Come Hither': The Performance of Tragedy in a Secure Psychiatric Hospital*. London: Jessica Kingsley Publishers, 1992.

Culture2030Goal campaign, "Culture in the Implementation of the 2030 Agenda: A Report by the Culture 2030 Goal Campaign" 2019. Accessed January 16, 2021. https://bit.ly/35 So. 2E34.

European Forum for Restorative Justice, "A Conversation" 2017. Accessed May 1, 2021. https://bit.ly/2xv7AO1.

European Forum for Restorative Justice. "Theatre Play *La Miranda del Otro*." 2019. Accessed August 1, 2021. https://bit.ly/3fgL2 So. 8.

Friends World Committee for Consultation."A Statement on Restorative Justice." 1990. Unpublished document.

Geese Theatre. 2019. Retrieved September 2, 2019. http://www.geese.co.uk.

Gussak, David. "Art Therapy with Prison Inmates: A Pilot Study." *The Arts In Psychotherapy,* 31, no. 4 (2004), 245–49.

Gussak, David. "Art Behind Bars." Accessed July 10, 2021, *Psychology Today*. https://bit.ly/2xu8f24.

Gussak, David. *Art and Art Therapy with the Imprisoned: Re-Creating Identity*. New York: Routledge, 2020.

Gussak, David and Marcia Sue Cohen-Liebman. "Investigation vs. Intervention: Forensic Art Therapy and Art Therapy in Forensic Settings." *The American Journal of Art Therapy* 40, no. 2 (2001): 123–135.

Harris, Audrey. "Kintsugi: the art of broken," in *Restorative Imagination: Artistic Pathways,* ed. Emanuela Biffi and Brunilda Pali, 36–40. Leuven, Belgium: European Forum for Restorative Justice, 2017.

Howard League. "History of the Howard League for Penal Reform" 2017. http://bit.ly/380GNbE.

Japan Traffic Culture Association. 2019. Accessed August 1, 2021. http://jptca.org/en/yoshida_sagenji/.

Jordanger, Vegar. "Healing Cultural Violence: Collective Vulnerability through Guided Imagery with Music," in *Music and Conflict Transformation: Harmonies and Dissonances in Geopolitics*, ed. Olivier Urbain, 136–154. London: I. B. Tauris, 2007.

Koestler Arts, 2019. Accessed July 31, 2021. https://www.koestlerarts.org.uk.

Lampen, Michael. "John De Rosen: Mural Master," in *Tales the Crypt: Archival pieces Michael Lampen, Grace Cathedral's Archivist*. Accessed May 3, 2021. https://bit.ly/2VYWfiv.

Liebmann, Marian. ed. *Mediation in Context*. London: Jessica Kingsley Publishers, 2000.

Liebmann, Marian. "'It Just Happened': Looking at Crime Events," in *Art Therapy in Practice,* ed. Marian Liebmann, 133–155. London: Jessica Kingsley Publishers, 1990.

Liebmann, Marian. "Letting Go and Getting Framed." *Probation Journal* March 1991, 25–31. London: National Association of Probation Officers.

Liebmann, Marian. "Giving it Form: Exploring Conflict Through Art," in *Arts Approaches to Conflict,* ed. Marian Liebmann, 152–175. London: Jessica Kingsley Publishers, 1996.

Liebmann, Marian. *Art Therapy for Groups, Second Edition.* London: Brunner-Routledge, 2004. Also translated into Hebrew, Czech, Chinese, Korean, Brazilian Portuguese.

Liebmann, Marian. 2007a. *Restorative Justice: How It Works.* London: Jessica Kingsley Publishers, 2007.

Liebmann, Marian. "Arts Approaches to Restorative Justice," in *Restorative Justice: How It Works,* ed. Marian Liebmann, 383–418. London: Jessica Kingsley Publishers, 2007.

Liebmann, Marian. *Art Therapy and Anger.* London: Jessica Kingsley Publishers, 2008.

Liebmann, Marian. "Art Therapy for Anger Management," in *Forensic Arts Therapies: Anthology of Practice and Research*, ed. Kate Rothwell, 69–85. London: Free Association Books, 2016.

Liebmann, Marian. "Using Visual Arts Approaches to Enhance Victim Awareness," in *Restorative Imagination: Artistic Pathways,* eds. Emanuela Biffi and Brunilda. Pali, 75–83. Leuven, Belgium: European Forum for Restorative Justice, 2017.

Liebmann, Marian. "Working with Anger Using Art," in *Curing Violence: How We Can Become a Less Violent Society*, eds. Phil Bowen and Stephen Whitehead, 172–181. London: Centre for Justice Innovation: The Monument Fellowship, 2018.

Liebmann, Marian. ed., *Art Therapy in Practice*. London: Jessica Kingsley Publishers, 1990.

Liebmann, Marian. ed. *Art Therapy with Offenders*. London: Jessica Kingsley Publishers, 1994. Also translated into Korean.

Liebmann, Marian. ed. *Arts Approaches to Conflict*. London: Jessica Kingsley Publishers, 1996.

Liebmann, Marian. *Art Therapy for Groups*. London: Routledge, 2004.

Liebmann, Marian. ed., *Art Therapy and Anger*. London: Jessica Kingsley Publishers, 2008. Also translated into Korean.

LeBaron, Michelle. In *Changing Our Worlds: Arts as Transformative Practice,* ed. Michelle LeBaron and Janis Sarra. Stellenbosch: Sun Press, 2018. Accessed August 4, 2021. https://bit.ly/2W3cz21.

Madeley, Harriet. *The Listening Room*. London: John Thaw Foundation, 2017. jobs

McKean, Anne and Kate Massey-Chase. eds., *Playing for Time Theatre Company: Perspectives the Prison*. Bristol, UK and Chicago, USA: Intellect Books, 2018.

National Criminal Justice Arts Alliance. Our Work. Accessed August 5, 2019.

Norman Rockwell Museum, 2014. Retrieved August 30, 2019, https://www.nrm.org/2014/02/golden_rule/.

Olusegun, David, Ade Ogunrinade, Ade."Music Education as a Pillar to Sustainable Development in Nigeria." *Journal of Economics and Sustainable Development* 6, no. 3 (2015): 83–86.

Quakers in the World. "Crime and Justice." 2019 Accessed January 9, 2021. http://bit.ly/3owoLEa.

Restorative Justice Council. "Could you forgive your son's killer?". 2019. Accessed September 1, 2019. https://bit.ly/3ddnCeI.

Rothwell, Kate. ed, *Forensic Arts Therapies: Anthology of Practice and Research.* London: Free Association Books, 2016.

Schiller, Friedrich. *Ode to Joy. "An die Freude."* Germany: Thalia, 1785, published 1786, 1808.

Scott, Simon. "The Music and Morality of Beethoven's Mighty Ninth," 2019. Accessed May 15, 2021. https://bit.ly/3mXtexQ.

Six Quakers. In *Quaker Faith & Practice, fifth edition.* Section 23.102. London: The Yearly Meeting of the Religious Society of Friends. Quakers in Britain, 2013.

Smulian, Mark. "Let Music Lead." 2020. Unpublished document.

Stephenson, Shelagh. *The Long Road.* London: Methuen Drama, 2008.

UCLG & Culture 21. "Culture in the Sustainable Development Goals: A Guide for Local Action." 2018. Accessed November 22, 2020. https://bit.ly/3qqB7PK.

UN Department of Economic and Social Affairs. Disability, "Envision2030: 17 goals to transform the world for persons with disabilities." Accessed January 17, 2021. https://bit.ly/35tYIVp.

UN doc. SA/RES/70/1 Transforming our world: The 2030 Agenda for Sustainable Development. 2015. Accessed July 24, 2021. http://bit.ly/3aQw99w.

UN News. "'Golden Rule,' iconic Norman Rockwell mosaic, rededicated at UN Headquarters." 2014. Accessed July 24, 2021. https://bit.ly/3fivSM0.

United Nations Information Service, "Art in Vienna UNO City," 2019. Accessed January 23, 2021. https://bit.ly/3o5DXqR.

United Religions Initiative. "The UN and URI Celebrate Their Anniversaries Together at Grace Cathedral," 2015. Accessed July 24, 2021. https://bit.ly/3fa4Qql.

United Nations Institute for Training and Research "UNITAR hosts seminar on Music Education and Sustainable Development," 2018. Accessed July 24, 2021. http://bit.ly/3mZFUV4.

United Nations Office on Drugs and Crime. "The Bangkok Rules," 2010. Accessed December 12, 2019. https://bit.ly/2KWlbkp.

United Nations Office on Drugs and Crime. "The United Nations Standard Minimum Rules for the Treatment of Prisoners. The Nelson Mandela Rules," 2015. Accessed December 17, 2020. https://bit.ly/3aWI4SS.

United Nations Office on Drugs and Crime. Kyoto Declaration, sections 22 and 23 "Draft Kyoto declaration on advancing crime prevention, criminal justice and the rule of law: toward the achievement of the 2030 Agenda for Sustainable Development," 2021. Accessed March 27, 2021, https://undocs.org/en/A/CONF.234/L.6.

Walker, Jamie. *Violence and Conflict Resolution in Schools: A Study of the Teaching of Interpersonal Problem-Solving Skills in Primary and Secondary Schools in Europe.* Strasbourg: Council of Europe, 1989.

Why Me?. "Impact of Restorative Justice explored on stage," 2017. Accessed September 1, 2019, https://bit.ly/2SwCKMl.

Williamson, David. *The Jack Manning Trilogy.* Sydney: Currency Press, 2002.

Afterword

Pedro R. David

THE SCOURGE OF WAR

The framers of the United Nations Charter dedicated it to "save succeeding generations from the scourge of war, which twice in our lifetime has brought untold sorrow to mankind, and to reaffirm faith in fundamental human rights, in the dignity and worth of the human person, in the equal rights of men and women and of nations large and small, and to establish conditions under which justice and respect for the obligations arising from treaties and other sources of international law can be maintained, and to promote social progress and better standards of life in larger freedom."

Save the first provision on the scourge of global wars, and the penultimate provision referring to international law, everything else Niccolò Machiavelli (1469–1527) and Charles-Louis Montesquieu (1689–1755) in one way or another witnessed or/and pursued in their philosophies, widely known across the world.

Regarding the scourge of world war, Karl Jaspers (1883–1969), a German philosopher (and criminologist by education), persecuted up to the end of World War II for his anti-Nazi sentiments, wrote in his book: "The atomic bomb created an entirely new situation. Either all of mankind will be physically destroyed or there will be a metamorphosis of the moral-political situation of man."[1]

Jasper's peer Carl Schmitt (1888–1985), German constitutional lawyer, intellectual Nazi supporter, categorically separated the political from the ethical. Rule of law can only be political, eschewed from the ethical component. Hence, personally, he neither admitted any moral responsibility for genocide, nor did he recognize the United Nations Charter's "principle of justice," a prototype of its current understanding of the "rule of law"—in the "heart" of the organization. He questioned the independence of judiciary. Its decisions should not depend on the personal convictions or opinions of an individual judge but be framed by the established institutions of judicial practice. It itself provides a criterion of practical rightness: "The criterion of right decision . . . is decided by the judicial practice itself. Practice yields its own specific criterion."[2]

Had Schmitt been not so detrimentally and categorically disinterested in the ethical conduct of power holders and judges, would he then have been immune to Edwin H. Sutherland's (1883–1950) findings about what enables the power holders' white-collar and organized crime? Had he been familiar with the 1984 United Nations Declaration for the Victims of Crime and Abuse of Power, would he still have intellectually dissociated himself from the contribution to Nazi genocide?

This is not a rhetorical question. In 1947, Schmitt—Nazi *Kronjurist* — could have been charged with intellectual "preparation of a war of aggression" before the International Military Tribunal's Great Chamber, where, I think, he still would have claimed that his scholarly work was "just a pure diagnosis . . . which I am still inclined to defend in front of any academic faculty in the world."[3]

What strikes me as a former UN official (and strikes me even harder as an ex-ICTY judge who adjudicated war crime; and the university law dean now) is that indeed anyone can blatantly argue that such a "specific criterion" may still apply notwithstanding fundamentally changed circumstances, as if the clause *rebus sic stantibus* could not have automatically invalidated the continuation of "judicial practice" that may eventually lead to genocidal consequences. What kind of "independent" judiciary is this, if lethally servile (if not blatantly self-serving) toxic *Weltanschauung* prevails? What kind of academic faculties there may be then? Who will defend whom? Will there be pursued or persecuted for the thesis of the supremacy of a global legal order of liberal democratic international justice?

Schmitt—the most prominent legal adviser of the Nazis—has provided ideological Nazi resource, as much as Edwin H. Sutherland criminological assessment of what it takes to become a serious criminal. Winston Churchill, the UK prime minister during World War II, and Henry Morgenthau in that time the US Secretary of Treasury and anti-Mafia and corruption official, have both been clear treating, respectively, Hitler as a gangster deserving an electric chair, and his soldiers as Mafia-type executors deserving no less dishonorable treatment. Goebbels and other intellectual Nazi instigators who held official capacity had, in fact, earned that treatment. Schmitt survived and as late as in 1985 he renewed his intellectual claims in the book *Der Hüter der Verfassung.*

In this volume, Yvon Dandurand and Jessica Jahn allude to overly self-serving interests of State Parties to the 2000 United Nations Convention against Transnational Organized Crime which for eighteen years could not adopt the assessment mechanism for its implementation. When they eventually did, they afforded themselves such a large margin of mutually protective guarantees that neither they nor their white-collar criminals, let alone the unassociated transnational organized criminals, can worry much about the prosperity of their businesses, hence about the superiority of the rule of law.

It goes without saying that after World Wars I and II tragedies, Machiavelli's and Schmitt's reasoning must have prompted Jaspers to call for a metamorphosis of moral-political situation of man. Jaspers sought to articulate and defend the notions of universal humanity and global citizenship in a world notably hostile to both.[4] Looking back at that UN postwar call, nowadays too little of its original inspiration has remained for a successful global transformation. The 2030 Agenda should serve as a wake-up call.

Jaspers as the successor to Kant's call for "universal peace" followed his concept of "enlarged mentality." Jan Smuts, holistic philosopher and general in one person, took it on the United Nations board as the head of the delegation of the Union of South Africa to the 1945 San Francisco United Nations Conference on International Organization. He successfully entered "larger freedom" in the Charter's preamble. Next, it was incorporated in the preamble of the Universal Declaration of Human Rights and into the United Nations 2015 Declaration, symbolically entitled "Transforming Our World: The 2030 Agenda for Sustainable Development."[5]

This still has been an unfinished agenda. In keeping with the content of this volume, "larger freedom" is also the Montesquieu's way to transform the world. For him the separation of powers and the independence of judiciary are key to counter arbitrariness of the rulers, protecting and expanding people's liberties.

Regarding thus the second provision of the Charter's preamble, by creating conditions under which justice and respect for the obligations arising from treaties and other sources of international law can be maintained, the United Nations is in a position to make people and peoples follow. In this context, as the former UN Interregional Crime Prevention and Criminal Justice Adviser, former judge, now professor and dean of the Law Faculty of the John F. Kennedy University in Buenos Aires (Argentina), I would like to share two observations: on justice, and on making it work.

JUSTICE

First, having gone through the dialogues between Montesquieu and Machiavelli which broadly address the question of the independence of judiciary and the challenges involved in its protection, I would like to refer to the

United Nations' "Human Rights in the Administration of Justice. A Manual on Human Rights for Judges, Prosecutors and Lawyers" (2003). From there one may draw extensive jurisprudence on the notion of judicial independence and impartiality, originally stipulated by the International Covenant on Civil and Political Rights (art. 14 (1)). Since the time of the publication of that manual until now, this jurisprudence has been even more extensive in member states, in the courts mandated by the regional intergovernmental organizations, but also because of the impressive output of the United Nations courts, including the International Criminal Court, and the recently officially closed International Criminal Tribunal for the former Yugoslavia in which I served as its *ad litem* judge.

I referred to the variety of member states, named some of them, pointed to international courts, and recognized here that Machiavelli was an Italian official and Montesquieu was a French academic. By this I wish to emphasize that claiming "specific" justice problems which elsewhere may only be misunderstood does not help to advance larger freedom. My own home country, Argentina, may be the best example of the vagaries of judicial independence that may be well appreciated elsewhere.

An 1862–1997 longitudinal study of judicial independence in Argentina[6] showed that the same formal judicial institutions may have di erent consequences over time—depending on party competition. The rule of law results from a balance of power between at least two political parties, neither of which has monolithic control, meaning that no highly disciplined party sustains control of both the executive and legislative branches. Competitive politics creates a climate in which an autonomous judiciary can emerge. One can see that divided government can strengthen democracy by promoting judicial independence. Over this long time, the establishment of the rule of law has not been a linear process, especially dramatic in the years 1976–1983 of military dictatorship ("Dirty War"). In sum, to the degree that a regime has a monopoly of political power, its commitments to judicial neutrality and the protection of rights of any kind are only contingent, but not truly credible.[7]

Not by coincidence I referred earlier to Montesquieu—the leading figure of the European Enlightenment. He adamantly criticized the abuse of power. Politicians say sometimes that these days Montesquieu would have turned in his grave had he witnessed the ongoing erosion of his principle of separation of powers, and destruction of the independence and impartiality of judiciary. In 1793, overzealous implementers of the sovereign will of masses profaned his tomb in *Église Saint-Sulpice* in Paris where he was buried. They threw his earthly remnants into a common grave in the Paris Catacombs. One year later, Georges Jacques Danton, one of the revolutionary radicals and Montesquieu's hastily reader, also found his posthumous destiny there.

For more than two centuries, Machiavelli's philosophy of governance had an armed upper hand. No wonder that in their course Maurice Joly's 1864 book defeated in France Montesquieu's arguments. Only in 1958 in the French "Fifth Republic" with its Constitution resuscitated Montesquieu's 1747 idea of the separation of powers. The 1958 Constitution begins with its invocation in the preamble of the 1789 Declaration of the Rights of Man. This, in turn, provides in article 16 that "A society in which the observance of the law is not assured, nor the separation of powers defined, has no constitution at all."[8] The French Constitution also contains a number of checks and balances, with an independent judiciary (Article 64).

The separation of powers was "blessed" in two papal encyclicals. In the 1891 *Rerum Novarum* by Leon XIII and in the 1991 *Centessimus annus* by John Paul II. In both they speak about "a healthy theory of State." Even if this looks like the Roman Catholic Church has been much quicker in institutionally recognizing the division of powers than a secular French state, Montesquieu's healthy theory of state should enjoy the license in any rule of law seeking or existing country in the world.

MAKING JUSTICE WORK

Second, however the above is laudable, there is a grain of truth in the statement, that law as a public good does not "descend upon societies from a Heaven of Higher Norms."[9] Therefore, I may say that the United Nations crime prevention and criminal justice standards and norms, be they even in the solemnly and ceremonially concluded declarations and treaties with institutional framework that legally and conceptually impacts national law, do not matter as much do earthly two factors. This is local public support for rights which they promote and envision; and technical assistance which operationalizes them.

Regarding *public support for rights*, it may make accountable governments and its officials for abuses against the weak, let alone for abuses against members of majorities. Machiavelli's disregard of either of the two, also of "plebs" or "masses" (as he respectively terms them in his "The Discourses" and in the "The Dialogue" by Joly)—because everything for his glory may be bought by propaganda—alerts now to the need of strengthening the political culture of vigilance. As Montesquieu and others say, constraint of men by other men is at best a necessary evil that keeps the government in check. In contemporary terms, this is not only about the separation of powers, but also about *glocal* civic education and activism, freedom of the press. Neither in Machiavelli's nor Montesquieu's time such vigilance existed, but surely it nationally had been in motion when Joly wrote his dialogue between the two of them.

Researchers suggest[10] that where this developmental experience is missing, institutional separation of powers or political fragmentation may hardly become a substitute which in political hegemony effectively protects individual and minority rights. Even less so, an independent court (if it exists) maneuvering among competing political branches. The bottom line from this research is that institutions not only provide solutions to commitment problems but also entail commitment problems. "For societies to enjoy a wide range of political, legal, and economic rights, either such rights must be self-enforcing, or the institutions that protect those rights—independent courts—must be self-enforcing. If democracies do a better, though still far from perfect, job of this than dictatorships, it is because power under such regimes is more likely to be fragmented or held in check by the public."[11]

Regarding *technical assistance for making justice work*, only if one stretches Montesquieu's views about "benevolent conquest" as an archetype of societal development aiming at enlarging freedom, then there is some platform to speak about operationalizing rights. This may involve introducing measures to motivate decision-makers, societies, communities and—first of all—individuals to take their lot into their own hands. In this sense matters Montesquieu's supportive opinion that if he knew something that would be useful to his nation and ruinous to another nation, he would not implement it. What could matter as well to Montesquieu as a philosopher emphasizing equality rights would be John Rawls's difference principle of distributive justice. According to him, injustice is permissible only if it benefits the worst off in a society (e.g., if it motivates to level up with others by creating legitimate opportunities to compete). As a former United Nations Interregional Adviser on Crime Prevention and Criminal Justice, I cannot stop reminding the technical assistance providers what in 1961 Mitchell Sharp, a high-ranking Canadian official, admitted: "If the primary purpose of our aid is to help ourselves, rather than to help others, we shall probably receive in return what we deserve, and a good deal less than we expect."[12]

However neither he, Rawls nor Montesquieu could have provided viable clues, how institutions may support one another in transforming mental models of any particular society. This now can be done by *developmental* assistance experts through training and education—in own countries and in countries receiving assistance.

The idea of transformative solidarity is very challenging in practice. Donors and recipients—they both pragmatically and paradigmatically should work out and offer advice geared toward the rights and goals of the 2030 United Nations Agenda and beyond. The United Nations is the only organization which may do this in the spirit of its laws extending beyond 2030, the laws that "ascend to a Heaven."

CONCLUSION

In conclusion, this last phrase in this Afterword written in Buenos Aires, close to Antarctica, was prompted by the finding of Intergovernmental Panel on Climate Change. Reportedly, this coldest, driest, and windiest continent warms up faster than the tropics. During that time, glaciers along the west coast of the Antarctic Peninsula have retreated.[13] In 2019, at the conference of the International Association of Penal Law in the Vatican City, Pope Francis considered whether to add an environmental sin "*Thou shalt not commit ecocide*" to church teachings. Continuing his message from the encyclic *Laudatio Si*, "he is determined to make Christians more observant of their moral obligation to demonstrate love of God and neighbor by adopting lifestyles that respect Creation and preserve our common home for future generations."[14] António Guterres, the present United Nations secretary genera in his own way warned: "We can either save our world or condemn humanity to a hellish future."[15]

The language of justice used in the UN Charter's Preamble well interplays with this postulated transformation. And so does the 2030 Agenda's Sustainable Development Goal 12.8 "to ensure that people everywhere have the relevant information and awareness for sustainable development and lifestyles in harmony with nature." Member states and individuals may appreciate that goal for mental model of transformation with a healthy theory of state. With this aim in mind, the readers of this book may wish to interpret the dialogue in hell between Machiavelli and Montesquieu on climate change and the rule of law, written by four eminent lawyers and civil society activists.

Pedro R. David, Professor of Law
Buenos Aires, Argentina, in Fall 2021

NOTES

1. Karl Jaspers. *Die Atombombe und die Zukunft des Menschen* (R. Piper & Co Verlag: München, 1958), 5.
2. Carl Schmitt. Gesetz und Urteil. Eine Untersuchung zum Problem der Rechtspraxis, 2nd ed. (Verlag C. H. Beck München, 1969), 100.
3. Adeel Hussein, Armin von Bogdandy. Carl Schmitt's International Thought and the State, *MPIL Research Paper Series* 34 (2018), 2.
4. Philippe Hansen. *Hannah Arendt: Politics, History and Citizenship* (Cambridge: Polity Press, 2003), 227.
5. UN doc. A/RES/70/1 Transforming our world: the 2030 Agenda for Sustainable Development 25 September 2015.

6. Rebecca Bill Chavez, John Ferejohn, Barry Weingast. "A Theory of the Politically Independent Judiciary: A Comparative Study of the United States and Argentina," in *Courts in Latin America* eds. Gretchen Helmke and Julio Rios Figueroa (Cambridge: Cambridge University Press, 2011), 219–247.

7. Gretchen Helmke, Frances Rosenbluth. "Regimes and the Rule of Law: Judicial Independence in Comparative Perspective," *Annual Review of Political Science* 12 (2009): 346.

8. "Declaration of the Rights of Man–1789," in AVALON Project. Documents in Law, History and Diplomacy, https://bit.ly/3smuNdf.

9. Steven Holmes, "Lineages of the Rule of Law" in *Democracy and the Rule of Law*, eds. Josè Mariá Maravall and Adam Przeworski (New York: Cambridge University Press, 2007), 53.

10. Helmke and Rosenbluth, "Regimes and the Rule of Law."

11. Helmke and Rosenbluth, "Regimes and the Rule of Law," 362.

12. Mitchell Sharp, "Canada's Stake in International Programs," *Dialogue* 1961, 47.

13. Intergovernmental Panel on Climate Change. The Physical Science Basis. Summary for Policymakers. Working Group I contribution to the Sixth Assessment Report of the Intergovernmental Panel on Climate Change, IPCC AR 6 WG I, Contribution of Working Group I to the Sixth Assessment Report of the Intergovernmental Panel on Climate Change Masson-Delmotte, V. et al., (Cambridge: Cambridge University Press, 2021), 6, 20, 21.

14. *Catholic Register* 2019.

15. UN News, The Now or Never to Save Our Planet or Keep Delaying Climate Action: Which Choice Will We Make?, October 3, 2021, https://bit.ly/2Ye2pzr.

BIBLIOGRAPHY

Catholic Register. Editorial: *Environmental Sin*. Accessed July 15, 2021. https://bit.ly/32AL9lr.

Chavez, Rebecca Bill, Ferejohn, John, and Weingast, Barry. "A Theory of the Politically Independent Judiciary: A Comparative Study of the United States and Argentina," in *Courts in Latin America* eds. Gretchen Helmke, Julio Rios Figueroa, 219–247 (Cambridge: Cambridge University Press, 2011).

"Declaration of the Rights of Man – 1789," in AVALON Project. Documents in Law, History and Diplomacy. Accessed July 15, 2021. https://bit.ly/3smuNdf.

Hansen, Philippe. *Hannah Arendt: Politics, History and Citizenship* (Cambridge: Polity Press, 2003).

Helmke, Gretchen, Rosenbluth, Frances. "Regimes and the Rule of Law: Judicial Independence in Comparative Perspective," *Annual Review of Political Science* 12 (2009): 345–66.

Holmes, Steven. "Lineages of the Rule of Law," in *Democracy and the Rule of Law* eds. Josè Mariá Maravall and Adam Przeworski, 19–61 (New York: Cambridge University Press, 2007).

Hussein, Adeel, von Bogdandy Armin. Carl Schmitt's International Thought and the State, *MPIL Research Paper Series* 34 (2018): 1–34.

Intergovernmental Panel on Climate Change. The Physical Science Basis. Summary for Policymakers. Working Group I contribution to the Sixth Assessment Report of the Intergovernmental Panel on Climate Change, IPCC AR 6 WG I, Contribution of Working Group I to the Sixth Assessment Report of the Intergovernmental Panel on Climate Change (Masson-Delmotte, V. *et al.*, Cambridge: Cambridge University Press, 2021).

Jaspers, Karl. *Die Atombombe und die Zukunft des Menschen* (München: R. Piper & Co Verlag, 1958).

Schmitt, Carl. *Gesetz und Urteil. Eine Untersuchung zum Problem der Rechtspraxis*, 2nd ed. (München: Verlag C. H. Beck: 1969).

Sharp, Mitchell. "Canada's Stake in International Programmes," *Dialogue* 1961, 47–48.

United Nations Office of the Higher Commissioner for Human Rights, Human Rights in the Administration of Justice. A Manual on Human Rights for Judges, Prosecutors and Lawyers (Geneva: United Nations, 2003).

UN News. The Now or Never to Save Our Planet or Keep Delaying Climate Action: Which Choice Will We Make?, October 3, 2021, https://bit.ly/2Ye2pzr.

UN doc. A/RES/70/1 Transforming our world: the 2030 Agenda for sustainable development 25 September 2015. Accessed August 15, 2021. https://bit.ly/2T9GK5O.

Index

About the Contributors

Megan Capp is a Canadian doctoral student at the UN-mandated University for Peace where her research focuses on protecting children whose parents are in conflict with the law. She holds a Master of Arts degree in Conflict Analysis and Management from Royal Roads University where her thesis focused on access to justice in the post-conflict environment. Her additional research interests include the pandemic's impact on justice systems—particularly for vulnerable groups—SDG 16, and justice metrics.

Yvon Dandurand is a criminologist, professor emeritus, School of Criminology and Criminal Justice, University of the Fraser Valley, Canada, as well as a fellow and senior associate of the International Centre for Criminal Law Reform and Criminal Justice Policy, a United Nations affiliated research institute. He specializes in comparative criminal justice research and his interests include justice for children, restorative justice, transnational organized crime, corruption, and international criminal justice cooperation.

Pedro R. David is a f. judge *ad litem* of the International Criminal Court for the former Yugoslavia (The Hague, the Netherlands); f. UN Interregional Crime Prevention and Criminal Justice Adviser; f. judge and president of the Argentine Federal Cassation Court (Buenos Aires, Argentina); dean of the Law School of the John F. Kennedy University (Buenos Aires, Argentina).

Newton Tavares Filho is a senior legal specialist at the Office of the Legislative Counsel, in the Brazilian House of Representatives. He holds a doctorate degree in constitutional law from the Université Paris 1 Panthéon-Sorbonne, as well as a Master of Law degree in International Legal Studies from the Georgetown University Law Center (Fulbright scholar). His work focuses on the judicial power, the legal profession, comparative judicial systems, and judicial activism.

Friedrich Forsthuber is the president of the Regional Criminal Court of Vienna and chairman of the Expert Group on Criminal Law of the Austrian Association of Judges. From 1981 to 1985, he studied Law at the University of Vienna (Master of Law). In 1990, he was appointed judge. Since 2018, he has also been active as chairman of the Association of Judicial History and Rule of Law.

Rita Haverkamp holds the endowed professorship of Crime Prevention and Risk Management at the Eberhard Karls University of Tübingen (Federal Republic of Germany). Before she worked as a senior researcher in the Department of Criminology at the former Max Planck Institute for Foreign and International Criminal Law. She is inter alia a member of the International Penal and Penitentiary Foundation (IPPF). Her research includes projects in Germany and in Europe mainly on safety and security, refugees and migrants, and the community-based crime prevention.

Jessica Jahn is an associate of the International Centre for Criminal Law Reform and Criminal Justice Policy (Vancouver, BC, Canada). She holds a postgraduate degree in criminal justice policy (MSc Distinction, LSE), for which she studied international cooperation to combat cybercrime. Jessica has worked on projects in Canada and abroad on maritime crime, penal policy, organized crime, international cooperation, access to justice, and the prevention of violent extremism.

Marian Liebmann, PhD, is restorative justice consultant. She has worked with offenders and victims of crime, for probation, mental health services and as director of Mediation UK. She has a BA from Oxford, an MA from Birmingham, and a PhD from Bristol University. She is also a qualified teacher, social worker, and art therapist. She has written/edited thirteen books on art therapy, mediation, and restorative justice. She was awarded Order of the British Empire in 2013, for services to art therapy and mediation in the UK and overseas. She is involved in local mediation services and helping Bristol to become a restorative city.

Mallika Mahajan, is chief commissioner of Customs and Indirect Taxes in the Ministry of Finance of India. She is frequently visiting professional at International Anti-Corruption Academy (IACA), Austria. She earned MPhil in History (Hyderabad, India) and holds a postgraduate degree in Anti-Corruption Studies (IACA, *magna cum laude*). IACA granted her a research fellowship in 2018 and published her thesis and research papers.

Eduardo Pinheiro Granzotto da Silva is a senior legal specialist at the Office of the Legislative Counsel, in the Brazilian House of Representatives, and a professor at the Brazilian Institute of Education, Development and Research (IDP). He holds a Master of Arts degree in International Peace and Security from King's College London (Chevening scholar), as well as a law degree from the Federal University of Santa Catarina (UFSC). Eduardo was trained at the Brazilian War College (ESG) in their Politics and Strategy programme and his work in Brazil focuses on the fields of public security and national defense.

Michael Platzer, PhD, is the co-chair of the Coalition of Faith-based Organizations for Crime Prevention and Criminal Justice of the United Nations Crime Prevention and Criminal Justice Programme. Michael Platzer worked for thirty-five years in the UN Secretariat in a variety of capacities including Division of Human Rights, Office of the Secretary General, Department of Technical Cooperation, UN HABITAT, Reconstruction and Development Support Unit/UNDP, and UN Office of Drugs and Crime. Since retiring, he has worked as advisor for the International Commission for Catholic Prison Pastoral Care, served as co-chair of the Alliance of NGOs for Crime Prevention and Criminal Justice, as well as the Vienna Representative of the United Nations Studies Association, and president of the International Association for Advancement of Innovative Solutions to Global Challenges, a nongovernmental organization in a general consultative status with the United Nations Economic and Social Council.

Sławomir Redo is a visiting professor of United Nations Law, member of the UN Studies Association, f. UN senior crime prevention and criminal justice expert and staff of the UN Office on Drugs and Crime (ret); university course lecturer on "The UN & Crime Prevention" and on "The UN & War Crimes Prevention." He promotes criminological education for the 2030 UN Sustainable Development Goals, especially crime prevention, civic education and climate change. He published eighty articles, five books, and coedited four others, including three bestsellers: *Women and Children as Victims and Offenders: Background, Prevention, Reintegration. Suggestions for Succeeding Generations* (2 vols.), *Refugees and Migrants in Law and Policy—Challenges and Opportunities for Global Civic Education*, and *Crime Prevention and Justice in 2030. UN and the Universal Declaration of Human Rights* (2016–2021).

Gerhard Reissner is the honorary president of International Association of Judges (IAJ), and representative of IAJ to the United Nations Office at Vienna (Austria); Doctor iuris, judge since 1982, last position president of a first instance court in Vienna. Former president of European Association of Judges, president of IAJ (2012–2014). Member and former president of the Consultative Council of European Judges, a consultative body of the Council of Europe. Expert Missions of European Union, Council of Europe or IAJ regarding, draft laws and projects on independence of judges, accountability of judges, evaluation, court administration, judicial reform strategies to several countries like Albania, Armenia, Belarus, Bulgaria, Czech Republic, Colombia, Egypt, Georgia, Italy, Kazakhstan, Morocco, Moldova, Montenegro, Serbia, Slovakia, Turkey, and Ukraine.

Diego García-Sayán is the United Nations special rapporteur on the Independence of Judges and Lawyers, judge of the Inter-American Court of Human Rights until December 31, 2015, and President for two consecutive terms. Former Minister of Justice of Peru during the democratic transition and the Minister of Foreign Affairs that proposed and promoted the Inter-American Democratic Charter in 2011 adopted in the Lima General Assembly. Member of the Permanent Court of Arbitration (The Hague). A professor of Law at Pontificia Universidad Católica del Perú. He has authored books on international law, politics, and development. He is the recipient of numerous honors, including awards from the governments of Peru, Bolivia, Colombia, Costa Rica, Ecuador, El Salvador, and Spain. In 2013, he received the Rule of Law Award from the American Bar Association for advancing human rights and the rule of law worldwide.

Wiliam Schabas is a professor of International Law (Middlesex University, London, UK), Officer of the Order of Canada, Member of the Royal Irish Academy, Member of the Board of Trustees of the United Nations Voluntary Fund for Technical Cooperation in the Field of Human Rights; president of the International Association of Genocide Scholars.

Pawan Kumar Sinha is the director of Academic Programmes at International Anti-Corruption Academy (IACA), Austria. He holds two postgraduate degrees in Economics (Delhi School of Economics, India) and Anti-Corruption Studies (IACA, *summa cum laude, the Best Master Thesis Award*). He has worked for over three decades in India's Ministry of Finance. He teaches Economics of Corruption, Asset Recovery, Collective Action, emerging technologies for anti-corruption, and Research Methodology at IACA.

Bernadette Somody is an assistant professor at the Constitutional Law Department of Faculty of Law, Eötvös Loránd University (Budapest, Hungary). Her research interests center on the mechanisms and methods of fundamental rights protection. She obtained her PhD degree based on a thesis on ombudsman institutions. She was formerly the director at the Eötvös Károly Policy Institute, worked for the Hungarian Parliamentary Commissioner for Fundamental Rights, and at the Office of the Commissioner for Educational Rights.

Murugesan Srinivasan is the professor and head of the Department of Criminology, University of Madras. He has to credit over sixty publications in reputed academic journals. His recent publications include a chapter on "Actualising the Right to Adequate Standard of Living: A Critical Examination of Green Criminology from an Indian Perspective" in the book *Crime Prevention and Justice in 2030* edited by Dr. Slawomir Redo and Professor Helmut Kury; and an article on "The application of routine activity theory in explaining victimization of child marriage" in the *International Review of Victimology*. He has conducted twenty-two research projects sponsored by both national and international agencies/institutions. He was an expert member of the Core Advisory Group for Criminal Justice System Reforms constituted by the National Human Rights Commission, India. Srinivasan was also part of the expert panel constituted by the United Nations Counter Terrorism Centre to prepare "Guidelines and Principles to Assist, Protect and Support Victims of Terrorism in Asia-Pacific."

Thomas Stelzer is dean and the executive director of the International Anti-corruption Academy (IACA), Austria. He was the deputy director of the Austrian Cultural Institute in New York, special assistant to the executive secretary of the CTBTO Preparatory Commission, and minister-counsellor at the Permanent Mission of Austria to the United Nations in New York. He also served as the Austrian representative to the governing bodies of the United Nations Development Programme (UNDP), the United Nations Children's Fund (UNICEF), and the United Nations Population Fund (UNFPA). He was Delegate to the Committee for Disarmament and International Security (First Committee) of the United Nations General Assembly. In 2008–2013, he served as United Nations assistant secretary general for Policy Coordination and Inter-Agency Affairs, Department of Economic and Social Affairs.

Cora True-Frost is the Bond, Schoeneck, and King Distinguished Associate Professor of Law at the Syracuse University College of Law (Syracuse, NY, USA). She is an expert in international law and constitutional/human rights law. Her primary research interests are at the intersection of international law and international relations, with a focus on how international standards and norms develop. Her scholarship draws on her experiences defending individuals accused of crimes against humanity and war crimes; leading the

NGO Working Group on Women, Peace and Security at UN headquarters to advocate to the United Nations Security Council, and working with disability rights organizations. In addition to her research and teaching, Professor True-Frost is the director of the *Journal of Global Rights and Organizations* and Impunity Watch News, a law review and human rights news reporting website.

Şerife Ceren Uysal is a human rights lawyer. During her practice in Turkey, she was working on many cases related to systemic human rights violations. She has been an executive board member of the Progressive Lawyers Association since 2012. She is the co-secretary general of the European Association of Lawyers for Democracy & World Human Rights. Based in Vienna since December 2016, she took up the position of guest researcher at the Ludwig Boltzmann Institute for a year. She was awarded the Dr. Georg Lebiszczak-Prize for Freedom of Speech in Austria. She is currently studying at the Gender Studies Master Program of the University of Vienna during which she has been focusing on gender issues within the context of human rights law.

Varsha Vijayan is the project coordinator of the Project on Juvenile Justice and Juvenile Psychology in partnership with UNICEF at the Department of Criminology, University of Madras (India). She has obtained her post-graduate degree in Criminology and Criminal Justice Science and Diploma in Juvenile Justice and Juvenile Psychology from the University of Madras. Recently, she conducted an intensive research on the "Psycho-social attributes of rape offenders." She has also made a presentation on "Trends in Sexual Victimisation of Children" at the Fourteenth United Nations Congress on Crime Prevention and Criminal Justice in March 2021. Her research interests include victimology, victim justice, and juvenile psychology.